# From the idyll to the novel:
# Karamzin's Sentimentalist prose

## GITTA HAMMARBERG

DEPARTMENT OF GERMAN AND RUSSIAN, MACALESTER COLLEGE, ST PAUL,
MINNESOTA

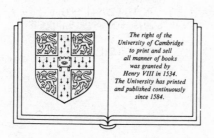

*The right of the
University of Cambridge
to print and sell
all manner of books
was granted by
Henry VIII in 1534.
The University has printed
and published continuously
since 1584.*

CAMBRIDGE UNIVERSITY PRESS

CAMBRIDGE

NEW YORK    PORT CHESTER    MELBOURNE    SYDNEY

Published by the Press Syndicate of the University of Cambridge
The Pitt Building, Trumpington Street, Cambridge CB2 1RP
40 West 20th Street, New York, NY 10011, USA
10 Stamford Road, Oakleigh, Melbourne 3166, Australia

First published 1991

Printed in Great Britain at the University Press, Cambridge

*British Library cataloguing in publication data*
Hammarberg, Gitta
From the idyll to the novel: Karamzin's Sentimentalist prose. –
(Cambridge studies in Russian literature).
1. Russian literature. Karamzin, N. M. (Nikolai Mikhailovich), 1766–1826
I. Title
891.78209

ISBN 0-521-38310-2

*Library of Congress cataloguing in publication data*
Hammarberg, Gitta.
From the idyll to the novel: Karamzin's Sentimentalist prose/Gitta Hammarberg.
p.   cm. – (Cambridge studies in Russian literature)
Includes bibliographical references and index.
ISBN 0-521-38310-2
1. Karamzin, Nikolaĭ Mikhaĭlovich, 1766–1826 – criticism and interpretation.
2. Sentimentalism in literature.
3. Russian prose literature – 18th century – History and criticism.
I. Title.    II. Series
PG3314.Z9S44  1991
891.78′209 – dc20      90-37705 CIP

ISBN 0 521 38310 2

# Contents

# Contents

# Preface and acknowledgments

Numerous studies have been devoted to the major Russian literary movements: Neoclassicism, Romanticism, Realism, Symbolism, Futurism, Socialist Realism, and so on. Russian Sentimentalism as a literary movement, chronologically following Neoclassicism and preceding Romanticism (and sometimes referred to as Preromanticism), spanning roughly the last quarter of the eighteenth century, has generated surprisingly few monograph length studies and none in English. Furthermore, the existing studies tend to focus on Sentimentalist poetry rather than prose. This is all the more surprising, given the crucial role this movement played in literary (and linguistic) evolution and in legitimizing prose fiction as a viable literary concern. Modern Russian prose fiction was indeed born during the second half of the eighteenth century, and Sentimentalist prose is intimately tied to the roots of the modern Russian novel. The present study aims to examine these roots by outlining a theory of Sentimentalism with an emphasis on prose, using modern theoretical concepts introduced by M. M. Bakhtin and V. N. Voloshinov, and further developed by other scholars.

The main part of this study is devoted to close readings of the short prose fiction of N. M. Karamzin, applying the theoretical principles developed. Karamzin, as the major representative of Russian Sentimentalism, has fared better as an object of study than the movement he represents. He has been widely studied as a writer, historian, journalist, political thinker, and linguistic innovator, reflecting the enormous influence he exerted in numerous areas of Russian intellectual history. Nevertheless, the lack of a modern, adequately annotated scholarly edition of Karamzin's complete works (such as the Academy editions of most other writers of his stature) is indicative of the comparative neglect of this major writer. Although 'Poor Liza' is still a staple on Soviet and Western course syllabi, and some of Karamzin's major works, such as *Letters of a Russian Traveller*, have received due attention, many of Karamzin's lesser works have rarely been studied and remain tucked away in inaccessible eighteenth-century journals. My concentration on short fiction and lesser works is partly theoretically motivated by the fact that precisely the so-called 'small form' (*malaia forma*), from prose idylls to all sorts of trifles (which will be closer defined in the course of this study), was tremendously influential and is arguably most representative of Sentimentalist prose. Partly I have selected short works for the methodological reason that close readings of long works would contribute few new insights about Sentimentalism or about Karamzin's prose that are not revealed in the readings of the short works. The Sentimentalist principles are the same regardless of length. Thus his *Letters of a Russian Traveller* will only receive peripheral attention and his twelve volume *History of the Russian State* is excluded from my analysis, although I believe that both works could fruitfully be discussed within my theoretical framework. My aim of presenting a representative selection rather than achieving completeness is also motivated by the fact that Sentimentalism as a literary movement is much more flexible than it has traditionally been given credit for. The lachrymose and narcissistic aspects of the movement have in general been emphasized to the neglect of its humorous, comic, parodic, and even frivolous aspects. Lachrymosity and narcissism, which certainly characterize a significant part of Sentimentalist fiction, are perhaps the main reasons both for the rapid demise of the movement and the subsequent disregard of, and even distaste for, Sentimentalism. The humorous and frivolous Sternian aspects of the movement will be investigated, not only to set the Sentimentalist picture straight, but also because they are crucial for understanding the origins of the so-called Gogol'ian strain of Russian literature. Karamzin played a more significant role in this continuity than has hitherto been realized.

The impetus for my study came from a reading of Karamzin's last work of prose fiction, *A Knight of Our Time*, in an eighteenth-century seminar at the University of Michigan. This made me realize that there was more to Sentimentalism than tears, sighs, and poor Liza. During several years, I studied Karamzin and Russian Sentimentalism in tandem with various twentieth-century theories of narration, supported by generous grants from the Horace Rackham School of Graduate Studies at the University of Michigan. This resulted in my 1982 Ph. D. dissertation on Karamzin and

Sentimentalism. Subsequent research was supported by the Bush Foundation and the Summer Research Laboratory on Russia and Eastern Europe at the University of Illinois. A Joyce Foundation Junior Faculty grant supported my 1988 sabbatical leave from Macalester College which allowed me to finish this book. I am most grateful to these institutions for their support.

I thank my teachers, colleagues, and students at the University of Michigan and Macalester College, who have encouraged me, stimulated me, argued with me, distracted me, or in other ways made this book possible. In particular, I wish to thank Ellis Dye, Caryl Emerson, and Peter Weisensel for their careful readings and constructive criticism of the manuscript. The Study Group on Eighteenth-century Russia is gratefully acknowledged as the first public forum for airing some of my ideas on Sentimentalism. Among its members, my special thanks go to Anthony Cross for continued intellectual stimulation. For domestic as well as intellectual support and heroic introductions to several word processing systems, I thank Robert Hammarberg. My greatest debt of gratitude goes to I. R. Titunik, whose high standards of academic excellence and continued personal support have challenged and sustained me for over a decade. He introduced me to Voloshinov and Bakhtin well before their works came into vogue in the US, and he made me realize that frivolity and humor were, and are, distinct positive values in Russian literature as in American academia. To him I dedicate this book.

# Notes on the text

*Method of citation.* The full references to works cited occur in the Bibliography section at the end of this study, and references in the Notes follow the traditional author–title system. A special citation code is used for Karamzin's works, and the full reference, preceded by the citation code can be found in a separate section of the Bibliography.

Special orthography and punctuation are important aspects of Sentimentalist expression. Therefore the original orthography and punctuation have been retained in quotations of Sentimentalist works throughout this study unless otherwise noted, even in translated material where the original Russian punctuation might stretch the rules for English. My commentary and punctuation are enclosed within square brackets and my emphasis within quotations is noted. Thus, e.g., ellipsis dots or dashes, unless placed within square brackets, are original.

*Transliteration.* For the transliteration of Russian, the Library of Congress system (without diacritics) has been used consistently throughout this study. Old orthography and spelling have been standardized according to the principles established in the *Trudy otdela drevnerusskoi literatury*.

*Translation.* All translations are my own. In as far as possible I have used first editions of Karamzin's works of prose fiction, in order to reflect the original Sentimentalist style, which in many cases was toned down or in other ways altered in subsequent editions. When this has not been possible, I have substituted other editions, close to the first editions.

*Copyright.* Permission has been granted to incorporate versions of my previously published articles into the present study, as follows: Chapter 3 incorporates a version of 'Karamzin's "Progulka" as

Sentimentalist Manifesto', *Russian Literature*, 26 (1989), 249–66; Chapter 5 incorporates a version of 'Poor Liza, Poor Èrast, Lucky Narrator', *Slavic and East European Journal*, 31, 3 (Fall 1987), 305–21; Chapter 6 incorporates versions of 'Eighteenth Century Narrative Variations on Frol Skobeev', *Slavic Review*, 46, 3/4 (Fall/Winter 1987), 529–39; and 'Metafiction in Russian 18th Century Prose: Karamzin's *Rycar' našego vremeni* or *Novyi Akteon, vnuk Kadma i Garmonii*', *Scando-Slavica*, 27 (1981), 27–46.

# 1

# The literary and intellectual context

During the first half of the eighteenth century, prose fiction was not a recognized literary concern in Russia. The only kind of prose that was regulated by the ruling Neoclassicist movement was nonfictional, nonnarrative prose, such as the oration. The existing prose fiction, widely circulated in manuscript form, was, by and large, a carry-over from the seventeenth century: popular literature, tales of the 'Frol Skobeev' type, the so-called Petrine tales, as well as translated Western chivalric adventure tales and romances, usually referred to as prose of the 'Bova Korolevich' calibre. Such prose fiction was regarded by the literati as inferior mass literature, which met neither of the Horatian criteria for literature proper. It was, however, extremely popular among the masses (and, one has reason to believe, not only among the masses) and proved influential for the further development of Russian prose fiction.[1]

Throughout the latter part of the century, this kind of prose fiction was, on the one hand, collected and published in unchanged form, and, on the other, edited, adapted, embellished, and combined with other kinds of prose and published in this changed form. The fact of publication in itself, with the widening reading public it entailed, served as an impetus for the recognition of the 'legitimacy' of such prose fiction. Book printing also gave a decisive boost to the Russian translators of Western prose fiction.[2] Translation of Western novels had started on a small scale already in the 1730s in manuscript form. From the 1750s on, these translations were printed, and were, furthermore, carried out by professional translators (I. P. Elagin, I. Shishkin, and S. A. Poroshin among the most prominent ones). A group of translators united around the first private journal, *Idle Time Usefully Spent (Prazdnoe vremia v polzu upotreblennoe*, 1759–60), the title being indicative of their stand with regard to prose fiction.[3] Their systematic translation and printing of prose fiction was instrumental in furthering its literary status. The range of prose fiction translated during the second half

1

of the eighteenth century was astounding: Hellenistic and Roman novels, Medieval courtly romances, Eastern tales in the vein of *Arabian Nights*, works by Calprenède, Mme de LaFayette, and Prévost appeared next to Lesage's picaresque novels, works by Fénelon, Ramsay, and Terrason, as well as the novels of Richardson, Fielding, Rousseau, and Goethe. Thus prose fiction of the most varied types, from geographically and chronologically different points of origin, vied with the native and translated popular literature. Original Russian novels and tales, heavily influenced by both the old popular prose fiction and the new Western translations, began to appear in the 1760s from the pens of such writers as Fedor Emin, Chulkov, Popov, and Levshin – to name just the most prominent.

The translators, particularly Elagin, Poroshin, and Emin, were also fervent advocates of the merits of their 'new' prose, understood by them mainly according to their prime model, Prévost. The prefaces to their works constituted the main forum for publicizing their views. Their contention was that prose fiction should be regarded as serious literature on a par with poetry; it, too, served the recognized functions of art, namely to edify and entertain. Furthermore, they claimed, edification and moral teaching are best served when presented in an entertaining rather than purely didactic manner, which was, in their view precisely the advantage of the 'new' prose fiction.

The opposing Neoclassicist camp did not reject the novel outright, but only the particular type of novel that was propagandized by Elagin and his camp – particularly prose fiction with affinities to both 'Bova Korolevich' and Prévost. Exceptions were made for certain works by Fénelon, Barclay, Terrason, Swift, Cervantes, and, of ancient prose, for Aesop, Apuleius, Petronius, and some others. Indeed, some of the major Neoclassicist writers themselves translated and even wrote original prose fiction. Trediakovskii, in addition to Tallemant's *précieuse* novel, *Voyage de l'île d'Amour* (which he translated as early as 1730), also translated Barclay's *Argenis* (1751) and Fénelon's *Les Aventures de Télémaque* (1766), the latter, in verse.[4] Kheraskov wrote a series of original Russian historical-philosophical-political novels: *Numa, or Flourishing Rome* (*Numa, ili Protsvetaiushchii Rim*, 1768), *Cadmus and Harmonia* (*Kadm i Garmoniia*, 1786), and *Polydorus, Son of Cadmus and Harmonia* (*Polidor, syn Kadma i Garmonii*, 1794), all of which are utopian, characterized by lofty didacticism, 'teachings for rulers', and Enlightenment rhetoric.[5]

Emin's *The Adventures of Themistocles* (*Prikliucheniia Femistokla*, 1763) is indicative of the fact that the Elagin camp (Emin started out as one of the 'new' translators), by no means spurned such edifying lofty prose fiction.[6] Thus both some of the leading Neoclassicists and the proponents of the 'new' prose strove to legitimize prose fiction as viable literature. This striving for legitimacy was implemented both in Neoclassicist novels and in the Emin-type 'new' prose, as well as in the tale adaptations, mainly through the introduction of an authoritative, sophisticated image of author, serving to guide the reader to the correct moral interpretation of the works.[7]

Even though some authors, notably Chulkov, single out this pretentious image of author as a butt for their mockery, their own works also strongly feature an image of author. That this image was qualitatively different (a humorous, silly, frivolous, vulgar double-talking liar, a mocker of literary pretentiousness), does not alter the basic innovatory fact of introducing a prominent image of author in the text. This signal feature of all prose fiction of the era was to be particularly prominent and further refined by Sentimentalist authors who finally managed to gain for prose fiction the status as legitimate literature it has since had. Both the serious and the mocking varieties are developed in Sentimentalist prose and can be seen as precursors to the two major strains of Russian nineteenth-century literature: the 'serious' images of author such as those in Tolstoi's major novels, and the chatty, mocking ones such as abound in Gogol''s masterpieces. One of Karamzin's achievements was to create images of author that were fully acceptable to the age of sense and sensibility, by trimming the rough edges of both the pretentious preacher image and the vulgar Chulkovian mocker.

The prominence of image of author has been noted by scholars. For example, Serman, in his survey of eighteenth-century prose, comes to the following conclusion:

On the whole, the most important innovation for Russian narrative prose from the mid 1770s on, was the appearance of an author–narrator who directly addresses a reader with direct speech. This direct authorial speech is heard in all new literary genres – in 'diaries', 'notes', 'journeys'. *Journey from St. Petersburg to Moscow* joins the general movement of Sentimentalist prose precisely by the fact that its unity is created by a lyrical image of author–narrator.[8]

The question as to what such an image of author consists in will be one of the main topics of my investigation. One of the best studies of the problem of author in Sentimentalist poetry is Gukovskii's 1938 monograph *Studies in the History of Russian Literature and Social Thought of the XVIII century*, the second part of which is devoted to what he calls the Murav'ev–Karamzin branch of the Sentimentalist movement.[9] He bases his literary argument on the socio-historical conditions of the era (revolutions in the West, peasant uprisings at home). This social reality shook the very foundations of the preceding Rationalistic world view, the faith in absolute values, given *a priori*. Everything external to man came to seem unstable and unpredictable, and the only firm point in the universe was man himself. R. F. Brissenden in his excellent discussion of West European Sentimentalism makes similar points and argues convincingly that Sentimentalism can be regarded as a specific branch of Enlightenment philosophy. He points out that the individual human experience was seen as the source of all knowledge and values. The point of departure for philosophical thinking was shifted, accordingly, from a metaphysical to an epistemological theory. A theory of what a person knows and how he comes to know it replaced, or was considered primary to, a theory about the ultimate nature of the world.[10] This shift from 'world' to 'perceiver of the world' also lies at the basis of what Gukovskii labels Sentimentalist solipsism, the guiding principle of the new literary movement:

Doubt about the truth of what to the fathers seemed the sole truth – that is the point of departure for the attitudes and world view of the Murav'ev–Karamzin school [ . . . ] The scepticism and relativism led inevitably to a solipsistic understanding of the world. In the final analysis, the writer and thinker places himself at the center of the world. The universe is shaped for him not according to the laws of a logical scheme, but according to the laws of his personal perception precisely as an individual person.[11]

A new subjective attitude toward art accompanied the new subjective philosophy. Art was both conceived and perceived in terms of personal experience and emotion, and the solipsistic principle became basic to Sentimentalist prose. By the same token, the poet's mission as an official intellectual leader and teacher was regarded with scepticism in favor of a subjective aesthetic experience. As Gukovskii aphoristically puts it, 'they [the Sentimentalists] see in a work of art only the individual, in this lies their weakness, but they *see* the individual and in this lies their strength'.[12]

Brissenden provides an interesting analysis of the complexities which arose in defining the nature of personal experience, the details of which need not concern us here. As a general tendency, two poles emerged, one emphasizing Feeling (Sensibility) the other emphasizing Reason (Sense). The former was in general afforded more attention and, in some cases, primacy. That emphasis was a natural consequence of the fact that the latter had reigned supreme in the preceding Rationalist philosophy. A balance of the two aspects of experience was held to be ideal, and, as Brissenden points out, definitions of the two extremes frequently came to overlap, particularly towards the end of the century when terms such as 'reasonable feelings' gradually came to indicate a common, supra-individual principle which was seen to inform both. The relative prominence of Feeling and Reason, and the awareness of individual experience was, however, less important than the crucial stress on the sanctity of individual experience and, consequently, on individual judgments of the physical and moral universe.

The logical consequence of the solipsistic principle would be a completely relativistic or subjective ethics (or lack of ethics) and, indeed, as is pointed out by Brissenden, 'it is a short, and some would argue, logical step from something like the humane scepticism of David Hume's ethical position to the bleak and anarchic moral nihilism espoused and advocated by the Marquis de Sade'.[13] The philosophers of the era were aware of the problem, and their debates came to focus increasingly on questions of whether the moral sentiments of the individual had any intrinsic authority, such that they have universal validity, and whether the moral sentiments of man in general at their core agreed or disagreed with the traditional precepts of Christian morality.

That Karamzin was deeply concerned with the consequences of solipsism and even, as it were, took the principle to its de Sadean limits, is attested by some of his last prose works, notably 'My Confession' ('Moia ispoved''). As Brissenden points out, however, the belief in the solipsistic principle was held along with a belief in a second principle: that of sympathy. The sympathetic principle states that a human being is inherently benevolent, or at least capable of acting benevolently, given the opportunity. According to this principle, human beings are by nature able to sympathize with each other, to identify in some way with the experiences of their fellow humans. Such innate sympathy was held to be basic to the formation of moral attitudes, and to be the factor which enabled humans to communicate in the first place. Sympathy was also viewed as the basis of social cohesion. For many thinkers (Brissenden names Shaftesbury, Hutcheson, Hume, Adam Smith), this was so fundamental a belief that it entered into the very definition of a human being, and its opposite was something inconceivable. Statements such as the following by Hume were characteristic: 'A creature, absolutely malicious and spiteful, were there any such in nature, must be worse than indifferent to the images of vice and virtue. All his sentiments must be inverted, and directly opposite to those which prevail in human society.'[14] That Karamzin relied on the sympathetic principle as well, is abundantly clear from his stress on man as active perceiver with the sympathetic ability to co-create, a concept I hope to show is crucial to Karamzin's Sentimentalism. The principle is repeatedly voiced by Karamzin both in his articles and in his fiction. Gukovskii quotes Karamzin's axiom, 'a bad person cannot be a good author', and one could cite a similar Karamzinian definition of the reader: 'Bad people do not even read novels.'[15] In a work published in 1797, 'Dialogue on Happiness' ('Razgovor o shchastii'), the following words echoing Hume's statement are uttered by Filalet, who plays the role of a more authoritative teacher to the sceptical Melodor: 'A total villain or a person who loves evil because it is evil and hates good because it is good, is, if not a bad poetic fantasy, at least a freak outside Nature, a being, inexplicable by natural laws.'[16]

This is not to say that Karamzin, or the other Sentimentalist thinkers, were oblivious to the existence of evil. Indeed, the belief in the sympathetic principle was often accompanied by a pessimistic belief that a person, although good, somehow creates the conditions which prevent him from fulfilling his good impulses. As Brissenden expresses it:

An awareness of the problem was usually not enough to destroy the optimistic belief that if only the right circumstances prevailed man could live up to his expectations. At the same time, however, the contemplation of the evil and inimical conditions – 'the world' – in which the benevolent impulse was forced to operate was accepted as a legitimate source for melancholy. The Sentimental tribute of a tear exacted by the spectacle of virtue in distress was an acknowledgement at once of man's inherent goodness and of the impossibility of his ever being able to demonstrate his goodness effectively.[17]

This kind of belief lies behind most of Karamzin's narrators, and is particularly forcefully expressed in 'Bornholm Island' ('Ostrov Borngol'm'), where, as we shall see, the stress is on sympathy between author and reader by way of describing its absence in the 'world'. For the most part, the existence of pure evil as such was not acknowledged by Karamzin, who preferred to refer vice to human weakness, imperfection, error, or an inability of the human mind to fathom the larger divine design which, by definition, is good. This leads us to the source of human sympathy, which by most Sentimentalists was seen as God (or Nature), who had implanted a spark of his absolute goodness in man. This idea is expressed by Karamzin (or his narrators and personages) from many different angles: as conscience, as a recurring Wielandian curtain image, and as faith in a larger divine design ('Bornholm Island'), and is most eloquently stated in 'A Promenade', which contains a passage curiously reminiscent of Yorick's famous apostrophe to the great SENSORIUM:

Dear sensibility! source inexhausted of all that's precious in our joys, or costly in our sorrows! thou chainest thy martyr down upon his bed of straw – and 'tis thou who lifts him up to HEAVEN – eternal fountain of our feelings! – 'tis here I trace thee – and this is thy divinity which stirs within me – not, that in some sad and sickening moments *my soul shrinks back upon herself, and startles at destruction* – mere pomp of words! – but that I feel some generous joys and generous cares beyond myself – all comes from thee, great SENSORIUM of the world! which vibrates, if a hair of our heads but falls upon the ground, in the remotest desert of thy creation.[18]

The same source of goodness is also the source of aesthetic perception and creation in Karamzin's aesthetics. The third Sentimentalist principle, what I will call the pleasure principle, is seen as the result of a recognition in one's self of this 'divine spark', that is, the recognition of one's own goodness. Pleasure may be prompted both by goodness in the 'world' and by various evils (provided one's own conscience is clear). Since man is naturally inclined towards his own pleasure and towards avoiding pain, it follows that he is also naturally inclined towards goodness and beauty. This idea was expressed with particular force in Karamzin's 'On the Sciences, Arts, and Enlightenment' ('Nechto o naukakh, iskusstvakh i pros-veshchenii'):

Whosoever, through the myriads of glimmering spheres, spinning in the blue celestial space, can spiritually ascend to the throne of the invisible divinity; whosoever hears his voice in thunder and in Zephyrs, in the stir of seas and – in his own heart; whosoever sees the world in an atom and in the world – an atom of boundless creation; whosoever in each flowerlet, in each motion and deed of nature feels the breath of the highest bliss and in scarlet celestial lightning kisses the hem of Savaoth's raiment: that person can not be a villain.[19]

The 'divine spark' also serves as our conscience, and alerts us to the presence of evil in ourselves. Such ideas were expressed by most of the major philosophers of the era, among others by Albrecht von Haller, both as a physiologist (his treatise on sensibility and irritability in animals) and as a poet (his meditation 'Über den Ursprung des Übels', written in 1734 and translated into Russian by Karamzin in 1786). The pleasure principle is also fundamental to Karamzin's aesthetics, since moral goodness is equated with beauty.

It is true that Karamzin, particularly in his *Aglaia* period and in some of his later works, paid more attention to existing evils – as did most Sentimentalists after the French Revolution.[20] That does not mean, however, that Karamzin during that period of his life (or indeed ever) subscribed to a belief that human nature is innately evil. It would seem, on the contrary, that his attention to evil (or human weakness, in Karamzin's system) stemmed from a firm belief in the inherent goodness in the human being, and in a possibility of awakening an awareness of the pleasure in goodness and pain in evil through art, education, philanthropy, enlightened monarchy, etc.[21]

As the solipsistic, sympathetic, and pleasure principles became prominent, the very nature of literature and its function in society was changing. Initially an organ of official (artistic and other) ideology practised in exclusive official and literary circles, it became a personal enterprise of private salons and intimate gatherings of a few friends aiming to move the audience's (and the poet's own) sensitivities. Tears and pleasant thoughts, rather than loud applause, became the desired effect of art. Trifling forms, practised in intimate society and previously not regarded as literature, gradually became sanctioned as literature.

It is one of the paradoxes of the era that, while all the personal aspects of literature came to be acknowledged as desirable, the actual practice of literature was simultaneously developing in an increasingly impersonal direction. Owing to a number of factors, such as a rapidly increasing literacy, bookprinting, translation, the emergence and ever wider circulation of literary journals, the author no longer could take a personal contact with his readers for granted. Earlier in the century authors knew their readers, either personally or by virtue of the fact that they were part of the same cultural elite. Manuscripts were circulated among friends and acquaintances or read aloud in select groups, official or strictly private, and there was always the assurance of a known audience. Publication (even after that became an option) was simply irrelevant and often deemed undesirable (Murav'ev's reluctance to publish, being a case in point). Economic gain did not enter the picture, since few authors lived solely by their literary work – they were supported by patrons, were independently wealthy, or were employed in positions ('real' or token) which gave them ample time to write.[22]

Thus, during the Neoclassicist era, while the distance between actual authors and actual readers was close, and there was a personal relationship between them, literature itself was conceptualized supra-personally. As has been demonstrated most convincingly by Gukovskii, the hierarchical system of genres (as opposed to the author's individuality) and the imitation and perfection of models (as opposed to individual innovations) were the artistic criteria *par excellence*. The very names of authors were thought of generically and ranked accordingly (The Russian Racine, The Russian Pindar). Poems, entire collections of poems, and entire novels, appeared anonymously. Works migrated freely, the same work could reappear in different journals and could be freely 'improved' and edited with or without the original author's approval. The work's origin and publication data were irrelevant. Genre also determined the composition of collections (the Novikov edition of Sumarokov's works is a good example), and even titles were often strictly generic. Thus the personality or identity of author and reader were not, *per se*, *literary facts*.[23] Towards the second half of the eighteenth century, and particularly from the

1780s on, this situation gradually began to change. Writing came to be regarded as a respectable profession, not only translating and publishing, but also creative writing as such. The author's name appeared more frequently on the title page, and the titles themselves often included a reference to the author's 'I' (Karamzin's *My Trifles* [*Moi bezdelki* ], and 'My Confession' ['Moia ispoved''], Dmitriev's *My Trifles Too* [*I moi bezdelki*], I. Bakhtin's *I Too Am an Author* [*I ia avtor*], are symptomatic). Works came to be read according to author (rather than genre).

Karamzin was one of the first authors in Russia to live exclusively by that profession (until 1803 when he became court historian and devoted himself exclusively to his *History of the Russian State*). Lotman points out that while most of Karamzin's friends divided their lives between art and government service, Karamzin demonstratively declined any government appointments in order to devote himself to writing.[24] Not only did he participate as an editor and contributor–translator in the *Children's Reading for Heart and Mind* (*Detskoe chtenie dlia serdtsa i razuma*, one of Novikov's publishing ventures), but he single-handedly published two major journals, *Moscow Journal* (*Moskovskii zhurnal*, 1791–2), and *Messenger of Europe*, (*Vestnik Evropy*, 1802–3) as well as various literary almanacs and 'pantheons'. Karamzin also established close connections with a French journal *Le Spectateur du Nord*, published in Hamburg. His own works appeared in it in translation, and he also contributed articles about Russian literature, thereby introducing Russian literature to the European audience.[25] As editor of the journals he always signed his work (either by full name or real initials, from advertising to title page to footnotes). Although the individual works in the journals were frequently unsigned, or signed by curious pseudonyms, real or made-up initials, or strange orthographical signs, some were clearly identified. It is revealing that Karamzin, in the final issue of *Messenger of Europe,* felt compelled (by popular demand) to identify previously unidentified works, acknowledging most of them as his own.[26] Even so, many of them, particularly the works in *Moscow Journal*, remain unattributed to this day. Krylov and Klushin stressed identification of their own works even more radically (not to say polemically), and always signed them in their journal, *St. Petersburg Mercury*.[27]

Lotman, in *Sotvorenie Karamzina,* repeatedly makes a very

important point about Karamzin's professional activities, namely
that virtually all his literary undertakings were perceived as pro-
vocative and even presumptious by his contemporaries – friends
and foes alike. Not only was his early retirement from government service in favor of literature highly unusual, but Karamzin
himself flaunted this act in his poetry. His various poses in life and
art (as Parisian fop, for instance), his choice of previously taboo
themes (incest, intimate love, various political themes and trivial
matters) for literary treatment, were all seen as somehow audacious. His journals were demonstratively private. They were
neither officially funded, nor did they represent any official body
(as was customary), but they were the product of individual free
enterprise, and most contributions were either Karamzin's own or
presented 'through' his editorship. Lotman shows the revolutionary significance of these literary acts and, more importantly, of
the very image of author in society that Karamzin introduced.
Equally important is the image of author created by Karamzin
within various texts – in my terminology, the sensitive narrator-
person of specific poems and prose works, the professional
narrator–editor of the journals, the narrator–close–friend of the
almanacs.[28]

Karamzin was also a fervent advocate of extending literacy to all
social classes, to women, and to children (*Children's Reading* was,
notably, the first children's journal in Russia). He devoted numerous articles to this topic, such as 'On the Introduction of National
Enlightenment in Russia' ('O novom obrazovanii narodnogo prosveshcheniia v Rossii'), 'Why are there Few Writers of Talent in
Russia?' ('Otchego v Rossii malo avtorskikh talantov?'), 'On the
Sciences, Arts, and Enlightenment' ('Nechto o naukakh, iskusstvakh i prosveshchenii').[29] He included numerous articles on
various aspects of pedagogy in both his journals. His pantheons
served the important function of popularization – foreign and
Russian works were made more accessible to the general public.
Karamzin strongly advocated reading as a pastime – whatever form
it might take, and supported the reading even of the most
(officially) frowned-upon novels, such as Fedor Emin's *Inconstant
Fortune, or the Voyage of Miramond* (*Nepostoiannaia Fortuna, ili
pokhozhdenie Miramonda*), in 'On the Book Trade and Love for
Reading in Russia'.[30] Lotman argues convincingly that Karamzin
indeed *created* the reading public of his era, particularly the woman

reader. That the circle of actual readers of prose fiction had increased immensely already by Karamzin's time is an established fact,[31] and Karamzin both widened the circle and molded it according to the spirit of the era.

The gradual detachment of the author from his reader, their mutual real life distance and lack of shared situation, and the transfer of reading to a solitary 'silent register' (Voloshinov's felicitous expression), ran counter to the prevailing personalistic views of literature, and the reconciliation of the two tendencies became one of the major problems and challenges for the authors. As B. H. Bronson has expressed it:

There, of course, lies the heart of the problem: how to establish an understanding, a mutual give-and-take, reciprocity of emotional, intellectual, moral response with a person or persons never seen. The old assurance from proximity has been taken away at a difficult time: just when the literary profession, as a profession, is beginning to walk by itself, and when imaginative prose is trying its powers in many new directions. A solid, tangible public would have been fortifying at such a moment.[32]

The problem was solved to a significant degree by simulating the desired intimate and/or oral situation within the literary structure itself by recourse to various increasingly ingenious devices for creating images of author and reader and their shared situation. Thus the author and his audience, as well as their relationship, became a fiction, a *literary* fact.

Gukovskii moves from the general intellectual context, to the literary work itself, and draws the textual corollaries from the subjectivist paradigm and prominence of author as literary fact. Language was viewed as a means of signifying not the concrete referent, but the poet's relationship to it. Referential language gave way to subject language as the ontological referent itself became problematical. Emotive and expressive features of language came to be foregrounded. The attitude to language had repercussions on the lexical, syntactic, and semantic levels of the work. A special emotive lexicon was favored, based not on logic, but on personal perception. Thus, for example, ornamental and emotive epithets rather than concretely descriptive ones were preferred, and the associative power of a word was stressed to the detriment of exact reference. On the syntactic level, elaborate periphrastic means replaced direct simple signification. Words were combined into emotive leitmotifs and musical tonalities, often disregarding logical linkage. Themes became apolitical, ahistorical, and thoroughly personalized. They were not systematically developed, but rather alluded to in vague ways, often distorting the theme proper in the traditional sense. The poet's personality and experience became prominent themes, as did his activities, i.e., art itself, poetry, dreams, imagination, inspiration, creation, and so on.[33]

The old Neoclassicist paradigm, correlating theme and style, the old conception of genres as a preconceived neatly organized hierarchical system was cast aside, and in every aspect of literature the voice of the speaker became the decisive factor. Gukovskii, like Brissenden, stresses an important aspect in this new subjective paradigm, namely that the shift from general *a priori* schemes to a solipsistic basic principle does not entail a shift from the abstract to the concrete. The 'I' of a poet became subjective but not individualized or concretized. One poet's 'I' does not differ significantly from that of another poet. The solipsistic focus is not empirically based, but is, rather, a supraempirical, generally applicable notion. Furthermore, in Gukovskii's view the range of moods and tonalities that tended to be favored by Sentimentalist poets was rather limited to the melancholic, dejected, blissful, sweet emotions, fostered by turning away from the horrors of reality to the peaceful havens of nature and intimate circles of friends.

As we have seen, the subjectivist intellectual tenor of the era, and the epistemological bent of Sentimentalist philosophy, had wide-ranging repercussions in the area of late eighteenth-century Russian literature. The concrete mode of its existence in society was undergoing change, its aims and functions were radically altered, its practitioners (authors and readers) were perceived differently, the ruling Neoclassicist canons were questioned and ultimately replaced by an entirely new system. New intellectual principles, here summarized as solipsism, sympathy, and pleasure, helped to shape both the Sentimentalist system of literature and the very structure of individual works. One of the most important new developments in the field of literature was the legitimation of prose fiction, accomplished after much debating during the Sentimentalist period. There seems to be general agreement among the scholars who have studied these matters that the *differentia specifica* of a Sentimentalist work of literature – be it prose or verse – lies in the new solipsistic emphasis on author in the work. It is precisely this *differentia specifica* that I propose to investigate, in particular the ways in which it was shaped in prose fiction, first as a theoretical concept, as part of the structure of narrative prose fiction, and second, as applied to the prose fiction of N. M. Karamzin, the foremost Russian Sentimentalist writer and thinker.

# 2
# Theory of Sentimentalism

## A BAKHTINIAN THEORY OF NARRATOR

The validity and implications of the claims made for authorial dominance in Sentimentalist fiction depend on how 'author' is defined. I shall view 'author' as a constitutive element of narrative structure, following a narrative theory developed by M. M. Bakhtin and V. N. Voloshinov, complemented with insights of Jakobson, Doležel, and Titunik, and, to a lesser extent, V. V. Vinogradov and modern speech act theory (henceforth SA theory) as represented by J. L. Austin, John Searle, and H. P. Grice.[1] The major advantage of the Bakhtin–Voloshinov theory is that the pragmatic framework of analysis is wholly appropriate to literature as a *sui generis* human activity, without reducing it to language, psychology, philosophy, and so on. Linguistic, psychological, and other aspects of a literary work are not thereby denied; they are simply relegated to a lower level of analysis, conditioned by, and subordinate to, properly literary categories.

On the most general level, literature is seen as a specific sphere of human socio-verbal interaction and thus operates within a set of conventions (or norms) peculiar to that sphere. A work of literature is defined as a 'turn' in this interaction, an 'utterance' in the full pragmatic sense of the term, or as a line or retort (*replika*) in a dialogical chain of utterances. As a 'turn', it is a separate unit, and its borders are clearly defined by the alternation of speakers. It thus has the property of being finalized (*zavershennost'*), it is a complete integral whole. As part of a dialogue, it relates actively to preceding and subsequent utterances, and has the property of 'addressedness' (*obrashchennost', adresovannost'*). It responds to (affirms, contradicts, mocks, and so on) previous utterances, and simultaneously anticipates possible reactions by future speakers. The utterance is thus dialogical in an external sense. The utterance is dialogical in an internal sense, as well, in that each word is used anew in a new

15

context which may contradict, affirm, or in some other way relate to previous usages.

For a work of narrative fiction, this inner dialogicity becomes particularly important in that utterances by other speakers (personages) are more or less explicitly incorporated within the single whole utterance by the present speaker (author) – with all the dialogical relationships which that entails. A work of narrative fiction is what Bakhtin terms a 'secondary' or 'complex' speech genre, and what Voloshinov speaks of as *chuzhaia rech'*: 'speech within speech, utterance within utterance, but at the same time speech about speech, utterance about utterance' ('rech' v rechi, vyskazyvanie v vyskazyvanii, no v to zhe vremia eto i rech' o rechi, vyskazyvanie o vyskazyvanii')[2].

These insights are of crucial significance for the Bakhtinian methodology. An analysis of a narrative text (and thus 'author') must proceed from the recognition of its socio-ideological nature as a whole utterance (in verbal as well as extra-verbal dimensions), which is a link in a chain of other utterances, to the investigation of its intrinsically social nature – its constitutive elements (author, reader, and personage) and the interrelationship among them. The special dialogical nature of these interrelationships is the primary object of analysis as the factor which determines all other aspects of the work. The work must be seen as an author's evaluative stance with regard to other utterances by both previous and subsequent speakers. This makes the author both speaker and listener simultaneously, and his utterance both his own and another's simultaneously. This fundamental dialogicity is predicated of each and every utterance in literature.

As a *literary* utterance it occurs within a set of relatively stable norms and conditions of the specific socio-ideological sphere of literature. Literature is a complexly organized form of cultural exchange, and the literary utterance is organized as a complex (secondary) speech genre. Its particular form is thus more complex and at the same time freer than that of a simple (primary) speech genre, such as a military command which is predetermined by conventional formulae for getting the listener to do something. A literary utterance is less standardized and is particularly conducive to stylistic individualization, which directly enters into the author's intention. It is characterized by the fact that 'it is wholly completed by the creation of the artistic work and by its continual recreations

in co-creative perception and it does not require any other objecti-
vations'.[3] Its point is thus to display its own style (or lack of style).[4]
Style, however, is a function of the dialogical relationships between
author and other speakers, and thus these relationships themselves
become the 'topic' of a literary work.

The key question in the Bakhtinian approach to literature
becomes how to decipher the internal and external dialogicity – the
relationships between the author's utterance and utterances of
others, or the different degrees of 'otherness'. How does the author
receive and process utterances of others and fuse them into a single
whole utterance, in the full chronotopical[5] and axiological dimensions? The structure of narrative prose fiction, specifically, is
treated most extensively in Bakhtin's *Problemy poetiki
Dostoevskogo*, particularly the fifth chapter, and in a work written
in 1934–5, 'Discourse in the Novel' ('Slovo v romane').[6] The
*differentia specifica* of the novel (in its wide sense referring to prose
fiction in general), lies in its artistic *exploitation* of the heterolingua-
lism, heteroglossia, heterovocalism (*raznoiazychie, raznorechie,
raznogolositsa*) and profusion of styles that characterize language–
speech in its live reality. In this, it is opposed to other more
canonized (and canonizable) genres, notably the epic, which are
determined by the opposite, centripetal tendency towards a single
standardized and regulated language. This Babel of utterances and
utterance types, tied to specific systems of values, opinions, world
views, and so on, enters the novel as the speech of others, and is
organized by the author into a single artistic whole, his novelistic
utterance:

The prose writer does not purge words of intentions and tones, alien to
him, he does not destroy the seeds of social heteroglossia embedded in
them, he does not eliminate the images of speakers and speech mannerisms
(potential personages–narrators) glimmering behind the words and forms
of language, but he arranges all these words and forms at different
distances from the ultimate core of meaning of his work, from his personal
intentional center.[7]

The primary distinction in Bakhtin's system is thus drawn
between author's speech and another's speech, and within the
latter, different degrees of 'otherness', depending on greater or
lesser authorial interference, greater or lesser proximity to the
author's 'ultimate core of meaning'. Speech can enter the novel in
three basic forms: direct univocal author's speech, represented or

object speech (personage speech, also univocal), and bivocal speech, author's and another's simultaneously. Bakhtin terms the first category variously 'monologue', 'direct author's speech', or 'direct object oriented speech' (*priamo predmetno napravlennoe slovo*), or 'univocal speech' (*odnogolosoe slovo*).

Direct author's speech must be such that the reader can recreate the intended referent, no more, no less. It must thus contain enough shared information for the reader to understand it, but no information about the author or the communicative situation itself. Stylistically too, it must satisfy only the referential task and not be conspicuous and draw attention to its own style. Furthermore, it is what constitutes the referent, the world represented by the author. In this sense it has the status of a Logos, it is the Word of creation, the Word whereby the world comes into existence. This entails that it be authoritative, that it express the 'truth' about the created world for the reader, lay out the brute facts, however improbable from the point of view of the reader's real world. Thus the reader (for the duration of his performance as a reader–co-creator) must subscribe to the same truth and understand the created world within the author's framework, within his 'ultimate core of meaning'.

Another most important feature of direct author's speech is that, as the language of creation, it cannot itself be seen as part of the created world, nor can the author or the reader be part of the world they themselves create. This leads to the controversial question of the ontological status of the author and reader and their utterance. It also involves the question of the possibility of a wholly neutral language which refers strictly to a reality outside the speaker and listener, without simultaneously referring to the users of language and their situation. Bakhtin is aware of this problem, and one of the threads that run through his works from the 1920s to the 1970s is this different attitude to language from the point of view of aesthetics (or the humanistic sciences, as he was later to generalize) and of natural science. While natural science aims for a non-evaluative language, aesthetics is by its very nature an evaluative act: it consciously evaluates an already evaluated reality. The aesthetic utterance, first and foremost, actively confronts others' evaluations and objects, as opposed to the scientific utterance whose ideal referent is the unverbalized world. It should be emphasized that Bakhtin fully recognizes that a literary utterance cannot but evaluate, and cannot but refer back to a speaker's evaluative (as well as cognitive and chronotopical) stance in the world. How then can this be reconciled with the concept of direct author's speech as defined above? This question has direct bearing on the concept of 'image of author' as used by Vinogradov, and the question of proximity between author and personage.[8]

Bakhtin asks to what extent one can speak of an 'image' of author in Vinogradov's sense. He concludes that such a concept is a *contradictio in adjecto*. In a work of literature, the so-called 'image' of author, albeit an image of a special kind, is an image nevertheless, and as such is part of the represented world, and in turn has a different author who created it. Borrowing a set of theological dicta, Bakhtin makes three functional distinctions:

(1) Primary author: *natura non creata quae creat*
(2) Secondary author: *natura creata quae creat*
(3) Personage: *natura creata quae non creat* [9]

Ontologically speaking, the primary author (and reader) exists, of course, in the real world, but he is also in the work as a whole (insofar as it is a whole utterance as described above). He is in a position, tangential to the real world and the created world, as Bakhtin expresses it.[10] He is in the work only as a representing principle, not as a personage within the created world. He is the carrier of the 'ultimate core of meaning' of the work as a whole. His direct speech, as Bakhtin has described it, is always neutral speech, it is another's speech which has ceased to be perceived as the speech of another (it is both 'another's' and 'own'), and which expresses the norms for the particular kind of utterance that is being uttered.[11] In this sense it is the authoritative background against which any speech in the created world must be measured. Such speech is not created by the author, but is used as a means in his own creation, and the author simply fits the pattern normally assumed for 'author' and does not materialize into an 'image'. From this it follows that direct author's speech is extensively used mainly in periods when the author is in fundamental agreement with the literary norms, when literature itself and authorship are firmly entrenched in society and firmly canonized, such as in the Neoclassicist period. When this is not the case, the author is less likely to speak directly and tends to resort to Bakhtin's third kind of speech, and, as it were, to create his own alternative images of author, genre and literature. He speaks 'through' secondary authors (narrators) or personages, and makes artistic creation itself (which has somehow become problematical) his theme, part of his created world. I will attempt to show that this is the case with the Sentimentalist period in Russian literature, when, as we saw, fundamental changes in ideology and literature, as well as the conception of authorship were taking place.[12]

The second type of speech that enters a literary utterance is 'represented speech' or 'object speech' (*izobrazhennoe ili ob'ekt-noe slovo*), in its purest form, the direct speech of the personages. It is also univocal and strictly oriented toward its referent, but is at the same time itself the object of the author's speech. It is used within the author's utterance, not so much for its referential aims, but as an object, a peculiar 'speech–thing', as speech which serves the purpose of characterization and creates an image of the speaker. It stands out stylistically, and the author displays this style either predominantly for its socio-typical, or for its idiosyncratic features. It is described as univocal because it retains its own referential meaning, the author's intention does not 'penetrate it from within', does not change its tone or meaning. The author does not relate to this type of speech as to speech by a speaking *person*, he does not engage in any kind of dialogical relations with it, but he simply displays it as he would an object. It is like direct author's speech in its direct referential aim, but contrasts to it functionally. It is speech on a different plane than direct author's speech, and is reported within his utterance and controlled by his 'ultimate core of meaning'. It enters the real world not on its own, but as part of an artistic, literary utterance.

The third type of speech that enters the novel structure is 'bivocal speech' or 'speech oriented towards another person's speech'. This category is by far the most interesting, and is, in Bakhtin's view, the type of speech most characteristic of modern narrative prose fiction. It is the only type of speech fully adequate for the represen-tation of another world. It describes this represented world both from the outside by the tangential outsider–author, and simultane-ously from the inside by the personages that populate it. It is thus speech that is both the author's and another's, both creating and created simultaneously. It is other's speech which the author engages dialogically in the full sense of the word. Under the bivocal rubric, Bakhtin discusses a number of phenomena that have this

property in common but differ among themselves according to the
nature of the dialogicity. Any of the traditional compositional
categories may have this quality. Furthermore, the two voices (and
two intentions, two accents, two languages) interact in various
ways: another's speech may be either active and influence the
author's speech, or passive and itself be subject to influence by the
author. Other previous literary utterances and the reader's anticipated responses are particularly important in this respect. The
active type of interaction has several subtypes: hidden internal
polemics, polemically colored autobiography and confession,
hidden dialogue, etc. Within the passive type there are two major
modes of interaction, what Bakhtin calls 'unidirectional bivocal
speech' (stylization and *skaz* are the main types), and 'heterodirectional bivocal speech' where the two intentions clash, move in
opposite directions (parody and parodic *skaz*). Finally, the speech
of another may be physically present or simply implied.

Bivocal speech, in all its varieties, thus occurs on a spectrum
between two poles: on one end of the spectrum it tends towards
confluence of the two voices into direct author's speech or direct
personage speech; the other end of the spectrum tends towards a
total separation between the two voices into two independent
univocal utterances (direct author's speech and direct personage
speech). The style of a work as a whole is defined in terms of
relationships between these basic types of speech contexts.

The *differentia specifica* of Sentimentalist fiction, as opposed to
earlier literary narrative genres (notably the epic), can be reformulated more precisely as the presence of bivocal speech, i.e. the
emergence of a secondary author, what I shall call 'narrator' and a
secondary reader, what I shall call 'narratee', as part of the
represented world. Bakhtin's basic distinctions can be fruitfully
used to define these concepts.[13]

'Narrator' and 'narratee' will be viewed against the background
of a *theoretical norm* of a two-utterance structure, consisting of
direct univocal author's speech (henceforth author utterance) and
univocal personage speech (henceforth personage utterance), as
defined functionally and stylistically. This basic method has been
developed in different contexts by Doležel and Titunik utilizing the
insights of Bakhtin and Voloshinov, in conjunction with a Jakobso-
nian communication model of the utterance.[14] Jakobson distinguishes between two constitutive parts of an utterance: speech

event and narrated event, each with its own set of participants and each correlating with specific functions and verbal features. In the two-utterance norm for narrative texts, the author utterance's *speech event* is unmarked or unfilled, and the personage utterance's *narrated event* is unmarked or unfilled. What this means is roughly that the author utterance reveals nothing about its speakers (Bakhtin's univocal author's speech), whereas the personage utterance functions mainly to reveal facts about its participants, their situation, their relationship, values, and so on (Bakhtin's univocal personage speech).[15]

The author utterance performs the function of reporting and control, it selects and organizes the material. This includes discursive and descriptive statements, phrases introducing and identifying the personages and their utterances, specifications as to intonation, gesture, setting, and so on. In SA terms the author utterance is a speech act of the declarative–representative type, an assertion of the truth with the force of creating a world. Other representatives (hypothesizing, suggesting, insisting) are excluded, as are all directives, commissives, and expressives, all of which impart information about the author–reader situation.[16] The author utterance must thus always be taken as authoritative, objective, and non-evaluative. I shall follow Titunik and refer to all these functions together as the *'reporting function'* of the author utterance, stressing its relational aspects with regard to the personage utterance. In such an utterance, speaker and listener (author and reader) are purely implicit presences. The personages function as the active agents of the non-verbal as well as verbal actions which comprise the narrated event.

The narrated speech event (the personage utterance) may express subjective, idiosyncratic evaluations, attitudes, opinions, conjectures, and so on, with respect to the narrated events they are part of. The personage utterance is, in principle, not authoritative. In other words, the personages may perform the full spectrum of speech acts, but their statements are always contingent upon the author utterance for their veracity and values. The personage utterance is thus always *reported in function*. This functional opposition correlates with, and complements, a verbal opposition between the two utterances: the author utterance is *unmarked* by speech event features, whereas the personage utterance is *marked* in this respect.

Speech event features are elements of language which serve to provide information about the participants in the speech event, their utterance in progress, contact, proximity, personal relationships, chronotopical relationships, and the like. Since the author utterance is characterized by a strict reference to the narrated event, these elements are lacking. Thus the norm narrative text can be summarized as a structure of two functionally and verbally distinct utterances:

(1) The author utterance which is functionally *reporting* and verbally *unmarked* by speech event features
(2) The personage utterance which is functionally *reported* and *marked* by speech event features.

As a norm, the reporting function is thus always correlated with an absence of speech event features, and the author is perceived only implicitly by his *de facto* carrying out the reporting function. The reader is similarly implicit as a co-creator or co-reporter (perceiver) in Bakhtin's sense, and is not explicitly referred to in the text. A narrator (and/or narratee) emerges by what Doležel describes as a 'neutralization' operation, and what Titunik describes as a disruption of the two-utterance structure by the interpolation of a third kind of utterance which is characterized as a combination of authorial and personage functions:

(3) Narrator utterance, which is *reporting–reported* in function and *marked* by speech event features.

Different types and degrees of 'narratorhood' will emerge against the norm, depending on the extent to which authorial function (focus on the referent) is carried out in conjunction with personage function (being the referent). The fact that personage function is added to authorial function entails stylistically marked speech. Narrator can thus be seen as a transformation from 'author' to 'author-as-personage'. The narrator utterance is distinguishable from the author utterance, whose function it models, by the presence of speech event features. This type of triple utterance structure will result when the author (and/or reader) performs personage functions (Doležel's interpretation or interpretation and action function) in addition to the authorial reporting function – with a resulting marking of the speech event, or, conversely, when a personage in addition to his normal functions takes on the reporting function. In either case there occurs a combination of authorial function and personage function, and in either case the speech event will be marked in the narrator utterance. Narrator may tend towards, but not coincide with, the pole of author, or towards the pole of the personages. Whatever the case may be, the narrator differs from both author and personage in the combination of function and verbal features.

The functional relationships between the utterances are of a dynamic nature, best described as categories of speech reporting in Voloshinov's sense: direct discourse, indirect discourse, and quasi-quoted (or represented) discourse, and their modifications.[17] These forms entail, respectively, authorial transmission, transformation, or a combination of transmission and transformation of the personage utterance. The clearest manifestation of the norm occurs in the case of direct discourse, which conjoins the author and personage utterances by conjunctionless coordination, and which leaves the personage utterance intact in its original form, clearly set apart from the author's utterance. The two utterances in this case are also set apart graphically, by special punctuation, and they are identifiable not only functionally–verbally but also compositionally. However, the norm prevails even when this is not the case, as long as speech event features, when they enter a 'compositionally speaking' author's context, can be assigned to the personages based on contextual information. This stresses the important point that compositional forms do not automatically determine the borders of the utterances (although they often do in fact coincide), but that the definition is purely functional/verbal. The utterances may thus 'compositionally' overlap, interpenetrate, and transform each other, without a narrator emerging.

By the same token, the participants of the narrator utterance may be explicitly introduced and identified by the reporting author utterance (the proper reporting clauses, setting description, punctuation, etc.), or they may be identified and set apart from the author and reader only through their own speech event, or they may be simply equated with 'author' and 'reader' of the work as a whole, with a reporting author utterance wholly lacking in its explicit form.[18]

Despite the anthropomorphic terms used, the three main categories of speech, outlined above, are functional–verbal categories, and are not strictly tied to either compositional forms or *a priori* persons. This is particularly obvious in the distinction between 'named' and 'unnamed' narrators. In the following, the traditional terms will be used to stand for referential totalities generated through functional–verbal qualities of the text, and their status as 'persons' is only inferred and used as a convenience. Depending on the concentration of speech event features in the reporting context, the narrator and narratee will be more or less perceptible, more or less like the norm author and reader, or more or less fully delineated as personages. Their communicative situation and relationship will be more or less detailed, and their proximity will stand out to greater or lesser degree. The speech event features will also vary in kind and distribution so that different aspects of the images will be stressed: features relating to narrator/narratee personalities, to their functions as 'author/reader', to their present utterance, and so on.

This kind of disruption of the norm text has been characterized as a device whereby the author and reader are made part of the topic of the message as a whole, just as the personages are part of that topic.[19] This is, in a sense, a fictionalization of reality, which, as we saw above, was called forth by the increase in distance between real authors and readers during the late eighteenth century. Being a device of fiction, however, it precludes any direct identification of narrator and narratee with the real author and reader; the former two are always fictional constructs by the latter. It could also be viewed as a device whereby fiction is made to seem like unmediated reality, since the participants of the narrator utterance and their situation are made to resemble and simulate a real author and reader and their ideally intimate situation. It is the contention of this study that this device is a signal feature of Sentimentalist fiction, and that the essence of Sentimentalist solipsism resides precisely in the fact that author, reader, the act of authorship, and the communicative event, are made part of the topic of the works, in other words, that a narrator utterance is strongly featured. Indeed, this topic often became the main topic to the detriment of traditional plots and personages. A corollary of this is that with author and reader as prominent protagonists (as narrator and narratee), the act of reporting itself becomes a major narrated event. Not only the act of writing 'this work', but the motivations for doing so, the preparations and circumstances preceding the writing, the sources, and so on, may turn into a fullblown plot.

The fact that Sentimentalist readers not used to this device perceived the narrator utterance as direct author utterance which they were used to from Neoclassicist prose, attests to the innovatory nature of the device. They were in fact fooled by the simulation of intimacy. There is ample evidence to this effect in the controversy over the 'new' prose mentioned earlier. One such instance is the uproar caused by Fedor Emin's 'autobiographism' in *Miramond*, where the 'author' in his preface identifies himself explicitly with one of the personages, Feridat.[20] An even more telling example is the response to Rousseau's *La Nouvelle Héloise*, when two of the real readers actually began a correspondence with Jean-Jacques himself, signing their letters Julie and Claire – literally extending fiction into real life. Rousseau's reactions are equally telling: by keeping up his end of the correspondence he maintains the fiction, while on the other hand, he soon became suspicious about its real life status and indeed began to suspect that his correspondents were neither Julie nor Claire, but men of the enemy persuasion who wanted to make him into a laughing-stock. He suspected them (unjustly) of various base real life motivations beyond their fiction. This incident caught Karamzin's fancy and eight pages of *Messenger of Europe* are devoted to a review of the published letters – yet another twist, reinstating art which had entered life, back into art, replete with reviews.[21] That the narrator was often interpreted as a real person by readers of Sentimentalist fiction is further borne out by such phenomena as Wertherian suicides, and, in a Russian setting, pilgrimages to the pond of poor Liza. In our investigation of Karamzin's works we will see numerous other examples of this phenomenon. Lotman pays particular attention to Karamzin as author, Karamzin as narrator (especially in *Letters of a Russian Traveller*), Karamzin as politician and historian, and Karamzin as a real historical person whose whole life was ultimately determined by aesthetic (and thus also moral) criteria.[22] Romantic Byronism in the succeeding era is the climax of this tendency to model one's life on art.

## TYPOLOGY OF VERBAL FEATURES MARKING NARRATOR/ NARRATEE

Narrator and narratee are integral parts of the functional–verbal text structure and are defined as referential totalities generated by a specific combination of functions and verbal features. The solipsistic principle of Sentimentalism can, accordingly, be reformulated as the presence of a dense concentration of speech event features in the reporting context of the work. Speech event features thus become crucial in an investigation of narrator and narratee in Sentimentalist prose: they are the signals of a fictionalization of author and reader within the text, and will also allow us to move from the abstraction of textual models to the concrete level of actual texts. My next task is thus to identify certain features of language which provide us with information about speaker and listener and their situation, while also being used in the telling of a story.

More or less complete typologies of such features have been designed for different purposes by Jakobson, Doležel, and Titunik, and are here further developed and adapted to my specific focus on Sentimentalist prose fiction. The organization of my typology reflects the three main aspects of narrator which emerge as most prominent in Sentimentalist prose: narrator and narratee as personages in their own right, narrator in his relationship to narratee, and narrator and narratee as 'author' and 'reader' of their own narrated event. The fact that a narrator is simultaneously part of a story, part of a communicative situation, and teller of a story, makes a rigid separation of these aspects and features quite artificial. Nevertheless, I think that different Sentimentalist works are characterized by a predominance of different aspects of narrator. The typology which follows is not meant to be exact or quantifiable in exact terms, and the categories will overlap, complement and reinforce one another. Although certain features may well serve as stronger markers of narrator/narratee than others, I see no need for my present purposes to rank them. My view will be that the stronger the concentration of the features listed, the more prominent will be the images of narrator and narratee that emerge and the lesser will be the focus on personages and the story proper.

## Features which characterize narrator and narratee as personages

### Emotive and expressive features

Besides interjections, 'the purely emotive stratum in language',[23] exclamations, self-apostrophes, rhetorical questions, diminutives, superlatives, elliptical constructions, aposiopesis, praeteritio, special rhythms, special intonations (marked by italics or other special typeface, punctuation, or word order), serve to a large extent to reveal the narrator's emotional state either at the moment of narration or in general. A certain class of speech acts, expressives, have as their point to express various psychological states of the speaker, and are in principle excluded from the author utterance. Whenever they are explicitly perceptible (by any of the devices mentioned or by explicit indications of performative usage) they mark a narrator.

The role of these features need hardly be stressed for Sentimentalist fiction. Karamzin's own statements of literary credo as set forth in, for instance, 'What does an Author Need?', are quite explicit on this score.[24] The first and foremost quality in an author is a sensitive, compassionate heart which responds emotionally and intellectually to beauty and harmony, as well as to the sorrows and misfortunes of mankind. Since 'the creator is always depicted in his creation, and often – against his will', his emotions will obviously be one of the prime features in this depiction. If these emotions are lacking, and the author instead possesses a 'heart of steel', his art cannot achieve its proper effect, which is to evoke the appropriate sensitivities in the reader. Art must depict a 'heart bleeding for the misfortunes of mankind', not the 'cold darkness of [the author's] soul', and must evoke a similar emotional response in the similarly sensitive reader's similarly sensitive soul. Thus it is obvious why the expressive and emotive features become all-important in a work of art. As Karamzin expressed it: 'Style, figures of speech, metaphors, images, expressions – all this moves and captivates when it is animated by feeling.'[25] This stands in sharp contrast to the Neoclassicist requirement that a work contain a specific style, figures, etc., according to predetermined norms for the genre.

### Subjective semantics

Here belong mainly adjectival and adverbial modifiers (and particularly the comparative and superlative degrees, 'grammatically', as well as semantically), but also certain nouns (kinship terms, proper names, invective nouns, and the like), 'extreme' numerals, and certain verbs and their combinations, which evaluate things

either 'factually' (small/large, beautiful/ugly, right/wrong, hero/
villain), or 'modally' (with regard to reality, possibility, conditiona-
lity, causality, desirability, necessity). In order to qualify as speech
event features they must reflect the narrator's subjective view,
differ from 'public opinion', and not be literary clichés. Whatever
they refer to, they also reflect back on the narrator's person, his
values, morals, knowledge, capacities for judging, and so on. In SA
terms, any speech act which is evaluative is excluded from the
author utterance, which can only contain what can crudely be
termed 'neutral' statements or assertions of truth. Therefore,
explicit markers to the contrary, such as those listed above, and the
corresponding performative usage of verbs such as suggest, hypo-
thesize, believe (which indicate different degrees of commitment to
truth), or suggest, insist, swear (which indicate the speaker's
interest), cannot be taken as issuing from the author, but are
markers of a narrator and his evaluation. All these means are
extremely prominent in Sentimentalist fiction and frequently
appear in unusual concentration – double, or even triple modifiers,
repetitions (often of the polyptotonic kind) of the same expressions
over extended segments of the text, special accumulations of
superlatives and diminutives or words of an inherently superlative
or diminutive nature, such as 'billions', 'myriads', 'all', 'most
often', 'huge'.

## Linguistic speech characterization

By this is meant *kind of speech* (dialects: professional, social,
regional; idiolects: idiosyncrasies, anomalies, pathological defects,
speech distortion, mispronunciation, repetition of tag words, mala-
propism, folk etymology); *manner of speaking* (oral or written);
*style of speech* (high bookish, officialese, conversational, intimate,
vulgar). Any linguistic deviation within the narration from the
standard written language codified for the genre will serve, besides
its purely referential purposes, also to characterize a narrator.
Linguistic speech characterization used to differentiate narrator or
personages is (to make a rather broad generalization) not exploited
by Karamzin, beyond the well-known striving to avoid coarseness
and vulgarity of any kind, as well as bookish 'pedantry' and to write
the way people (and especially women) of the educated class speak
– or at least ought to speak.[26]

## Features which characterize the narrator's relationship to the narratee and their situation

### *Allocutional features*

Forms in vocative function are substantival, pronominal, and adjectival forms explicitly used to single out, name, and describe the addressee and to gain and retain his attention. They may range from a single noun or proper name ('Reader!'), to a noun combined with a pronoun ('My friends!') or with an adjectival epithet ('Gentle reader!'), to more extended combinations of the above, as well as appositions or extended relative clauses. Karamzin, in practically all his works, makes his narratee's presence explicitly felt. Indeed, there are examples of works which in their entirety are extended allocutions with the most elaborate vocative forms. For instance, 'Dedication of a Grove' ('Posviashchenie kushchi') begins with the following elaborate construction: 'Fair, eternally young, multifarious, winged goddess, flowering *Fantasy!*' In cases such as this, the narratee is not only named, but her qualities are described, and frequently even her actions and general situation. The narratees addressed are quite varied and often encompass, besides the narratee of the work as a whole, also the personages and even the inanimate setting, thereby animating it. Often the narratee is the narrator himself or some aspect of him, and the effect is one of peculiar soliloquy, or curious divided forms of address, which erase the borders between speech event and narrated event. The vocative forms are seldom neutral to the narrator's own emotions, and thus also serve as emotive, expressive features, as discussed above, as well as markers of social deixis and phatic function.

Expressives, commissives, and directives are speech acts which include reference to the speech event. Expressives are defined by Searle as speech acts which express the psychological state of speaker or hearer, such as: thank, apologize, congratulate, condole, deplore, welcome. In addition to revealing facts about the narrator himself, they also tell us something about the narratee and the relationship between them.[27] Expressives are extremely well developed in Karamzin's works, and, in at least one instance, an expressive determines the very form of a work: 'The Bird of Paradise' ('Raiskaia ptichka') is an extended compliment to the narratee. Apologies of various kinds are also prominent, and particularly in Karamzin's later works, they are used in a light playful tone. Commissives, which mainly reveal the narrator's intention, may also inform us about the narratee.

An even more obvious form of marked speech event is a more fully developed dialogue where the narratee actually 'gets the floor'. This happens when his responses are anticipated or his previous utterances recalled by the narrator who 'quotes' or simply implies the narratee's lines. It can take the shape of quoting the whole line or more subtle 'narratee-words', used by the narrator as if in quotation marks, often actually marked by the appropriate punctuation or singled out by special orthography within the narrator's own speech, or even in such extreme forms as the blank pages that Tristram Shandy leaves for his narratee to 'put his fancy in'. Devices such as fragmented stories, or, on a smaller scale, elliptical constructions or summaries, can be seen as part of the same phenomenon. Besides their emotive function noted above, they also reveal the narratee's presence. He is assumed to be able to 'fill in the blanks', or this ability may at least be pointed to. Sometimes further actions by the narratee are indicated, as when the narrator suggests that the narratee 'demand a more detailed explanation from his favorite eighteen-year-old girl friend', or 'leave us and not read our story which is intended only for sensitive souls'. These sorts of relationships point to the important shifts in roles between narrator and narratee, which both Bakhtin and Voloshinov so adamantly stressed: the speaker as listener and the listener as speaker. These kinds of shifts are of the utmost importance in Karamzin's fiction.

## Deixis

The most prevalent devices for revealing the narrator's and narratee's anchoring in a common communicative situation, more or less distinct from the narrated event, can be discussed under the label of deixis: personal, temporal, spatial, and social. Deictic aspects of language are defined by Fillmore as:

lexical items and grammatical forms which can be interpreted only when the sentences in which they occur are understood as being anchored in some social context, that context defined in such a way as to identify the participants in the communication act, their location in space, and the time during which the communication act is performed.[28]

Both deixis and elenxis (defined as relationships strictly within the narrated event without reference to the speech event) are possible in the narrator utterance, while the author utterance can include only the elenctic forms.[29]

The first and second person forms of verbs and personal and possessive pronouns define narrator as addresser and narratee as addressee, and shift when their roles shift. Only third person forms may occur in the author utterance. In Sentimentalist fiction first person narration was particularly popular, owing to the personalization and fictionalization of 'author', and the influence of new literary genres, such as autobiographies, memoirs, confessions, diaries, and journals of various kinds where this form is natural.[30]

All three verbal tenses (past, present, future), temporal adverbs or adverbial phrases, adjectival phrases (now, then, tomorrow, before, after, three years ago, last summer), are used relative to the narrator's time position. They may also denote the narratee's time position, but need not. In other words, the 'encoding time' may be different from the 'decoding time', or the two may simply be indicated as 'coding time'. The narrated event is strictly past tense, and thus only past tense indicators are allowed in the norm author utterance. Even in cases where present tense forms are used, they refer to the past (historical present) or to an atemporal, eternal time frame (discursive or existential present, stressing the fact rather than the time). Karamzin's works display quite interesting shifts between past tense, historical or existential present, and present tense proper, indicating subtle changes in the narrator's simulated participation or emotional involvement in, and evaluation of, the narrated events, personages, or phenomena. Bakhtin makes a good case for distinguishing the epic from the novel in terms of a present time center in the novel and a past one in the epic.[31] This is somewhat similar to describing the novel in terms of both deixis and elenxis, and the epic in terms of elenxis exclusively. I shall return to this question below in the context of the narrator's control function.

Spatial adverbs, adverbial phrases, adjectives, adjectival phrases, and demonstrative pronouns (here, there, this, that, up, down, right, left, near, far) indicate the location of the narrator, narratee, or both, as a spatial reference point. Some of these can be used elenctically and can thus occur in the author utterance, but others have only deictic reference and mark a narrator. The most clearcut case of dependence on the communicative situation is demonstrated by what Fillmore calls 'presentatives'.[32] In Russian certain demonstratives are of this nature, such as *von, vot,* and are used strictly gesturally so that they must be perceived together with the gesture, and in written texts cannot be understood without more explicit situational information. Certain verbs of motion (English 'come/go', in Russian expressed by means of prefixes, such as *pri-, u-, vos-, niz-*) are other examples of spatial deixis, which often require some knowledge of the concrete utterance situation. Indeed, perception is often referred to in asides, such as *vidite, znaete, zamet'te, predstav'te sebe,* which in a single form unite personal, spatial, temporal, and social deixis, as well as the vocative function mentioned above. Karamzin's works tend to be explicit in giving detailed deictic information about the location of his narrators and narratees. Often the location of the narrator coincides with that of the narrated events, and indeed, the narrator's visit to a certain locale is often what provokes the telling of the story in the first place. This tendency towards spatial proximity between the narrator, narratee and personages contributes significantly to the general impression of intimacy and sympathy between them, stressed also by other (for instance, emotive) means.

Some of the devices for person, time, and space deixis which serve to establish the functional, spatial and temporal parameters between narrator, narratee, and personages, can also serve to indicate the social realities of the speech event. The personal and possessive pronouns are a case in point. Paul Friedrich points to ten factors which determine the appropriateness of Russian *ty* or *vy* (and these factors, consequently, can to some extent be inferred from the pronouns used in the text): the topic of conversation, the social context, the age or sex or generation of the partners, their kinship relationships, their shared membership in a dialect or social group, juridical and political authority on the part of either, and the degree of emotional solidarity between them.[33]

Social relationships can also be revealed by proper names, titles, kinship terms, and by the use of specific speech levels (polite, honorific, humble, cringing).[34] Distinctions between male and female, young and adult, addressees can also be made explicit in the language of the narrator utterance, but can only be implied in the author utterance. This was of particular importance during the

Sentimentalist period, and is amply illustrated in the numerous discussions about female readers and writers both in Karamzin's own criticism and in the Shishkovite counterstatements and parodies of the Karamzinian 'effeminate' language. Certain features of language were linked to male speech (various forms of 'pedantry', stemming from the old literature, learned prose of a chancery hue, business formulae, as well as low and vulgar expressions), and should be avoided, so as not to offend the sensitive readers (women being the models).[35]

Walter Ong, among others, has stressed the social implications of even such humble elements of language as the definite article, closely related to demonstratives. Ong sees the use of 'the' or demonstratives such as 'that X' (when implying 'that X which you and I know so well') as an important device for establishing companionship between Hemingway's narrator and narratee.[36] The same device is extremely frequent in Karamzin's works, the most famous instance being the opening lines of 'Natal'ia, the Boyar's Daughter' ('Natal'ia, boiarskaia doch''): 'Kto iz nas ne liubit tekh vremen' ('Which one of us does not remember those times'). Various means for glossing and explaining the narrated events can also be seen as indicators of the narrator's perception of his addressee – his level of education, general knowledge, linguistic and literary competence. Similarly, comparisons of something alien to the narratee with something familiar to him (or vice versa) are frequently used by Karamzin as a traveller when describing something foreign in terms of something Russian, and signal speech event. In general, Karamzin's works stand out in striking contrast to previous fiction through their intimate, sympathetic narrator–narratee relationships – as would be expected, given the intellectual climate of the era. The two are usually on the same level in all respects, and perhaps because of this near identity, their positions can so easily shift.

## Phatic features

Closely related to the above are elements that 'serve to establish, to prolong, or to discontinue communication, to check whether the channel works [ . . . ] to attract the attention of the interlocutor or to confirm his continued attention'.[37] This is most overtly expressed by ritualized formulae of various kinds. Of a similar nature are the narrator's means for creating suspense, keeping his reader from yawning, and when explicitly referred to, they mark the speech event. Such devices are quite fancifully laid bare in some of Karamzin's works, notably 'Natal'ia' and *A Knight of our Time* (*Rytsar' nashego vremeni*).

## Features which mark the narrator/narratee's author/reader function

### Discourse deixis

By this I mean any devices that refer to the narrator utterance in progress, or metalingual elements in the wide sense. These devices range from brief indicators, such as 'the former', 'the above', to more elaborate constructions. They may refer to the discourse point as a general coding time: 'In the last paragraph we saw', or as decoding time: 'In the last chapter you saw.'[38] All such instances refer to some temporal or spatial point in the narrator utterance. Some such references are peculiar to written discourse ('above', 'below'), often including reference to the act of writing itself (trembling hands that cannot hold the pen, tears falling on the sheet of paper, illegible handwriting, and other clichés of epistolary writing, prominent also in Karamzin). Others contribute to sustain an impression of oral delivery ('what I just said', 'next you will hear'). These lay bare the narrator as writer or speaker and the narratee as reader or listener.

There are, however, elements which refer more explicitly to authorship: any references to literary genres ('Ah! why am I not writing a novel, but a sad true story?'), literary devices ('this striking comparison', 'this rhetorical figure'), literary composition ('may these lines be the introduction or foreword'), references to readers of novels, readers of this tale, and so on. Such devices of consecutive literary analysis are well developed, especially in Karamzin's later works. Another type of discourse deixis is the use of glosses, footnotes, editorial devices, and various other explanatory material, as well as remarks (corrections, rewordings) qualifying the utterance in some way ('to put it plainly', 'in brief', 'by the way').[39]

Any information pertaining to the genesis of the story (pre-reporting or encoding information) or to the reception (post-

reporting or decoding information) is part of the same phenomenon. Pre-reporting information can consist of allusions to the
narrator's sources. In Sentimentalist fiction, old manuscripts,
ancient chronicles, tales or myths, letters, sad events told by a
friend, and the narrator's own memory are typical sources, frequently elaborated at great length. Information about how the
narrator came by the story, his own circumstances at the time, his
mood, location, what effects the story had on him, how it was told
to him, is typical. Other types of pre-reporting information pertain
to what inspired the present telling, why the story is pertinent now –
some nature scene or some incident reminds the narrator of this
story, ancient gravestones prompt him to recollect the sad fates of
the persons buried, a melancholy mood may match the mood of the
story, the narrator may be overcome by inspiration, or the narratee
may simply request a story. The story may even be explicitly
revealed as a turn in a parlor game, as in the case of Karamzin's
'The Deep Forest' ('Dremuchii les'). Frequently these motifs are
compositionally organized as more or less independent 'overtures/
epilogues' (as Gukovskii aptly has termed them), preceding and/or
concluding the story proper as its reporting clause. This reporting
clause may be expanded into a story in its own right on a par with
the real story. Often the reporting clause not only introduces and
concludes the story, but constantly interrupts its telling, and itself
colors the core story. In some cases, the core story even becomes
incidental to its telling.

In this type of story about the genesis (or further fate) of a story,
certain elements tend to prevail, which, on the one hand, exceed
normal reporting acts (representation, description, etc.) but, on
the other hand, are more limited in range than the traditional
personage actions, and are not part of the sequence of actions in the
core story. In other words, they consist of something more than
author's speech acts and something less than personages' speech
and non-speech acts, although they overlap with both. This is fully
consistent with the definition of narrator in terms of functions. In
his analysis of a work by Komensky, Doležel aptly describes a
somewhat similar configuration of actions as 'narrator motifs,
N-motifs'.[40] In the case of a genesis story, the motifs, as we have
seen, have to do with the narrator's sources and the obtaining of
them. Certain types of actions become highlighted: *perceptive*
(reading, listening, seeing, noticing, hearing, observing,

eavesdropping), *interpretative* (condemning, approving, understanding, analyzing, pondering, questioning, doubting), *emotively
responsive* (loving, liking, being moved, feeling sorry, weeping,
being amazed, being awestruck). All of this amounts to nothing but
the normal functions of the addressee. In many Sentimentalist
works, the narrator is indeed also a (secondary) narratee, and the
narratee, in turn, frequently a (secondary) narrator – which once
more stresses the precarious balance between speaker as listener,
listener as speaker, and utterances that are both the author's and
another speaker's simultaneously. This is most emphatically the
case in Karamzin's 'Bornholm Island' ('Ostrov Borngol′m'), as I
will show.

Some utterances, besides commenting on the utterance itself and
its sources, tend to compare the present manner of telling to other
past or possible ways of telling the *same* story ('Poor Liza',
'Natal′ia'), or *similar* stories ('My Confession', *Knight,* 'The
Beautiful Princess', 'The Deep Forest'), often parodying the genre,
style, or other literary features. In this case the narrator's role is
three-fold: he is featured as narratee, re-narrator, and as literary
critic. Occasionally he even resorts to the use of professional jargon
as a critic. In these variants of pre-reporting motifs, the narrator
himself is featured as narratee or critic of *others'* stories. In the case
of post-reporting motifs, reference is made in the narrator's story to
the reception of the *same* story which is now in progress. Information about the further fate of the narrator's story (or parts of it)
may be included. Such information consists of speculations about
who may read it, remarks about the narrator's own rereading, and
the projected effects the story may have. Not surprisingly, the
Sentimentalist narrator in these cases too, often turns out to be the
narratee (his own addressee), or, as it were, reincarnated as a
reader who responds, feels, and acts, precisely like the narrator.
Thus the discourse deictic devices are highly indicative of Sentimentalist solipsism.


## Poetic language

By this is meant any obvious 'artistic' manipulations of language:
poetic figures and tropes, rhyme, rhythm, intonation, stanza or
chapter division, musical quality, euphonic devices, purple
patches, literary allusions, inasfar as they somehow deviate from

the prevalent literary norms for the genre. Against the background
of the *slaveno–rossiiskii* norm for prose fiction, one of the most
important features of the Karamzinian 'new style' was the formation of a so-called poetic style.[41] The lexical composition of the
poetic style partly coincides with the 'high' lexicon retained from
the *slaveno–rossiiskii* style. All elements of the poetic lexicon can in
certain contexts be 'high', but not all the 'high' elements can be
poetic. This special stylistic layer did not previously carry out the
poetic function it acquired in the Karamzin system, although
indications are that already Trediakovskii thought along the same
lines. The new function was wholly determined by the author's
attitude – not by any *a priori* criteria. Any object, any theme, can
be poeticized, and, in fact, the less inherently poetic the object is,
the more necessary it becomes to poeticize it by recourse to the
appropriate poetic lexicon, specific syntactical means, etc. Thus,
for instance, common prostitutes in Karamzin's style become
'nymphs of joy'. Poetic means are to be found both in narrator's
speech and personage speech, both in written and spoken discourse, both in literature and non-literature. Poetic diction does
not, in principle, need any motivation whatsoever, but is part and
parcel of the speaker's perception of reality. The Karamzinian
style, as a rule, gets an overall poetic coloration. Although the
poetic elements are more pronounced in verse than in prose, the
fact is that there is no great difference between Karamzin's verse
and his prose; his prose, too, is properly poeticized.[42] Karamzin's
own discussions of literature testify to the fact that this was indeed
an important aspect of his literary credo. For example, in the
foreword to the second volume of his almanac *Aonidy* in 1797,
Karamzin speaks out against lofty bombastic pathos, traditionally
high important themes, as well as against writing according to
predetermined models of any kind. Instead he advises the budding
author to write about his own experiences, subjects close to his
heart:

The true poet finds a poetic side in the most ordinary things: his task is to
gloss everything in living colors, to impart to everything a witty thought, a
tender sentiment, or to embellish expressively an ordinary thought, an
ordinary sentiment, to show the nuances which are hidden from the eyes of
others, to find imperceptible analogies, similarities, to play with ideas, and
like Jupiter (as the wise Aesop said) at times *make the petty great, at times
the great, petty*.[43]

Furthermore, the poet must not write in general terms, but show his theme as it relates to his own character and situation, for, Karamzin points out, such subjectivism helps to convince us of the truth and often deceives us – but such deceit, in Karamzin's view, is the triumph of art.[44] One can hardly find a better description of the Sentimentalist author's poetic function and of the devices which make the author as poet perceptible to the reader (i.e., which mark a narrator–poet).

Vinogradov points out that abstract lexicon came to be linked mainly to spheres of emotional–psychological and ethical concepts, that socio-political ideas were often expressed in the style of idylls and religious symbolism in florid, ornamental language, that periphrasis became especially favored, and that a specific range of adjectives, adverbs, and nouns which expressed the most nuanced emotions, moods, and experiences was developed.[45] It was, however, largely by syntactic means that the poetization of the ordinary came about, and syntax was perhaps the area where the Karamzinian reforms made themselves most strongly felt. The prevailing convoluted, oratorical, declamatory syntax, inherited partly from the Latino-Greco-Germanic scholastic and chancery styles, was abandoned in favor of a simpler syntax based on more natural and logical linkage of ideas. The phrase structure was significantly altered, and the means for conjoining clauses were drastically changed. Subordinate conjunctions were reduced in number, and coordination (with or without conjunction) became the preferred method. Frequently clauses were joined together into lengthy chains, often by tautological conjunctions ('*Ia khotel by, chtoby [ . . . ] i chtoby [ . . . ] khotel by, chtoby [ . . . ] chtoby [ . . . ] i chtoby [ . . . ] khotel by, chtoby [ . . . ] khotel by, nakonets, chtoby [ . . . ]* ' is rather typical). Word order was standardized, and thus inversion became a viable means for marking poetic speech. All this entered the famed Karamzinian *period*. Various kinds of symmetry, parallel lexical chains, anaphora and epiphora, refrains, repetitions, contrasts, euphonic repetition, expressive, exclamatory, interrogatory, and intonational modulations, created an amazingly rhythmical and emotionally expressive cadenced prose, quite close to verse and orchestrated in accord with the narrator's shifting moods. One must note, however, that this subjective poetic character of Sentimentalist prose, on the one hand soon turned conventional, and that there developed a certain set of stock phrases, typical images, typical emotions, which came to be viewed as poetic. On the other hand, the poetization could turn into an exaggerated and mannered periphrastic mania in the hands of the imitators of Karamzin, and even provoked his censure.

## Narrator's transmission/transformation of his narrated event and narrated speech event

Closely related to (and partly overlapping with) the previous categories are features in the narrator's speech event which reveal his authorial control function. Control implies selection and organization of the material, introduction and characterization of personages and events, specification of manner of speech, intonation, and gestures. As soon as this control is made explicit and draws attention to itself it may be seen as a mark of narrator.

Bakhtin made the selection and delimitation of topic a major point in his distinction between the epic and the novel.[46] The epic topic is predetermined national legend, set in the absolute past and separated from the author and reader by absolute, epic distance, pre-evaluated as an officially and generically canonized idealization and piously accepted by author and reader as part of their world view, and known to both as a finalized and resolved whole. It is based on 'impersonal, indisputable legend, universality of evaluation and point of view, which excludes any possibility of a different approach, a deep piety with regard to the object of representation and the very word about it as the word of legend.'[47] The point of reference is located in the absolute atemporal past. Thus the epic world is wholly finalized and resolved (*zavershen*) as a real event of the distant past, but also as an idea and as a value. It cannot be changed or re-evaluated, but rather, everything else is conceptualized in terms of its norms, according to the values of 'origins', 'ancestors', 'the first', 'the beginning', and other such categories as axiologically superlative. Memory, not cognition, nor invention, nor experience, is the basic creative source.[48] What this means is that personal invention, experience, and so on, are wholly irrelevant to authorial function – the epic author's single most important function is to keep memory alive, to carry on tradition and eternalize what is predetermined as being worthy of it. The epic narration is thus representation *sub specie aeternitatis*. Authorial control of the topic is also wholly irrelevant as an artistic category, since the author can only choose which part of the legend to tell (and, indeed, must limit himself to a part since it cannot be retold in its entirety). This choice is, in itself, not artistically significant, since any part reiterates the predetermined structure of the whole. Thus the epic topic, like direct univocal author's speech, is wholly beyond the author's control; it simply expresses the norm, in the canonized generic form, and the author's control of his topic is assumed as an implied given fact.

As soon as his control is somehow topicalized or laid bare (beyond epic clichés to this effect) either positively (affirming that he in fact controls his story) or negatively (stressing his lack of control), this must be seen as marking a narrator. Explicit references to scientific, artistic, literary, or other authorities or sources can be seen as indicators of the narrator's personal control (if he questions, contradicts, parodies them) or his personal lack of control (if he simply affirms them or uses them didactically). Any excessive stress on the truth of what is told, similarly marks a narrator, since the author's statements are by definition assumed to express the truth. Similarly, references to the narrator's knowledge or ignorance of events or phenomena, explicit hypothesizing, guessing, and all the devices of subjective semantics or deixis, besides their other functions, also may reveal the narrator's control.

Most importantly, however, whenever the topic selected is not part of legend, when the axiological and chronotopical center shifts to a nonfinalized and nonresolved present, as a 'process of becoming' in Bakhtin's sense, a wholly new type of artistic information emerges with a stress on what is new and unknown to the reader, on what the narrator knows but the narratee will find out only through the narrator's utterance. Thus the narrator's control of what to tell, when to tell it, in how much detail to tell it, which parts to emphasize, and so on, become artistically viable devices and potential topics in their own right. Any explicit exploitation of the addressee's expectations by different devices for withholding information or providing excess information or information out of sequence, marks a narrator. Excess information can take various forms (ornamentalism and elaboration, empty 'filler' words, repetitions, belaboring, emphasizing, explaining, rewording previously made points or common truisms), and may develop into lengthy digressions – most famously laid bare in Sterne's digression on digressions. Introductory or parenthetical phrases such as 'it must be said', 'as is wellknown to everyone', 'without doubt', 'of course', 'strictly speaking', reveal the narrator's hand, as do digressions–resumptions frequently explicit in Karamzin's works: 'But this is not the point'; 'But we will anticipate this messenger and see what is happening in the capital'; 'Let us return to Moscow – there our story began and there it must also end'; 'The reader will forgive me this digression'; 'Now the reader must know that [ . . . ] but we don't want to reveal the future in advance.'

The narrator's control is perhaps even more poignantly laid bare in what he chooses *not* to tell. This may be expressed as ellipsis, by means of aposiopesis or praeteritio – devices frequent in Karamzin's works: 'But I cannot describe all that they said on this occasion'; 'But what pen can now describe his emotions'; 'I heard nothing more'; 'she barely dared to believe her ears and . . . but I throw down my brush. I'll say only that'; 'by the way, there is no great need to know it'. The most telling manifestation of control is ellipsis on a larger scale within the very plotline itself, namely fragmentation as a conscious literary device. Fragmentation in the sense that the story breaks off without giving the narratee a conclusion is most strikingly used in 'Bornholm Island', 'Liodor', and *Knight*. In Sentimentalist fiction the fragment became a most important form.

Similar means highlight the narrator's explicit control of his narrated speech event, but there are, in addition, the specific devices for transformation and re-contextualization of 'originally autonomous' personage speech, usually discussed under the label 'reported speech'.[49] Basically, the tendency in Karamzin's works is for educated, refined narrator's discourse to penetrate and transform the personage speech stylistically so that the two utterances are hardly distinguishable in terms of language. On the other hand, the narrator is prone to analyze his personage's speech in terms of the context in which it occurs – gestures, accompanying the speech, tone, facial appearance, bodily position, and so on, are incorporated in great detail into the narrator's reporting contextualizing clause. This is, of course, particularly true of the emotive aspects of the utterances – his own and those of the personages most often being identical. Thus the narrator's reporting clause in most cases presets the narratee for the desired emotional perception or empathy for the personages.

Although most of these features in combination with authorial function are used prominently in all of Karamzin's works, one can discern a certain evolution. The earliest works in an idyllic mode tend to define the narrator and narratee as sensitive personages and are particularly good illustrations of the first group of speech event features. Works related to what I will call salon practices, are especially good illustrations of the intimacies of the narrator's relationship to his narratee and thus of the second group of features. Karamzin's last, most mature works, while incorporating most of the features listed, use the third group of features to particular advantage and create 'professional' images of narrators who tend to mock other literary works. I shall therefore investigate Karamzin's prose both 'typologically' and chronologically, beginning with the early idylls.

# 3
# The literary model: the idyll

The middle echelon of the Neoclassicist genre–style hierarchy, and particularly the idyll, became increasingly important during the third and last, Kheraskovian, period of Neoclassicism. The idyll was also one of the genres that gained most attention among the Sentimentalists, and Karamzin's first venture into prose fiction was his 1783 translation of Salomon Gessner's idyll 'Das hölzerne Bein'. The choice of the idyll genre was highly symptomatic of the era and can be seen as the common ground between the two literary movements and as the prime literary model for Sentimentalist prose. The emergence of a prose fiction that centers around the narrator can be elucidated to a significant degree by a closer look at the idyll as a literary form.

'Poetry' ('Poeziia') written in 1787, is one of Karamzin's earliest statements of literary credo.[1] The pastoral poets are particularly prominently featured: Bion, Theocritus, Moschus, Virgil, James Thomson, and, in a section added later, the 'Alpine Theocritus', Salomon Gessner. Of sixteen named poets six are famed mainly for their pastoral poetry. Karamzin's omissions, as has long been noted by scholars, are equally characteristic, particularly the complete absence of French and Russian names, which can be interpreted as a rather blatant slap in the face of the Neoclassicist movement. This, together with the prediction in the same poem that a new era is dawning for Russian poetry, indicates a wish to break with the ruling literary system by drawing on the pastoral tradition, which, although part of Neoclassicism, as well, was to play quite a different role in Sentimentalism. The function of the idyll is different in the two literary movements. This crucial difference is often ignored in discussions of the roots of Sentimentalism.[2]

P.A. Orlov's recent study of Sentimentalism is revealing in this connection. The role of the Kheraskovite circle is stressed, particularly their practice within the mid-style echelon. In his discussion of Kheraskov's poem, 'Pleasant Night' ('Priiatnaia noch'')

Orlov refers to it as a 'typical Sentimentalist idyll' because it contrasts nature to city (civilization), it shows the poet's task to be an evocation of a world of sweet experience, and it stresses the poet's wish to become one with nature. That, Orlov shows, is accomplished mainly by means of emotive epithets oriented towards the pleasure of the title. All of this amounts to a description not only of a 'typical Sentimentalist idyll', as Orlov puts it, but equally appropriately of a 'typical Neoclassicist idyll'. It conforms perfectly to Sumarokov's rules for the idyll, as expressed in his 'Instructions' ('Nastavlenie').[3] This is of course to be expected since Kheraskov was of a Neoclassicist persuasion. More surprising are perhaps the affinities of Sumarokov's rules for the idyll (and other mid-style genres, such as the elegy) to Sentimentalist idylls and indeed to any of Karamzin's statements of poetic credo. Sumarokov's guidelines for the mid-style genres provide a practically complete description of Sentimentalist poetics as a whole. His advice against the use of 'loud' words, unpleasant to the ear of the reader, against a 'magnificent voice' when speaking to shepherdesses, against overly learned or crude language, against turning a shepherd into a peasant or a courtier, and for natural simplicity are reminiscent of Karamzinian pronouncements on style.[4] Sumarokov's advocacy of emotional involvement and personal experience of the heart, as more important than deep thoughts, is wholly supported by Karamzin, and became one of the main tenets of Sentimentalist poetics. The traditional pastoral themes were also to become extremely productive for Sentimentalist authors. One can thus say that the Neoclassicist mid-style echelon, and especially genres such as the idyll, form the common ground between the two movements. However, the basic and crucial difference, overlooked by Orlov and others, is the divergent function of such genres within the respective literary systems: in Neoclassicism, the idyll filled the generic and stylistic function of a middle echelon in a system which in its entirety was much more comprehensive. The Kheraskovian emphasis on the middle echelon, with its tendencies to neutralize the opposition between high and low and to do away with the specificity within the middle echelon, can thus be seen as preparing the ground for Sentimentalism. The Kheraskovites' practice cannot, however, be seen as 'Sentimentalism before Sentimentalism' – to cull a phrase from Sakulin – unless one ignores the total framework within which their idyll practise was conceptualized. This would be tantamount to ignoring such seminal contributions to Russian Neoclassicism as Kheraskov's epic, 'Rossiada'.

In Sentimentalism, the idyll as chronotopical and axiological form set the tone for the *entire* system, and the old distinction between 'high', 'middle', and 'low' lost its relevance in all respects: generic, stylistic, and so on. The idyll values were now stated not for a specific genre in a specific style, but were predicated of the entire literary system. Temporal, spatial, and axiological parameters on all levels of artistic structure were conceptualized in terms of the idyllic *locus amoenus* with an emotive poet–shepherd and a reader–shepherdess in its center.

The idyll space, the *locus amoenus,* can be seen as an extension of the poet's harmonious, beautiful soul. It is the externalization of an inner world, an artistic vision, rather than actual outward reality. It is a 'beautiful, shaded natural site. Its minimum ingredients comprise a tree (or several trees), a meadow, and a spring or brook. Birdsong and flowers may be added. The most elaborate examples also add a breeze.'[5] These are the topoi of the pastoral genres since Theocritus and Virgil, and occur practically unaltered in Sumarokov's eclogues and idylls and Gessner's idylls. The same olive trees, laurel branches, myrtle, rosemary, balsam, the same violets, roses, and hyacinths grow in Gessner's Swiss idylls and Karamzin's Russian ones as in Theocritus' Sicilian ones – only occasionally transformed into their northern counterparts. It is immaterial whether the poet's 'actual' surroundings be Sicily, the Valley of Tempes, the Zürcher See, the environs of Moscow, or a Caucasian village – in his idyllic conceptualization, the world is populated by the same nature spirits, mythological gods, satyrs, nymphs, shepherds, and shepherdesses as always populated the idyll. What Kesselmann points out about Gessner's idylls is equally true of all pastoral poetry:

Space is spiritualized, it does not consist in an objective quasi-nature which is located outside man, but it is already systematized and brought into a spiritual order by man and thereby simultaneously planned and shaped [ . . . ] Space is in Gessner always a spiritually adapted nature and subjectivized human space for living.[6]

In his discussion of the idyll, Bakhtin distinguishes between the love idyll (the basic kind), the idyll of work (tilling the soil, fishing, and the like), the idyll of work or craftsmanship, and the family idyll.[7] In all types of idyll there is a tendency to demarcate an intimate living space. The grove or cave is made inhabitable by soft mosses and grasses, it is decorated by flowers and vines. Hedges, rivulets, an impenetrable forest, or an inaccessible mountain range surround it, creating a kind of pleasant island where man lives a sheltered life tending the herds, tilling the fertile soil, fishing or creating simple artefacts (wooden jugs, flower wreaths, shepherds' staffs). He has ample time to contemplate the beauty of the setting and cultivate love and friendship in an intimate circle of loved ones. The same spatial pleasure principle is in force whether the setting be a grove, a cave, a shepherd's hut, a country estate, or a drawing room.

This small scale externalization of the poet's soul can be seen as a microcosm of the world at large – a world of peace and harmony structured as a patriarchal society, where all are brothers and everyone is happy with his lot. The larger picture, which is typical of various utopias from classical antiquity to Fénelon and Kheraskov, does not, however, enter the idyll proper – what occurs outside the *locus amoenus* is simply not relevant. Space is miniaturized in the manner of rococo painting. It is no coincidence that Gessner was first and foremost a painter and that handbooks on miniature painting were quite popular in Russia at this time.[8] Spatial parameters in idylls are reduced to understandable dimensions and do not, in general, include abstract structures such as society or nation, but are limited to what is accessible to the poet's senses – physical (tactile, auditory, visual) or emotional–spiritual.

In terms of artistic structure this means that the distance between the poet's speech event and the narrated event is either nonexistent or minimal. The poet is himself either the main personage or an observer at close quarters who shares the temporal, spatial, and axiological parameters with his personages. Thus the devices of unnoticed observing or overhearing a declaration of love or a lovers' quarrel, watching nymphs bathe, and the like, have become topoi of the genre. The description of the setting follows the poet's eye, ear, and nose, and the events described are strongly colored by his mood. This explains the typical idyll epithets such as pleasant, sweet, cool, aromatic, light, tender. The immediate 'here', as sensed by the poet through his rose-colored glasses, also determines the distribution and amount of detail in the description.

Objects tend to be described in minute detail – down to the individual veins on flower petals and the smallest insect. (Interestingly enough, the prominence of botanical phenomena is also reflected by the extended sections on how to paint specific flowers in the miniature painting handbooks, mentioned above.) Sensual data are obligatory in idylls: the purling of a brook, the fragrance of a violet, the singing of a nightingale, the buzzing of a bee. Some depth is added by the introduction of distant echoes of the shepherd's song, river banks or mountains, as well as astronomical and meteorological phenomena. However, there is a definite tendency to reduce and humanize these global phenomena as well: besides frequent recourse to personification, the moonlight serves to light the shepherd's path, dew is the favored drink, the prevalent winds are light breezes or Zephyrs who play with the shepherdess' hair, small cupids are sitting on silvery clouds, and so on. This has the effect of foreshortening. All these 'concrete' spatial details do not make the description realistic, but are abstract and artificial topoi of the genre, part of literary tradition.

The temporal parameters of the idyll are, in a sense, as artificial as the spatial ones. Idyllic time, as opposed to linear, historical time, or to the absolute epic past, is a cyclical, eternally recurring present. The idea of cultural progress is lacking, and although the idyll values are derived from an Arcadian Golden Age, this past is not perceived as past, but is eternally renewed in each moment, each hour, each day, and each season. If space is an extension of the poet's soul, time, in turn, is an extension of space, in that it is determined by cycles in nature. In Bakhtin's terms, the unity of place neutralizes all temporal borders in individual lives and their phases. There are no absolute beginnings or ends. Death is juxtaposed to birth (for instance, the topos of children playing on graves), old age to extreme youth, winter to spring, and sunset to sunrise. The focus is on the smaller temporal segments, the 'now', and each fragment is representative of the whole. One can thus with Brukhanskii speak of a 'completed literary fragment'.[9] Although all ages are present in the idyll, no personage is actually seen growing old, nor is there any character development. Furthermore, all ages are of equal value, and the same values (sensitivity, love, friendship, virtue) are shared by all age groups, reinforcing the overall harmony. Villains are rare and obstacles few. The conflicts depicted usually have a happy outcome or are seen as outside intrusions which ultimately serve to set the inside happiness into sharper relief.

The narrated events that make up the plot are few and basic: birth, death, meetings, and partings, and there is a tendency here, too, to focus on the minutiae of life – eating, drinking, singing, a good deed. This is a far cry from the epic focus on significant peaks of national history, feats of valor, complex adventures, battles, and victories.

The idyll plot is brief, but to compensate, it extends laterally in the structure of the work. The narrated events can be said to emanate from (and compete for the reader's attention with) the speech event which prominently expresses the events within the poet's soul – the 'stirrings of his heart', his moods and emotions. The speech event makes up the innermost circle in a concentric spatial configuration of events. The structure is roughly as follows: the poet's pleasant mood, the 'event' of a shepherd's song, the song of a nightingale, the echo, etc.; or the poet's happy expectations for meeting his beloved, the 'event' of the meeting (a brief teasing dialogue, an embrace, a kiss, ecstatic happiness), nearby satyrs and nymphs frolic, birds fly in pairs, cupids smile, and so on. A single sustained mood colors all of the 'circles' in this configuration – the mood of the poet matches the mood of the personages, the mood of the nymphs, satyrs, and birds.

The idyll may be strictly lyrical, narrative, or dramatic. In the case of a narrative form, the reporting function (narrating events, describing settings) may be limited to a minimal reporting clause (subject and a *verbum dicendi* or *sentiendi*) or take the form of the most extensive indirect (and even quasidirect) reporting of events, most of which are speech acts, thought acts, or emotive acts. Whatever the form, there is never a great difference between the poet's speech and that of the personages – the same kind of expressive language is used by both. Emotive epithets, diminutives, personifications, superlatives, sound repetitions, parallelism, etc., are typical, as are speech acts characteristic of personage (rather than author's) speech: exclamations, benedictions, questions, and so on. Thus the image of the poet–narrator is quite prominent. The poet performs personage function to a significant degree – another logical consequence of the actions themselves which are predominantly of the internal kind. The converse is also true – the personages often perform author function in that they themselves are singers, poets, or storytellers. This is particularly true of the singing contest type of idyll, where the very nature of poetry is discussed by the personages themselves. Other forms of art are also frequently the topic, particularly in the sphere of the decorative arts and crafts – woodworking, gardening, flower arranging, and the like. This easy transfer of functions and features between the speech event and the narrated event is, as was stated earlier, one of the signal features of Sentimentalist fiction.

The idyll contrasts with the epic in all aspects of artistic structure. In terms of the proximities between and within speech event and narrated event, the epic is characterized by epic distance, whereas the idyll may be seen in terms of idyllic identity. The epic values are conceived in terms of history (the past, firsts, origins, ancestors, national history), those of the idyll are seen in terms of the eternal present, the 'here and now' of the speaker (the moment, the family, love, immediate nature). Although the idyll world is poet centered, this does not mean that it is more concrete in any sense; it is just as abstract as the epic world. It is personal but not individual, and all idyllic poets and personages share the same essential characteristics.

That the idyll rather than the epic was the favored mode of Sentimentalist appreciation of art, is neatly demonstrated by the reception of Virgil among the Sentimentalists. Virgil is, of course, famed as both an idyllist and as an epic poet. Among the Russian Sentimentalists, there is a pronounced preference for the idyllic Virgil, the disciple of Theocritus and the forerunner to Gessner.[10] Even when Virgil's epic is discussed, there tends to be a wholly idyllic appreciation of it: 'The philosophy of his [Virgil's] era softens Homer's lines, and the moving love of man, tender passions, and enlightened generosity in the Aeneid take the place of the fierce bravery of the Iliad. His narration is constantly animated by sensitivity.'[11]

The claim can thus be made that the idyll properties best met the demands of Sentimentalist solipsism, sympathy, and pleasure, and that the idyll became the prime literary model for the new prose. Sentimentalist prose works can, by this token, best be viewed as idylls or as transformations of the idyll in contrast to the epic, retaining the basic idyllic principles outlined. A similar claim has indeed been made in a seminal article by Skipina, 'On the Sentimental Tale', and further developed by Cross.[12] Although one may disagree with Skipina's Formalist linguistic bent and the simplified causality it implies, her arguments for the link between the Sentimental tale and the idyll are solid. The Sentimental tale is seen as a reaction against all aspects of the novel as practised in eighteenth-century Russia: against the genre as a large form (*bol'shaia forma*) with a stress on a well-developed plot, against its coarse, confused, and complex syntax, and against the lack of taste in lexical selection. The pleasure principle (*priiatnost'*) became the new rallying point in the reaction against all the above aspects of artistic structure. The same principle, in Skipina's view, governs the idyll and the pastoral. Furthermore, she points out, the very orientation of the small form (*malaia forma*) is toward style rather than plot, which is true also of the idyll. This orientation, she concludes, made the idyll the most appropriate model when the aim was a reform of style.

If one takes Skipina's argument a step further and views style in the framework of utterance (rather than narrowly 'linguistically'), it becomes obvious that a 'focus on style' entails a focus on the narrator, narratee and their situation. The idyll genre provided the chronotopical model par excellence, and idyllic values corresponded perfectly to the social, philosophical, ideological, and linguistic developments of the era: the shift in emphasis from ontology to epistemology as described earlier.

### KARAMZIN'S EARLY SENTIMENTALIST IDYLLS OF VICARIOUS EXPERIENCE

It is not surprising that Karamzin began his prose career in the idyllic mode. His primary model was Salomon Gessner, most famed for his prose idylls. Gessner's idylls took a middle road between the erotically excessive Anacreontic rococo poetry and the somewhat too rustic aspects of Theocritus, and eschewed the overly mannered elegance of the French idyllists. He infused his own idylls with a sound dose of conventional morality and pietistic religiosity, all of which applies in equal measure to Karamzin's works.[13] Gessner proved particularly influential on his Russian disciple in the area of style. His German was as refreshingly innovative to his readers as was Karamzin's Russian to his. Hibberd's description of Gessner's style points out most of the features that have also been used to describe Karamzin's famed *period*.[14]

The evidence of Karamzin's fondness for Gessner has been documented in characteristic detail by Cross, and there is no need to rehearse his data here. Suffice it to point out that, in addition to 'Das hölzerne Bein', Karamzin almost certainly also translated Gessner's 'Idas, Mycon', which appeared in 1789 in *Children's Reading*. His translation of another Gessner-idyll, 'Die Zephyren', appeared as late as 1796, which indicates that Karamzin's fondness for the genre did not abate.[15] Neither of the above works demonstrates any unusual feats of translation nor any significant modification of the originals. Another idyll, translated by Karamzin is more interesting. This is a work entitled 'Gessner's Death' ('Gessnerova smert''), footnoted as an idyll, translated from a French (*Mercure de France*) translation of a German original. It is a most befitting tribute to the foremost idyllist of the era: an idyll about the death of the idyllist. Shepherds and shepherdesses erect an altar of smooth stones under ancient oak trees, a 'modest Mausoleum' to their beloved singer. All file past the altar covering it with cypress wreaths, and each dedicates his own wreath personally. Their dedications are, respectively, to: 'Harmonious singer of our Cantons'; 'friend of tender jokes'; 'wise and sensitive Gessner'; 'humane judge; good citizen and true friend, tender father; best husband; most virtuous . . . '[16] After this, all fall to the ground, weep, are silent, and, in typical idyll fashion, 'felt a light trembling in the surroundings – a trembling which was the sign of Nature's participation in the death of her favorite poet'.

This is an interesting testimony of the reader reception of the image of idyll author created by Gessner, turned here into main personage in a work like his own idylls. It shows that the idyll author is perceived almost entirely as a personage with all the qualities most esteemed by Sentimentalists, rather than as a skilled poet in any technical sense, although the genre itself was quite comfortable with poetic skill as a theme. It also shows how easily an author of idylls may be turned into a personage in an idyll – a kind of proof that there is little difference between the two in features and function. Art tends to be projected into life, and life is viewed in terms of art.[17]

This type of narrator is dominant in Karamzin's early works, whereas in some of his later works there is an increased stress, often in a playful vein, on the more technical 'writerly' aspects, not, however, excluding the personal emotive aspects. In the Sentimentalist image of author, the human aspects were always to take precedence over technical skill.

To his translation of the idyll about Gessner's death, Karamzin appended his personal tribute: 'a tear, a sigh, a song' in prose and verse, attesting to his love for Gessner from childhood on. The verse part of that tribute was later included in his credo, 'Poeziia', written two years earlier, but published only in 1792. For Karamzin, Gessner was 'the Alpine Theocritus', 'the sweetest singer of songs', who ecstatically sang innocence, simplicity, and pastoral customs, and who with his song 'captivated all tender hearts' – Gessner's own precise aspirations as a poet.

Several of Karamzin's original early works conform to a significant degree to the idyllic pattern outlined (although only one is explicitly labelled an idyll), while at the same time indicating Karamzin's further modifications of the genre. Such works are, chronologically listed: 'A Promenade' ('Progulka'), 'Innocence' ('Nevinnost''), 'The Flood. A Fragment' ('Navodnenie. Otryvok'), 'Palemon and Daphnis. An Idyll' ('Palemon i Dafnis. Idilliia'), 'Night' ('Noch''), and 'The Countryside. A Fragment' ('Derevnia. Otryvok'), all of which were published between 1789 and 1791.

In most comprehensive studies devoted to Karamzin's fiction,[18] these early 'idylls' have not been analyzed in depth, and, if mentioned at all, have mostly been dismissed in a paragraph or two. Articles have appeared about some of them, stressing for the most part, however, aspects of the works peripheral to the present discussion. The negligible amount of attention that they have attracted is perhaps deserved if one compares their artistic value to Karamzin's later works (or applies more modern tastes in literature), and understandable, if one considers the problems of attribution and the considerable amount of groundwork devoted to that problem alone. Most of them are unsigned or cryptically initialled, and most of them were not included in later collections of Karamzin's works – neither in those supervised by Karamzin himself nor those compiled by later scholars.[19] This corpus of early idylls may be expanded when more work in this area is done. The present study makes no attempt at attribution (nor does it aspire to completeness), and previous attributions will be accepted. Some of the works under consideration are also quite modest in size and content, and have perhaps therefore been slighted. But, since the

Sentimentalists extolled all manner of trifles, that in itself would seem to be all the more reason for investigating the works.

A notable exception to the above is Cross who convincingly establishes Karamzin's early interest in, and experimentation with, the idyll, from his first mention of Gessner to his last works.[20] Cross's scope, however, does not allow for detailed analysis of the texts themselves. The present chapter is an attempt to investigate further and expand some of his and Skipina's ideas on the subject, stressing artistic structure, and placing the works within a coherent theoretical framework as precursors to Karamzin's later works. I hope to show that the idylls provide both interesting insights into the 'roots of Sentimentalism', and a crucial link to the sentimental tale proper. They are good examples of experimentation with various aspects of style and structure which were later to be modified, perfected, and even parodied by the author. I shall therefore allow myself some close analysis of the works and leave the question of artistic merit aside.

## 'Palemon and Daphnis'

'Palemon and Daphnis' is, as Cross has pointed out, a 'skillful adaptation' of Gessner's idyll 'Der Sturm'.[21] The two illustrate the same moral ('Be content with your lot') by means of a similar picture of shepherds watching ships perishing in a storm (the fate of those who are not content with their lot and leave their native shores). Their structures are similar: a brief narrator's overture, introducing and situating the main personages (their names changed from Battus and Lacon to Palemon and Daphnis), followed by a 'dramatically' structured dialogue (the personages' lines are introduced simply by the name of the speaker), and a concluding brief epilogue by the narrator – a common enough idyll structure. Aside from this basic skeleton and some similarity in images (at least some of which consist of topoi of the genre and are by no means specific to either Gessner or Karamzin), Karamzin's idyll is quite different from Gessner's. This is true both with respect to internal structure and emphasis – even the moral of the story is differently conveyed. Leaving Gessner aside, let us turn to Karamzin's version.

The narrator relates almost neutrally and laconically the actions of the two shepherds: 'Palemon and Daphnis sat'; 'Palemon and

Daphnis sat silently and watched'; 'finally Daphnis said to Palemon [dialogue follows]'; 'they got up and left'. There is no description of their looks, personalities, characters, previous actions, or relationships, nor is there any overt indication of the narrator's attitude toward them. Their immediate setting is identified simply as a high rocky seashore, and their final destination as their hut 'where love and peace awaited them'. The description of their field of vision is quite different: it utilizes evaluative epithets, personifications, metaphors, similes, and the like. It is a cheerful picture of the calm sea on a sunny day, and reveals the poetic narrator as a keen observer and appreciator of beauty. His description is organized by the principle of zooming in from the general to the particular: sun, sky, water, ships, sails, sailors, 'inhabitants of the wet element', and 'pearly shiny bubbles', each logically related to the next by proximity. This cheerful picture, animated by color, motion, and sound, provides the setting and the main personages for the sailor story which is revealed through the shepherds' dialogue. The personages in the narrator's story thus also perform the function of (dramatically) narrating a story. The narrator reports a vicarious experience, his overture functioning as a reporting clause for the shepherd story (ending with 'Daphnis said to Palemon: [ . . . ]', a clear identification of addresser, addressee, and *verbum dicendi*). The narrator's utterance relates clearly and unambiguously to that of the personages as direct discourse. The shepherds perform both personage function (in 'Palemon and Daphnis' as a whole) and reporting function (as well as addressee function since the dialogue format posits each in turn as listener) in the sailor story. Their dialogue, as would be expected, reveals as much about the speakers themselves as it reveals about the sailors. Moreover, their function as narrators is carried one step further: they project themselves into the future when they will tell the identical story to their children. They imagine themselves performing the present narrator's exact function in their future telling of a vicarious experience (that of Palemon and Daphnis junior).

The narrator's overture is not entirely neutral. Not only does his joyous picture serve as a sharp contrast to the ensuing description of the disaster (by Palemon and Daphnis), thus stressing its gravity, but the possibility of disaster is predicted by the narrator's concluding image: pearly shiny bubbles are bound not to last. Thus the narrator's concrete description on a metaphorical level presets his narratee's expectations with regard to the following story and its interpretation. The narrator's wider experience as a person (he knows that the happiness he describes is ephemeral) prompts him to tell the Palemon–Daphnis story, just as their present experience prompts them to plan (and, as it were, rehearse) a subsequent re-telling of the *same* story to their children.

'Palemon and Daphnis' is structured around one major opposition: between the idyll world and the outside world, between what the shepherds have and what they do not have, symbolized by land and sea, respectively. This opposition is described in terms of the physical events that transpire at sea and the corresponding intellectual and emotional reactions which take place in the minds of Palemon and Daphnis on land. The advantages represented by the sea are conceived of idyllically, and undergo several stages of evaluation and re-evaluation.

The title indicates the focus of the story as a whole: Palemon and Daphnis, rather than the sailors. It is thus *their* idyll that justifies the subtitle of Karamzin's story, not the sailor story. The narrator reports the actions of the shepherds, as we saw (sitting, watching, speaking) and their location (the high rocky seashore) as well as the meteorological conditions (sunny day, light breezes) on land and sea. The sea is depicted in positive terms with, however, the metaphorically ominous conclusion (bubble image). The shore is, at this point, not evaluated.

Once the shepherds' dialogue begins, their actions, besides speech, include mainly observing the sea and evaluating the life of the sailors in terms of their *imagined* actions, which Palemon and Daphnis thereby report through their dialogue. The joyous seascape conjures up entirely positive images of the sailors' life: the pleasure of 'flying to the distant lands we have heard so many wondrous things about, but which neither our fathers nor children have visited' and the pleasure of 'always breathing new air and always seeing something new'. The new and distant is thereby initially assigned a positive value, as compared to that which is familiar and close. The wondrous and fictional is also assigned a positive value as opposed to reality as they refer to the pleasure of 'seeing with one's own eyes that which surprises us in stories'.

When the shepherds further develop their *imagined* reality, a note of hesitation can be detected, and the evaluation is no longer entirely positive. Leaving for distant lands entails the disadvantage

of 'parting with one's friends, one's loved ones – –'. The note of
hesitation is conveyed rhythmically and intonationally by the
elliptical conclusion. The advantage is, however, a joyous
homecoming, embraces of friends and loved ones: 'the minute of
reunion rewards them [the sailors] for a year of separation'. The
evaluation at this point is clear: a year abroad equals a minute at
home. It is, however, still positive, although the advantages of life
at sea are now seen not in terms of travel for its own sake, but rather
in terms of intensifying the values that prevail at home.

Travelling furthermore gives the returning sailor and his loved
ones the pleasure of wondrous stories about Hesperian gardens
(golden apples of the far West), crooked Cyclops (Hesiod's *storm*
genii, *thunder and lightning*, Homeric unpleasantries), Lestrigonian *cannibals*, Scylla and Charybdis (mythical *rocks, threatening
the safety of seafarers*). The storytelling situation, the close
narrator–narratee communion with family and friends is extolled
(an idyllic value), while the stories themselves consist of the
un-idyllic stuff that makes up epics and adventure novels. A close
look at the topics reveals that whatever their fascination may be in
fiction, for the most part they stress the dangers of sailing, namely
what makes a reunion most unlikely. The evaluation at this stage is
still presented in a positive way, with, however, ominous hints of
impending disaster (like the narrator's bubble image).

Next Palemon and Daphnis move to observation and evaluation
of the *real* sailor reality, and report the events at sea through highly
emotive comments (exclamations, interjections, apostrophes to the
gods: 'Oh!'; 'Ah!'; 'Gods!'; 'Dear Gods!') and exhortations to each
other ('Look'; 'Do you see'), rapid brief sentences, few conjunctions, highly charged verbs of motion, emotive epithets of horror
and threat ('horrid', 'black'). In this way the narratee finds out what
both shepherds see first-hand, and would not need to tell each other
('the sun is setting', 'the storm is raging', which from Palemon's and
Daphnis' point of view is informative only insofar as the lines
express their respective emotions or serve the phatic function). For
the most part, however, their lines, although somewhat artificial,
convey first and foremost emotive and evaluative information
relevant to Palemon and Daphnis themselves, and the events at sea
are reported (for the benefit of the narratee of 'Palemon and
Daphnis' as a whole) through the veil of emotive, expressive, and
evaluative information (for the benefit of Palemon and Daphnis as

alternating secondary narratees *and* for the narratee). This kind of
clumsy artificiality is the drawback of 'dramatic narration' through
personages in general. This property may have contributed to the
fact that Karamzin in his later works gives his narrator a greater
role, taking over more of the reporting function while retaining for
both his narrators and personages many features of expressive
emotive speech, and retaining a close contact (as between Palemon
and Daphnis) between his narrators and narratees.

In 'Palemon and Daphnis' the highly emotive report of the sailor
reality is followed by an equally emotive description of the
*imagined* consequences (future tense), and finally the emotions
directly address the culminating horrors that actually occur. The
*real* joyous seascape of the narrator's overture now turns into its
opposite with a kind of crescendo reporting. Day → night; sunshine
and light breezes → raging storm, thunder, and lightning; the sea at
repose → raging elements; the sailors' bustling about and song →
hard work (lowering the sails, securing the mast) → raising their
hands to the skies, pleading for salvation → drowning; the shiny
bubble → jet black waves with whitetops. Finally the ships are
swallowed up by the raging elements: the shiny bubble has burst,
the threats of Cyclops, Scylla, and Charybdis have been realized,
and what had seemed exciting story stuff is a tragedy in real life.
The *imagined* homecoming of the sailors turns into its opposite as
Palemon and Daphnis next envision the consequences of travel
(future tense, wholly imagined events). The pleasures previously
imagined fail to materialize. There will be no joyous return to
family and friends, no happy reunion, no storytelling. Instead,
mothers will wait in vain on the shore, children will be orphaned,
the sailors' bodies will be washed by the salty waves, hungry whales
will swallow them, birds will peck at them (the Lestrigonian image
realized, albeit not by humans). Thus all the most cherished idyll
values are shattered for the sailors.

The shepherds' attention finally turns away from the sea, and
their lines consist entirely of expressions of their own states and
about their idyllic setting. The moral is stated (not to say over-
stated) most emphatically in their highly emotive final lines. They
pray for the gods' forgiveness for having envied the sailors and
coveted what they did not themselves have. They express their
hope and resolve always to be content with their lot, thus strongly
affirming the traditional idyll values: the 'dear sunset', the 'sweet

kisses and embraces of Chloe and Phillida', their 'flocks of sheep', 'playing the reed pipe', being a 'consolation to their fathers' and 'a joy to their mothers', 'playing with, amusing, fondling, and kissing their children', and implanting in them the same idyll values by sharing with them their own experiences, namely telling them the story 'Palemon and Daphnis'. The development of the dialogue in this section is quite interesting and indicative of the manner in which later Karamzinian *narrators* speak. The two are in complete agreement in their emotions and evaluations. This is conveyed by the frequent use of first person plural *my*, and by the fact that the meaning of Palemon's lines is repeated in Daphnis' lines in semantically, syntactically, and intonationally parallel constructions, with synonymous variations in lexicon only, and with some intensification in the expression, which is also accomplished by sheer accumulation. For instance, when Palemon says: 'Forgive me', Daphnis echoes: 'Forgive me, forgive me', with the same general idea completing both lines. Palemon's: 'Let us always' (followed by a vow always to treasure the dear sunset and the kisses of Chloe) is repeated in Daphnis': 'Let us always' (and a vow always to be content with tending sheep, playing the reed pipe, and the embraces of dear Phillida). After a few lines of such anaphorical parallel reiteration, the dialogue changes – Daphnis does not finish his line, but Palemon finishes it for him: Palemon: 'And when we have children – '; Daphnis: 'Dear children'; Palemon: 'then – '; Daphnis: 'then we will [ . . . ]'; Palemon: 'We will [ . . . ]'; with abundant anaphora, anadiplosis, epiphora, and parallelism. This gives an impression of unison speaking, from which it is only a step to speech by a single person (a kind of hidden dialogicity) and to Karamzin's subsequent narrators who retain all the basic features of Palemon's and Daphnis' combined speech. In this section of the text they no longer speak to each other so much as jointly give vent to their emotions, addressing the gods, the powers that be, or seemingly no one. Their speech is made up exclusively of hortative, optative, and promissive constructions. Given this construction of the dialogue, the moral is first stated by both consecutively, then by both in unison, and, finally, once more by their committing themselves to re-telling the story to their children when the youngsters will some day sit on the rocky seashore, watching ships at sea, and so on. Not only do they commit themselves to doing so, but they actually go through a brief synopsis of the future story,

thereby summarizing 'Palemon and Daphnis'. The choice of audience is also interesting. Children, as we have seen, were becoming
a literary fact during the Sentimentalist period. *Children's Reading*
was the first Russian journal with children targeted as readers,
children also make up the audience within Karamzin's later 'The
Deep Forest', and Karamzin was later to use child heroes in his
works, as we shall see. The focus on children can be seen as part of
the tendency towards miniaturization characteristic of the idyll
chronotope.

Today's reader may wince at the heavy-handed moralizing, but
the fact is that the moral is quite skillfully integrated into the story
and spoken by the personages themselves as part of the 'plot'. This
must be seen against the background of items such as the philosophical novels or the adventure novels still read during the late
eighteenth century (not to mention certain allegedly Sentimentalist
works, such as Fedor Emin's *Letters of Ernest and Doravra* [*Pis'ma
Ernesta i Doravry*] in which such moralizing makes up whole
chapters, and is often spoken by the preachy narrator himself).

This section of 'Palemon and Daphnis' ends by Palemon feeling
cold and urging Daphnis to return to their hut. The narrator
concludes with one sentence reaffirming the main idyll values:
'They got up and went to their hut where love and peace awaited
them.' Thus the protagonists are safely back within the heart of the
idyll world. They had strayed to its peripheries (the seashore, a
typical dividing line) where an enticing vision and flights of fantasy
had led them into wondrous lands beyond their pale – wondrous
visions which ultimately leave them cold and only serve to reaffirm
what they had all along.

Compared to Russian Neoclassicist idylls and eclogues,
'Palemon and Daphnis' demonstrates the further fate of the genre.
It is structurally close to some of Sumarokov's 'dramatic' eclogues,
but is vastly embellished and complicated by didactic elements.
Sumarokov's eclogues and idylls were limited to the topic of love –
or occasionally friendship. Subsequently, the possible topics were
expanded to include all types listed by Bakhtin. The setting was
similarly expanded (besides the grove and the hut: the house, the
village, the landowner's estate, etc.). Poetic prose took the place of
verse. The plots were allowed more variation, and later the
narrator's role became vastly expanded and personalized, ultimately leading to a bifurcation similar to what Gukovskii described

for the Kheraskovites' elegies.[22] Furthermore, non-idyllic values came to intrude more and more until in some Sentimental tales the idyll values are not only threatened (to be affirmed in the end), but in extreme cases the outside values prove more powerful and most often the idyllic values come to be at least questioned, if not conquered or inverted. The narrator's contemporary reality 'novelizes' the idyll. This is not yet the case in 'Palemon and Daphnis' however.

Cross interprets 'Palemon and Daphnis' as an allegory of the French Revolution and a warning to the Russians to be content with their lot.[23] One may also be justified in reading it as a statement *about literature*, a kind of apologia for the idyllic mode of writing, as opposed to epics or adventure novels, and thus as part of the narrator's external dialogue with other writers. Shipwrecks and wondrous adventures were the stock-in-trade of the latter genres from Homer to Kheraskov and Fedor Emin, where the heroes, in contrast to the sailors in the present work, are miraculously saved from storms, Cyclops, Scylla and Charybdis, and Lestrigonians, and live to bring home Hesperian apples. Such tales are, as we saw, part of Palemon's and Daphnis' enticing vision, but are rejected in favor of telling the children a simple idyll, stressing the age-old pastoral values. The same choice was made by Karamzin himself in, for example, his *Letters of a Russian Traveller* and several other works describing miniature journeys. *Letters of a Russian Traveller* stresses the disadvantages and advantages of travel in very much the same manner as does 'Palemon and Daphnis' (parting from friends, reunion, spellbinding one's friends with exotic tales). Karamzin's traveller–narrator, we might note, poses as a youngster and a pupil, as Lotman demonstrates, and we can relate this to the new literary emphasis on youth.[24] Some of the 'stories' told by the later traveller are like the exotic adventures of the sailors and all are permeated by the narrator's self. Some of them are themselves typical idylls. Most importantly, however, the very epistolary structure is motivated by a wish for contact with the loved ones – a kind of surrogate for, and recreation of, the intimate heart-to-heart situation in the idyll hut.[25]

'THE FLOOD. A FRAGMENT'

'The Flood' is another idyll inspired by Gessner and 'very probably' written by Karamzin.[26] It is an idyll in the narrative mode, although

Karamzin does not label it as such. Most of the work is taken up by the narrator's narration, and the personages do not carry on a sustained dialogue. The flood is depicted as a major disaster, but is also the reason for the happy outcome of the love story which makes up the kernel of the plot.

Young Milon, described as a virtuous shepherd (and named accordingly) by the none too impartial narrator, watches the tragedy of a flood from the top of a hill next to his 'modest hut' and weeps over the fate of his brothers for, as the narrator informs us, 'he considered all people his brothers'. He sees a chance to save an old man and a young woman. They turn out to be his beloved Daphna, and her rich but cruel father, Amint, who had opposed their marriage, and even forbidden them to see each other, due to Milon's poverty. Milon not only saves their lives, but also offers Amint (who lost all his riches to the flood) all he owns: his hut and his flock of sheep, which had remained unscathed by the elements. On this 'day of Divine Wrath', the old man realizes the futility of riches and the full value of Milon's pure heart which cannot be destroyed by a flood, begs Milon's forgiveness, and the two lovers are happily united as the flood abates and the sun breaks through the clouds.

The main stress of the work is obviously not on this trite love story but on its moral and its telling. The structure is somewhat similar to that of 'Palemon and Daphnis': a narrator tells about a shepherd who watches a disaster from a safe spot on dry land. The shepherds and the other personages, however, serve the action function to a much greater degree by performing a more developed series of physical actions. The inner actions, which in 'Palemon and Daphnis' were mainly performed by the two protagonists, are here taken over by the narrator to a significant degree. This narrator functions and speaks much in the same way as Palemon and Daphnis (combined into one speaker), and his role is thus expanded as compared to the former idyll. He reports and emotes over a similar observed event (here 'actual' rather than 'imagined' at all stages of the way), and the damage of the flood is evaluated by the narrator in terms very similar to Palemon's and Daphnis' evaluation of the storm victims. 'The Flood' is a good illustration of Karamzin's later (1794) advice to authors: 'You want to be an author: read the history of the misfortunes of the human race – and if your heart does not overflow with blood –

drop your pencil – or it will depict for us the cold darkness of your soul.'[27]

By these criteria, the narrator of 'The Flood' certainly qualifies for the Parnassus. His narration begins with a meteorological gradatio, which builds up to flood, disaster, and death. Dense mists → clouds → a strong rain → rapid streams → rivers → waters → furious waves → the cruel elements, is the graduated sequence of phenomena and epithets. The action sequence is built up on the same principle: are agitated → darken → turn grey in the clouds → pour → roar → swell → rise from cloudy banks → swallow, and the color scheme develops from dark to grey to black as the narrator's agitation grows meteorologically. The introduction of personages is construed on an opposite principle of degradatio: first a general commotion, then a more precise 'pale villagers', next three sets of pairs: a frightened father and young son (male action), a young couple (action by youth), and finally young Milon, a virtuous shepherd (a single youth named and characterized). Through this is conveyed, besides the events of the story, also how the narrator's emotions intensify the higher the flood gets and the more individualized the personages get. The initial description highlights the speed by which the flood accumulates, and is organized as a rapid enumeration of nouns and verbs. Once the flood is at its peak, the narrator gives vent to his full personal involvement through emotionally loaded similes and personifications (watery death pursues the fleeing people as a grey wolf with open jaws pursues lambs), exclamations, apostrophes to the personages, rhetorical questions, and personal interpretations of the lives and fates of the dying personages. Parallelism in motion is highly developed, and all motions aim at 'reaching': rivers are pursued by winds, people by death, (like) lambs by the wolf, the father reaches out for his son, the mother tries to hold on to her baby, and finally the young couple freezes in a deathly embrace, thus having reached each other, but in vain. The narrator stresses what the flood deprives the populace of in idyllic terms very similar to what we already saw in 'Palemon and Daphnis'.

The emotionally charged intonations are also accomplished by utterance structure. Utterances are left unfinished, pauses replace conjunctions, interjections interrupt the normal syntax, and, above all, there is a very skillful use of repetition (synonymous and polyptotonic) and contrast of highly expressive lexicon: 'her warm heart already feels the mortal cooling of her beloved, – feels, and loses all feelings'; or: 'is it long since they tenderly clasped each other [ . . . ] Now they embrace with despair, embrace for the last time, freeze, and float dead – – '[final ellipsis original]. The narrator, although not named even by an 'I', is very much present 'here and now' as the narration is conducted in the present tense for the most part. The narrator himself is light on moralizing directly (although not totally alien to sententiae). The main moral of the story is left to be pronounced by Amint, and is all the more effective as it comes from a reformed sinner. The stress is on strictly idyllic values, the various generations, family relationships (father–son, mother–child, young couple, among the casualties; father–daughter–son-in-law, among the survivors), intimate acts of affection, good deeds on a personal level. Heroism is downplayed – even in the case of Milon's deed as a life-saver.

The idyll world is threatened (first by Amint's social prejudices and then by the flood), but its heart is preserved, and it is the virtuous shepherd together with his modest hut and his loved ones who are saved to carry on the idyllic life. The non-idyllic values (symbolized by Amint's riches and opposition to true love) perish with the flood, and Amint himself is the first to reaffirm the true value of a good heart. A modest life of love and happiness goes on, and the raging elements give way to abundantly flowing tears of happiness. It is, indeed, typical for the idyll that there are no villains strictly speaking within the idyll world, and potential villains are either nipped in the bud or have at least some redeeming features. This is also the case in most Sentimental tales, although the happy aspects, as we shall see, will be more clearly ascribed to a narrator's own idyllic world and the tragic aspects will be further elaborated in the world of the personages which is often presented as an idyll manqué. By the 'fragment' subtitle, 'The Flood' becomes even more explicitly symbolical of the Biblical flood and the human condition at large, and expresses the narrator's belief in Christian brotherhood, love and personal virtue – in none too subtle terms. The potentials of the fragment as an artistic device were to be realized with much greater finesse in Karamzin's later works – an issue to which I will return later.

## KARAMZIN'S EARLY SENTIMENTALIST IDYLLS OF PERSONAL EXPERIENCE

The works I shall next turn to represent a near-exclusive focus on a lyrical narrator and perhaps the apogee of Karamzin's solipsism. They are: 'A Promenade', 'The Countryside. A Fragment', and 'Night'.[28] Their general artistic structure is the same: first person narration (where the narrator is also the main personage) and a narrated event, the plot of which is exceedingly scanty in terms of physical action, 'events' in the ordinary sense. The plots consist almost entirely of speech acts, perceptual acts, cognitive acts, emotive acts, and 'non-acts' or states. This kind of structure is most conducive to interpenetration between the author utterance and the personage utterance since the 'person' of the speaker is the same on both levels, and the internal actions are well suited to minimize the chronotopical distinction between the two utterances. At times it is therefore impossible to distinguish whether the narrator speaks in his capacity of author or personage, and in most cases the dialogue between the two contexts is spoken in unison, or is at least couched in an aura of agreement and support rather than polemics. In all these works, the personages are also to a greater or lesser extent depicted as poets or narrators, another fact which contributes to the neutralization of the opposition between speech contexts.

## 'A Promenade'

'A Promenade' has been characterized by Sipovskii as a 'sentimental poem in prose', the 'first' of its kind in Russia.[29] The poem can be further specified loosely as an idyll of the craft–work type, the craft in question being the creation of poetry.[30] It is Karamzin's most explicit early statement of artistic credo implemented in fictional form. 'A Promenade' both expresses and implements many of the most basic tenets of Sentimentalist poetics, such as the solipsistic focus on the narrator, the pleasure principle, the role of sense and sensibility, the Sentimentalist view of mimesis, and the history and function of poetry. Its topic may be summarized as the creation of poetry and the poetry of creation. In many respects it runs parallel to Karamzin's other fictional statements of artistic credo such as 'Poetry', written two years earlier, and 'Proteus, or a poet's contradictions' ('Protei, ili nesoglasiia stikhotvortsa'), published much later, in 1798–9. It stresses the same values, traces the same history, with the same artistic preferences.

The history of poetry is quite comprehensively drawn from divine Creation of the world (the original poem),[31] man's first hymns to Creation, similar hymns by the rest of the animate world, hymns by ancient sages and bards, to contemporary poets, such as Wieland, and even to poet brothers on other planets. The poet in 'A Promenade' joins this chorus with his own hymn (a rather mediocre four lines of verse). Despite the cosmic scope, 'A Promenade' is structured around the present century and the I-personage's creative activity. The rest of poetry serves the sole function of input into his hymn. Furthermore, it is not the hymn itself as a finished artefact, that is the main topic (and thus its mediocrity is of little consequence), but the process of creating it. Due to the near identity between personage and narrator, the same process is at the roots of the I-narrator's creation, namely 'A Promenade' as a whole, and poetry is ultimately centered around the I-narrator. Thus, the plot can be seen largely in terms of discourse deictic encoding and decoding motifs with an almost exclusive focus on the qualities required of the Sentimentalist author for poetic utterance and of the Sentimentalist reader for its reception.

The 'promenade' of the title refers literally to the I-personage's physical walk in nature, but applies equally well to a spiritual walk in nature as a set of poems, his own and others'.[32] It is in this spiritual walk that the I-narrator participates as fully as the I-personage. This bisemic reading of the title is immediately suggested by the epigraph, consisting of the second and third lines of Thomson's 'Hymn' at the conclusion of his *The Seasons*:

> Forth in the pleasing Spring
> Thy beauty walks, Thy tenderness and love

The promenade also proceeds with a volume of 'my Thomson' in hand. 'A Promenade' is structured as a slow-motion physical walk with frequent stops which depict the spiritual wanderings of the mind, emotions, and fantasy, which in turn have as their topic the 'beauty, tenderness, and love' created by God and re-created by Thomson, Young, and others. Taking his cue from Thomson's lines, the narrator begins by stating his preference for the season of spring in a one-paragraph overture:

No season is as pleasant to me as spring. When the beneficial sun, risen to the sign of Taurus, begins to shed the clearest light on earth, when little by little, warming the snowy masses with its rays, it extracts from earth a tender greenery with its mysterious magnet: then I feel a pleasant change in my whole being, and a quiet joy feeds my heart. It seems that the sun's rays penetrate my very imagination, and warm it with their flame; for at this time it is more ardent than at other times. I can then see, hear, feel, and think better. (161)[33]

This overture is poetically structured in a manner which was to characterize the majority of Karamzin's later Sentimental tales: rhythmical prose, accomplished by anaphoric repetition of syntactically parallel clauses. It is implicitly and explicitly subjective: epithets, such as 'pleasant', 'beneficial', 'clearest', 'tender', 'mysterious', are coupled with an overt description of the beneficial effects of spring and sunshine on the speaker. This description is carried out in the imperfective present tense, stressing the eternal nature of the effects of spring. When the ensuing narration switches to a preterite description of one such spring day, it is already abundantly clear that what follows is simply a metonymy of the present narrator's usual surge of creativity every spring. Indeed, the story is precisely an elaboration on his imagination, his 'seeing, hearing, feeling, and thinking' at their most intense. The impression is that thoughts of poetic creation, divine nature, self-awareness, and so on, are as much on the mind of the 'I' now as they were during his past walk.

After the lyrical overture, which can thus be seen as a synopsis of the story of the specific walk, the preterite of narration of that walk ensues. Generally speaking, 'A Promenade' consists of narrative segments in the past tense (author or narrator speech) alternating with segments in the present tense which, for lack of a better term, can be called digressions (personage speech and/or narrator speech). With the exception of the tense difference, the former can hardly be distinguished from the latter in features or function.[34]

The main function of the narrative segments is to report the actions of the I-personage (the only human protagonist physically present), and to provide the chronotopical setting for the plot. The concrete setting and the physical actions (mostly verbs of motion) are described with the utmost economy. They are not important for their own sake, as is immediately made clear: 'I [ . . . ] set off for a walk out of town. I fell in thought, forgot myself, walked and did

not know whither' (162). Most of the important actions reported
are those of perception (it is the personage's eyes, ears, nose, and
touch, that are active rather than the whole person) and, above all,
those of cognition, emotion, inner states. The concrete setting is
equally de-emphasized. The narrator informs us that the spatial
movement is away from town, to a grassy river bank, the top of a
hill, and back to town. Beyond this, there is little specific description, and the narrator is concerned mainly with global phenomena,
such as the sun, and abstract features of the setting, such as light,
shadow, sound, motion, and particularly the 'pleasures' (*priiatnosti*
and *udovol'stvii*) that surround the poet. The narration is far from
objective reporting, and clearly reveals an emotive, sensitive
narrator–person as much as it reveals his story, if not more.

The same type of lexicon, syntax, and semantics, characterizes
the narrative sections and the digressions: rhythmical prose, parallelism, repetition, metaphorical turns of phrase, emotive and evaluative (mostly solemn) lexicon, dynamic enumeration, and exclamation. Often the I-narrator comments on his story explicitly, at times
generalizing its contents to apply to the human condition as he sees
it. At times he pits the events in the story against his own past experiences (outside the walk). After the description of how he listened to
Philomela's song, he comments: 'Never did Marchesi and Todi sing
so pleasantly to me' (173).[35] Occasionally he comments directly on
his own function as author: 'But can I describe the pleasure of falling
asleep like this!'; 'This can only be felt' (173), obvious resorts to
discourse deixis, stressing on the one hand, the inadequacy of language (an authorial dilemma) and, on the other hand, the intensity
of the experience (a personage privilege). This type of bivocal
deictic commentary became extremely frequent in Karamzin's later
works, and was subsequently more fully developed into a topic in its
own right by Karamzin's successors – one need only think of Zhukovskii's famous 'Inexpressibility' ('Nevyrazimost'').

Frequently the manner of narration itself tangibly reproduces the
phenomena described, most notably the sleepy intonations
whereby the personage is described as trailing off to sleep: 'sleep
began to close my eyes, – and its tender touch was so pleasant, so
pleasant . . . ' (173, sleepy ellipsis original). These instances of
personage type speech are interspersed within the narrator's past
tense segments and are clearly attributable to him as he re-lives the
past walk at the time of his present narration.

The present tense digressions expressing thoughts, fantasies, emotions, and the like, are characterized entirely by personage speech features, as is to be expected if they originate with the I-personage within the walk story. These segments are, however, not always clearly attributable to him. In some cases such attribution is made, as in the case of the paean to the sun which is introduced by an explicit reporting clause: 'Looking at it for some time, I thought: [paean]' (162). Similarly, the hymn to the Creator at sunrise is introduced by a clearcut reporting clause: 'I fell to my knees in reverence, and on a heartfelt impulse, I broke into song: [hymn]' (174). In other cases, the attributions are more vague, as in the postpositive reporting clause identifying the digression on poetry: '[digression on poetry] Thus dreams an ardent imagination' (168). This could refer either to the present of narration (compare the stress on the narrator's imagination in the overture), or to the past of the walk, or, for that matter, to the sensitive person in general. The major digression on silence, the universe, and the Creator, is equally ambiguously attributed and could be voiced either by the I-personage within the story or by the I-narrator *à propos* the topic. Such examples can be multiplied, but suffice this to show the subtle nature of the transitions between narrator's and personage's speech contexts. The narrator, in addition to his reporting function, also carries out the personage functions of evaluating, emoting, and the like.

As for the personage's speech (where it is identifiable as such), the dialogue which the I-personage carries out (with partners present only in spirit, not in body, or with inanimate partners, such as the sun personified) also 'reports', so that within the general narrative structure there are miniature 'stories within the story'. Thus, for instance, within the reported paean to the sun, while addressing the sun, the personage also reports a story about how some sage five or six thousand years ago pronounced similar panegyrics to the sun (directly quoted, 162–3). The personage thus also performs a dual function as personage and as a secondary narrator. Furthermore, the secondary stories essentially echo the main story, the topic on all levels being poetic creation. The structure of 'A Promenade' as a whole can be seen as centered around the I-narrator's present creation in all respects. The process of his creation is metonymically elaborated in terms of his own past creation of the hymn, and the same process is extended *spatially*:

the paean to the sun by Indian and Arabic sages, savage tribes on the other side of the globe, culturally more advanced poets on distant planets; and *temporally*: ancient sages, a specific hymn sung five or six thousand years ago (directly quoted), the Biblical singer of Creation (Genesis directly quoted), Thomson (*The Seasons* quoted as epigraph), Young (Cynthia from his *Night Thoughts* apostrophized), Wieland, Homer, and Ossian. It is thus also repeated at all stages of culture. It is echoed by non-human singers (birds in general, Philomela, and the 'herald of morning'), and ultimately it all harks back to and imitates the original Creation, nature thus being the main and eternally renewable poem. Nature is being imitated, as are the other models, but it is important to stress that this imitation takes the form of reliving the very process of Creation; the emotions and thoughts that inspire poetic creation at all stages of history and at all locales are the same.

The physical movements of the I-personage, his (and the I-narrator's) emotions, moods, and thoughts, are synchronized with the movement of the sun (and thus the outward appearance of nature), and each phase is linked to specific moods, specific aspects of creation and reception, and to specific poets exemplifying them. The concentric compositional structure of 'A Promenade' with the poet's inner essence at its center thus fully replicates the topic of poetic creation, conceptualized as egocentric. The universe is depicted as 'one great house' of poets, close and distant in time and space, presided over by God, the first poet. It is seen entirely according to the imagination of the present poet, depicted both as ideal author and, above all, ideal reader, according to Sentimentalist poetics.

In this Ptolemeian universe everything revolves around the poet–center, around his internal space. Not only does the sun move and the earth stand still, but, on a smaller scale, too, the poet is the center of gravity towards which everything is attracted or away from which everything recedes. The choice of vocabulary and syntax is as egocentric as the plot, theme, and compositional structure. A few examples will demonstrate this: 'the sun's rays penetrate my very imagination' (161); 'Lightness, freedom, joy, poured into me with the air. The pleasures of evening crowded around me' (162); 'the birds sang [ . . . ] and with the harmony of their songs delighted my heart' (164); 'all objects hid from my eyes, all disappeared for me' (165); 'awe flows through all my nerves' (166); 'But how many vital pleasures too the picture of a nocturnal sky can pour into my heart! What a spacious field is opened up for the actions of my intellect!' (168–9). Nature is lit up by the sun so that the poet may enjoy its beauty, it is darkened so that he may fully perceive himself without distractions, and it is lit up by the moon and stars so that he may perceive it on the grandest scale.

The poet's creative act in all its aspects is described as imaginative co-creation of the original divine Creation of nature. In order to co-create, the poet must first be able to appreciate fully and with all his senses, all of Creation, as well as subsequent poetic re-creations by his predecessors. A keen perception of the surrounding nature and poetry is thus the first tool of the poet's trade. The second tool is a sensitized heart and mind, which allows all the sense data to be internalized as they are perceived.[36]

Beauty is most fully appreciated when contrasted to its absence. As the sun begins to set, this absence is graphically depicted: birds cease singing, evening shadows close up around the poet, and finally there is nothing external left to occupy the poet's senses. Everything has been internalized and the poet can now fully concentrate on self-perception. This inner self-awareness can be fully realized as the 'highest ecstasy of joy' only by an innocent and virtuous heart. Thus goodness is seen as the third tool of the trade, and poetry is seen as an inherently ethical venture. This equation between ethics and aesthetics was, as we saw earlier, one of the marks of the intellectual climate of the era. This idea is most emphatically expressed by the poet of 'A Promenade' in his apostrophe to 'sacred silence' which gets at the very roots of Sentimentalist solipsism, nowhere in Karamzin's works as fully described as here. To show the solemn style, I will quote this apostrophe in Russian:

Священная тишина, ужас сердца порочного, стихия не-винности, убежище мудрых, святилище добродетели! да не трепещет сердце мое в твоих объъятиях! или да будет трепет его высочайшим восторгом радости! Буди благословенна, тишина уединения! и в то время, как все видимое творение погружается в глубоком сне, возбуждай меня к священным размышлениям, к ближайшему собе-седованию с сердцем моим, и утишай в нем всякое волнение, произ-водимое бурями общежития. Да пробудятся все духовные силы мои, и да чувствую во глубине души своей, что я существую!... И се растекается сие животворное чувство по всей внутренности моей! Ощущаю живо, что я живу, и есмь нечто отделенное от прочего, есмь совершенное целое. (165)

(Holy silence, horror to a vicious heart, element of innocence, refuge of the wise, shrine of virtue! may my heart not tremble in your embraces! or may its trembling be the highest ecstasy of joy! Be blessed silence of solitude! And when all visible creation is sinking into a deep sleep, awaken me to holy meditations, to the most intimate communion with my heart, and silence in it every agitation, brought on by the storms of society. May all my spiritual strength awaken and may I feel in the depth of my soul, that I exist! . . . And this life giving feeling is [now] flowing throughout my insides! I feel vividly, that I live, and am something separate from the rest, am a complete whole.)

The poet addresses silence (i.e., an *absence* of sound) which he panegyrically personifies in terms of all the qualities desirable in his own self: innocence, wisdom, virtue (prayed for and granted!). He further prays that he may be granted 'spiritual strength', 'sacred thoughts', the 'most intimate conversation with my own heart', and 'a sense that I exist' (all of which is already in progress, being done at the moment, and, as it were, divinely sanctioned, as that prayer too is granted). In essence, the poet addresses his own conscience (which is clear), and his own consciousness of self (which is already at its peak). He speaks with himself, about himself, and, as it were, 'speaks himself'. He is alone, and consequently metonymizes himself so that he may communicate with himself. Thus the passage is largely auto-suggestive, wishful thinking, while at the same time addressed also to Silence and to the powers that be. The solemn Church Slavic optatives and imperatives, the sustained religious lexicon, and the urgent intonations thus combine into a curiously mixed prayer–auto-suggestion to the circumstances, the powers that be, and (mainly) to the poet's inner self, that they may all combine into the desired spiritual constellation. This most fervent prayer–auto-suggestion is punctuated by a moment of absolute silence (graphically designated by ellipsis dots and also evoked by the preponderance of sibilants and 'hushers'), suggesting that all powers are indeed absolutely concentrated on this single aim of the poet's spiritual self-awareness. The slow solemn intonations culminate in the most exalted exclamation of joy: 'I feel vividly that I live', directly expressing that his prayers have been answered, so to speak, *in medias res*. It is followed by another ecstatic apostrophe to the sense of existence, another even more overt expression of the poet's own present feeling. It is difficult to imagine a more solipsistic passage.[37]

Next follows the actual expression/description of the poet's 'sacred thoughts' and his 'communion with his heart'. This religiously stated heightened self-awareness, coupled with total darkness in the surroundings and the single sound of water, enables the poet to imagine the Creation of the world. Together with the 'Hebrew bard' (Genesis 1.2 is quoted), the poet vividly experiences the primordial void (the deep, the ocean) as his own non-being, his death, with a beating heart and a feeling of awe (*uzhas*). The Divine 'Let there be light' is then recaptured on a personal level with an exhortation by the poet to himself: 'But be consoled!' and the thoughts of the consoling phenomenon of the life-giving force of the sun, expressing a firm belief in a spiritual afterlife.

Night in the midst of nature is depicted as the environment furthest removed from worldly vanity and as the time when the poet's heart and mind are most receptive to poetry. The thoughts of his own life – death – rebirth in terms of divine Creation lead him to recall Young's *Night Thoughts* on the same themes. This results in another prayer, this time to Young's Cynthia, that she might grant him the same inspiration that was granted to Young, Homer, and Ossian. He also re-enacts Wieland's spiritual insights and through Wieland he experiences his own spiritual essence, his 'kinship with blessed spirits', when his physical being is completely de-emphasized and his actions are entirely spiritual. Indeed, he envisions the day when he can fully discard his corporeal trappings and see the 'full light that surrounds the throne' of God.[38]

The poet's mind (*razum*) is as highly sensitized as is his heart, and he tries to fathom the infinitude of the universe, and thus the full magnitude of Creation. This foray into science is as Sentimentally solipsistic as were his forays into poetry: the poet not only imagines other more perfectly developed poet brothers on distant planets, but tries to see the earth (and himself) through their eyes. They are all seen as brothers in the same house of poetry.

The poet of 'A Promenade' can thus empathize with the creators of the most inspired poetry: with God as the Creator of nature, with Moses as the first poet of Creation, with Young, the foremost contemporary singer of night, with Homer and Ossian, with Wieland, whose spiritual insights he shares, and even with extraterrestrial poets. He re-lives what they felt when they created their poetry, and projects the effects of night and nature as described in their poetry on himself. This is a picture of the poet himself as the

ideal Sentimentalist *reader*, and the ideal effect of poetry is seen as
an evocation of the same emotions in the reader as those which
were felt by the poet himself when he created his work. Complete
self-awareness, which allows the most vivid imagination and an
ability to project oneself completely into the place of another and
thus to co-create, is the poet's fourth and most essential tool. 'A
Promenade' in its own fictional way illustrates the three major
principles of Sentimentalist philosophy: solipsism, sympathy, and
pleasure.

The promenader also displays a certain amount of narcissism
when he proceeds to thank the Creator for being properly endowed
in an apostrophe to the Creator which in all its humility is
nevertheless quite self-congratulatory:

Благодарю Тебя за то, что Ты сотворил меня, и сотворил человеком;
что Ты даровал мне способность чувствовать и рассуждать –
чувствовать свое и Твое бытие, рассуждать о Тебе и себе самом, –
рассуждать о свойствах Твоих и моем назначении по видимому
мирозданию, делу рук Твоих, и по собственному моему существу!
(172)

(I thank Thee for creating me, and creating me as a man; that Thou
gave me the ability to feel and reflect – feel my own and Thine
existence, reflect on Thee and myself, – reflect on Thy qualities and
my significance, on the visible universe, created by Thy hands, and
on my own existence!)

Since this passage is not clearly attributable only to the past
I-personage, it may also be read as the present I-narrator's expression of gratitude for the ability to do what he is in fact in the
process of doing.

The exalted rapture precedes, and is the cause of, the state of 'a
certain oblivion' in which the poet can for the first time fully
appreciate the quiet and pleasant song of Philomela, which corresponds to his own feelings of sweet, tender pleasure. The sweet and
pleasing song of the nightingale is favorably contrasted to the
operatic singing of Marchesi and Todi. He thereby subtly censures
the present state of the arts as 'unnatural' artificial culture, and
stresses a general Sentimentalist preference for what is natural to
what is artificial and conventional.[39]

After his 'pleasant oblivion' with his soul completely at peace
(symbolized by a three-hour slumber), the poet is prepared to greet
the rising sun and thereby participate in the re-creation of the world

with his own hymn. It is sung spontaneously in unison with all the rest of nature as birds suddenly burst out singing at sunrise. After lingering at the site a few more minutes, the poet is invigorated and returns to town, Thomson in hand, now opened to the *concluding* pages of his hymn. 'A Promenade' can also be seen as the story of the poet's personal reading and co-creating of Thomson's 'Hymn' from beginning (we recall that the second and third lines made up the epigraph) to end.

Sentimentalist poetics, as outlined in 'A Promenade', contrasts to the Classicist conception of imitation of nature and models. It is abundantly clear, that Sentimentalism rejects neither imitation nor Reason, as is frequently claimed in textbook accounts of the movement. The Sentimentalists do not see imitation in terms of formal properties of the work as a finished product. It is not important for them that the work adhere to (and preferably, perfect) artistic rules for genre or style, determined *a priori* and sanctioned by tradition as absolute ideal properties of a specific type of work. The Sentimentalist view of imitation, as outlined in 'A Promenade', stresses that the poet as ideal reader co-experience the emotions, states, and thoughts which prompted the 'models', thus making them his own. It is less important that he study or imitate the formal characteristics or use the same kind of imagery and style as the model. The stress is predominantly on creative process, rather than end product. Therefore the Sentimentalist poet can wish that 'my dreams were like those of Homer' without wishing to be an epic poet, a 'Russian Homer'.[40] Imagery, style, and genre were seen entirely as a mirror of the poet's soul, and the poet himself was necessarily mirrored in his own fiction, whatever the genre.

Similarly, Reason was seen as a property of the poet himself, rather than as a general property which organized the world and art into neat systems. The important factor was that *all* the poet's personal creative faculties, both senses and sensibilities, both *sviashchennye razmyshleniia* and *sobesedovaniia s serdtsem* were fully engaged in the creative process, and consequently were reflected in the work itself so that the reader would become equally engaged in co-creative reading.

'A Promenade' is both a fiction and a manifesto of Sentimentalist principles which were to change relatively little during Karamzin's subsequent career. The frenetic pitch and the solemnity of actions

and emotions (and the correspondingly lofty style) do not contradict Sentimentalist poetics, although it was the mellower moods
which came to dominate in later practice. The exaggerated mystical
elements of the individual's communion with God and the Spirits,
the *Misteriia Poezii,* and the equally exaggerated worship of sun
and light, no doubt derived mostly from Karamzin's Masonic
connections, and were later to abate.[41] However, the pronounced
stress on the individual's inner experiences as the true source,
subject, and aim of poetry was to remain the guiding principle for
both Karamzin and his followers. The individualistic stress is more
profound than a mere matter of themes or stylistic devices or a new
language – it pervaded all aspects of art and was implemented in the
very structure of the works. In particular the idea of author as
reader, is crucial to an understanding of Sentimentalist poetics. It is
mainly these latter aspects of Sentimentalist poetics that 'A Promenade' demonstrates with unusual force and clarity. It is also
Karamzin's first Sentimental journey – albeit on a miniature scale –
and his later account of his grand tour was to echo the structure of
'A Promenade'. The larger opus is no less a 'promenade' both in
the concrete chronotopical dimensions and in the spiritual realm,
the latter wholly informing and penetrating the former.

## 'The Countryside. A Fragment'

'The Countryside' is, in many respects, similar to 'A Promenade'. It
describes the narrator's stay at his country estate, where he has
travelled for a rest (from city life and travel), thus repeating the
movement from city to country in 'A Promenade'. From the
physical premises of the estate he sets out on several walks into the
environs, thus multiplying the walk of 'A Promenade'. Here, too,
the walks take place both physically and spiritually (one of the
walks, with Thomson in the hand of the walker), but in 'The
Countryside' there is a comparatively greater stress on the former
aspect. Where 'A Promenade' emphasizes that the narrator is part
of the universe of spirits and poets, 'The Countryside' is mainly
concerned with the minutiae in the immediate setting. Where the
former poet's vision was telescopical, the poet in 'The Countryside'
is more fond of a microscope. Where the former poet is communi-
cating with distant planets, the latter turns his attention to the fine
veins and motley petals of minuscule flowers. The basic solipsistic

structure is not altered thereby – each poet, as it were, still holds his instrument, and it is still the poet's inner space that makes up the center of the concentric configuration. Poetry itself, which in 'A Promenade' was the near-exclusive topic, is but part of the topic of 'The Countryside', which, in addition to solemn reflection on the universe and poetic creation, also shows its poet engaged in more prosaic activities: botanizing, eating, and swimming. Their reading matter is at once the same (Thomson) and different (Gresset and LaFontaine, who take the place of Young, Wieland, Homer, and Ossian). Both Gresset and LaFontaine are famed for their writing in light, humorous, and at times even irreverent tones.[42] The choice of reading is a consequence of the temporal setting in each work: 'A Promenade' is a night walk, whereas the main actions in 'The Countryside' unfold during the day, with an overlap at each end. A hot summer day obviously makes for lighter reading, whereas Young and Ossian in particular, are geared towards night moods. The poetic production of each poet differs accordingly: whereas in 'A Promenade' the inspiration results in a modest hymn to Creation, 'The Countryside' yields 'brief notes' (directly quoted, as was the hymn) for the poet's herbarium.

'The Countryside' has a bipartite composition: the first part is a lyrical overture and the second, set apart by a subtitle 'My Day', describes the narrator's activities from dawn to dusk. This bipartite composition is not, however, an adequate description of the artistic structure of the work as a whole, which is more complex and also more consciously structured than has hitherto been noted.[43]

'The Countryside' is a typical Sentimentalist idyll where the narrator's self dominates the structure. The overture consists of almost pure speech event, revealing the narrator's own emotions and opinions. 'My Day' relates his actions during one day. This binary distinction between opinions–emotions and actions is by no means pure, and although the opinions–emotions are concentrated in the overture and the beginning of 'My Day', they strongly interpenetrate the core of actions as well. The narrated core events in 'My Day' also beg to be read on three different levels: as a concrete description of a specific day (a single day, but one representative of a succession of identical days), as a more general, more abstract reflection, where 'day' metaphorically refers to the narrator's adult life (as opposed to the 'morning' of his childhood and the 'evening' of old age), and, finally, as a further extension of the latter level to symbolize the 'ages of man' in a historical sense. The latter two levels generalize the opinions–emotions of the overture to a universal philosophy, the first level, on the other hand particularizes them to apply to a single day, the narrator's personal minor acts of little general consequence. The narrator closely identifies with the values of childhood (both his personal childhood and a distant past idyllic Golden Age). 'My Day' is thus a fragment of several larger temporal units: the calendar cycle, the human cycle, and the historical cycle. The country estate is similarly a fragment of the world, which also contains the city. The country is a symbol of nature as opposed to city artifice, – 'culture' in a derogatory sense, similar to its derogation in the judgement of Marchesi and Todi in 'A Promenade'. The focus of the work as a whole is, however, on daytime, on adult life, and on the present mature stage of mankind.

The overture of 'The Countryside' is almost entirely made up of the narrator's expression of his mood, his likes, and his dislikes. Neither the setting nor the events are directly reported, but can be gleaned from emotive vocative constructions, exclamations, rhythmic and euphonic outpourings of thoughts, memories, emphatic evaluations, and the like. It begins with an expressive–declarative speech act uttered in explicit performative form as an apostrophe to all the topoi essential to the idyllic *locus amoenus*:

Благословляю вас, мирные сельские тени, густые, кудрявые рощи, душистые луга, и поля, златыми класами покрытые! Благословляю тебя, кроткая речка, и вас, журчащие ручейки, в нее текущие! Я пришел к вам искать отдохновения. (58)

(I bless you, peaceful country shades, dense, bushy groves, fragrant meadows, and fields covered with golden grains! I bless you, meek rivulet, and you purling streamlets flowing in it! I came to you to seek repose.)

These basic elements, the grove, the meadow, and the river, already here multiplied by plural forms and near synonyms (not only *luga* but also *polia,* not only *rechka* but also *rucheek*), are elaborated throughout the work as a whole: *topographically* (gullies, valleys, hills, hillocks, riverbanks, plains); *botanically* (all conceivable formations of vegetation: groves, forests, bowers, tall trees, bushes [six types of trees are named: aspen, birch, lime, elm, willow, and oak]; branches, leaves, tall grasses, balsamic grasses, soft mosses, grains [rye and barley are named], and flowers [the cornflower is named]); *ornithologically* (birds in general, the lark is named); *entymologically* (dragonflies and bees); *meteorologically* (light breezes, the refreshing shade of trees, crystalline rivers, the noonday heat, clouds, sunshine); and *mythologically* (playful Zephyrs and motley Sylphides, i.e., the minor mythological nature spirits, obligatory in the idyll). The effect of foreshortening is produced through the attention to the minutiae: leaves of trees, berries from the bushes, a single feather, and the precise details of flower petals. As the narrator himself puts it, 'everything huge is disagreeable to country simplicity'. Stylistically, this preference is implemented in a striking preponderance of diminutives: *rechka, rucheek, malen'kie dorozhki, berezki, tropinka, domik, nizen'kii, okoshka, kustochka, veterok, listochka, ovechka, travka, korzinok, tsvetochki, tonen'kie zhilochki, kraeshki, chashechka, bumazhka,* not to speak of words which inherently denote smallness. An emotive flashback to the narrator's childhood and an equally emotive reference to the 'youngsters of mankind, the children of wild Nature, those simple-hearted folks of yore', can be seen as part of the same tendency towards miniaturization, characteristic of the idyll in general. Since diminutives in Russian carry connotations of endearment, this miniaturization contributes to creating a sensitive image of the narrator.

Another characteristic of the work as a whole is the pervasive synaesthesia: sounds, smells, tastes, textures, colors, and temperatures are expressed in nouns, verbs, and adjectives. The addition of shepherds, shepherdesses, flocks of sheep, fertile fields, newly cut grass, the scythe, and the reed pipe complete the idyllic picture.

After the initial benedictions of, and reunion with, his *locus amoenus,* the narrator waxes lyrical in a passage which reveals his relief and joy over the newfound solitude in nature:

> Давно уже душа моя не наслаждалась
> такою тишиною,
> таким совершенным уединением,
> такою совершенною свободою.
> Я один –
> один с своими мыслями –
> один с Натурою.
> (59, line arrangement added)

(It has been long since my soul enjoyed / such silence, / such complete solitude, / such complete freedom. / I am alone – / alone with my thoughts – / alone with Nature.)

The passage demonstrates the typical Karamzinian intonations – his famed *period*. It can almost be read as a poem in free iambics. Almost every 'line' is anaphorical, and almost every line has its syntactic parallel. Owing to repetition and lexical choice, the passage is strongly euphonic (*sovershennym, sovershennoiu, svobodoiu, s svoimi*), and the predominant sounds are sibilant, evoking the 'sound' of silence, which furthermore, owing to the construction of the passage, can be perceived as synonymous with solitude, freedom, thoughts, nature, and, ultimately, with the 'I'. The dash, indicating an intonational pause, is also extremely typical of Karamzin. Similar passages can be found in all of Karamzin's works, although, particularly towards the end of his career, he tends to use them as targets for his humor and parody.

The narrator's state of mind, and the great world of nature which provoked it, remind him of his childhood on the edge of (civilized) Europe, where his 'spirit was formed in natural simplicity', where 'the great phenomena of nature' received his first attention, and where a clap of thunder formed 'the basis of his religion'. The natural *naiveté* stressed in this section and its exact imagery are repeated almost verbatim more than ten years later in one of Karamzin's last works, *A Knight of Our Time,* but (as I shall show in my analysis of that work) in an entirely different non-serious context. In 'The Countryside' the narrator is dead serious.

The passages analyzed so far, perform two functions, important for what follows. First, they imply another, less peaceful and simple setting, for which the narrator's 'natural upbringing' was interrupted and which he is glad to have left behind 'now' as an adult. Second, they establish his personal stance in the conflict between nature and culture which is developed into a polemically tinted (more or less hidden) dialogue concluding the overture. This 'dialogue' expresses the philosophy that underlies his daily activities explored in 'My Day'. Although Karamzin's narrators in general are fond of stating their own opinions and evaluations, the narrator of 'The Countryside' is singularly vocal in this respect. He speaks directly, unequivocally, and emphatically for more than two pages. Even his reported physical actions are first and foremost expressions of his evaluation ('I see [ . . . ] I walk past'), as are his intellectual actions ('I compare'). He gives vent to his likes and dislikes directly ('I love [ . . . ] love'; 'gives me an unpleasant feeling'), his pleasures ('more attractive to me', 'for me there is no pleasure'), his intentions ('I will never be'), his wishes and desires ('I don't want [ . . . ] here's what I wish', 'I don't feel like'). He states his opinions categorically, and often in general, almost aphoristic turns of phrase: 'In the country every artifice is unpleasant', 'Man ponders and destroys', 'Wilderness is holy to me', 'Everything huge is disagreeable to country simplicity.' Elaborate metaphors and similes are developed to drive home a point: a transplanted and trimmed tree is likened to a prisoner, and he, in turn, to a 'man without love'. All this obviously extolls nature and condemns culture. The following oppositions are established: the garden, the avenue, flowerbeds ↔ the aspen grove; French and English gardens ↔ the meadow, forest, river, gully, hill; sanded garden walks ↔ a path trodden by a shepherdess; a large house ↔ a small low hut; the view from a window ↔ being out in the fields. The whole tirade gives the impression of being polemically addressed to a narratee who sides with culture and needs to be converted. Although only the narrator's 'lines' are actually verbalized, his opponent's 'lines' are implied by certain features of the narrator's speech. The speech of another has penetrated the present utterance and makes it bivocal. The emphatic 'No, no! I'll never [ . . . ]' implies that someone is either incredulous or has suggested that the narrator might [ . . . ]. After explaining that he prefers wild nature to ordered gardens, he concludes: 'My groves will remain untouched – let them get overgrown by tall grass!' Where the dash occurs one can easily imagine an objection to wild groves, and when the narrator says: 'So there won't be a view from the windows – true – but then, one doesn't need a view. It is much better [ . . . ]', he seems to be conceding a point to the narratee whose objection he repeats and tries to counter.

The entire overture is strongly marked with practically all types of speech event features, including traces of an interlocutor. It serves almost the exclusive function of revealing the narrator's personality and opinions, and to persuade the narratee to accept, or at least understand, his system of values against those that are typical of adult city dwellers. The narrated events that follow in 'My Day' emerge logically as a demonstration of the narrator's principles. They provide a kind of experiential proof for his side of the polemic, and each experience provokes him to further elaborations of his opinions and further expressions of rapture over nature and simplicity. The events reported are the narrator's habits. The thoughts reported occur to him every day, and there is no distance between 'author' and 'personage' – they have fully congealed into one image of narrator. The tense used is the present, encompassing both speech event and narrated event. The reporting and acting subject is the same 'I', the thoughts and opinions uttered could have occurred during the actual day or at the time of writing, and the values professed during the walks described are still treasured at the moment of writing. Indeed, one could say that the entire work is an elaboration of the speech event parameters, particularly the speaker himself and his wider setting.

The narrator's activities at sunrise serve to remind him of childhood in general as a time of naive innocence, his own childhood, and the early stages of human history. His activities at sunset similarly conjure up an image of a specific old man and thoughts about his own future and death, as well as the future of human history. The events of the day are arranged by the principle of strict symmetry from sunrise to noon and from noon to sunset, each half of the day mirroring the other, and, in turn, reflecting the greater cycles of nature. In each half similar events are reported, similar settings used, similar emotions provoked, and similar style and vocabulary used.

'The Countryside' is a good demonstration of Karamzin's views of the poetic function as seeing the extraordinary in the ordinary, most explicitly stated in his (later) foreword to the second book of *Aonidy*. Most of the actions are exceedingly prosaic (eating, drinking, reading, swimming, and gathering flowers), but are endowed with almost magical capacities to give the sentient human pleasure. Their importance is raised to the level of global phenomena, such as the movement of the planets. Seeing the essential in the ordinary everyday is typical for the idyll.[44] By way of demonstration, the narrator of 'The Countryside' shows that all that nature has to offer is vastly superior to all that 'artificial' culture has produced. A simple dish of raspberries is far superior to elaborate banquets, the simple rustling of leaves to the pleasures that cultural centers of the world can offer, fields of ripe grain to a painter's canvas. There is more pleasure in perceiving the fragrance and the perfect beauty of a small flower than there is in knowing the schemes of a Linné. The opposition between nature and culture, and the advocacy of the former in the overture is sustained in the second part of the work as well.

The emotive–reflective manner of narration established in the overture carries over into the report of daily activities in 'My Day'. As I mentioned, its inception and conclusion coincide temporally with the conclusion and inception of 'A Promenade' respectively, and the two works are complementary. The solemn reflective mood of the narrator during his night walk in 'A Promenade' also characterizes the narrator of 'The Countryside' before and after his daily activities. A similar lofty, metaphorical and heavily Church Slavic style can be discerned in both. 'The Countryside's' narrator personifies the rising sun as 'the radiant groom of nature' appearing while people (cultured city dwellers) are still sleeping. The narrator reflects: 'And man sleeps through these solemn morning hours, when white clouds on their gilded crests, from the depths of the ocean carry the radiant groom of Nature, greeted by loud choirs of living creation!' (62). We are reminded of the similar images of the void, night, and Creation as well as the morning birdsong in 'A Promenade'.

The narrator next reports his own actions: 'I kneel silently!' – a narrated event, but the exclamatory intonations, the present tense, and the first person forms, are typical of speech event. Two rhetorical questions express the narrator's reflections on the 'not surprising fact' that already the 'youngsters of mankind, the children of wild Nature, those simple-hearted folks of yore' worshipped the same magnificent luminary (compare the reflections on primitive ancient sun-worshippers in 'A Promenade'), thereby mentally extending the events of his own day into the historical dimension mentioned. The description of sunset is identically structured and couched in the same solemn style with analogous imagery. From his vantage point on a high sandy riverbank (compare 'A Promenade', 'Palemon and Daphnis', and 'The Flood') the narrator watches the evening sun in its 'quiet grandeur' and 'tender greatness' as it reaches the gates of the West and 'glimmers behind a thin gilded wavy cloud – kindles it with its rays – appears once more in all its fullness – casts a glimmer and a shine on earth – and hides. Now there is a scarlet afterglow in the West' (67).[45]

An extended simile follows, echoing the personification at sunrise: the setting sun is compared to a 'wise virtuous man', reaching the end of his days after a long life as a 'beneficial luminary for moral beings', and whose fiery imagination (like the sun's rays) has cooled off, but whose mind remains light. His memory will shine after he is gone like the afterglow of the sun (compare the thoughts on afterlife in 'A Promenade'). The narrator's physical action repeats his kneeling at sunrise, whereupon follow a prayer and further reflections on life and death, vice and virtue, reflections comparing the state of mankind to the light and shade in nature. The radiant innocence of childhood has developed into the calm wisdom of old age – both visions provoked by the 'great phenomena of nature' which laid the foundation for the narrator's education, and which still inform him during his adult return to the country.

The transitions from and to the solemn reflective level, and to and from the specific quotidian activities related occur naturally, since the metaphorical vision is also the concrete sunrise and sunset which begins and concludes 'my' day. They are accomplished, again, by analogous imagery at both ends. In the morning, the narrator waxes lyrical over the fresh morning air, the 'sea of fragrances' that extends between earth and sky. Next, he beholds the idyllic morning activities of shepherds and shepherdesses: the herds dispersing on the hills, the scythes glistening on the fields, the lark singing above toiling villagers, and the 'tender Lavinia' preparing breakfast for her Palemon – nature seen in wholly Thomsonian colors (we might note that Karamzin had earlier translated Thomson's 'Lavinia'). A morning walk in the fields and a return to his quiet abode, where a glass of thick yellow cream awaits him, completes the picture of early morning. The description of early evening mirrors that of morning. The narrator hears the shepherd's reed pipe and sees the sheep returning to their folds while the villager lingers in the fields. A pleasant cup of tea 'in the clean air' is extolled because the 'evening aromas pour into my cup' (we are reminded of the centripetally moving pleasures in 'A Promenade'), and inspires the narrator to go and view the sunset. The narrative sequence of air, shepherds, herds, villagers, drink, walk, is thus reiterated in images either identical, synonymous, or analogous, and in the same rapturous tones.

The same kind of symmetry can be seen in the entire description of the day – morning and evening 'coming together' at a noon-hour swim. The swim is a concrete everyday correspondence to the allegory of the sun rising out of the ocean and the sunset watched from the riverbank. The combination of heat and cold and a complete stillness in nature further centers the event beyond its compositional centrality. The swim is preceded by a walk to a grove, 'Thomson in hand', and a leisurely and pleasant hour of reading and contemplating. The narrator interrupts his reading, places his book next to a raspberry shrub, directs his glance upwards, and contemplates the high trees and the lush greenery of the branches, the pleasant play of light and shade, and the rustling of the leaves, 'so different from the city, the Paris, London noise' – echoing his preference for wild nature to *French* and *English* gardens, voiced in the overture. A similar reading session takes place after his swim, repeating with slight variations the imagery of the earlier description: he sits in the shade of an elm tree (grove), reads Gresset and LaFontaine (Thomson), lets the book fall from his hand (sets the book aside), as he trails off into a pleasant slumber, is awakened by light Zephyrs, and later receives a basket of fresh raspberries (raspberry shrub) brought by his faithful gardener. The simple meal is greeted by a rapturous: 'How pleasant and refreshing these juicy fruits of generous Nature are! Oh! can one *not* love her for all she does to please and pamper man!' As in the case of other such emotive outbursts, it is impossible to determine whether the words were spoken at the actual moment of eating, or at the moment of writing and remembering, or, for that matter, whether the reporting is concurrent with the events.

The narrator's glance mimics the allegorical and concrete movement of the sun: before the swim the sun is moving towards its zenith, and the narrator's glances are turned upwards towards the leaves and branches; now, as the sun is headed down, he turns his attention down to the wildflowers and grasses, and sets out to botanize.[46] The nature/culture opposition is further developed in the ensuing description. He does not approach the flora in order to gain any formal scientific insights, he simply wants to enjoy what nature has to offer, and her beauty needs no learned adornment. His main reactions are to admire and wonder at the perfect beauty and delicacy of each fragrance, each petal, each minute 'little cuplet'. The botanical specimens are then brought home, examined, preserved, and provided with labels. The narrator eschews the genus and species information proper to a herbarium, and instead writes what amounts to a miniature prose poem for each plant. One such label is quoted in full, *as an example*, introduced by the following reporting clause: 'not being a learned Botanist, I write brief notes on each plant. For example: [note]'. Although this is a case of directly quoted speech, it is by no means clear that he wrote the actual label during the day described. Rather it is cited as an example of something he is in the habit of doing, and is perhaps making up at the moment of narration. The impression is again one of concurrent reporting. The note and the description of the botanizing excursion are focused on describing not the phenomena themselves, but the impressions they make on the observer. The label, after briefly describing the coloration of 'these' flowers, 'pleasant for the eye but even more pleasant for the nose', continues as an elaborate address to a familiar second person *ty,* and a suggestion that the addressee take a sunset walk to 'that dark grove'. In effect, it is addressed to the narrator himself for a later recollection and/or re-experience of 'today's' walk.

The brief note is a wholly unscientific fiction – a good example of a Sentimentalist trifle. Its introduction into 'The Countryside' serves to double the description of the narrator's pleasure, and to complete the description of his literary activities with his own writings. This fits the general development which characterizes 'My Day' as a whole, from 'greenery' to 'fruition': sunrise → sunset, green leaves → picked flowers, raspberry shrub → ripe berries, reading and inspiration → own creation, all of which on the minute daily scale echoes the allegorical development from radiant groom → old sage, innocence → wisdom.

The birth and childhood imagery at the beginning is also developed to its logical conclusion in the death imagery at the end: in addition to the sunset/old man simile, there is a narrator's epilogue where flashes of lightning (mirroring the clap of thunder in the overture) and the light of the moon reveal to the narrator a ruined old church and mossy gravestones, which provoke his final reflection: 'Thus darkness and light, vice and virtue, storms and lulls, grief and joy, together rule in our world!' This reiterates and resolves the initial nature/culture polemic in somewhat resigned tones, stressing, however, the narrator's pleasure in perceiving the natural harmony of things. The passage lays bare the allegorical aspects of the piece, a speech event comment on the 'story' just told, in the discourse deictic manner.

Thus 'My Day' is, like the overture, centered around the narrator, his moods, thoughts, emotions. The events are narrated not for the purpose of describing an actual day in the life of the narrator, but for the main purpose of demonstrating his *poetic perception* of such a day. There can thus be no question of 'realism' (except light touches, such as native Russian vegetation), nor any serious attempt at describing real Russian landowner life.[47] The countryside is a variant of the idyllic *locus amoenus* existing for the sole purpose of evoking different pleasurable sensations in the narrator as personage, as author–personage, and as personage–author. Nature is there to please all his senses: seeing, hearing, smelling, touching, and tasting. The other personages provide him not only with idyllic views and pleasant sounds, but also with his culinary delights. 'The Countryside' is both a return to a personal childhood and a return to nature in a more Rousseau'an sense, and the adult outside world of culture exists only as a negative backdrop which does not penetrate the actual *locus*. It is a typical Sentimentalist landowner-idyll, reminiscent of, for instance, some of Murav'ev's prose works ('The Suburban Dweller', 'Emile's Letters'), and, although it has the structure of a prose poem, it has traces of an epistolary work, particularly the polemical section of the overture.[48] One could well regard it as a letter from the narrator to one of his friends who is spending the summer in the city – despite the lack of formal epistolary characteristics.

## 'Night'

'Night' is the most lyrical and verse-like of Karamzin's prose idylls. It consists of three larger cycles, each comprising four stanza–paragraphs. The first cycle consists of the poet's invocation to the elements of his *locus amoenus* to comply with his desire to meet his beloved. The second cycle consists of four digressions from the present story line *à propos* its main topic, love – extensions in time and space of the narrator's *locus* and his emotions. The last cycle represents love as a *fait accompli* and the poet's expression of his own love and his benedictions to love in general. The piece as a whole may be seen as a poetic sublimation of an erotic core event, another characteristic that Bakhtin posits for the idyll. Here the *locus amoenus* serves its most basic idyll function: it is the setting for a lovers' rendezvous.

Each element of the *locus* is invoked to lead the beloved Chloe (perhaps the most traditional name for a shepherdess) to the dewey moss where her lover awaits her: the moon to light her path, the brooklet's purling to serve as her guide, the violet's fragrance and the nightingale's song to further attract her. Each invocation is a directive speech act, implemented by imperatives expressing the speaker's entreaties and optatives expressing his desires. The elements are invoked by elaborate vocative constructions, paraphrastic and/or provided with epithets of a panegyrically descriptive nature. Thus, in addition to their 'normal' function of address, the vocative constructions serve to describe and praise the addressees, and to convey the addresser's exalted state. The moon is addressed as *prekrasnoe svetilo nochi*, the brooklet as *kristal'nyi rucheek, rezvo tekushchii po zelenemu lugu, i tonkoiu penoiu svoikh malen'-kikh voln okropliaiushchii golubye tsvetochki i miagkuiu travku krasivykh berezhkov svoikh*, the vegetation more briefly as *fioli nochnye; tsvetushchie dreva; kazhdaia travka*, and the nightingale as *perveishii iz pevtsov krylatykh*. The entreaties are stated in familiar imperative forms (except of course where plurals apply): *Iavisia i prolei, rassei; zhurchi, shumi, i bud' veselym vozhdem; dyshite, dyshite, pitaite vozdukh; kuris'; poi, ne umolkaia* and optatives of the more solemn Church Slavic form (*da* + present tense verb): *da ne boitsia ona; da vozvyshaetsia pesn' tvoia; da uslyshit tebia moia liubeznaia; volshebnye treli tvoi da privlekut ee*. These forms reveal a mixed address: the imperatives are directed to the respective elements of nature (personified), the optatives to unnamed powers, the Creator, the Gods, Fate, Circumstances, or whatever – all of which combine to express the intensity of the poet's desires. The double imperatives contribute to the same effect of urgency (*zhurchite, shumite; dyshite, dyshite*). This is very similar to the poet's apostrophe to silence in 'A Promenade', although the element of autosuggestion is missing, and the emotions are different. The main plot actions of the personages (Chloe arriving, her lover waiting) are built into these directive speech acts as their motivational complements (if such a term may be coined). For instance: *Rassei nochnye teni i strakh liubeznoi Khloi, idushchei k svoemu drugu*, where the main burden of the expression is on the imperative (*rassei*), and Chloe's action complements the imperative causally, the action conveyed as a participial, almost adjectival, description of Chloe, rather than as an overt direct report of action. The actions themselves (directly 'reported' only in one case) provide a refrain to each stanza, reiterating and further developing the preceding refrain. The 'tune' is slightly altered each time:

[1] любезной Хлои, идущей к своему другу. – Да не боится она
[2] любезной Хлои, идущей к своему другу! Здесь, на мураве оро-
    шенной, дожидается он прихода ее.
[3] я жду моей любезной,
[4] моя любезная [ . . . ] да привлекут ее в мои отверстые объятия!

The poet's view of the personages becomes gradually more
ego-centered: lovely Chloe/she → lovely Chloe → my lovely one,
and: her friend/he → I → my open embraces. Most interesting is the
shift in focus from Chloe to the first person poet–lover, and, within
that, the shift in the reference to him from third person forms (her
friend/he) to first person (I/my lovely one), effecting a change from
what initially seems a narration of vicarious experience to one of
personal experience – a most overt case of coupling the function of
author with personage function. The speech acts used are characteristic of personage speech, as is the consistent use of lofty
Church Slavic lexicon, teeming with participial constructions and
complex coordination and subordination, with poetic devices such
as inversions, figures and tropes, the pervasive use of diminutives
and the rhythmical cadences themselves.

The second cycle consists of four digressions from the main
narrative: the poet's four visions of love, chronotopically extending
his present emotion as well as his expectations and apprehensions.
All the digressions (idylls or elegies within the idyll) are related to
the present idyll causally as possible outcomes of the present
situation, by the theme of love and by means of temporal and
spatial deixis. The deictic means link each paragraph anaphorically
to each of the others (and are further repeated within each stanza):

[1] Ночь тиха [ . . . ] подобно той [ . . . ] узрела в первый раз
    [+ the past tense Diana–Endymion love idyll]
[2] Там на отдаленном холмике [ . . . ] Там [ . . . ]
    [+ the present tense Acast family idyll]
[3] Там, в темной зелени высоких елей [ . . . ]
    [+ the past tense Phillida elegiac idyll]
[4] Там, между миртами [ . . . ] там в первый раз
    [+ the past tense first stage of the present Chloe idyll]

The four digressions also progress towards the temporal, spatial,
and emotional center of the poet's ego. The first, a vision of happy
love, takes place at night (at a similar hour as in the present idyll),
but long ago, on the distant Carian mountains. The second one, a
vision of familial and altruistic love, takes place 'on the distant hill,

beyond the palm grove' (only the general topography is visible), and lingers on till the present time. The third one, a vision of the unfulfilled love of Phillida, took place long ago, but spatially closer, in the dark greenery of the high trees (individual trees visible), and continues to have its repercussions in the present, when lovelorn shepherds place flowers and shed tears on the grave of poor Phillida. All of these are visions of vicarious experiences of love, which, however, have personal significance for the lovelorn poet. The fourth vision is a vivid recollection of the poet's own first experience of love for his Chloe in the near past, in the immediate vicinity 'among the myrtle bushes' (individual shrubs, 'right here'). This last vision is interrupted by immediate reality: a rustling in the laurel bushes, which heralds Chloe's appearance. Thus a natural transition is effected back to the present idyll, the poet's speech event, which coincides temporally and spatially with his narrated event. The transition is formally accomplished by ellipsis dots and a 'but': ' . . . but I hear' – a device which was used by Karamzin for the most part of his career.

The tempo of the first two cycles can be described as slow, corresponding to the phenomenon described: the poet's waiting. The invocations, although urgently and impetuously stated, are done with the utmost detail and poetic ornamentation, and the digressive idylls are the poet's leisurely reflections on similar situations as he whiles his time away. In both cycles, the paragraphs–stanzas consist of lengthy, complex, and mostly complete (grammatically speaking) sentences, linking several clauses by coordination and subordination by complex conjunctions and participles. In fact, the entire second cycle serves essentially the function of retarding the present plot. The last cycle is significantly faster in tempo. This speed-up is accomplished mainly by a rapid succession of brief clauses separated by pauses (as if to catch a breath) indicated by a dash or a semicolon, and by grammatically incomplete sentences signalled by ellipsis dots, or simple coordination by the conjunction $i$. They are essentially enumerations with very little poetic ornament. The first stanza in this cycle is a good illustration of the speed-up in tempo as compared to the first cycle, which it reiterates. It consists of the poet's agitated report, showing that his entreaties have been answered – in one single sentence: 'Vysoko vzoshel iasnyi mesiats; svetlo blistaet zhurchashchii ruchei v svoem techenii; dereva, tsvety, i travy islivaiut svoiu ambrosiiu;

gromko poet solovei na vet'vi rozmarinnoi'. The earlier periphrastic designations of the *same* phenomena, their diminutive forms,
the qualifying epithets, inversions and metaphorical turns, are
replaced by simple 'normal' designations (*mesiats* instead of *prekrasnoe svetilo nochi; solovei* instead of *perveishii iz pevtsov krylatykh*). The subsequent events are then reported in brief clauses
consisting basically of subject + predicate, joined by a dash or a
semicolon, with the final clause in the *period* attached by the
conjunction *i*: 'Serdtse moe b'etsia; ja smotriu i slushaiu – shorokh
priblizhaetsia – razdeliaiutsia vet'vi – vecherniaia rosa oblivaet
menia – i Khloia v moikh ob"iatiiakh'. All the wishes and desires of
the poet are fulfilled, and his agitated emotions are rendered
mainly intonationally by phrase-structural means. This is a clear
illustration of the subjective perception and description of idyllic
nature – its countenance changes entirely in accordance with the
perceiver's emotional state.

The second stanza in this last cycle culminates in the lovers'
meeting, and is reported in similar 'rapid' syntax with the bare
lexical essentials in terms of motions and emotions. The erotic
agitation is conveyed solely by means of syntax, while the lexicon is
sublimated (repeating some of the imagery of the idylls interpolated in the second cycle), and Cupid most conveniently enters at
the climax, bringing the two lovers back to life – a typical device of
rococo anacreontics.

The third stanza is a report of the subsequent affections and
emotions of the two lovers using similar utterance structure. It ends
with the poet reporting that he 'blesses allmighty Love' – which
actual speech act makes up the last stanza of the cycle and the poem
as a whole.

In the concluding stanza the poet addresses 'Love, love, reason
and aim of our life!' through a declarative–expressive speech act of
benediction, pronouncing all those who are touched by love blessed
– thereby expressing his own state most ecstatically by indirection.
The benediction is interrupted in mid-stream, marked by the now
familiar ellipsis dashes and a 'but', concluding the work with a
metaphorical statement to the effect that the poet is falling asleep
and expects new 'pleasures' in his dreams.

In 'Night', as in 'A Promenade' and 'The Countryside', there is
no compositionally differentiated narrator. Whatever 'reporting'
can be discerned is carried out by the main personage, and is

characterized by practically all the features typical of personage speech (with the exception of dialect). In the basic idyll type the main hero was a shepherd, and his main preoccupation was a direct expression of his own love for a shepherdess – in words and deeds, either directly to her, or, in her absence, to his *locus amoenus* which reminded him of her. Song (or other forms of art) served the same basic function of expressing love (or friendship), but could also become an end in itself (as in the case of song contest idylls). The hero in 'A Promenade' is such a singer; his function as poet, rather than shepherd, is stressed, and poetry is the object of both his reflections and his actions. The hero of 'The Countryside' is a shepherd-turned-landowner among shepherds and other idyllic accoutrements, sharing all the pleasures of the shepherd's life but none of his responsibilities. He is also a consumer and producer of poetry in his own right; the grazing flocks, the tender shepherdesses, and so on, provide him with a pleasant backdrop for his poetic and other activities. The hero of 'Night' is closest to the pastoral – he **is** Daphnis (although not named), the lover of his Chloe (named), with, however, a more reflective disposition, himself 'subverbally' quoting four other idylls. The poet in 'A Promenade' sings about poetry and utters his own hymn. The poet of 'The Countryside' sings about the simple life as he lives it and writes a botanical trifle. The poet of 'Night' expresses his own love in idyll form, tells three other love idylls, and finally sings of Love as a general blessing.

# 4

# The extra-literary model: salon trifles

During the last quarter of the eighteenth century, literature changed to fit the new epistemologically oriented intellectual currents. The borders between literature and non-literature ('life' in the broad sense) were shifting: life entered art and what were previously regarded as facts of life, trivial from a literary point of view, now became sanctioned as literary facts. The literary legitimation of prose fiction, as we saw, was a case in point. The fictionalization of author/reader, i.e. the emergence of narrator/ narratee as constitutive elements of narrative structure, was part of the same phenomenon. Partly this fictionalization was accomplished by drawing on existing *literary* genres which were still viable in terms of temporal, spatial, and axiological 'fit' to the era, namely the old middle genres, especially the idyll. Facts of life became aesthetic facts through 'idyllization'. The idyllic chronotope as we have discussed it, was characterized by temporal, spatial, and axiological miniaturization, reduction, or, one might say, trivialization. 'Less' became 'more'. Events, trifling from a literary point of view, such as promenades, botanical expeditions, simple pleasures, and good deeds, now became the prime literary topics. The topics became strongly personalized by a prominently featured vicariously or personally involved narrator and narratee cast in the idyllic mold.

Literary genres were, however, only one of the models for the new literature. *Quasi-literary* and even *extra-literary* speech genres became as important as the idyll and a great deal of 'crossfertilization' took place. What I analyzed earlier as the idyll chronotope has its extra-literary counterpart in what I shall term the salon chronotope. The idyllic *locus amoenus* has its analogue in the intimate chamber or salon of fashionable society. Many of the new prose pieces took their inspiration from the most trivial salon practices and 'personal speech genres'. Russian salons of Karamzin's era (such as they were) were not as 'official' nor as influential as the classical French seventeenth- to eighteenth-century models. In the following, I will use the word 'salon' in the broad sense of friendly gatherings of literary and other artists, relatives, family, and friends in the private homes of educated society.

Quasi-literary and extra-literary genres such as letters, confessions, diaries, society anecdotes and gossip, compliments, and invectives, served as important prototypes for reinvigorating literature and particularly for creating a narrator/narratee framework of intimacy. Already in the 1920s Tynianov made this important point. Citing the foreword to Karamzin's *Letters of a Russian Traveller*, Tynianov stresses the role of the extra-literary letter in the late eighteenth-century literary renewal.[1] He also emphasizes the role of other speech genres: 'Salons, conversations of "dear women", albums, quatrains, rondos, acrostics, charades, bouts-rimés, and games are transformed into an important literary phenomenon'.[2] Lotman in his inspired discussion of Karamzin's *Letters of a Russian Traveller*, particularly those devoted to France, emphasizes the literary significance of extra-literary oral factors, such as the interaction between the actors and the audience at the theater, cafe and street conversations, society gossip, salon practices, revolutionary oratory (and particularly oratorical behavior, gestures, tone of voice, and the like), and printed everyday extra-literary phenomena such as newspapers, revolutionary brochures and leaflets, caricatures, posters, and popular prints.[3] He discusses the classical seventeenth- to early eighteenth-century Paris salons and their late eighteenth-century successors which (the real) Karamzin might have visited and which were transformed into a kind of composite literary picture in *Letters of a Russian Traveller*. The transformation from life to art reveals much about Karamzin's artistic method. Lotman's discussion is interesting also for what it reveals about a more general role of salons in shaping new literary forms. Karamzin's attitude to the contemporary French salons was ironic and, according to Lotman, he preferred the livelier atmosphere of the street, the cafe, and the political assemblies. The same kind of irony is also directed against Frenchified Geneva salons in 'The Suicide'.[4] The irony seems to be directed mostly towards the official, artificial, and superficial aspects of salon life, and although his attitude to salons, in Lotman's view, is cold, that does not deny the enormous influence of salon practices on literary forms made popular by Karamzin. The emphasis on intimacy and friendship, lightheartedness, wit, polite educated conversations, and amusement were to become important elements in Karamzin's trifles.[5] The intimate gatherings at the estates of the educated Russian provincial gentry can be seen as an interesting cross between the more official salons in the capital, and the provincial estate idylls we have analyzed. Znamenskoe, the estate of the Pleshcheevs, was one setting for such gatherings, and Karamzin participated in them actively, especially in 1793–5. Lotman calls this period Karamzin's 'Znamenskoe period' and contrasts the difficulties connected with writing and publishing in the 'official world' to the creative influence of the 'small world' of Znamenskoe on Karamzin's literary trifles. In particular, he singles out the 'literaturization' (*oliteraturivanie*) of the letter and the parlor game.[6] I shall return to both these phenomena later in the context of specific works.

The emphasis on the 'dear women' in Tynianov, and in the literary and linguistic discussions of the day, are an indication that an important re-evaluation of gender issues in literature also took place during the period. Women were important as trendsetters of the 'refined taste', 'refined speech', 'refined manners', and sensitivities in general that were especially treasured in the salon setting. Elizavetina, in her discussion of the (extra-literary) memoir and autobiographical writing in the period before Sentimentalism, makes an interesting comparison between the autobiography of Princess N. B. Dolgorukaia and those of male writers, such as Ia. P. Shakhovskoi. The former emphasizes the most intimate and personal aspects of her life, while the male authors of autobiographies tend to present themselves in terms of their government careers in order to show their part in important historical events, or to depict themselves as typical of their social set.[7] It is clear that the female model was to be more influential on the Sentimentalist literary canon than the male writing. Women writers (Mme de Genlis [whom the young Karamzin translated], Mme de LaFayette, Mme de Scudéry, Mme de Staël [whom Karamzin met], Anna Radcliffe) were very popular in Russia at the time and female readers were important in real life and were even seen as the primary readers, particularly of the new literature. Women were frequently cast as narratees. As hostesses of, and guests in, salons, women were also seen as the prime practitioners of the personal salon genres, a fact that no doubt influenced the popularity of these genres as models

for the new literature. Uspenskii discusses the importance of
women's speech for the new style in the wider context of a general
orientation towards *usus*, spoken language (as opposed to the older
written *slaveno-rossiiskii* language, scholastic, stilted, and considered unsuited to refined society) and high society tastes in
general as defined by 'delicate' and 'refined' women. Many pronouncements by the Karamzinists are cited where budding authors
are encouraged to imitate the speech of the 'dear women' of
society.[8] However, most pronouncements of this nature also
caution the budding authors that Russian women still do not speak
perfectly (nor even Russian!): 'The dear women on whom we
should only need to eavesdrop in order to adorn a novel or a
comedy with amiable felicitous expressions, captivate us with
non-Russian phrases.'[9] The budding author was faced with a
dilemma: on the one hand, he ought to write as the 'dear women'
spoke, on the other hand, he first needed to provide them with
Russian models of how to speak elegantly and sensitively. One of
Karamzin's major accomplishments was precisely that he managed
to create not only the models (female personages, narrators, and
narratees within his works), but also, as Lotman emphasizes, the
appropriate reading public, prominently including women. This is
an indication of the ultimately *male* definition of woman in a society
and an enterprise that was still profoundly dominated by men. In
this context, we might also recall the new emphasis on children and
childhood. From a literary point of view, lesser genres, lesser
genders, lesser age and sophistication, are akin to Rousseau's
'noble savage', and the whole tendency towards trivialization as a
positive force of renewal in literature. The fact that the literary
image of woman had little to do with Russian reality, and was often
in fact defined by a male imagination, should not obscure the
importance of gender in Sentimentalist literature, although today's
feminists may recoil at what women were implied to lack (strength,
scholastic aptitude, importance in heroic events from the national
past, professional skills, etc.), and at the derogatory gender slurs
(effeminacy) applied to the Sentimentalist writers by the opposition. Lotman makes an important point related to the re-
evaluation of gender by the Sentimentalists. Women were regarded
as particularly sensitive, emotional, and weak ('delicate' in a more
positive wording). All these qualities, including weakness, were
highly treasured as the most *human* qualities of human beings.[10] As

we shall see, weakness became equated with strength in a sense, but this very quality was also at the root of human tragedy, as will be borne out in, for instance, 'Liodor', 'Eugene and Julia', and 'Bornholm Island'. We might note that the same semantic ambiguity colors much of the most favored Sentimentalist vocabulary – another instance that could be linked to woman is 'tender' (*nezhnyi*). 'Woman' was the gender analogue to the trivial, the ordinary, the insignificant, the frivolous, the small form, that characterized the new literary idyll and salon chronotopes. This focus on woman also gave rise to interesting semantic shifts.[11]

The cult of friendship was one of the most characteristic expressions of salon society. Salons (in my definition) were intimate gatherings of family, friends and like-minded acquaintances. Both men and women participated in evenings of literary readings, musical performances, dinners, or simply to exchange social chit-chat and gossip, play games, court eligible partners or show off the latest fashions. Social graces and sensitivities were naturally stressed and even displayed, compliments made to the ladies, or witty verse written in their albums. The letter or note was one of the links to one's friends during absences, and the letter became one of the major models for literature during this era. Epistolary novels were common, as were travelogues in letters addressed to one's dearest friends. Karamzin's *Letters of a Russian Traveller* consists ostensibly of his letters to the Pleshcheevs – although actually it is a literary work, carefully researched and prepared for publication.[12] Here the most astounding variety of impressions from Karamzin's Grand Tour of Europe (natural beauties, visits with the foremost European writers and scholars, theater life in the capitals, anecdotes and tales heard on the way, and so on) is 'trivialized' by being framed by the typical epistolary formulae addressing the dear friends, reminiscences about the common past, thanks for letters received, and the like. The single letter also became a popular literary form, which indeed saw its all-time heights in Russian literature among Pushkin and his friends a few decades later. Karamzin's 'Bornholm Island' is one of many works among Karamzin's *œuvres* that consist of a single letter (to a friend or friends, to 'the editor', to a friend in the country, or others). During a salon evening, books would be inscribed with friendly personal dedications, besides the traditional dedications in print to friends or to important personages or mentors. This, strictly speaking extra-

literary act, became a bona fide literary form in and of itself, quite
fancifully developed, as we shall see in Karamzin's 'Dedication of a
Grove'. Anecdotes were told in the salons about mutual friends or
enemies, about noteworthy events, about good serfs, and so on –
orally, without any claims to literary status. Such 'trifles' gradually
also became literary works in themselves and entered the literary
journals. Karamzin's trifle 'Frol Silin' is a precursor to this trend
and his 'The Suicide' is also defined by the typical markers of oral
anecdotes and gossip, while also commenting on the pros and cons
of salon life and the meaning of true friendship. One of Karamzin's
later works is simply entitled 'Anecdote'. Compliments to the
ladies also took on a new embellished literary life in 'Innocence'
and 'The Bird of Paradise', and even a word game became a literary
trifle in 'The Deep Forest'. The opposite of the compliment, the
invective, was also 'refined' and took on literary popularity in the
verse epigram. We might also note the pamphlet, another form of
invective which also gained increasing significance as literature.[13]
Caricature, yet another form of social invective, became popular
not only in visual form in the albums of fashionable ladies, but also
in written form. 'The Beautiful Princess' was labelled both 'an
olden fairy tale' and 'a new caricature', and the hero of 'My
Confession' brags about his skills in caricature drawing which he
considers a definite asset in composing his caricature-like confession. The conversations with the 'dear women' inspired the appropriate balance of sensitivity, elegance, flattery, flirtation, and the
feeling of 'addressedness' to a certain narratee in almost any of the
new literary trifles. Conversations have another important characteristic that was to define both the style and the form of literary
works, namely the fact that they are easily interrupted. Many lines
in Sentimentalist conversations end elliptically as we have already
seen, and whole stories may be interrupted in the midst of the plot
and published as fragments – a special trivialization of the plot to
which I shall return later in greater depth.

The importance of the insignificant and trifling as a major
innovatory force is borne out in many of the forewords and
introductions to Russian prose works of the most varied kinds.
Sometimes the trifling nature of the work is stressed simply to set it
apart from more weighty moralizing and teaching typical of the
older Neoclassical novels. For instance Fedor Emin warns the
reader of his *Letters of Ernest and Doravra* that 'for learned people

this booklet (*knizhka*) is a minor trifle (*bezdelitsa*)'[14] – despite the fact that this 'booklet' was a hefty four volumes of epistolary writing, including several 'philosophizing' letters of great length and pretension. Chulkov, in his preamble to his mammoth omnibus collection *The Mocker* (*Peresmeshnik*, 1766) also tongue in cheek, tells the reader that he releases this work 'not in order to become famous, for it can't seem like anything but a minor trifle (*nechem, ibo bezdelitseiu*) to the whole world'.[15] Many authors, in their forewords, stress their own lack of talent, and emphasize that they do not wish to teach nor to improve manners or morals, but hope that their work will provide entertainment and be a pleasant way for the reader to while away his or her free time, or that the work itself does not deserve any great attention.[16] Others stress the casual effortless way their work was put together from notes jotted down during trips, or written in some corner in the midst of profuse noise, or on little scraps of paper without plan or aim. Jones demonstrates how autobiographies and biographies towards the end of the eighteenth century also moved away from significant personages and events and became more intimate in nature. They too were influenced by 'the potency of the trivial', as Jones puts it.[17] Radishchev's *Life of Ushakov* and Fonvizin's confessional auto-biography are cases in point.[18] We are also reminded once more of collection titles even more prominently flaunting the trifling nature of the works: Karamzin's *My Trifles* (*Moi bezdelki*), I. I. Dmitriev's *My Trifles Too* (*I moi bezdelki*) and P. A. Pel'skii's *My Something or Other* (*Moe koe-chto*). Even the physical size of the works reflected the tendency towards miniaturization–trivialization. For instance, Karamzin in his correspondence with Dmitriev describes his plans for a Russian *Almanach des Muses* (Karamzin's *Aonidy*, modelled on French and German predecessors) 'in small format', as an annually appearing small booklet of verse which 'our ladies would not be ashamed to carry in their pockets'.[19] This letter reveals, besides the small size, also the intended woman reader and the personal manner of using the work: a woman would presumably carry the booklet on her very person and read it wherever and whenever she felt like it. The very act of reading was made more intimate and personal.

Not every writer, however, subscribed to this new pose, and there were still works written for the stated serious purpose of moral teaching. However, even the opponents of the frivolous triviality pose admitted that this was (alas) what the bookmarket demanded. One such opponent, A. L. author of *Dobrada the Fairy or An Image of Virtuous Conduct Towards One's Neighbor* (*Dobrada volshebnitsa, ili obraz dobrodetel'stva blizhnemu*, 1788) in his foreword describes the content of 'good' books demanded these days but which he himself cannot write:

They are insolent trifles (*bezdelki*) expressed with flippancy, old-time thoughts in a new style, adorned in new expressions and appropriated by whosoever dissipates them as by the Heir of the Universe himself: false rules, adorned by the name of Philosophy; a heap of audacious lies presented as true History; invented Anecdotes which are contradicted by the chronicles and history of the time, minor fables in verse and in the manner of songs; love trifles (*pustiaki*), catcalls to virtue, and so on.[20]

Even serious trifle practitioners, such as Karamzin, soon began to parody the insignificance pose, as we can see from one of his last works, 'My Confession', itself a trifle, parodying the pose in a phlegmatic amoral narrator who points to the proclivity of contemporary Authors to talk about themselves and their ability to make a mountain out of a molehill (*rasplodit' samoe nichto*).[21] B. Anastasevich in his 'Letter to a Friend from the Capital' ('Pis'mo k drugu iz stolitsy') writes about a new illness akin to heartfailure whose main symptoms are:

vertigo, frequent delirium from staring at the merest trifle (*na samuiu bezdelitsu*), hands that shake in order to leave on paper a reminiscence of a promenade in the field, in the garden, in the street, in the room, in one's pockets, about dressing and drinking tea, in a word, about every step taken awake or asleep or during a bout with a fever stemming from this illness. The abscess on the heart I mentioned is so delicate that the smallest impact on it by any of the five common emotions brings on a strong shock in the whole person and shows all of him in a melancholy or sometimes mellow mien. The infected weeps if out of carelessness he happens to *wipe the dust from the winglets of a moth*; he dreams that Hebe on Olympus treats him to nectar when he pours himself some liquid concoction of Chinese grasses. Any even somewhat *comely cowgirl* seems to him one of the Graces. In an anthill he sees a *well-run society of indefatigable citizens* [ . . . ] Those infected with this ailment call it *sentimentality* but those who are healthy call it by its old name *madness*.[22]

The negative evaluations of the Sentimentalist preoccupation with trivia bring out their literary importance with particular force. Lotman quotes A. I. Turgenev (a former admirer of Karamzin)

who in 1801 pronounced Karamzin's influence on Russian literature harmful.[23] It is even more harmful, in Turgenev's opinion,
because Karamzin writes so well and in such an interesting manner.
He goes so far as to hope that Russian authors should continue to
write worse and in a less interesting manner than Karamzin if only
they would turn to more important (*vazhneishimi*) subjects and not
preoccupy themselves so much with trifling matters (*melochnymi
rodami*). A letter written by Karamzin in 1815 (i.e. 14 years later!)
contains an interesting 'response' to Turgenev's opinions: 'The
difference between *trifling* (*melochnymi*) and so-called *important*
(*vazhnymi*) matters is small: only the inner motive and feeling are
important.'[24] Whether the trivial is positively or negatively evaluated, it is clearly a new force to be reckoned with on the literary
scene and in descriptions, such as those cited, we can indeed
recognize the new trifles.

It is important to stress that although real life speech genres
infiltrated and created new literary forms, these new forms themselves were not viewed as specific new genres: the idea of literary
genre was, as we have seen, not important. They were regarded
more or less agenerically as trifles, '*bezdelki*'.

### THE DEDICATION

## 'Dedication of a grove'

As should by now have become obvious, long elaborate apostrophes are frequently incorporated into Karamzin's early works.
Apostrophes, as we have seen, mark the speech event by making
explicit the addressee, the addresser, the utterance itself, and their
interrelations, with variations in proximity and in emphasis. Most
of the apostrophes in the works so far analyzed are addressed either
to concrete nature (the elements of the *locus amoenus*) or to
abstract phenomena, which are, for the most part, personified
(above and beyond the mere fact of being addressed), and frequently take the form of mixed address. Insofar as the addressees
are described in the process of the address, this description is
always strongly subjective, and always reflects back on the
addresser himself more than is usually the case even in address.
This results from the nature of the addressees chosen, who are
often of a global stature, such that they encompass the speaker

himself, or personify his own moods together with the general mood itself. Thus the speaker relates metonymically to his addressee (and/or vice versa), and by addressing the addressee as a whole he also addresses himself – or at least that aspect that they have in common. By apostrophizing Creation and seeing himself infused with the same spirit, he in essence addresses himself as well. By addressing poetry as a whole, he includes his own poetic creativity; by addressing Love, he includes his own present state. The same is true when he addresses more concrete phenomena – the sun, the moon, nature – the addressee is never wholly outside the speaker himself, or at least they share the essential traits, and their relationship, if not entirely solipsistic (and narcissistic, self-congratulatory), is always of the most intimate and personal kind.

Another aspect of apostrophes is that the address is always made for some purpose other than merely getting the addressee's attention or stating objective facts, i.e., they are undertaken by performing some speech act which itself marks the utterance as speech event: entreaties, requests, intentions, commitments, blessings, and so on, recognizable as such by typical formulae for performing these speech acts, by performative use of verbs, etc. Benedictions can be accomplished by pronouncing the words 'Blessed be those who' or by performative 'I bless you'. A commitment may be performed by uttering some formula, such as 'I will always' or by performative 'I intend to', and so on. Karamzin's apostrophes usually mark the acts performed by combinations of several such markers and thereby strongly stress, besides the addressee, the speaker himself and their relationship, the utterance itself, and its setting. Furthermore, in most cases several speech acts are performed simultaneously in one utterance.

'Dedication of a Grove' is of this nature.[25] The entire work is a protracted dedication–consecration in the form of an apostrophe to the goddess Fantasy. Even the title is discourse-deictic in the strict sense of referring to the speech act itself (not to the major protagonist nor the narrated events). It also refers to the object dedicated, which also happens to be the setting of the speech event. This is somewhat unusual for prose works, but by no means unique, particularly for the *malaia forma*. It does, however, stand out against the background of the most prevalent type of prose titles, particularly those of the eighteenth-century novels. The titles of novels were lengthy references to the hero and/or heroine, and frequently summarized the entire plot. In general, Karamzin's prose titles are brief, and many of them refer in idyll fashion to the hero or heroine or both, with little or no elaboration: 'Eugene and Julia', 'Palemon and Daphnis. Idyll', 'Liodor', 'Julia', 'Poor Liza', 'Natal'ia, the Boyar's Daughter', 'Frol Silin, a Virtuous Person'. Others refer to the setting ('The Countryside. Fragment', 'Bornholm Island', 'Sierra-Morena. Elegiac Fragment', 'Night', 'The Deep Forest') or the main event ('The Flood. Fragment', 'A Promenade', 'Athenian Life'). Some other titles are discourse-deictic in the narrow sense (*Letters of a Russian Traveller,* 'Anecdote', 'My Confession'), or make a discourse-deictic reference in the subtitle, as in some of the works already listed. Although such discourse-deictic titles were common in poetry, it was rare that a prose title consisted solely of the name of the speech act in the performative sense, such as 'Dedication of a Grove', where labelling it a dedication already makes it such. Furthermore, and more importantly, a dedication as such was not a canonic genre. Dedications were frequent enough during the era. Usually, however, they were appended to another work in the manner of forewords and introductions, dedicating that work to a (real life) patron or friend, often some important personage, a strictly speaking extra-literary fact. The written dedications ranged from highly formulaic and elaborate panegyrics to the addressee and correspondingly litotetic reference to the author or his work, or both, listing all possible superlatives applicable (or at least flattering) to the addressee, to a simple 'To NN'.[26] That the formulaic variety of dedication had become hackneyed is attested to by the fact that it was already being parodied, and thus was at least on its way to becoming 'serious' literary fact, but still as part of another, main, work.[27]

Sentimentalist authors frequently dedicated their works to close friends, often women. Karamzin's dedication of his almanac *Aglaia* is of this nature.[28]

'Dedication of a Grove' raises the dedication to the status of an independent prose work, an independent literary fact on a par with so many other trifles. It is also significant that the object of dedication is the idyllist's *locus amoenus* – in its dark, solitary, silent hypostasis: the grove, 'besprinkled by a foamy stream falling from a granite cliff'. Social flattery is blended with idyllic topoi in this work.

The work begins by revealing the female narratee in an elaborate panegyric vocative construction: 'Fair, eternally young, multifarious winged goddess, flowering *Fantasy!*'[29] Next the object of dedication is deictically referred to as 'this' grove (described also by three preceding epithets and an appositive relative participial construction, 'besprinkled by'). The address is concluded by a performative verb indicating the illocutionary force of the utterance ('I dedicate'). The familiar form of the second person pronoun (*tebe*) specifies the recipient of the dedication with the addition of yet another apposition, 'divine'. This introduction refers to the speech event – the narratee as perceived by the narrator, the present setting (also the object of dedication), the narrator, and the nature of the present discourse. The words themselves constitute the act of dedicating ('saying makes it so').

The concluding paragraph is a variation on the solemn formula that constitutes dedication ('May this solitary grove [for you love solitude] be your temple, delight of my life, flowering *Fantasy!* '), repeating one each of the introductory epithets for the goddess and the grove. The grove becomes a temple by the sheer force of words. The dedication is also a consecration, since the addressee is a goddess with various divine attributes. Her name is set off orthographically from the rest of the text, as befits sacred personages, and the style is appropriately lofty. The grove is declared a temple in mythological fashion.

A dedication usually extolls the worthiness of the addressee and expresses the hope that the humble gesture be accepted and that it might give the recipient pleasure. It expresses gratitude for past services to the addresser (or the addresser as part of a group, or of mankind in general), and the speaker's intention always to honor and revere the addressee, as well as his hope for future patronage – all of which pertains to the relationship between addresser and addressee.

The narrator of 'Dedication of a Grove', in addition to praising the narratee, praises his own gift. He states his intention (a commissive speech act) to sit 'here' in the grove, far from the world, in solitude and silence, and 'with gentle trembling of [my] heart heed the sounds of your approaching winged arrival', and expresses a promise (another commissive) to like her, whatever her guise might be. This is an extension into the future of the present speech event and its pleasurable aspects (pleasure for both, as Fantasy's liking for solitude is assumed, as are her future appearances). The narrator commits himself to a future position as narratee ('I will sit in silence and [ . . . ] heed') or silent perceiver and enjoyer of her appearances. He stresses his own future pleasure much more than hers. Next follows a lengthy listing, structured by anaphorically parallel constructions, of her guises which continues for over a page (two, if one counts the footnotes by the editor – Karamzin). This is interrupted by another vocative address, followed by another anaphorically parallel listing, this time of four good consoling deeds typical of Fantasy. After naming four of her appealing guises and four of her comforting deeds, the narrator makes clear that this is only a partial listing of her praiseworthy qualities and actions. He utters two rhetorical questions, concluding with another vocative sobriquet for her: 'But who can enumerate your guises? Who can enumerate your deeds, you who are worthy of temples and altars?' This kind of rhetorical question is a form of the modesty topos used in practically all of Karamzin's works, and is another discourse-deictic reference (in this wording), indirectly professing the narrator's and other speakers' inability to do the addressee justice. It is also another example of the inexpressibility topos, already seen in other works analyzed.

'Dedication of a Grove' then concludes with the variation on the dedicatory formula mentioned above. The work consists of a single protracted speech event, expressing the speaker's praise for his addressee's qualities, consecrating the grove as a temple to her, and stating his own commitment always to perform as her fervent worshipper in that temple, in other words, continuing to do what he is in the process of doing 'now'.

What is most curious is that the goddess Fantasy is a creature entirely in the eyes of the beholder, a quality or ability of the narrator himself (albeit with age-old mythological sanction). Fantasy or imagination is, in Sentimentalist poetics, one of the crucial abilities of a poet.[30] The narrator of 'Dedication of a Grove' in essence proclaims himself a poet: he will always sit in his grove, and Fantasy will always make her appearance. No doubt is voiced on this score, nor is the utterance a prayer for inspiration. The narrator, in a sense, assumes that he will always be able to fantasize, and with a trembling heart to boot. The work is entirely solipsistic: he addresses the poet in himself.

The qualities and actions of Fantasy make up a list of typical

Sentimentalist topics and values. Her qualities include: triumphant virtue, beauty, compassion for the suffering, grief (in the guise of quiet night, slowly descending as a Niobe onto the grave of 'my Agathon', with tear-filled eyes, sprinkling anemones and hyacinths on the grave in sad remembrance). Her comforting deeds are the following: removing the chains from a prisoner and allowing him to return to his fatherland and his family; transforming the leaden burden of life into a light feather, and sweetening an orphan's tears of sorrow with honey; elevating the last shepherd to the throne and making nations bow low to him. These deeds are already familiar from Karamzin's other works, and represent the stuff that Sentimentalist fiction is made of.

The reference to blossoms sprinkled 'on the grave of my Agathon' is particularly curious. It is more than a mere autobiographical reference to Karamzin's friend and fellow poet, A. A. Petrov, nicknamed Agathon, with whom Karamzin spent much of the spring and summer of 1791 when 'Dedication of a Grove' was written, and who at the time seemed to be *recovering* from a serious illness. It is also a curious prediction of the 'obituary', 'A Blossom on the Grave of My Agathon' ('Tsvetok na grob moego Agatona'), that Karamzin wrote in 1793, shortly after Petrov's death.[31] Karamzin's friends and contemporary readers would have been likely to recognize Agathon, a fairly frequent reference in his other works, as well. Lotman discusses Karamzin's long relationship with Petrov and the Agathon image in Karamzin's works. He reveals some interesting new facts about Karamzin's Petrov obituary (or 'elegy in prose', as he calls it). He points out that Karamzin's literary model may well have been one of the literary trifles, little known to contemporaries and now entirely forgotten, by the major German writer Jakob Lenz. Lenz's own work plays on the literary nickname Philotas (with allusions to a Lessing play). Karamzin's nickname for Petrov is an obvious allusion to Wieland's novel and, what is more interesting, his title echoes that of Lenz: 'On Philotas. A Violet on his Grave'.[32] Violets are, as we shall see, particularly important in other works by Karamzin, and are often linked to death, as, for instance, in 'Liodor'.

The use of mythological imagery does not contradict Sentimentalist poetics, as is often implied by scholars. As a rule, however, it is less used than in Neoclassicism, and it is usually the minor mythological figures that are favored. Here, however, the narrator's mood is solemn, and that is a sufficient motivation both for the mythological imagery and for the lofty style of the work (Church Slavic lexicon and constructions, complex phrase structure, participles, etc.). One might also note that Karamzin (in his capacity as editor of *Moscow Journal*) is no longer quite comfortable with the mythological imagery and deems it necessary to supply elaborate footnotes to practically every mythological reference for the benefit of eighteenth-century journal readers, not all of whom could still be assumed to be familiar with the Olympus.

Cross sees Herder's *Paramythien* as the model for Karamzin's mythological prose poems, and cites R. T. Clarke's description of them: 'an extremely free translation or paraphrase of materials from foreign literatures, especially the Classical, with far-reaching modifications to make them acceptable to contemporary readers'.[33] It would seem that it is mainly the trifle form and the solipsistic orientation which made 'Dedication of a Grove' acceptable to its contemporary readers.[34]

## THE COMPLIMENT

### 'Innocence'

'Innocence' is cited by Cross as another paramythological piece, reminiscent of Herder's 'Die Lilie und Rose', a translation of which had appeared in *Moscow Journal* one month before 'Innocence'.[35] It is an extended personification, a device highly treasured by the Neoclassicists (one need only think of all the personified virtues and vices in Neoclassical drama), but a personification with a decidedly personal and even autobiographical Sentimentalist salon twist.

The first (and longest) part of the work is an extremely stylized and lofty personification of 'innocence' (in Russian, conveniently of the feminine gender) in specific and detailed human terms. That is to say, 'her' body parts and coverings are human (*ochi, chelo, lanity, stan, odezhda, vlasy, grudi, nogi* [eyes, brow, cheeks, torso, clothing, hair, breasts, legs]), most of which are expressed with the Church Slavic denotations). Her actions are also human (*ulybat'-sia, shestvovat', ee stopy* [smile, walk, her steps]). These parts and actions, as well as the elements of the setting, are described in a highly ornate style, with all manner of figures, tropes, and traditionally sanctioned poetic devices. There are personifications within the personification, simple and extended similes, inversions (practically all personal pronouns appear after the nouns modified). Mythological imagery is used, and idyllic imagery is particularly prominent, to the effect that 'she' appears as a shepherdess. Floral similes, a white garb, flowers in her hair, hair let down, Zephyrs playing with her clothing and her hair, joy and tenderness – all this makes her appear as the ideal shepherdess as seen by her shepherd. Typical for the idyll are also the images of the various dangers that surround 'her': storms and darkness, poisonous snakes, thorny grasses – all of which are found in numerous idylls, and which were used by Karamzin in other works as well (for instance, 'Night').

The second part is an allegory of 'her' life on earth. She is named Innocence for the first time (except in the title), thus making the personification explicit. It is a view of the Golden Age, typical of the times (particularly as expressed in Masonic circles): Innocence lived on earth among shepherdesses in a past era when love and peace reigned among mortals, that is, until the Fall. At that time Innocence returned to her heavenly fatherland, and is since then rarely seen.

The conclusion consists of an unexpected 'autobiographical' statement: 'But I saw her in the image of lovely Aglaia'. This is the kind of salon twist to personification I referred to above. On the one hand, it fits perfectly within the allegory of the text, on the other hand, it is autobiographical in a quite literal sense. In the first part, 'she' was characterized as 'crowned by the flowers of Graces', and the address to Aglaia, one of the Graces, thus fits in well on the allegorical level. According to this reading, innocence would be personified specifically as one of the Graces, Aglaia, and the narrator's vision would be personal, yet acceptable in mythological terms. To contemporary salon society it was, however, abundantly clear that Aglaia was the name always used by Karamzin with reference to a specific mortal, namely Anastasia Ivanovna Pleshcheeva, one of Karamzin's closest friends. The Karamzin–Pleshcheeva relationship typifies an interesting aspect of Sentimentalist culture: friendship between a man and a woman. This relationship could be characterized as intense and tender non-erotic love. Pleshcheeva was older than Karamzin and already happily married when they met, and Karamzin was to marry her younger sister in 1801. Lotman makes the acute observation that

Karamzin transformed the relationship from a fact of his own intimate biography to a cultural fact of the era and to a literary fact. Karamzin demonstratively displayed their tender platonic friendship–love (and other writers followed suit) to the extent that it became part of the public domain and most of the readers would recognize the prototypes behind the literary masks. As Lotman points out, even the tsar 'advertised' his own feelings publicly and indeed, the very word *liubit'* underwent semantic change (from an initial meaning of 'love' to a later meaning of both 'love' and 'like'). This is also part of the re-evaluation of gender during the era, and Lotman makes some other interesting observations on this topic.[36] The mention of Aglaia in 'Innocence' invites a whole new reading of the preceding text: 'Innocence' is turned into a personal compliment to the author's (real life) ideal woman. One of the similes in the first part of the work adds further support for the auto-biographical interpretation, the comparison of 'her' breasts to a Swiss mountain, the Jungfer (footnoted), which links the work to Karamzin's *Letters of a Russian Traveller*, which were addressed in equally veiled terms to the Pleshcheevs, and one edition of which was also dedicated to them. Pleshcheeva was also the Aglaia addressee of several poems and the tales 'Liodor' and 'The Bird of Paradise', and she was honored with an almanac, *Aglaia*, named for her and dedicated to her.

This infusion of intensely personal tones into 'standard' personifications of abstract concepts was also evident in the apostrophes in, for example, 'Night', 'A Promenade', and 'Dedication of a Grove', where, however, the focus was on the narrator himself. Here it is directed mainly towards his narratee. 'Innocence' can be viewed as an example of a trifle that grew out of what was otherwise used as one of many devices within larger works (personification) or as a literary version of a salon speech genre (the compliment). It is also a good example of the kind of crossfertilization that took place between the idyll and the salon chronotopes.

## 'The Bird of Paradise'

'The Bird of Paradise' is another extended compliment to Aglaia, structurally similar to 'Innocence'.[37] It also utilizes personification (time flying), but eschews the mythological trappings of 'Innocence'. Instead, it utilizes a piece of native folklore which had entered the *Great Mirror* (*Velikoe sertsalo*), various *luboks*, Simeon Polotskii's *Garden of Many Flowers* (*Vertograd mnogotsvetnyi*) and some other works of literature.[38] In the first edition of *Moscow Journal* a footnote explains the source: 'The idea for this piece is taken from a Russian folktale and shows that we in Russia already long ago understood the wondrous effect of harmony on the human heart. I find in this fiction something poetic'.[39] Folklore in and of itself, it should perhaps be mentioned, was not yet at this time widely accepted as literature, and folktales were still viewed at best as a quasi-literary phenomenon. They too began to be treasured for their poetic potential during this period and were to flourish in literature during the succeeding Romantic era. Folklore is thus another example of the trivialization of literature, of the transformation of extra-literary fact into literature. Possibly the interest in folktales can also be linked with the re-evaluation of children and children's literature during this era. M. T. Kachenovskii, for instance, admires folk songs as 'native [Russian] works, as the inventions of simple minds, as innocent children's toys'.[40] I shall return to the subject of folklore later in greater depth.

The plot line is quite well developed in 'The Bird of Paradise'. A pious old monk goes into the deep forest to gather figs for a monastic meal, is captivated by the wondrous song of a bird, time flies without touching him, and when he returns to the monastery, a thousand years have passed and everything is changed. The monk is divinely enlightened, starts to explain to the present monks what he had experienced, but when he tries to elaborate on the sweetness of the song 'his tongue gets numb, his gaze darkens – he falls, and the holy spirit flies out of his mortal body'. A description of his tombstone concludes the plot, and the work as a whole ends with the narrator's apostrophe: 'Lovely Aglaia! I also do not feel time, when I listen to your singing!'

This apostrophe invites a reinterpretation (or at least a supplementary interpretation) of the whole work as an extended metaphor for the narrator–narratee relationship, equating the narrator with the monk and Aglaia with the bird, thus complimenting her singing. The Sentimentalist coloration of 'The Bird of Paradise' is rendered not only by the development of the inexpressibility topos, nor by the addition of gravestone imagery, nor by Karamzin's elaboration of the monk's feelings, nor even by the utilization of native sources, all of which has been emphasized in

studies of the work, but first and foremost by the reconceptuali-
zation of the work in personal salon terms. The piece, in Karamzin's version, is neither a folktale nor a piece of hagiography, but a
fanciful compliment – another trifle.

The original source is transformed stylistically in a manner
typical of Karamzin's works of the time, and it utilizes many of the
devices already described for the other works. The tempo, for
instance, is modulated so that the emotionally most tense moments
(the song and the final vision of the monk) are retarded by
elaborate poetic devices (repetition of synonymous clauses, metaphors, personification, periphrasis, etc.), whereas the intermediate
actions are speeded up in laconic enumeration with omission of
conjunctions and subject pronouns: 'Arrives, and sees – other
scenes, another church, other cells, and other monks; does not
believe his eyes, goes up to the abbot'. The tempo is retarded at the
moments when 'time stands still' for the narrator as well – another
case where the manner of narration reproduces both the mood of
the narrator and the events he reports. The present tense is also
used within the general past tense of narration, but here it is clear
that the present tense actions refer to the past of the story, and it is
thus used as a 'historical present' to create an impression of
involvement in a *vicarious* experience. Even that obviously vicarious experience is personalized, and the narrator is involved not so
much in the monk's experience for its own sake as for the fact that it
reminds him of his Aglaia and his own experience of listening to her
singing. It is a compliment on a typical salon activity. Some
interesting new evidence about the specific activities at the
Znamenskoe gatherings is presented by Lotman based on a newly
discovered 1794 booklet, published in French in Moscow under the
title '*Les amusemens de Znamenskoé. Lizes-le, ne-lizes pas*'.
Among the activities discussed is musical entertainment.[41]
Although 'The Bird of Paradise' precedes Karamzin's Znamenskoe
period, it is indeed likely that he heard Pleshcheeva sing at earlier
gatherings of the same kind since he had known her for a long time.

The old monk's state of rapture when listening to the birdsong is
reminiscent of 'A Promenade', and indeed, the theme of the ideal
Sentimentalist reader is here developed as an extended metaphor.
The reception of true beauty here, too, requires that the perceiver
give himself fully to the experience and forget all else – his
surroundings and his physical self. Just as the narrator in 'A

Promenade' feels close not only to birds, but also to the spirits and the Creator, so the old monk's listening is 'like heeding the eternal inhabitants of heaven'. By comparing the beauty of Aglaia's song to that of the bird and divinities (and thereby complimenting her), the narrator also tells us that he is a privileged listener to divine voices. He, of course, compliments not only Aglaia, but also himself as the ideal Sentimentalist perceiver who has the gift of full appreciation of art and beauty. Indeed, very little is said of the singing itself, and as is also clear from the footnote, the main focus of the work is the 'wondrous *effect* of harmony on the human heart' [emphasis added], i.e., the narrator's own sensitivity. 'The Bird of Paradise' is yet another example of narcissistic Sentimentalist solipsism, and is a double-edged compliment.


### THE GAME

## 'The Deep Forest'

'The Deep Forest' is subtitled 'a fairy tale for children', (*skazka dlia detei*) and is another example of how quasi-literary folklore material was accommodated to the literary tastes of salon society by using the extra-literary, and partly even extra-verbal, salon genre of a game.[42] It is literally a word game 'composed in one day on the following given words: balcony, forest, sphere, hut, horse, meadow, raspberry shrub, oak, Ossian, spring, grave, music'. The editor tells us in a footnote that the words were to be included in the story in the order they were given. We might note that in the first edition this rule of the game is not strictly observed: the order of 'hut' and 'horse' is reversed in the text. In subsequent editions, the *list* was corrected according to the text – perhaps an unintentional laying bare of the game as a device by changing the *rules* to fit the move already made.

In Sipovskii's opinion, the work 'has no historical–literary significance: it is a prank of the pen, – the result of social amusement'.[43] I disagree with Sipovskii's assessment, for its historical–literary significance lies precisely in its trifling nature. For it is literature, or at least it was clearly regarded as such at a time when trifles were given special literary value. It was even published earlier in French. Lotman in his discussion of the brochure '*Les amusemens de Znamenskoé*', points out some interesting facts about the French version of 'The Deep Forest', entitled 'La forêt noire'. It is signed by 'g. K\*\*\*' and was probably a transcription of Karamzin's oral improvisation. The Russian text which we know from the almanac *Aglaia* is not a direct translation but an adaptation of the French version, but, as Lotman points out, and as my analysis will also confirm, the oral aspects are carefully preserved in Russian as well.[44] In other words, the piece is definitely a result of some *literary* effort, despite its pose as a simple trifle. The brochure contains several other tales based on the same game by the other participants in the Znamenskoe gatherings, including another 'short story, in the genre of a lyrical monologue' by Karamzin, where Znamenskoe reality flows together with the idylls. Lotman includes the full translation, significantly shorter than 'The Deep Forest'.[45] From a literary point of view it is also significant that Karamzin himself included 'The Deep Forest' as one of eight *povesti* in the first edition of his collected works.[46] The others were: 'Poor Liza', 'The Beautiful Princess', 'Julia', 'Natal'ia', 'Sierra-Morena', 'Bornholm Island', and 'Martha the Mayoress', works whose literariness has never been disputed.

Based on the brochure, Lotman makes several interesting points in his analysis of the Znamenskoe setting and activities which are relevant to our present discussion. The contents of the brochure gives it the character of a family album, literature for an in-group and fully accessible only to the members of this group who can understand the circumstances of writing and the extra-textual situation. He cites as an example a play about the return of Aleksei Pleshcheev which is fully understandable only to his wife (who wrote it) and their children (also the audience within 'The Deep Forest'). Karamzin's literary almanacs were to preserve many of the traits of a family album. The homespun intimate and amateur character of the literary activities at the estate, in Lotman's view, served as a laboratory for the era's cultural life and was an important influence on the next generation of writers. 'Playing at literature grows into a literature of play.' The intimacy of these kinds of real life salons was simulated in Karamzin's other trifles as well by the introduction of a special personal narrator–narratee, as we have observed earlier. Lotman describes this larger phenomenon *à propos* Karamzin's almanac *Aglaia*:

But 'Aglaia' is addressed to the reader, i.e. to a stranger, an unknown person. Intimacy here is transformed into 'as-if intimacy', an imitation of friendly-direct communication. Between the writer and the reader whom he does not know personally, relationships are established which imitate friendly closeness. A type of relationship is created which in the future is made obligatory for the almanac (a certain shade of 'albumness') and which in principle is different from the functioning of a book.[47]

Sipovskii grants 'The Deep Forest' some interest in that it includes a number of fairy tale topoi, and thereby demonstrates that they were by that time already well-defined in Russia. Among such topoi, Sipovskii mentions the rabbit which guides the hero through the forest, the mysterious voice, the magic tricks, and the tendency to give a natural explanation for these tricks.

'The Deep Forest' is an unusually explicit demonstration of how a fairy tale was perceived during the time, and how it was transformed into literature according to Sentimentalist precepts. As part of the work, the mood and expectations are initially set for a fairy tale, but in the course of the telling they are frustrated one by one (not without humor), and instead of an old-fashioned fairy tale, the story that emerges is surprisingly like Karamzin's other works with a moral message, reminiscent of Marmontel's *contes moraux* and some of Gessner's most pietistic idylls. It is then both a fairy tale, a game, and a tale about the telling of a fairy tale and the audience it is told to.

The title, subtitle, and set vocabulary are indicative of this transformation. The title coupled with the subtitle leads one to expect a children's fairy tale about an enchanted forest. The set vocabulary and the game explanation tells us, on the other hand, that the tale is made up by the narrator for a specific occasion (and is thus not a proper folktale), and even how long it took him. The set vocabulary, furthermore, reads as the top of a frequency listing of Karamzin's idyll lexicon. We note that 'forest, hut, meadow, raspberry shrub, oak, spring', are nouns typical for describing a Karamzinian *locus amoenus*. 'Ossian, grave, music', are also high frequency Sentimentalist words, and only three of the twelve nouns listed ('balcony, sphere, horse') are neutral. None of the vocabulary items refers exclusively to a fairy world. Although the work is subtitled 'a fairy tale for children', the children are part of the work as a whole, which, I believe, is meant for older addressees who can participate in the game, and appreciate both the Classical allusions and the allusions to the current state of the world, as well as the play with literary tradition.

The inclusion of youthful listeners as part of the topic allows the author to feature prominently the voice of the narratee. Children are less inhibited in their actual participation in the telling, they are more prone to display their expectations and their reactions to the story, to interrupt the teller with questions, to voice their approval or disapproval, to demand explanations, and so on, i.e. they are ideal Sentimentalist *readers*. All these aspects of speech event dialogue appear prominently as part of the text.

Let us first turn to the fairy tale topoi. They are introduced as the children's wishes and expectations, the narrator's compliance with their wishes, and his further suggestive encouragement of their expectations. The wishes and expectations are explicitly derived and developed from the 'present' speech event, and the tale begins, as do practically all of Karamzin's works, with a dialogically structured speech event overture, describing the typical salon chronotope: the intimate familiar space of a balcony, the small circle of family and friends, the basic activities of eating and drinking, and intimate conversation.

The narrator's speech acts at the beginning of the tale are mainly directives, commissives, and expressives, and primarily impart information about his own and the listeners' inner states and about their interrelationships. The narrator reports events and describes settings only secondarily. He first invites the children to tea (a directive), and thereby secondarily informs us of the time and place of the telling. Next, he expresses their general mood in the resigned intonations of an extended sigh, while at the same time commenting on the gloomy weather (mainly an expressive). Next, he interprets the children's looks as a wish that he tell them a story (the children have subverbally performed a directive), and checks his interpretation with a question, 'Isn't it true?' (another directive), agrees to comply (a commissive), and concludes this dialogue with a request that they listen (another directive). This kind of 'dramatic' reporting is familiar from early works, such as 'Palemon and Daphnis'. The children's 'lines' in this dialogue are 'hidden'. They are indicated by ellipsis dots or dashes, or are repeated by the narrator ('You want that I [ . . . ]'), or simply implied by his 'answers' – all of which serves to reveal mainly the dynamics of the speech event – pre-coding motifs, in our terminology.

The gloomy conditions outside provoke a correspondingly gloomy mood. The children wish to hear a 'tale of yore, wretched or terrifying', from their secure vantage point of closeness, friendliness, and warmth. The aesthetics of horror is in force – a topic I will return to in connection with 'Bornholm Island'.

The attention moves concentrically from the immediate setting to the larger setting to the even more distant and unfamiliar. Similarly, the mood is developed from the happy news of tea time to the gloomy and sad mood instilled by the weather and the late hour to the prospect of a 'wretched', 'terrifying' story.

The narrator then makes the transition from speech event to narrated event very gradual by first directing the listeners' attention to the most distant and least familiar setting, still within view, however: the 'ancient, dense, dark forest'. He is capitalizing on the prevailing gloomy conditions outside (the 'threatening clouds, a black stormcloud, an ancient church, the howling wind'). He further enhances these gloom-inspiring conditions by repetition of the same 'terrifying' vocabulary in suggestive, almost hypnotic intonations, expressing both his own terror at beholding the forest, and simultaneously evoking the same mood in his listeners, based on what they see and hear ('Look at [ . . . ] how terrifying it looks! What black shadows [ . . . ]! You listen [ . . . ] – and feel the chill of terror in your hearts'). Once this mood is set and sustained, he is ready to describe the setting of the events and to 'report' his story (i.e. information, new to the listeners), still, however, in terms explicitly relating the story to the present. The setting is the same nearby forest as it existed ten centuries ago, 'ten times vaster, darker, and more terrifying'. No human set foot in the forest, and a certain legend 'frightened timid people even more'. The beginning of events is presented as local lore, according to which 'an evil wizard or magician, gossip (*kum* ) and friend of hellish Beelzebub (*Velzevul*)' lived and ruled in the forest. Spheres of fire and some huge, horrid monster moving around at night, illuminating about one hundred *sazhens* around him with his fiery eyes, had been spotted. Furthermore, 'a few thousand times' it happened that the brave horses that ventured into the forest came back wounded and bloody. We note the gradation in adjectives from 'normal' degree to comparative, to superlative and the numerical progression from one to ten, to one hundred, to a thousand. The dimensions of phenomena increase in proportion to the increasing fear – a device reminiscent of 'Palemon and Daphnis' where the boundless sea and the scary events were contrasted to the small scale idyll parameters of the speech event.

The frightened villagers conclude according to 'natural logic' (the narrator tells us, tongue in cheek), that the forest seethed with evil, supernatural magic. The listeners' fear is maintained by the narrator's aside: 'you will agree, my friends, that this was in fact very, very scary'. Thus the fairy tale expectations of inexplicable horrors are gradually set, and the frightening setting and evil personages are introduced.

Next, the good personages are introduced: 'a good old man and a good old woman' (likened by the well-read narrator to the old Phrygian couple, Phillis and Baucis, favored by the gods for their goodness), their only son, ideal in beauty, goodness, and intellect, quite in accord with fairy tale topoi. They live in a humble hut in 'our' village (we note the identity in locale between speech event and good personages). Their only problem is that the youth does not like any of the village beauties and does not want to get married – the typical problem of such a fairy tale and the typical fairy tale age of transition from boyhood to manhood.

So far the narrator's fairy tale consists of evil and good territory, evil and good personages, supernatural happenings, and the normal problems within the good territory. The two sets are so far clearly separated, and the obvious expectation is that a move across the borders will occur (from village to forest), with fear that such a move will have terrible results. The problem is most immediately the son's, and he is thus the expected primary victim. The next developments indeed fulfill these expectations. The supernatural is maintained in the form of a 'thundering voice' which resounds in the night and is heard by both parents and son. The voice tells the parents to send their son into the forest, and the son is told to enter it. Their reactions are predictably different: the parents are terrified and refuse to comply. They attribute the voice to 'some sort of hellish spirit wishing our ruin', in accord with the lore about the forest and its ruler. The son is more courageous and is eager to follow the dictates of the voice. His speculations about the speaker are, however, somewhat unorthodox for the fairy tale context: 'You heard a Heavenly voice, the voice of my Angel protector.' The 'religious' interpretation can be seen as part of the Sentimentalist transformation of ancient folklore.

The fairy tale pattern of threefold incremental repetition is followed as the voice resounds two more nights, the third time, with the significant addition: 'Woe to nonbelievers'. The parents are now converted to the son's interpretation, and realize that it is God speaking, for 'what evil hellish spirit could speak of the holy faith?' The youth (who was earlier described as 'an old man in intellect' according to the *puer senex* topos of both fairy tales and idylls) advises his parents to have full confidence 'in the dark paths of the highest Wisdom'. He sets off after a tearful farewell, equipped with a small charm which had been his great-grandmother's, and which had protected their humble hut no worse than the statue of Minerva protected Troy, as the narrator comments. The Classical references are as incongruous on the lips of a fairy tale teller as they are for the ears of his audience, and represent one of the traditional means of transforming fairy tales during the era. The religious theme is also somewhat odd in a fairy tale and the youth sounds more and more like the narrator of tales, such as 'Bornholm Island'. The religious interpretation of the supernatural is further developed in the following scenes, and is part of the tendency to give 'natural' explanations for 'magic' tricks.

From the point where the youth enters the forest (following a white rabbit, typical of fairy tales, but also of idylls), all the expectations of horror and evil, so carefully built up, are frustrated. The youth's adventures in the forest are entirely of the idyllic–Sentimentalist kind. In fact, the expectations are overtly frustrated by the narrator. For instance, when the youth unexpectedly arrives at an idyllic country house, he forgets all the striking features of the surroundings when 'he suddenly saw before his very eyes . . . ' The elliptical ending is filled in by the narrator's verbalization of the children's expectations: '"Some sort of monster?" you think – "some sort of dragon, snake, crocodile, or evil magician in a high hat, riding on a bat?" . . . No, my friends, something totally different, totally different'(109–10).

In the narrator's tale, the fairy tale monsters are replaced by a beautiful young woman 'who looked not like Venus, but like a pure Angel'. The image of female perfection is exactly like most of Karamzin's heroines: Julia, Liza, Natal'ia, Aglaia, and all the idyllic shepherdesses. One is particularly struck by the similarities to the personification of innocence, a resemblance strengthened by the old man's concern for her fate after he dies: 'innocence was left an orphan on earth'. Her dying father is equally typical of Karamzin's idyllic images of old age and wisdom, for instance, the old man/sunset metaphor in 'The Countryside'.

Before the old man dies, he speaks at great length to the young people, telling them the story of his own happy life devoted to the study of 'the secrets of wondrous Nature', and his love for his wife and daughter (an idyll within the fairy tale). He joins the two in a marriage, divinely sanctioned. The idyllic proximities characterize both his own life and his death, and a new idyllic cycle starts when the young couple begins married life together in the same idyllic setting as the parents, beauty and goodness joined once more. Thus the enchanted forest turns out to contain not an evil wizard, but a holy, wise man and his ideal family, and the expected tricks of evil magic are replaced by superior wisdom and the 'magical' beauty of divine creation.

Evil does not entirely disappear in this idyllic picture, and the youth's movement through the fearsome forest to its idyllic center is a fairy tale parallel to the old man's Sentimentalist movement away from 'evil and corrupted people' to the silent solitude and a personal life of virtue and 'holy contemplation', similar to many promenades and travels in Karamzin's other works. Thus this narrator, too, implants in his audience the moral that beauty and goodness are a personal, internal matter.

An interesting 'prediction' of the present speech event and the larger reality of which it is a part occurs in the old man's monologue. He predicts 'times of horror and fear [ . . . ] centuries of ruin and curse, in the midst of enlightenment and the greatest advances of the human intellect'. The reference to 'enlightenment' and the following description of the horrors indicate that it is the narrator's own era (ten centuries later, from the old man's point of view) that is foreseen, with horrors, such as the French Revolution and its bloody consequences. This unidyllic evil of the world at large is offset by the old man's consoling prediction of an idyll which persists on a personal level despite the horrors he has mentioned:

Thus, *one sensitive family circle, a community of most tender friends, having fled from the noisy world, will some day settle near this deep forest whose night will with time be illuminated by light; here, regardless of universal turmoil, it will enjoy love and holy friendship* . . . (114–15)

We recall that the narrator and the children are at the 'present' drinking tea on the balcony of a house in the village at the edge of the forest. That the old man's prediction of a future idyll refers to the present speech event, and that the present storyteller and children are in fact described in the prediction, is made even more explicit by the use of italics which call special attention to the passage and perhaps indicate special emphasis in the oral telling. Moreover, in subsequent editions a footnote is added (after the words 'deep forest' in the passage) which reads: 'There lived the Author in the family circle of his friends.' The addition of this note is clearly part of the literary transformation and is included for the benefit of the anonymous reader of the literary work – the in-group obviously did not need this kind of information. It is fairly evident that this idyllic transformation of a fairy tale is governed ultimately by the same solipsistic principle which characterizes all Sentimentalist fiction.

After the idyllic interlude, the story continues to a happy ending in the fairy tale mode. The tone, however, differs from the 'serious' fairy tale beginning, and the fairy tale topoi are treated with light humor. The two young people return to the parents left in the hut. The narrator adds in a musing footnote: 'we are led to believe that the white rabbit was again the guide'. When the old couple is unwilling to leave their humble hut for the house in the forest, the narrator turns to his listeners in a mock-surprised aside, and then resolves the problem by reintroducing fairy tale magic (which he had been at such pains to debunk!): suddenly a wind out of nowhere blows the hut away so that no trace of it is left. All move to the forest and live happily ever after. The narrator ends his fairy tale discourse-deictically: 'Here concludes the story of the *deep forest*'.

'The Deep Forest' does not, however, end there. The voice of the children is once more heard with a note of disappointment. Their expectations have obviously been frustrated, and they still expect a 'real', scary fairy tale. They want to know what happened to the evil wizard, the spheres of fire, and so on. The narrator provides his own 'enlightened' explanation: 'You should know that the rumor about the evil magician was one of those absurd fables which good people since time immemorial are so fond of.' A modern 'scientific', 'natural' explanation of the magic phenomena and events (but not of the rabbit or the strong wind) then concludes the tale. The narrator thus, in no uncertain terms, voices his opinion about folk legends and superstitions, just as the children had voiced theirs with respect to his moralistic idyllic substitute. The humor of 'The Deep Forest' is mainly engendered by the contrast between these opposing evaluations of two modes of storytelling. The structure of this trifle, contrasting an idyllic narrator–narratee framework and an idyllic tale of his own ancestors with a non-idyllic backdrop (superstitions, fear, horrors in the outside world) anticipates what we shall see in some of Karamzin's serious Sentimental tales. The humor in 'The Deep Forest' resulting from a clash between two kinds of stories and two modes of storytelling is similar to more elaborate Sentimental fairy tales, such as 'The Beautiful Princess', and also anticipates later parodies of various narrative practices.

## THE ANECDOTE

### 'Frol Silin, a Virtuous Person'

'Frol Silin, a Virtuous Person', an account of the good deeds of a Russian peasant, instantly attracted a great deal of attention.[48] It was translated into at least German, English, and French soon after its publication. In Russia it was widely imitated, and similar pieces subsequently flooded practically every literary journal, including Karamzin's own journals. Indeed, special sections were created in the journals of so-called Russian anecdotes, and the genre's popularity even resulted in special anecdote collections.[49]

Not only did 'Frol Silin' generate a spate of imitations, but the work itself became a topic within other literary works, serious and parodic, from a fable by A. P. Benitskii, 'The Ox and the Sheep' ('Byk i ovtsa', 1807), to Dostoevskii's *The Village of Stepanchikovo* (*Selo Stepanchikova*, 1859).[50] Indeed, Frol Silin, apparently a real peasant, was himself regaled with I. I. Dmitriev's reading of the story about him, and his reactions were even documented (second-hand) by Karamzin in connection with his republication of 'Frol Silin' in *My Trifles*, and by M. A. Dmitriev in his memoirs of his uncle. In Karamzin's version 'the good old man wept and said "I'm not worthy of this, I'm not worthy of this!".'[51] In M. A. Dmitriev's version 'To Frol Silin it seemed extremely absurd that people wrote about him in a book: he somehow did not believe it and, it seems, wondered whether they weren't playing a joke on him and whether they weren't reading from memory what hadn't been written at all.'[52] The difference between the two accounts is interesting: Karamzin's version stresses the emotive response and thus sustains the Sentimental image created in the story. Dmitriev's account seems a more realistic account of an uneducated peasant, suspicious of the written word. It also fits his uncle's description of the real Frol Silin, who not only had a red nose from a certain fondness for the bottle, but whose life apparently was more in the vein of Fedor Emin's heroes: illegitimate son of a peasant woman who was abducted by robbers but later escaped – not without money – and who himself, according to local lore, was somewhat of a sorcerer.

If Frol Silin was surprised by the fiction about him, Karamzin was no less surprised by the further fate of his story. Reviewing the French translation in 1803, he thinks it funny that the translator, Coiffier, not only sees 'Natal′ia, the Boyar's Daughter' as a 'Marmontelian tale (*rasskaz*)', but that he furthermore makes 'Frol Silin' out to be another tale (*povest′, conte* ), and inferior to the other work. Karamzin concludes the review with the following remark: 'Good Frol the Simbirsk peasant is still alive: won't he be surprised that his name and deeds have become famous in Paris and Germany?'[53] The implication is that the work was not meant to be a *povest′, conte*, and therefore is not comparable to 'Natal′ia', or even important enough to merit worldwide attention. It was simply a 'description of Frol Silin's good deeds'. Notably, Karamzin himself did not include the work in a single personally supervised edition of his collected works. He did, however, include it in *My Trifles*.

Since then it is, curiously enough, the genre of 'Frol Silin' that has been widely debated. Coiffier, as already mentioned, calls it a *conte* (corresponding to the Russian *povest′* or *rasskaz*). N. I. Grech calls it a 'true tale' (*istinnaia povest′*), but feels compelled to explain that he includes it among 'fictitious tales' (*vymyshlennye povesti*) because 'its story is entirely romantic and it is in general more akin to tales (*povestiam*) than to "History" (*k "Istorii"*)'. Sipovskii calls it a 'small tale–anecdote' (*povestushka–anekdot*). Of more recent commentators, Blagoi anachronistically calls it a sketch (*ocherk*). Stepanov refers to it alternatively as a *povest′* and an *anekdot*, reflecting the late eighteenth- to early nineteenth-century reception. Finally, fictitious 'critics' also had their say: in Foma Opiskin's opinion, 'this is a great epic! This is a purely national work' (not, of course, to be read as Dostoevskii's opinion). It is that opinion that comes closest to the most recent attempts to define its genre, those by Cross and Orlov. Cross sees it as the 'sentimental version of the classical ode, with prose replacing verse and a peasant extolled instead of a prince' or a 'prose counterpart to the lofty panegyric ode, an experiment consistent with his [Karamzin's] belief that the epic [?!] also could be written in prose'. Orlov, in an article devoted specifically to the generic definition of 'Frol Silin', views it as a Sentimentalist version of the Classicist panegyric oration (*pokhvalnoe slovo*), to which genre, in his opinion, it corresponds mainly compositionally.[54]

The generic labels applied to 'Frol Silin' could, no doubt, be further multiplied. What is most curious about the whole issue is that it is so entirely alien to the ageneric basis of Sentimentalist poetics. Generic labels were simply not important, and even though one may find features in the work reminiscent of all the genres mentioned, that in itself indicates its ageneric nature. Karamzin's own comments and publication decisions about the work, furthermore, make his ageneric intentions abundantly clear. One of the points Stepanov makes would seem closest to the historical situation. He points to the fact that the anecdote, in the Russian eighteenth-century view, was in transition between extra-literary fact (oral and written) and literary fact properly speaking. Even when written, it was mostly considered part of the 'lowly' literature of the vulgus, and when it entered literary journals it was relegated to the end, among other trivia. Before 'Frol Silin', written anecdotes were mostly of foreign origin and had foreign subject matter. As a Russian and a literary variant of the anecdote, 'Frol Silin' was, no doubt, an important link in this historical chain, inspiring what was later to become a bona fide literary genre. For Karamzin it was, however, another *bezdelka*, literary, but its specific genre was irrelevant.

'Frol Silin' is a good demonstration of Karamzin's literary method, precisely because we do have a description of the real prototype for the hero. One must, of course, approach the question of the 'real' Frol Silin with some caution. The information we have is either secondhand or childhood memories, and need not necessarily correspond to historical fact. Nevertheless, the location of the events tallies with fact – the Karamzins and the Dmitrievs both had estates in the Simbirsk district, and both authors spent their childhood in that area. Given this location, Frol's life as depicted by the Dmitrievs is not as farfetched as it may seem. At the time of Karamzin's childhood the area was still at the edge of the Russian empire, and bordered on lands populated by Bashkirs and other tribes. The peasants were gradually resettled further and further into the territories acquired by the Russians, and the area was by no means safe.[55] The abduction of a peasant woman by robbers in such a setting, as well as the further adventures and alleged prosperity of her child, seem not at all unlikely. If one thus considers Dmitriev's account more or less true, what Karamzin chose to focus on is certainly striking: *not* on Frol's adventurous life, nor on the local lore about him, but on his sincere religiosity, his good deeds to needy neighbors, his acting as a father to two serf girls whom he freed; *not* on his legendary riches, but on his thrifty and cautious habits – all of which is fully consonant with the trivialization of literature that we have noted.

In terms of structure, 'Frol Silin' is reminiscent of idylls such as 'The Flood' with a sympathetic shepherd watching a natural disaster ravaging the idyll world. In 'Frol Silin', the good peasant (Frol) replaces the good shepherd (Milon), and the unnamed narrator in the idyll takes on the autobiographical flesh of an 'I'. The flood is replaced by its opposite, a drought, no less perilous for the populace. 'Frol Silin' is certainly not a realistic sociological description of a Russian village (nor was it meant to be), but a vast idealization in a typically Sentimental mode, an anecdote adapted for a refined salon audience. Nevertheless, with its Russian setting and Russian accoutrements (albeit very schematized), it is intensely patriotic – a trait eagerly picked up by the later imitators.

'Frol Silin's' structure is relatively simple, its Sentimentalist coloring most overtly revealed by the addition of a narrator–narratee context, introducing and concluding the report of Frol's good deeds. As is usually the case in Karamzin's works, the narrator's presence intrudes into the reporting of events, but at least some of them are allowed to speak for themselves more directly than usually. Conversely, the setting of the events and their main protagonist in turn enter the narrator's speech event: the time and the dismal conditions are introduced in the overture as the narrator's childhood memory, and Frol – alive or possibly dead – enters the narrator's future plans in the epilogue as an imagined addressee and/or object of his veneration. Strictly compositionally speaking, the overture and the epilogue comprise roughly half of the text, and even if one, in addition, counts only the most overt narrator's evaluations and comments interwoven with the reporting of events, it is clear that the narrator dominates the text structure.

Frol's actions, first and foremost, give the narrator an opportunity to describe his own emotions and actions and concurrently comment on his own telling of the story. The narrator's self-description is divided between a description of his reaction to events and the matter of properly showing his respects to Frol. His authorial function is stressed more overtly and in a more technical sense than in most of Karamzin's other early works. Notably he presents himself not as a poet, but as a reporter of actual true events – a device (discourse-deictic encoding motif) which was to become extremely important in Karamzin's later fiction. He is not a poet, yet utterly sensitive and knows poetry enough to come across as well-read and also knows the world enough to come across as well-travelled – the kind of pose one can well imagine in eighteenth-century salons.

The first lines of the overture, two optative constructions and a discourse-deictic statement of intention, serve to differentiate the present work from the traditional forms of praise, the traditional worthy objects of praise, and the traditional practitioners of praise: 'Let the Virgils glorify the Augusts! Let the eloquent flatterers praise the magnanimity of the Famous! I want to praise Frol Silin, a simple villager and my praise will consist in a description of his deeds known to me' (31). The narrator's words, we might note, were repeated almost verbatim by Karamzin, the editor of *Messenger of Europe,* twelve years later in his critique of Coiffier.

A contrast is established between official praise and flattery according to rank and abstract qualities, and simple description of personally known genuine deeds, which need no artful elaboration but will, as it were, be allowed to speak for themselves. One is here reminded of Gessner's invocation to his Muse. In his introduction to the idylls, called 'An Daphnen', he begins with the following lines distancing himself from the epic: 'Nicht den blutbespritzten kühnen Helden, nicht das Öde Schlachtfeld singt frohe Muse; sanft und schüchtern fliesst sie das Gewühl, die leichte Flöt' in ihrer Hand'.[56]

Next in 'Frol Silin' follows a description of the time and the conditions which make up the setting for Frol's deeds, the memory of which still at the time of the telling calls forth the same 'heartfelt shudder' in the adult narrator as he had felt as a precociously sensitive child (we note again the inclusion of a child as a narratee). The 'shuddering of the heart' is reflected in the manner of description, an anaphorically structured chronological enumeration of the evils that befell the villagers, much like those in the idylls. The narrator's own sympathetic suffering is stressed, as is the narratee's sensitive heart – too sensitive to bear further gruesome details, as the narrator tells us. The delicate sensitivities of the 'dear ladies' in the salon would seem to be the measure for what is fit to tell.

Frol Silin is introduced as one of the villagers who lived through the disastrous year and 'maybe lives even now'. His good qualities are enumerated in another anaphorically structured passage, positively contrasted to the description of the general situation and the average villager. Frol is reminiscent of Milon in 'The Flood', not only in generous deeds, but also in his very manner of expressing his relationship to those less fortunate. The narrator makes a point of telling us that 'good Frol called them his brethren (brat'iami)' and of directly quoting Frol's own addresses to the villagers: 'Listen brothers (bratsy)'; 'No brothers (bratsy)'.[57] This demonstrates that Karamzin did make some attempt at speech differentiation between his narrator and his personage. Although neither Frol's nor the villagers' directly quoted lines are in any sense real peasant dialect, bratsy is certainly more colloquial than the narrator's brat'ia, and the personages' speech is consistently kept simple and familiar.

Frol's first deeds are described in detail, with a strong element of evaluation and some overt comments by the narrator. Thus, the peasants' surprise at Frol's generosity is ironically commented upon by the narrator's somewhat jaded explanation: 'for both in cities and in the village magnanimity is a rare phenomenon' – a comment particularly ironical since the 'magnanimity of the Famous' was the topic of the 'eloquent flatterers' mentioned in the overture and since the existential present (est') makes it obvious that behavior (in city or village) has not changed much since the narrator's childhood. It is also clear that the narrator has seen both cities and villages and is no peasant himself. The narrator's second overt intrusion is a comment on Frol's weeping and gazing at the sky: 'what he saw there – is known to him, not to me'. This foreshadows a discourse-deictic device which Karamzin's later narrators were to use much more effectively and humorously – here it is somewhat misplaced.

Frol's first deeds consist of feeding the hungry during the 'year of hunger' and refusing to accept the grateful villagers' repayments. His deeds are extended temporally (factually and hypothetically) up to the present of the narrator's speech event. Three more altruistic deeds are briefly and 'factually' reported in one paragraph each, without any narratorial evaluation or intrusion to speak of. For each deed, Frol's concrete gifts are carefully noted: grain to feed the hungry (with the actual amounts mentioned), two rubles and a scythe each to fourteen households ravaged by fire a few years later, a horse to other villagers also made destitute by fire at another time, and freedom and a good dowry to two serf girls. The philanthropic idealization of a peasant might impress sensitive upper class society at a time when serfdom was beginning to be felt as a problem in Russian society.

The epilogue consists of an apostrophe to Frol, who if still alive 'then surely you are even now doing good and raising your celestial rank'. This extends (hypothetically) the narrated events to the present of the speech event and the narrator's evaluation, and contrasts Frol's 'celestial rank' to the 'earthly rank' of the 'Augusts' and the 'Famous' of the overture.

The narrator next reveals that his information about Frol is secondhand and belated (encoding motifs), but he vows to visit either Frol in person and bow down to his virtue, or his grave on which he will shed a tear, place a white stone and 'with my own hands I will carve on it the words: *Here rest the ashes of a virtuous person*'. The narrator's projected actions are highly idyllic and reminiscent of, for instance, the idyll description of Gessner's grave.

The last paragraph reinstates the wider perspective of a well-travelled narrator, and a 'magnificent temple *to great men*, men who surprised us with their gifts (*darovaniiami*)' – footnoted as Westminster Abbey with its monuments to famous English authors. This temple is contrasted to a hypothetical 'temple consecrated to the good people of mankind' (in later editions, 'the good genii of mankind'). The initial contrast is reiterated: abstract official greatness as opposed to concrete goodness, the 'giftedness' of famous men to Frol's carefully enumerated concrete gifts. The former merit the conventional raising of one's hat, the latter – heartfelt tears, the highest possible tribute by the Sentimental narrator to his virtuous hero.

# 5

# Serious Sentimental tales:
# narrator as narratee

The literary potentials of the idyll and the trifle as I have described them, were to find their fullest and most creative realization in the most developed form of Sentimentalist prose fiction: the Sentimental tale. As we have already seen, the idyll and the trifle were by no means mutually exclusive concepts, but shared the basic Sentimental chronotope of solipsistic intimacy, pleasure, and sympathy. There was a great deal of interaction between idylls and trifles. This ageneric trend continues with the Sentimental tale and the label is used here mostly as a heuristic device to facilitate our discussion. Nevertheless, I believe one can make a qualitative distinction between humorous and serious Sentimental tales. Within the latter, what I shall call the 'complete fragment' most directly develops properties inherent in the idyll, and the 'incomplete fragment' can be seen as a development of certain trifle potentials to their limits. I should stress, however, that these divisions are not meant to reflect genres as perceived at the time.

On the most general structural level, a Sentimental tale shall be viewed as a trivocal (or sometimes bivocal) utterance. It is the account of a narrator's present personal re-experience of a past personal experience as narratee of an earlier (thus twice removed) vicarious love intrigue. The core love story is doubly framed by two sets of narrators/narratees, a primary (present) and secondary (past) narrator/narratee. Thus the easy switches in roles we have noted between narrator and narratee are especially highlighted in Sentimental tales.

The inclusion of two storytelling situations within a single tale allows Sentimentalist writers to revel in all aspects of their own craft, to indulge in focusing on its full dialogical nature. Both participants in the dialogue of storytelling are important, the narratee is as important as the narrator. Frequently the part of narratee is in fact even more emphasized. This emphasis becomes doubly solipsistic in that the present narrator is most often presented as the same person as the past narratee so that the tale is largely centered around 'I then' and 'I now', the 'I' who heard the story in the past and retells the same story in the present. Even if there is not an identity in person there is always an identity in personality of narrators and narratees. As might be expected, it is the Sensitive Person who performs actively both as teller and perceiver. Furthermore, the identity in personality also extends to the personages in the core love story. This makes Sentimental tales highly self-reflective and prone to be read as metapoetical statements about Sentimentalist art in general.

The present narrator often re-experiences the narrated events (or their first telling) *in situ* and he (and the narratee) personally knows one or several of the protagonists in the love story. All are, or were, close friends and the cult of friendship seen in the idylls and trifles continues to be celebrated. The narrator might meet the personages at an epilogue stage, hear their story, weep over their graves, or simply reminisce about the past. Thus a 'real' connection is established between the narrator and his story (or stories). The story's (or stories') verisimilitude is thereby sanctioned, and the image of narrator/narratee is thereby anchored in time and space. Coding motifs tend to become as prominent as the requisite senses and sensibilities of narrators, narratees, and personages. The storytelling situations are always emotional events, and the idyll or salon chronotope is observed. The same range of sensibilities that characterized the idylls and the trifles already discussed is further elaborated in the Sentimental tales, and they contain some of the best descriptions of the Sentimentalist ideals for artistic creation and, particularly, reception.

The present narrator dominates the text in that his characteristics are extended to all levels within it: both to other narrators/ narratees and to personages. His moods, emotions, opinions, and their modulations and shifts give the Sentimental tales their fundamental lyrical unity. Most often the mood is a mixture of joy and sorrow, an aesthetically pleasurable melancholy. The narratorial dominance may be compositionally reflected in the already familiar overtures, epilogues, and intermittent asides, comments, exclamations, questions, and apostrophes, especially at peak moments of the love story. Frequently the overture is a thumbnail sketch of the narrator's worldview while also comprising a synopsis of the story to follow or containing ominous foreshadowings of events to come.

We should stress, however, that the narrator's dominance extends beyond composition; his voice, his evaluations, and his emotions, color all reported events, as well. As in the idylls and trifles, the narrator's utterance always has a dual focus on narrating itself and narrated events.

The stylistic unity is facilitated by the fact that the narrated events and personages are, relatively speaking, limited in number and scope, as compared to the *bol'shaia forma* of the novel, although somewhat more complex than we saw in most idylls and trifles. It is mainly in this respect that Karamzin's Sentimental tales differ from the prose of his predecessors.[1] Such unity was seldom successfully achieved even by his epigones.[2]

The vicarious love story at the core of a Sentimental tale always consists of a thwarted love idyll which reflects the narrator's own sorrow and melancholy moods. The tragedy of the lovers (the failed idyll) is, however, usually mitigated by the true idyll between narrators and narratees. One could say that the tragedy of the failed idyll at the core is aesthetically sublimated in the narrator's own idyll. The nuanced double tonalities (pleasurable melancholy) stem precisely from the simultaneous double focus on core story and frame story, or, in Bakhtin's terms, the bivocal or trivocal utterance structure.

The active personages in the love story are more like the narrator than were the idyll and trifle personages. Instead of the shepherds and shepherdesses, the peasants, monks, abbots, and more or less abstract Graces and Fantasies of the idylls and trifles, they tend to be more 'normal' (Russian) youngsters with a social upperclass background much like that of the narrator – or for that matter, a young Karamzin. They still, however, retain the essential characteristics of the idyll and trifle personages and are by no means realistic. Similarly, the settings may be more precisely specified (Moscow, Gravesend, Bornholm, Sierra-Morena), but they still retain the general properties of the earlier settings to the extent that they too are not realistic and Moscow differs little from the island of Bornholm.

The physical events in the love story are all closely connected to the love intrigue (meetings, partings), and complex adventures are eschewed. For the most part the focus on inner psychological 'events' is retained from the idylls and trifles. As we have seen, that makes the actions of the personages very much like the actions of the narrator/narratee. The personages are, in fact, also identical in person to subsequent narrators with the resulting chain reaction of storytelling. In this sense, the Sentimental tales could be said to be akin to the salon speech genre of gossip. The love plot itself is rather trite. It develops from a first meeting between the protagonists to mutual attraction, to passionate love, a conflict, and a catastrophe which leads to the separation of the lovers (parental obstacles, social taboos, sickness, death, suicide), occasionally followed by a belated repentance by the person guilty of disrupting the idyll. The rising–falling emotive curve is in idyll fashion echoed in the surroundings. While in most Sentimental tales the love idyll is flawed by the intrusion of non-idyllic elements into the idyll world, some are disrupted by flaws inherent in the idyll and salon chronotope themselves: a delicate sensitivity can actually be physically debilitating. Delicacy, weakness, and tenderness are, as we pointed out earlier, some of the concepts that were re-evaluated during the Sentimentalist era. The Sentimentalist heroes and heroines may be flawed in some respect, and, by the same token, the villains, if introduced at all, tend to have some redeeming features. The virtue we have seen so far in more or less pure form, in the Sentimental tales increasingly becomes a virtue in distress. Sentimental tales are, by this token, characterized not only by greater nuances in narrator and narratee and narrating voices, but also by greater psychological depth in personages than what had been the case in earlier literature.

The physical events are, as we saw, trite in and of themselves and the love triangle is quite predictable. Often they are not overtly reported at all, but conveyed by hints and allusions, and the inexpressible, the inexplicable, the unspeakable, and the mysterious, must be contemplated and resolved by the narratee, whose role becomes much more active than before. Orthographic expressive means reach unprecedented density, and ellipsis dots and dashes, italics, exclamation and question marks punctuate the text with unusual frequency.[3] Various kinds of elliptical devices are used extensively in all Sentimental tales, thus linked to the trifles and idylls by their trivialized plot and trivialized telling (in the sense of ellipsis). However, the potential of 'being interrupted' described for salon conversations, is most fully developed in what I have labelled 'incomplete fragments'. Here the plot of the story is literally left unfinished. The story is never told completely.

The fragment is indeed a bona fide Sentimentalist form and many of Karamzin's works are explicitly subtitled 'A Fragment' (*otryvok*) – 'The Flood', 'The Countryside', and 'Sierra-Morena', being the most notable examples. None of these works are, however, left unfinished. In terms of basic love plot they are all 'complete'. 'The Flood' is a complete love idyll with a happy ending; 'The Countryside' is a complete day in the life of the narrator; 'Sierra-Morena' is a complete love story with a tragic ending. On the other hand, they are all, together with the other Sentimental tales, as we shall see, presented as fragments of a larger narrator–narratee framework (ethical, religious, psychological, allegorical, and so on) that framework itself made part of the topic of the work as a whole. The label 'fragment' here serves as a signal to the reader to turn his attention not only to the core story, but also to what the story is a *fragment of*, i.e. another indicator of a solipsistic focus on narrator and narratee. I shall call the Sentimental tales with a complete love plot 'complete fragments'.

The structure is somewhat different in the case of 'Bornholm Island', 'Liodor', and the later novel, *A Knight of Our Time* (and one could add a verse tale, the *poema* 'Il'ia Muromets'), where the basic plot itself breaks off *in medias res*. I shall call these tales 'incomplete fragments'.[4] This form, too, has its markers, most frequently expressed in words to the effect that the story is to be continued, or that the narrator for some reason cannot tell more, or that further details are simply too gruesome to reveal. These kinds of wordings are even more blatant pleas for reader (or narratee) involvement both with the personages and the narrator himself. In a sense the reader is himself invited to fill in the blanks, ponder the problems posed, or in general contemplate the situation, and thus to function not only as narratee, but also as co-creative narrator and to take a more active part in the dialogical enterprise of storytelling. This is, of course, fully consonant with solipsistic Sentimentalist poetics as we have already discussed it, emphasizing the process of creation rather than the end product created.

## COMPLETE FRAGMENTS

### 'Eugene and Julia, a Russian True Tale'

'Eugene and Julia' has been hailed as the first Russian Sentimental tale, and its subtitle has, since Sipovskii, led to various speculations about its Russianness and its true (and even autobiographical) status.[5] Attempts have been made to identify foreign sources, and Sipovskii pointed to its affinities to the tales of Mme de Genlis (translated by Karamzin for *Children's Reading*), a connection which is upheld by most scholars, and even narrowed down to her tale 'Eugénie et Léonce', which Cross sees as Karamzin's closest model.[6] Similarities to Gessner have also been stressed, but the consensus seems to be that it is an original work, rather than a translation or adaptation.[7]

Its links to de Genlis on the one hand, and to Gessner on the other, are indicative of its structure: it is neither a simple idyll nor a typical Sentimental tale, but forms a bridge between the two. Its roots are firmly implanted in idyllic soil, and in many respects it is remarkably like 'A Promenade' (which appeared in the same issue of *Children's Reading*) and the later idyll 'The Countryside'. Unlike any of Karamzin's early idylls it does, however, have a developed vicarious love plot which aligns it with Sentimental tales such as 'Poor Liza'. Many of the motifs of 'Eugene and Julia' were to be further developed in later Sentimental tales.[8]

An image of narrator is not yet developed temporally or spatially and is not linked to a concrete 'I', which is the case in Karamzin's subsequent Sentimental tales. Thus the temporal–spatial distance between the narrated events of the love story and the speech event of its telling is not specified, nor is the speech event itself significantly elaborated into a subsidiary plot, let alone a main plot. The narrator's actions are not referred to, and the telling itself is in no way motivated. Thus coding motifs, which were to become one of the hallmarks of Karamzinian narrators, are almost entirely lacking. Nevertheless, there are some examples of discourse deixis, and, above all, the love story is a thoroughly subjective, emotive, and aesthetically organized idyllic vision. A narrator is felt as an amorphous source of the emotions, opinions, and evaluations with respect to the vicarious love story, much like the unnamed narrators in Karamzin's idylls of vicarious experience.

The acting personages are three, all idealized figures, much like the shepherds and shepherdesses or sensitive poets of the idylls and trifles. The complete absence of villains or even minor negative qualities in anyone or anything is conspicuous even when compared to the Sentimental tales where absolute villains are rare. Mrs L is the ideal mother whose life is devoted solely to the happiness and

education of her children (Julia is an orphan 'adopted' by Mrs L).
Eugene and Julia are ideal children, affectionate to their mother
and each other, compassionate to those in need, sensitive to nature
and the arts, perfect in mind and body, and beloved by all,
including house servants and peasants.

The idyllic setting consists of the gentry estate variant of the *locus
amoenus*, an aestheticized version of a Russian estate. It is
described in terms of the same general topography, botany, and
meteorology that characterize 'A Promenade' and 'The Countryside', and the same intangible range of 'innocent pleasures', 'pure
joys', 'pleasant views', 'ambrosiac aromas', 'spirit of Nature',
needed to satisfy all the senses of the sensitive personages. This
idyllic setting is a world unto itself, sheltered from the outside
world, the existence of which is only alluded to by Mrs L's youth in
Moscow, Eugene's studies abroad, unfounded fears that Eugene
might be corrupted by staying abroad, and, significantly, the road
that leads Eugene *back* to his village. Indeed, Eugene's absence
only enhances the love the two women feel for him. In his absence,
his letters and thoughts of his return are the major pleasures of the
two women, and Eugene's 'first and most pleasant thought' while
abroad is the memory of the women and their tearful parting, with
Julia's promise always to remain his 'most tender friend'. Their
mutual affections are only strengthened as he returns 'with greater
knowledge and unspoiled feelings'. As in Palemon's and Daphnis'
dream visions, the idyllic values are merely intensified by the
separation.

The tale, consistently maintained in the past tense (disrupted
only occasionally by clearly marked exclamations and apostrophes
by the narrator), begins by introducing and situating Mrs L and
Julia in the solitude of the country estate and describing their
peaceful life in complete harmony with nature. A detailed 'hourly'
description of a summer day from sunrise to sunset (various
tendernesses, walks, enjoyment of nature), followed by that of a
winter day (reading 'the true philosophers' and Eugene's letters), is
temporally extended in a summarizing 'thus flowed days, months,
and years'. The moods are synchronized with nature: tender joy in
summer, languid melancholy in winter, pleasant tears and joyous
expectations at the thought of Eugene's return in early summer.
The narrative tempo is modulated from slow to fast according to
the approaching return of Eugene; slower, the further it is in the

future, faster, as it approaches, and rapid when it finally occurs. The technique is already familiar from the idylls and trifles.

The next scenes are devoted to descriptions of how the old brother–sister relationship of their childhood is re-established – thereby also serving to describe the childhood which heretofore was not the topic. Julia's shy smiles and the 'strong stirrings of her heart', Eugene's insistence on the familiar *ty*, and his assurances of his constant thoughts of the women while abroad indicates their mutual love. The walks and preoccupations of Mrs L and Julia are now repeated in threesome, each spot providing fond memories of childhood. Mrs L helps the youngsters recall their childhood virtue: a strawberry picking event with Eugene helping Julia to fill her basket, and a Good Samaritan deed by the two helping an old man in distress. Mrs L thus reports part of 'this' story in the form of two interpolated miniature idylls (compare, for instance, Gessner's 'Das hölzerne Bein', and 'Menalcus und Alexis').

A night walk recalls 'A Promenade': a starry sky makes them marvel at the greatness of God, and the sound of a waterfall calls forth a discussion of immortality. The latter is a rather ominous foreshadowing for those readers who recall thoughts of void and death with similar imagery in 'A Promenade' (which association must have occurred to most readers, since the two works appeared in the same issue of *Children's Reading*).

The indoor activities of the two women are now repeated and amplified by new French, Italian, and German books, and sheet music brought from abroad by Eugene. Julia sings and plays the harpsichord, and is particularly moved by Klopstock's song, set to music by Gluck.[9] This provokes an emotional apostrophe from the narrator: 'Gentle, tender souls! you alone know the value of these Virtuosi, and to you alone are their immortal works dedicated! One of your tears is for them the greatest reward' (153). The narrator's reference to his personages' sensitivities and simultaneous expression of his own emotions also allows him to express the Sentimentalist credo of artistic reception.

Later in summer, on Eugene's twenty-second birthday, Mrs L tells them that the time has come for her lifelong wish that the two become husband and wife. The mood is set idyllically by birds singing and 'all objects smiling' when Eugene wakes up, two turtle doves kissing outside Mrs L's window, and Julia appearing in the typical guise of a shepherdess (white dress with rose colored ribbons, hair let down, joyously smiling). The joy on all sides is shared by the narrator who apostrophizes the innocence and virtue of the Golden Age in a way that foreshadows Karamzin's conception of a lost Arcadian innocence, as expressed in his later 'Innocence'. In both works the narrator views innocence as a fragment of a more perfect age, anachronistically transplanted for a brief moment into the personages' and his own less perfect era.

The joy of Eugene and Julia (and the narrator) is, in idyll fashion, echoed in the surroundings: besides the birds and 'objects smiling', the servants are overjoyed, and the whole scene 'would have made Raphael throw down his brush' and is a 'sight for Angels' – as the ecstatic narrator interprets it.

The narration at this peak moment is disrupted by the longest narrative digression in the text, commenting on the expected happy ending and foreshadowing the actual ending. The digression highlights the narrator's authorial control function, and articulates his own faith in divine Providence. The events to come are rationalized as the mysterious ways of the omnipotent, wise God, which, although at times incomprehensible to mortals, must nevertheless be accepted on faith. A similar belief will subsequently be stressed by Karamzin in 'Bornholm Island'. Eugene's 'ecstasy of highest joy' reminds us of 'A Promenade', where the identical expression is used in a section preceding the narrator's imaginary death. Here it leads to Eugene's real illness and death.

The grief of the mother and the wife-not-to-be is shared by all: servants and peasants carry the casket and participate in the funeral hymns. The narrator utters his own eulogy, thus participating *in absentia* as if *in presentia*: 'Farewell, flower of virtue and innocence! Your ashes rest in the embraces of our common mother; but your spirit, which is your true being floats in the countless joys of eternity, awaiting your beloved with whom you could not here be joined in eternal union. Farewell!' (160–1).

The embraces of the protagonists referred to at all stages of the text (147, 151, 154, 155) are now figuratively extended to *mother* nature. The earthly pleasures are transferred to a spiritual plane of immortality, where an eternal idyll awaits the ill-fated lovers. Thus the tragedy is sublimated aesthetically by the narrator in a spiritually consoling matriarchal ending. Thoughts of a posthumous reunion sustain Mrs L and Julia for the remainder of their solitary lives. Posthumous reunion is one of the topoi of Sentimentalist writing and can be seen, for instance, in Goethe's *Werther* and Karamzin's 'Poor Liza'. The topos could be seen as another indication of the fragment mode: life on earth is seen as but a fragment of a larger more perfect design. It is interesting to note that the past Arcadia is seen as patriarchal, whereas the future is matriarchally described – perhaps an unintentional indication of the shifting gender evaluations during Karamzin's era.

The conclusion of 'Eugene and Julia' reiterates some of the initial imagery: Julia is now as preoccupied with flowers as she was then. Now, however, they grow on Eugene's grave, watered by her tears. Another idyllic topos is introduced: youth rejoicing by the grave, celebrating the arrival of spring. This topos affirms the cyclical force of renewal which informs the idyllic conception of the world.

An epilogue is added: a young man passing through the village hears the sad story, visits Eugene's grave, and in pencil writes an epitaph (in iambic hexameter) on a white stone – later to be properly inscribed on marble: 'This flower of paradise could not blossom forth in this world. It withered, dried, broke off – and was carried back to paradise' (162).[10] The epilogue differs from most Sentimental tales where the narrator will personally take the place of the 'young man' visiting Eugene's grave, after hearing his sad story. The tale as a whole differs from other Sentimental tales, mainly in the fact that the narrator's presence has not yet congealed into the fully developed image it was later to become. The complete lack of conflict is also unusual. The matriarchal set-up is singularly effective in preventing any conceivable sin. Parental obstacles are obviously excluded, since only one parent is involved, and she serves as a single parent for both lovers. Furthermore, she herself has long prepared for the union. Seduction is out of the question, since the two are brought up together according to the same pious morals, and the transformation of brotherly–sisterly love to erotic love is simply a question of age and sexual maturity. The two types of love are completely reconcilable, since Eugene and Julia both are, and are not, siblings. The tale thus eschews the paradox of incest which often lurks in the background for Sentimentalist lovers. In 'Poor Liza', for instance, Erast's ideal of a brotherly–sisterly love is irreconcilable with the erotic feelings that develop, and Erast's dilemma is precisely that he cannot be both brother and husband to Liza. In 'Bornholm Island' the incest taboo is indeed implied as the main obstacle in the love story. In 'Eugene and Julia' the tragedy is, ironically, a result of the positive characteristics of the personages. Extreme happiness is too much for Eugene's highly developed 'delicate' sensitivity, and the idyll is thwarted from the inside, by properties inherent in the idyllic conception.

## 'Poor Liza'

'Poor Liza' is, as Bulich phrased it, Karamzin's 'recollection from the world of Gessner's idylls, brought back to him perhaps by a real story by an old woman in the environs of Paris, but not by a real Russian event'.[11] As has been pointed out by several scholars, the tale is, however, no longer an idyll pure and simple; the very essence of the Golden Age myth and the contemporary literature inspired by it are questioned.[12]

The idyll as reality and as literature is made the theme of a Sentimental tale. The theme of the idyll as reality is centered around Liza. Her reality can be seen as an idyll of the mixed type in Bakhtin's terms. Her father is described as an ideal peasant, much like Frol Silin.[13] Her mother on several occasions describes her life with 'my Ivan' as a perfect love–family idyll, ending only by his death in her arms two years earlier. His death is, in a sense, at the root of Liza's subsequent troubles. Since then, Liza's mother's foremost concern is that Liza recreate the idyll of her own youth by marrying, and thus continuing the idyllic cycle. Liza herself is part of the family idyll, transformed after her father's death by including elements of a labor–craft idyll. Her preoccupations are perfectly within that tradition (picking flowers and fashioning them into bouquets, weaving, knitting). Her second meeting with Erast relates to the idyllic topos of offering drink to a traveller – the fresh milk, the earthenware pot, the careful drying of the glass, are entirely traditional.[14] The mutual love and intimacy between mother and daughter complete Liza's idyllic reality.

The setting of Liza's idyll with its simple hut, its flocks of sheep, shepherds and their reed pipes, its meadows, and groves, matches the idyllic *locus amoenus*. This world is, however, no longer sheltered from the outside: Liza must cross the river to Moscow in order to sell her flowers. She meets Erast, which leads to several lovers' meetings in the idyllic setting, but with one important un-idyllic consequence: Liza's mother is not to be informed. In itself, that is not contrary to the idyll tradition (we are reminded, for example, of Sumarokov's eclogue 'Agnesa'[15]), but it is featured in such a way as to become a major moral issue for Liza, gradually developing into an all-pervasive feeling of guilt. Liza is caught in a dilemma between her mother's pious morality and Erast's love. She does not understand (or at least, does not admit to herself that she does) why the two are incompatible.

Erast's attitude to Liza's mother is ambiguous. On the one hand he likes her, and he particularly likes to listen to the stories she tells of her own life. On the other hand, knowing that she might be suspicious of his intentions towards Liza, he does not want her to know of their relationship. Liza obviously does not understand the necessity for secrecy, but complies with Erast's wishes. Their meetings are kept illicit – after her mother is asleep or away from the hut. Thoughts of her mother, however, lurk in the background of each meeting like the voice of conscience. They make Liza interrupt her third meeting with Erast, and subsequently keep her from following him to the war.

Liza's mother herself sends somewhat contradictory signals to Liza with regards to Erast – inadvertently, since the match between the two is, to her, simply unthinkable and not an issue. On the one hand, she warns Liza about evil city people who might take advantage of a peasant girl. On the other hand, she immediately takes a liking to Erast. Her topics of conversation are interesting: when the three are together, she speaks either of her own husband or of a desired suitor for Liza. She praises Liza's good qualities to Erast. When alone with Liza, her topic is the same, with additional praise for Erast. Indeed, after the mother's first meeting with Erast, she turns to Liza with the intriguing wish that Liza's husband be just like Erast: 'Ah Liza! how kind and good he is! If only your fiancé would be like that!' (237). She, of course, means someone *like* Erast, not Erast himself. At this point (after Liza's second meeting with Erast when she is already attracted to him) Liza objects to her mother's wish: 'Mama! Mama! how could that be? he is a *barin*, and among peasants – ' (237). The rest remains unsaid, as if her mother's statement had further fired Liza's own wishful thinking with regard to Erast. Liza has a sleepless night, and in the morning (before her third meeting with Erast) her thoughts still revolve around the same subject. A pastoral vision of a young shepherd, tending his flock on the river bank, playing his reed pipe, leads Liza to project Erast into the shepherd's place, and to imagine how she would encourage his love if he were in fact a shepherd. She barely has time to dismiss her thoughts as 'A dream! A dream!'[16] when Erast miraculously materializes before her very eyes in a boat on the river. He takes her hand, kisses her, and actually takes the place of the imaginary shepherd–Erast of her thoughts, his actions as idyllic as those of the real shepherd. Liza herself is still so enthralled by her dreams that she is powerless to resist his advances.

Her mother's constant preoccupation with marrying Liza off, and her wish that Liza accept a marriage proposal from a well-to-do peasant, finally precipitate Liza's fall. Liza cannot but reject the suitor despite her mother's tears and worries, and despite the fact that she cannot explain to her mother the real reason for her rejection. To Erast's promise that he will live with her inseparably, 'in the country and in the deep forest as in paradise' (notably *after* her mother's death), Liza objects that Erast cannot be her husband because she is a peasant girl. Yet, even with this awareness of their social differences, Erast's assurance that a 'sensitive, innocent soul' is all that matters, sets Liza at ease. Her dream reality has an irresistible grip on her, and she gives herself to him, heart and soul – and body. Thus Liza acts fully in keeping with idyllic love, and her vague awareness of the non-idyllic outside reality (where social differences do matter) is not fully understood, or is at any rate suppressed. She follows her heart, and places complete trust in Erast, whom she loves for himself, not for his social station. She, furthermore, knows that her mother is fond of Erast, and wants her to marry. The only idyll value she compromises is her intimacy with her mother. After Liza's fall, her main feelings are not guilt for her transgression, but fear of losing Erast and guilt for deceiving her mother. When Erast later leaves her, Liza does not mourn her loss of innocence, but her loss of Erast's love. Her last thoughts before her suicide are of her mother, however, and the fact that she was guilty of betraying her trust.

The topic of the idyll as fiction is centered around Erast, a point to which I shall return below. In brief, Erast is of (un-idyllic) urban gentry background, a habitué of salon society where erotic conquests are as proper as reading the latest idylls and novels. He is caught between a social reality that no longer satisfies him and fictional ideals that he cannot fulfill. From his first meeting with Liza, he is aware of this social reality, conveyed in the text as a vague voice of public opinion which guides his actions no less than do his idyllic readings. He lets Liza go when passers-by stop and laugh at them knowingly (or so the narrator interprets the situation). He knows that his own past behavior would have warranted a salacious interpretation of the situation. He later goes to war not only for the glory, but also because otherwise 'everybody' would have considered him a coward. He also suspects (justly) that Liza's mother would have misread his intentions with regard to Liza, because young men of his class were, in fact, wont to take advantage of peasant girls. The idyllic illusion cannot be sustained in such a society, and must be kept strictly between himself and Liza. It is, from the very beginning, a highly artificial situation. Furthermore, although his generosity to Liza and her mother is genuine, its commercial expression is alien to idyllic values, as is his later marriage for riches. All indications are that while Erast's actions are sincere enough, he is at least subconsciously aware of his own (and his society's) limitations, and is not fully convinced that he can play the parts he has embarked upon.

The narrated events of 'Poor Liza' can thus be summarized as a clash between the idyll world and the outside world. Liza's father dies, and with him the old patriarchal world of the idyll. Liza is caught in a dilemma between a *poor widow* (idyll reality, suspicious of outside reality) and Erast (outside reality in idyllic clothing). Erast is caught in a dilemma between a *rich widow* (outside reality with its social and commercial conventions) and Liza (an idyllic fiction, materialized with a non-fictional eroticism taking its toll). Even on this level, 'Poor Liza' is significantly more complex than anything before it. The complexity does not result from the plot itself, which is simple, not to say trite, but from the problems it poses: the mixture of vice and virtue in each of the personages, the relation between fiction and reality, the complexity of the emotions described, the social, and ultimately ethical questions. This has long been recognized by scholars. Orlov notes the role of Liza's mother.[17] Berkov pleads the case for '*bednyi Erast*'.[18] He points to the final paragraph as a key to a deeper interpretation than the tale has traditionally afforded (the traditional reading held to be sympathetic to Liza and the peasant class, and hostile to Erast and the gentry). On Berkov's view 'the five lines of the epilogue of "Poor Liza" comprise the synopsis of a large psychological tale, whose hero is "poor Erast."' The epilogue referred to by Berkov reads as follows:

Erast was unhappy to the end of his life. After he found out about Liza's fate, he could not be consoled and regarded himself as her murderer. I met him a year before his death. He himself told me this story and took me to Liza's grave. – Now, perhaps, they have already been reconciled! (263–4)

These lines are indeed crucial for an understanding of 'Poor Liza'. They perform the normal epilogue function of extending and summarizing the narrated events, temporally and ethically.[19] Erast, too, is punished: he is unhappy till the end of his days, considering himself Liza's murderer. One might add that he also, indirectly, caused Liza's mother's death, and, no doubt, the unhappiness of his wife, thus having ruined the lives of three women. The important thing, however, is that Erast has since acquired a conscience and sincerely repents his past conduct. Although this cannot bring Liza back, virtue has triumphed, and the libertine streak in Erast is reformed. By telling his story, he is in essence making a confession and is entitled to forgiveness. 'Poor Liza' thus ends with the narrator's forgiveness and his affirming the possibility of an idyll on a spiritual plane, much like the conclusion of 'Eugene and Julia'.

Most importantly for the present purposes, however, the epilogue functions as a postpositive reporting clause, laying bare the complex narrative structure of the tale as a whole. It is revealed as an utterance of a trivocal structure: a personage utterance (Erast, Liza, and Liza's mother speak), Erast's subsequent oral narration–confession to the narrator, and the narrator's written re-narration to the narratee.

The importance of the epilogue in terms of narrative structure has been recognized by Garrard, who correctly points out that 'Liza is seen through the eyes of an admiring narrator, who never knew her. If we follow the frame of the story, he is looking back at her through the eyes of a repentant Erast.' Yet, Garrard's analysis based on this crucial insight is not entirely satisfactory. He faults Karamzin for switching from first person to omniscient narration, for hesitating 'between omniscient narrator, participant, and witness or acquaintance as his mouthpiece', for not providing a steady point of view. He sees the epilogue as a 'belated effort to frame the story and create an epic situation for the narrator'.[20] This analysis, it seems to me, suffers from the 'either/or fallacy' that underlies early point of view approaches: namely, that only a single point of view (be it omniscient, first person, or whatever) can be operative at any one point of a narrative. This excludes any simultaneous bivocality in Bakhtin's sense, and oversimplifies narrative structure. 'Poor Liza' *in its entirety* is told by the first person narrator, and there is no switch in Garrard's sense. The epilogue does, however, reveal the trivocal structure. It explains the account of events accessible only to a participant in the Liza–Erast story. It also explains the idyllic style and the fact that even Liza speaks in a manner unlike the uneducated peasant girl she is. Her speech is filtered through *two* subsequent reports. Only vestiges of her 'autonomous' utterance are left, most notably her (and her mother's) use of the word *barin* to refer to Erast. Similarly, Erast's original utterance is filtered through his own subsequent report and the narrator's final report, which, although in many respects similar to Erast's own direct speech, adds a light irony. Thus, most events are reported bivocally, and the two voices of the narrator and Erast are heard at times as a single voice, at times as two distinct voices. In some cases the narrator adds original reporting in sections compositionally set apart (notably the overture, epilogue, and some asides and digressions). But even when not set apart compositionally, his voice is always present. This is not only a matter of linguistic features; each voice implies a certain evaluation as well. The narrator's evaluation often, but not always, coincides with that of Erast (either as young protagonist or as a more mature and repentant teller). Karamzin cannot be charged with inconsistencies in narrative method, and his method is fully motivated by the triple source of utterance.

In the following, I will try to show that the narrator is one of the most important 'personages' in 'Poor Liza' as a whole. He is precisely a 'fully realized' narrator, and, furthermore, the only entirely positive personage in the tale, its true hero, in a characteristically solipsistic manner. To be sure, I do not wish to belittle the psychological or social interpretations of the tale, but I believe that its full *aesthetic* significance cannot be grasped without a closer look at the 'lucky' narrator. It is to the narrator and his speech event that we must now turn.

Its title already indicates the tale's double focus: both Liza's misfortunes and the narrator's compassionate nature. It is, furthermore, ambiguous in that it could also refer to Liza's economic state; poverty is what leads to her first meeting with Erast and their subsequent seller–buyer relationship. Thus, the first fact we know about the narrator is that he is compassionate to a woman in distress. The same epithet is repeated seven times within the text (229, 230, 242, 255, 257, 262, and 263); six of these refer to Liza, one to her mother. They are uttered by the narrator, by Liza herself, and by the villagers. Notably the epithet is not used by Erast in his directly quoted speech. The reference to the mother as *bednaia vdova* (230) is made in the immediate context of the family's financial state of affairs.[21] It contrasts to Erast's wife, referred to as a *pozhilaia bogataia vdova* (260). The contrast between the two may be seen as part of the major oppositions of the tale: city/country, rich/poor, gentry/peasant, outside world/idyll world. The first reference to *bednaia* Liza after the title serves to reinstate the title at the end of the narrator's overture, and signals the transition to the Liza–Erast story proper, which now resumes. Here the tale is further specified as 'vospominanie o plachevnoi sud'be Lizy, **bednoi** Lizy', amplifying the title's indication of the narrator's emotive involvement both in intonation and in epithets. The other uses of *bednaia* occur in the context of Liza's fears of being deceived by Erast: 'uzheli ty obmanesh' **bednuiu** Lizu' (Liza, 242); after Erast has told her that he has to leave: '*Liubeznyi, milyi Erast! pomni, pomni svoiu bednuiu Lizu*' (Liza, 255, italics original); after she has in fact lost him: 'i Liza, ostavlennaia, **bednaia**, lishilas' chuvstv i pamiati' (narrator, 257); before her suicide: 'skazhi, chto **bednaia** Liza velela potselovat' ee' (Liza, 262); and after her death: '*tam stonet bednaia Liza!*' (villagers, 263, italics original).

It is notable that, in general, the epithets used by the narrator to describe Liza are of an emotive and positively evaluative nature, rather than strictly descriptive (*bednaia, prekrasnaia, liubeznaia, nezhnaia, usluzhlivaia, robkaia, milaia, blednaia, tomnaia, gorestnaia*). Some of them are clearly used in unison with Erast, who uses, e.g., *milaia* and *liubeznaia* in his directly quoted speech as well – a case where the two narrative voices coincide. Furthermore, the narrator at the more emotional moments uses double, and even triple, epithets when he refers to Liza (*prekrasnaia, liubeznaia; blednaia, tomnaia, gorestnaia; ostavlennaia, bednaia*) and thereby particularly emphasizes his own emotive involvement. Interjections, repetitions of her name, special orthography and punctuation, and other rhythmical and intonational means similar to those used in Karamzin's idylls serve the same purpose.

The epithets used by the narrator in reference to the other personages are less effusive (in quantity and in quality). The most frequently used epithet for Erast is the neutral *molodoi*. Liza's mother is most frequently also referred to by age as a *starushka*, but with a greater frequency of positive epithets than in the case of Erast. Only once (except purely descriptively) does the narrator use a double epithet with reference to Erast, and that a negative one apostrophizing Erast at an emotively charged moment as *bezrassudnyi molodoi chelovek!* (247).

Even this cursory survey of the epithets used tells us where the narrator's sympathies lie: Liza and what she stands for are certainly both more positively and more intensely evaluated. That, of course, gives us some idea of what sort of man the narrator himself is.

The first four pages of the tale make up a typical Karamzinian mood-setting overture. Is is a further development of a method already familiar since 'A Promenade'. It provides a wealth of information about the narrator. It is indeed *his* mood that is reflected, and this mood saturates the whole story from beginning to end. The narrator describes his own walks out of the city, and thereby describes both his external and internal landscapes, both his physical settings and habits and his intellectual–emotional make-up. The overture simultaneously provides a synopsis of the Liza–Erast story, thus making that story an integral part of the narrator's external and internal landscapes. Or, conversely, the memory of that concrete story is particularly conducive to intensifying the narrator's awareness of his own emotions, opinions, and character, and is thus especially pleasurable to him. 'Poor Liza' on the most general level, can be seen as a picture of a rather hedonistic narrator, who revels in his own aesthetic sensitivity, which, according to Sentimentalist poetics, is tantamount to his own virtue. Therefore the fact that he can find the most intense pleasure in remembering what, objectively speaking, is a tragic story is not as paradoxical as it may first seem. By fully giving himself up to all his emotions, grief as well as joy, and empathizing with the full range of vicarious experiences (with his own conscience clear), he can experience his own virtue, and everyday objects and events take on an aesthetic aura. 'Poor Liza' is, by this token, the story of the narrator's aesthetic experience of virtue in distress.

The narrator begins by describing himself and his own quest for aesthetic experience. The tense used throughout the overture is the existential present, stressing the fact more than the actual time. The actions are denoted by the imperfective aspect of the verbs, with a stress on their habitual nature. Words such as 'often', 'most often', 'every summer', 'almost always', 'sometimes', and plural time references such as 'gloomy autumn days' are used to the same end: to describe the narrator's *general* habits in a time frame which includes, but which is wider than, the present specific speech event. From the very beginning, the narrator's exceptional nature is stressed: he knows the environs of Moscow better than any other Muscovite, he walks there more frequently than anybody else, and so on. His rural walks have no other aim than to find 'new pleasant places' and 'new beauties in old ones', in other words, they are undertaken solely for aesthetic pleasure.

From the general description of the walks and the general itinerary of pleasant places and beauties, the description turns to the narrator's favorite spot: the hill with the Gothic towers of the Si-nov monastery – a vantage point not unlike other spots for aesthetic enjoyment in Karamzin's idylls. The difference from the idyllic vantage points is that the Si-nov hills open up a wider field of vision, encompassing both pristine idyllic nature (as the views from the high river banks of 'Palemon and Daphnis', 'A Promenade', 'The Countryside', or the setting of 'Night') and a concrete, non-idyllic urban landscape (not just a symbolic ocean as in 'Palemon and Daphnis', nor the bucolic pastoral villages beset by natural disasters in 'The Flood' and 'Frol Silin'). The narrator of 'Poor Liza' thus has a wider world view (both literally and philosophically) than the previous narrators.

The fact that Moscow and some concrete landmarks are introduced does not, as is frequently claimed, imply a realistic description: there is nothing specifically Muscovite in the view itself, nor is it meant to be taken in the guidebook sense.[22] The view is mainly meant to evoke *aesthetic* pleasure. The field of vision is characterized in terms borrowed from the arts: 'images', 'majestic amphitheater', 'grandiose picture', 'sad pictures'.[23] Rothe points out the topoi of other Karamzinian nature descriptions, and comes to the following conclusion:

The landscape is clearly also not realistic. It is a carefully structured description whose reference to the framing round of the amphitheater is sufficiently clear. Under Karamzin's pen, every landscape looks the same as Moscow on the Moscow River looks here, whether it is located on the Thames, the Saône, or the Elbe. A landscape which did not offer him this structural possibility, did not become the subject of his literary art.[24]

The initial description is predominantly visual, and it moves from right to left, from near to far, concentrically expanding the narrator's physical setting. This is signalled by deictic markers such as 'on the right side', 'below', 'on the other side', 'over there', 'further', 'further still', 'in the distance'. These indicators are understandable to the narratee only if he shares the narrator's vantage point. The demonstrative deictic 'there' and 'here' anaphorically repeated in the third paragraph of the overture, similarly indicate a narratee who can follow the pointing motions of the narrator.

The description is divided between unidyllic 'culture' and idyllic 'nature': on the one end, far right, Moscow; in the middle, below, fields, a river, a grove of oaks, ancient elms; further on, the Danilov monastery, and further yet, Sparrow hills (i.e. all the idyllic elements, including the typical borders: a river and hills), and on the far left again, 'culture': Kolomenskoe with its tall manor.

It is interesting to see how the setting is described. Moscow is an *uzhasnaia gromada domov i tserkvei*, and is characterized by superlatives (*gromada, velichestvennaia, velikolepnaia, beschislennye*). The predominant color is gold. It is, furthermore, characterized as *alchnaia Moskva*, nourished by the entire fertile Russian empire, a domain of magnificent dimensions, huge quantities, riches, gold, and hunger or even greed. The populace does not figure in the picture, except indirectly – through houses and churches which imply people. The picture is thus one of awesome and impersonal external grandeur. The Moscow River is the dividing line. Its urban, commercial aspect is evoked by large boats laden with goods for the greedy city; the bucolic aspect of nature is indicated by the light oars of fishermen in rowboats.

Idyllic nature is described (as expected) on a smaller scale: the topography is quite detailed, down to the multi-colored flowers, the description abounding in diminutive forms. It is also more personal and more animated, including living beings: herds grazing, young shepherds singing under trees. The narrator is closer to the idyll both physically and 'sympathetically'. Such then is the picture of the narrator's aesthetic view of summer in general, the time of year mentioned twice (225 and 226).

The most interesting fact about this part of the overture is its complete temporal, spatial, axiological, and thematic coincidence with the Liza–Erast story. It is indeed the amphitheater where the narrated events will be staged. The narrated events occur over an entire summer. The narrator's initial vision covers the same territory as does the story, and, furthermore, does so in the same sequence: Moscow (Liza's and Erast's first meeting), the flowering *luga* (their second meeting in Liza's home, situated in the midst of the fields, *sredi zelenogo luga*), the river with its boats (their third meeting, when Erast arrives in a rowboat), the groves (most of their subsequent meetings), the city (their final meeting).

Thematically and acoustically, this part of the overture also outlines the major developments of the Liza–Erast story. The Erast theme is linked to Moscow. His final appearance in a *velichestvennaia kareta*, his living quarters, the *ogromnyi dom* with its *kabinet*, the **gold** of the ten **imperials**, cannot but recall (in terms of lexicon, sound, and sense) the general *velikolepnaia kartina*, the *uzhasnaia gromada domov*, the **golden** color, the *Rossiiskaia Imperiia*, of the overture. Similarly, Erast's arrival in a **rowboat** on the Moscow **river**, the *shum vesel* and the *lodka* containing Erast, cannot but recall the narrator's initial view of the *prozrachnaia reka, volnuemaia legkimi veslami rybachikh lodok, ili shumiashchei*. Furthermore, both the 'greedy' and the commercial aspects of boats carrying goods to the *alchnaia Moskva* foreshadows Erast (who 'thought only about his own pleasure', who repeatedly stated his wish to be the only buyer of all of Liza's wares, and who finally paid her off and married a widow for her riches) and the trips to Moscow by Liza, laden with flowers and craft items. Thus Erast as protagonist in the Liza–Erast story is only a singulative instance of the narrator's general perception of the world.

The Liza theme, besides her role as victim of urban commercialism, is evoked by the idyll, by 'nature' in the overture. Her flowers, her pastoral vision of a single shepherd, a single flock, and her dream, are already present in plural form in the overture. Furthermore, like the shepherds who sang *prostye unylye pesni*, in the overture, Liza herself *tikhim golosom pela zhalobnye pesni* (234). If we scrutinize the third paragraph of the overture, we find an ever stronger evocation of Liza's and her mother's tragedy. This paragraph consists of a more particular excursus into the narrator's internal landscapes in spring and in autumn in a close-up of the same locale on the Si-nov hill. The Liza–Erast story begins in spring and ends in autumn in the nearby spatial setting. The overture now turns to autumn and the narrator's sorrowful mood evoked by meteorological conditions (*mrachnye dni oseni; strashno voiut* **vetry**), the *opustevshii monastyr'*, and the overgrown **graves**. He visits this setting specifically to *gorevat' vmeste s Prirodoiu* and to listen to the *glukhoi ston vremen* which makes his heart shiver. In the end of the Liza–Erast story, Liza's **grave** is near a pond *pod* **mrachnym dubom**, and their hut **opustela**. In it *voet veter*, and the villagers believe that *tam* **stonet** *bednaia Liza*. The parallelism to the overture is striking, and Liza's tragedy is clearly part of a larger set of analogous motifs which provoke the narrator's melancholy pleasure.

The rest of the third paragraph is taken up by pictures formed in the narrator's imagination. The setting conjures up the image of an old monk, whose piety, constant prayers, and feelings of illness and impending death run parallel to Liza's mother, both thematically and lexically. The next image is that of a young monk *s* **blednym** *litsem, s* **tomnym** *vzorom*, who from within his lonely cell watches joyous nature without being able to participate in that joy, and who dies a premature death. This imagery is very similar to the description of Liza and her premature death, her inability to participate in nature's joy without Erast at her side (especially 239–40), down to an identity in epithets used to describe Liza during her final autumn as **blednaia, tomnaia** *gorestnaia podruga* (256).

The pictures on the monastery gates (showing miracles that had occurred in the monastery, such as **fishes** falling from the sky to feed the inhabitants, and the image of the Mother-of-God setting the enemy to flight) can be associated with Liza's hope for a miraculous transformation of Erast into a shepherd (further strengthened by the analogy between Erast and **fishermen** in rowboats). Erast's generous payments for Liza's wares also miraculously alleviate Liza's and her mother's poverty, and Liza's suitors are turned away as was the enemy. The thought of the 'sad history of the fatherland', of those times when Tatars and Lithuanians with fire and sword ravaged the environs of the capital, and the *neshchast-naia Moskva, kak bezzashchitnaia vdovitsa* expected help from

God, are evocative of the ravished Liza and her defenseless widowed mother. The fire and sword can be seen as analogous to Erast's actions in love and war.

The rising–falling emotional curve of Liza's love story echoes that of the overture. Both initially stress the pleasurable and the joyous, and both end on a sad note. The same rhythmic and intonational means (coupled with lexicon, syntax, and semantics) of conveying emotive involvement and response on the part of the narrator run through both the overture and the Liza–Erast story, the latter filling in all the nuances and subtle shifts as elaborations on the general curve of the overture. The means are the same as for the idylls and trifles, with the difference that 'Poor Liza' manages to sustain the emotive modulations for over thirty pages of text – that in itself a feat – while the idylls and trifles are significantly shorter. The concentration of devices is also quite amazing – Brang, for example, counts over sixty anaphorical constructions, many of which are single, but several of which are double or even triple.[25]

Thus the general physical panoramic view, the more detailed close-up imaginary view, and the still more particular Liza–Erast story combine into an increasingly detailed map of the narrator's aesthetic response.

The fourth paragraph of the overture both summarizes the narrator's experience and serves as a transition from the general to the particulars of the Liza–Erast story. The transition is facilitated by the identity in chronotope of the speech event and the narrated event, and is a logical culmination of the gradual progression from general to particular. The sad fate of poor Liza is revealed as that memory which most often attracts the narrator to the locale of the Si-nov hills. It is clear that the Liza–Erast story is an *aesthetic object* among other such objects. In light of this, one wonders why Garrard is 'first led to believe that the narrator probably took part in the events'.[26] The events of the Liza–Erast story are equated with the fates of an old monk, a young monk, the history of the fatherland, and the like, as 'objects that move my heart and make me shed tears of tender grief' (229). All these events are clearly significant to the narrator as *vicarious* experiences, which he likes to relive emotively and aesthetically. The narrator, in typical Sentimentalist fashion, is thus first and foremost described as an active, imaginative perceiver of his surroundings, fully responding with heart and mind. It is precisely the recognition of his own capacities to respond aesthetically (and thus also ethically) to nature, to culture, to actual pictures on the monastery gates, to imaginary historical events, and to an actual recollection by Erast, that gives him pleasure. Thus it is also puzzling that Garrard is 'disturbed by his [the narrator's] effusiveness' and wonders why the narrator 'feels so strongly about the fate of "poor" Liza'.[27] The narrator himself, in no uncertain terms answers these questions: 'Ah! I love those objects that move my heart' – the aesthetic raison d'être of *all* Sentimentalists. Besides the objects and events that provoke the full range of emotions, those emotions themselves, the resulting pleasure in the narrator, and the narrator himself must thus be included in a list of topics of 'Poor Liza' as a whole.

The narratee also strongly figures in the text as part of the narrator's reality, as a close friend standing by his side, following his eyes, his pointing finger, and co-experiencing his emotions. The direct addresses to the narratee within the story, and the references to, and omissions of, 'that which is obvious to everyone', further maintain the illusion of a close relationship between narrator and narratee. The aim of the Sentimentalist author, as we have seen, is to move his reader to full co-experience of artistic creation. Since the beautiful is equated with the good, such co-experience will also instill in the reader virtuous thoughts, emotions, and actions. The reader is featured within the text as a narratee, and the narrator himself is also often featured as a perceiver or narratee. That the readers of Karamzin's time fully identified with the created image of narrators/narratees is evident from the pilgrimages to 'Lizin prud' – art was thus projected into real life. Interestingly enough, there were no actual Liza-suicides in Russia. As opposed to the German readers of *Werther,* who re-enacted a personage-experience (i.e., that of Werther as a personage, not as I-narrator), the Russian readers re-enacted the narrator's experience of the story – a testimony to the success and the importance of Karamzin's image of narrator.

The personages in Sentimental tales are, as we have seen, often sensitive 'clones' of the narrator–narratee. 'Poor Liza' is no exception. The narrator's aesthetic 'joy-in-tears', for instance, is echoed by Liza. After Erast announces that he is leaving, he tells Liza that he does not want her to cry without him. Liza, in turn, accuses him of cruelty for wanting to deprive her even of this *joy.*[28] Erast's reaction of unfeigned *pleasure* to Liza's mother's tales about her

late husband and his sad demise is perhaps an even more poignant
example of a personage who, like the narrator, responds with joy to
vicarious grief.[29]

The narrator thus presents himself directly in the overture and
indirectly, as mirrored both in narratee and personages. He also
provides abundant information about himself in his retelling of the
Liza–Erast story. His own emotions, attitudes, opinions, and
evaluations of events and personages are consistently featured
together with the facts of the story. He frequently reveals his own
conception of personages and events (factual and modal) in motivations qualified by 'perhaps', 'in fact', and similar expressions.
Other motivations are aphoristically phrased and introduced by the
causal conjunctions 'for' or 'because', and expressed in an existential present tense, notably the famous motivation for Liza's
mother's tears, 'for even peasant women know how to love' (230) –
the actions thereby explicitly demonstrating the narrator's worldview. His emotional involvement in the vicarious events is correlated with the plot. The emotional peaks, besides being described
by all the 'poetic' devices of rhythmic prose (modulated by intonation, tempo, sound quality), also elicit the narrator's apostrophe
to personages and narratee, his exclamations, benedictions,
rhetorical questions, elliptical emoting, and the like. As an
example of how such a peak moment is rendered, consider the
famous passage describing Liza's loss of innocence:

> Она бросилась в его об ъятия –
> и в сей час надлежало погибнуть непорочности ! –
> Эраст чувствовал необыкновенное волнение в крови своей –
> никогда Лиза не казалась ему столь прелестною –
> никогда ласки ее не трогали его так сильно –
> никогда ее поцелуи не были столь пламенны –
> она ничего не знала,
> ничего не подозревала,
> ничего не боялясь –
> мрак вечера питал желания –
> ни одной звездочки не сияло на небе –
> никакой луч не мог осветить заблуждения –
> Эраст чувствует в сее трепет –
> Лиза также,
> не зная, от чего –
> не зная, что с нею делается . . .
> Ах Лиза, Лиза!
> где мать твоя ? [this line was deleted from later editions]

Где Ангел хранитель твой?
Где – твоя невинность?
(250, line arrangement added)

(She threw herself in his embraces – / and at this hour virtue was to perish! – / Erast felt an unusual agitation in his blood – / never did Liza seem to him as charming – / never did her caresses move him so strongly – / never were her kisses as ardent – / she knew nothing, / nothing did she suspect, / nothing made her afraid – / the darkness of evening fed desires – / not a single starlet shone in the sky – / no ray could shed light on the delusion – / Erast feels a tremble – / Liza also, / not knowing from what – / not knowing what is happening to her . . . / Ah Liza, Liza! / where is your mother? / Where is your Angel protector? / where – is your innocence?)

The devices used are the same as in the earlier idylls and trifles, but significantly more concentrated – even as emotional peaks go. The passage is framed by exclamatory evaluation–emotion, and within the frame there is a single sentence (or rather, a Karamzinian *period*) with anaphorically structured and syntactically parallel and partly synonymous clauses, occasionally with inversions (*laski ee – ee potselui*) and a general gradatio effect corresponding to the heightened emotions (*Liza – laski ee – ee potselui; ne znala – ne podozrevala – ne boialas'; mat' tvoia – Angel khranitel' tvoi – tvoia nevinnost'*). The clauses are expressively set apart with dashes and commas, and the *period* ends elliptically. The ellipsis and the repetition double the sense of inexpressibility and inexplicability of the strong emotions, in addition to stressing Liza's innocence. The erotic climax is thus conveyed by highly emotional dialogical means. The shift in tense from the past of narrated events to the present (*Erast chuvstvuet*) is almost imperceptible and suggests a mounting immediacy, as if the narrator (and narratee) were present. The narrator's introductory and concluding exclamations and questions not only confirm Liza's loss of innocence, but also inform us of the narrator's own attitudes to the event (labelled *zabluzhdenie*), and convey his condolences.

Seen in their proper temporal framework, Karamzin's erotic scenes are described with a great deal of finesse and psychological acuity – something that was sorely lacking in the pathetic, moralistic descriptions of similar scenes in previous prose fiction.[30] The narrator in describing Liza's fall voices a rather conventional moral with an appeal to the same precepts as those expressed by Liza's mother. He lightly censures Liza for forgetting these principles and her mother (*Gde mat' tvoia?*). The passage cited is set apart from the rest of the story as the only occasion when Liza's mother does not interfere (in one way or another) in Liza's relationship with Erast. The narrator's evaluations are made less obtrusive through various means of indirection. Frequently they are addressed to the personages themselves. Thus, for instance, he evaluates Erast's brotherly intentions towards Liza with a gently chiding apostrophe: 'Foolish young man! do you know your own heart? Can you always answer for your movements? Is reason always tsar over your emotions?' (247). As in the previous example, direct moralizing is eschewed in favor of paternal advice in the dialogical form of questions. Erast and Liza are partly absolved from guilt. There are indeed few sections where the narrator turns direct moralist. Even the most moralizing passage ('the fulfillment of *all* desires is the most dangerous test for love', 252) is prefaced dialogically as a truism already familiar to the narratee: 'whosoever knows his own heart, will agree with me that [ . . . ]'. The narrator does not presume to teach his narratee, but again assumes a narratee cut from the same cloth as he himself. In fact, Erast, too, is presented as acting just like a youthful narrator or narratee might have acted in the same situation, and his waning love for Liza is made a rather universal phenomenon. Finally, even Erast's basest behavior does not elicit direct moralizing. On the contrary, it elicits an apologia for the *narrator's* own inability to condemn Erast, accompanied by the impotent tears typical of the Sensitive person in his contemplation of human distress: 'My heart bleeds at this minute. I forget the man in Erast – I am ready to curse him – but my tongue does not move – I look at the sky, and a tear rolls down my face. Ah! why am I not writing a novel but a sad true story!' (260). This outburst reveals the narrator as author and his subtle polemics with the novels of the era. By pronouncing himself physically incapable of cursing Erast, he implicitly distances himself from the overt didacticism and moralizing so typical in the literature of the era. The point of the tale cannot simply be reduced to a 'moral' condemning promiscuity, but includes an analysis of the narrator's own emotional and professional response to the events.

The narrator, in his authorial function of control of the whole, is revealed through various discourse-deictic devices, such as the use of the verisimilitude topos in the passage cited ('Ah! why am I not writing a novel but a sad true story!'), the inexpressibility topos ('I throw down my brush, I will say only that'), the timing of the formal introduction of Erast after he has already appeared as a personage ('Now the reader ought to know'), and the subsequent resumption of the story ('Let us return to Liza'), as well as the disclosure in the epilogue of his source. Foreshadowings (another device marking narrator) of the tragic ending, already present in the overture, are also frequent within the Liza–Erast story itself, not least in the all-pervasive symbolism. Liza's business of selling flowers is perhaps the most obvious symbol: the fate of her flowers is like that of her virtue, picking flowers being a traditional euphemism for sexual liberties. The bouquet Erast does not buy is thrown in the river, metonymically foreshadowing Liza's suicide in the pond.

Although the narrator's voice frequently coincides with that of a repentant Erast–narrator, his own voice, divergent from Erast's, is also quite evident in his telling. Erast as a narrator is not only his source, but also a personage in a double temporal and ethical sense. The narrator sees Erast from a vantage point more encompassing than Erast's and is thus, in Bakhtin's terms, able to 'finalize' Erast into an aesthetic image, seeing both Erast's range of vision (*krugozor*) and his full surroundings (*okruzhenie*).[31] He describes and evaluates Erast's externals and his life as a whole, including his death, in a way not possible for Erast himself. An important part of this *okruzhenie* is ironical. Irony is one of the major means whereby the narrator judges Erast's behavior in general and another avenue leading to an image of the narrator. He judges Erast's betrayal of Liza by answering his own rhetorical question (or, if one will, a projected narratee question), 'And thus did Erast deceive Liza having told her that he will join the army?' (260), with a firm 'No, he actually was in the army, but instead of fighting with the enemy, he played cards and lost all his estate.' This is followed by an explanation of how he came to marry, and concludes with another question 'But can all this exonerate him?' The passage is marked by irony, first because card playing instead of fighting for one's fatherland is certainly as bad an offense as lying, second, because Erast's lying or not lying is not the main issue. His real betrayal lies in abandoning his 'true love'. The irony of Erast's commercial transaction of paying Liza the ten imperials (and what amounts to selling himself to the rich widow) is that in doing so he follows one of the basic precepts of Liza and her mother: not accepting something for nothing. The ultimate irony is, of course, that Liza and her mother, despite their moral convictions, are punished. That the story is nevertheless strongly moral can be seen from the epilogue where the narrator (like Liza's mother earlier) subscribes to the notion that virtue is rewarded in the afterlife; true virtue is thus seen as a spiritual quality.

Irony is also displayed by the narrator in his evaluation of Erast's reading matter: idylls and novels. The idyll, as we have seen, enters 'Poor Liza' in two important ways: as reality (centered around Liza) and as literature (centered around Erast). Leaving aside the idyll as reality, let us now turn to the idyll as fiction and look closer at the narrator's irony with regard to that literary genre. Erast is an avid reader of idylls and novels, and, as we have seen, an equally avid listener to Liza's mother's idyllic recollections. Liza steps into his life like an image from his books. He eagerly grasps the opportunity to cure his boredom with the more sublime pleasures of nature and its 'pure joys', which he knows only from idylls and novels. He wants to pride himself on Platonic love, pure enjoyment of nature, simple pleasures, good, unselfish deeds, and generosity, all qualities that we have seen repeatedly in the idyllic hero. In other words, Erast wants to live an idyllic fiction, ultimately an egoistic desire to see his own altruism. As the narrator expresses it, 'Erast delighted in his shepherdess – so he called Liza – and, seeing how much she loved him, *he seemed all the more amiable to himself*' (247, emphasis added). His idyllic intentions weaken when he finds out that he cannot live up to his ideals and begins to harbor erotic feelings toward Liza, feelings 'which he could not *take pride in* and which were no longer new to him' (252). Still, he maintains the idyllic topos for a while: for example, he promises an Arcadian future 'in the deep forest'. A concrete marriage proposal would have been too prosaic for his poetic vision.

The war provides a convenient excuse for Erast to leave Liza while continuing to live according to literary models. It fires his imagination anew. Erast, still caught up in a world of fiction, sees himself as an epic hero, valorously defending his fatherland while winning for himself honor and glory. His idyllic vision becomes fused with the values of the novels he has read (honor, glory, great deeds in battle, death for the fatherland – values which, as we have seen, contradict the small scale idyll values). When he has failed both as an idyllic and an epic hero, he finally reverts to his old ways, dismisses Liza 'with a sigh', and cruelly pays her off. His idyll with Liza turns into another erotic conquest. His epic plans for the war turn into another spree at the card tables.

The Liza–Erast story is couched in the diction of idylls and romances, both the direct speech of the personages and the narration itself. At times the narrator directly acknowledges Erast as the source of the idyllic diction. For example, when he refers to Liza as a shepherdess, he provides a gloss in his own voice: 'so he called Liza', thereby referring the endearing sobriquet to Erast. The description of their innocent love teems with idyllic clichés: Zephyrs and the hands of the 'dear friend' playing with Liza's hair, the presence of 'chaste and bashful Cynthia', and so on, the narrator and Erast both following idyllic tradition. Erast's direct speech to Liza is equally cliché-ridden. The *idyll* is particularly evident in his promises of future happiness in the deep forest, the value of a pure innocent soul, and the like. The *novel* is particularly evident in the description of his plans for the war. Both instances are ironically revealed as style without substance, in that they so blatantly clash with Erast's actions. The idyllic coloring of Erast's speech decreases with the waning of his attraction to Liza. Thus his last dialogue with her is wholly unidyllic and as businesslike as his base transaction itself.[32]

Sometimes the irony is expressed in parenthetical commentary on Erast's thoughts or words. For example, seeing Liza as the personification of idyllic purity, Erast decided to leave high society 'at least for the time being', as the narrator ironically interjects. The section most clearly attributable to the narrator and most indicative of his irony with regard to Erast as a reader of literature, is contained in his formal introduction of Erast to the narratee (238) – an introduction which Erast himself obviously did not include in his narration, in person, to the narrator. Liza's beauty is said to have made a deep impression on Erast, a statement immediately followed by a description of Erast's readings, thus implying a causal relationship:

He used to read novels, idylls; had a fairly vivid imagination, and often mentally transported himself to those times (real or unreal) when, according to the description of Poets, all people wandered carefree on meadows, bathed in pure springs, kissed like turtle doves, rested under rose and myrtle, and passed all their days in happy idleness. It seemed to him, that he had found in Liza what his heart had long been seeking. 'Nature beckons me to its embraces, to its pure joys' – he thought, and decided – at least for the time being – to leave high society.(238–9)

The irony of this passage is more complex than has generally been recognized.[33] To be sure, it is directed against the idylls and novels, their mannerism, as well as their unreal subject matter. However, the description of the idylls also reads like a synopsis of Karamzin's idylls. Karamzin, the author, is not exempt from this narrator's irony. Furthermore, the narrator's own daily activities, as described in the overture, are quite close to those of people who *bespechno* **guliali po lugam** [ . . . ] *i v shchastlivoi prazdnosti vse dni svoi provozhdali* (compare the overture's *nikto bolee moego ne* **brodit peshkom**, *bez plana, bez tseli – kuda glaza gladiat – po lugam i poliam, po roshcham i kustochkam*). The irony is thus directed, at least partly, against the narrator himself, as well as against other Karamzinian narrators, such as the leisurely promenaders of 'A Promenade' and 'The Countryside'. Indeed, Erast to a certain extent replicates the narrator's quest for idyllic beauty in the Moscow environs, away from the city.

One of the differences between the narrator and Erast is that while Erast tries to transform art into life, the narrator transforms life into art. The latter succeeds, the former fails. The egocentric aim of both is pleasure, although in one case the pleasure is aesthetic, in the other it is largely physical. The narrator's perspective is also wider, encompassing both idyllic and unidyllic vistas, a perspective Erast could see only in retrospect. The narrator's wider, more balanced perspective is reflected in his style. The most overt clichés are lacking in the sections where the narrator speaks in his own voice only. Erast's and other idyllists' mannerisms are the main target of the irony, directed at the rift between idyllic clichés and a truly aesthetic idyllic vision. Erast is faulted for his failure as a Sentimentalist reader, and the idyllists, similarly for a failure in true aesthetic creation, which must proceed from inner conviction, not ornate external form. Part of the blame is thus placed on the authors of mannered literature. Erast's main tragedy is that he fails in perceiving literature, as well as reality, aesthetically and thus also ethically. He tries to be an idyllic hero and an epic hero only according to the formal recipe of the idylls and novels. The distance between the 'lucky narrator' and 'poor Erast' as personage in the Liza–Erast story is thus largely aesthetic. It is the distance between the ideal Sentimentalist reader and a naive reader. The distance between the narrator and Erast as (secondary) narrator is smaller, and Erast's subsequent realization that his fiction has been serious reality from Liza's point of view, explains why the narrator cannot condemn him outright.

To summarize, there is more to 'Poor Liza' than the double tragedy of Liza and Erast. In the image of the narrator Karamzin presents the ideal of the Sensitive Person, lucky enough to be endowed with the full arsenal of emotional and artistic sensibilities. These sensibilities allow him to respond fully to everything, from the Moscow environs to the tragedy of Liza and Erast. He is, in other words, the ideal Sentimentalist reader of texts in the wide sense. In this respect he is presented as superior to Erast. The same sensibilities allow him to transform both the Moscow environs and the fates of Liza and Erast into aesthetic objects. This makes him the ideal Sentimentalist author. Since these aesthetic sensibilities are equated with virtue in the Sentimentalist canon (consider, once more, Karamzin's famous dicta: 'A bad person cannot be a good author' and 'Bad people don't even read novels'), the narrator ultimately presents himself as the ideal Sensitive Person. Furthermore, he derives immense pleasure from the realization that he himself possesses all the requisite sensibilities and from his experiences of artistic response and creation. The light irony – and especially self-irony contained in the subtle literary polemic discernible as another dimension of the story – at least partly mitigates the self-congratulatory stance of the lucky narrator as a paragon of Sentimentalist virtue.

## 'Sierra-Morena'

'Sierra-Morena' was originally editorially subtitled an 'Elegiac Fragment from the Papers of N', a subtitle omitted in later editions.[34] It appeared in the second book of *Aglaia* as the first of thirteen numbered items, all of which were written (although not signed) by Karamzin himself, directly following a poetic prose dedication to Pleshcheeva, 'To the friend of my heart, the only one, the priceless one.' The dedication sets the tone for the almanac as a whole: it voices a general disenchantment with the world at large, but, significantly, with a consoling personal framework to counteract the pessimism. All the other works in the volume stress some positive aspects of life (like the dedication): close friendship or love, the power to create imaginary ideal worlds, the healing powers of nature, God, and so on. In this respect the dedication is

programmatic, stressing positive aspects as the ultimately significant reality despite the sad general situation. The following lines
from the dedication are particularly pertinent:

> We live in a sad world; but whoever has a friend
> fall down on your knees, and thank the Omnipresent one!
> We live in a sad world, where innocence often suffers,
> where virtue often perishes; but man has a consolation – to love!
> Sweet consolation! . . . to love one's friend, to love
> virtue! . . . to love, and to feel that we love![35]

The existence of evil in the world at large is ever more pervasively felt as a topic in Karamzin's works, and the idyllic aspects
are less and less featured. Nevertheless, the small world of a
personal idyll of either intimate relationships with a small circle of
friends in some sheltered corner of the world, or communion with
God or nature, is the cure advocated in theme as well as in
structural implementation. Ultimately, the idyll is reduced to an
exclusively internal world of imagination. Auto-communication is
featured (for instance, in 'Athenian Life' ['Afinskaia zhizn'']) as a
measure preventing the outside evil from penetrating the sensitive
self. Thus one's thoughts, emotions, and imagination make up the
last bastion affirming idyllic values despite the outside horrors.

   'Sierra-Morena' differs from all the other *Aglaia* works in that
this consoling framework is lacking. Its loss is indeed part of the
theme of the work. The tale is a description of the fall of the idyll. It
is perhaps this difference which prompted Karamzin, the author–
editor, to add the subtitle, attributing the unmitigated pessimism to
N, and stressing the fact that it is a fragment, not the entire picture,
which, one might speculate, would feature some positive consolation to the love tragedy. But that is left for the narratee to
ponder, as in the case of all such 'complete fragments'. In this case,
the general context of *Aglaia*, leading from N to the editor, would
seem to set the narratee on the path to a positive view of the greater
whole of which 'Sierra-Morena' is a fragment. The tale is fragmentary in a different respect, as well. It poses problems and paradoxes
which it does not resolve. One such problem is the question of guilt
and punishment which looms particularly large behind the narration of events. All three personages are in one sense innocent,
and in a different sense guilty. Yet all are punished, rightly or
wrongly.[36] We might also note that it is a positive quality – an
excessive capacity for love – which ultimately leads to the tragedy.

In this sense 'Sierra-Morena' is akin to 'Eugene and Julia'. The fragment is 'complete' in the sense that the plot is fully developed.

As it stands, 'Sierra-Morena' describes the narrator's (N's) path from the first stirrings of love to the 'happiest minute' of his life (coinciding roughly with the mid-point of the text) to total alienation and utter existential despair (the present state of the narrator). It can be seen as a double elegy: that of Elvira (mourning the loss of her beloved Alonzo, temporarily relieved by her love for the narrator) and that of the narrator (mourning the loss of his beloved Elvira). The first love tragedy both enables the second to take place and is at the same time, the cause of its tragic ending.

Structurally, 'Sierra-Morena' is a compression of the triple utterance structure. The present account in 'Sierra-Morena' is the direct consequence (without the temporal ellipsis of tales such as 'Liodor' and 'Bornholm Island') of the past personal experience. The present situation adds no new intimate narratees–friends, only mute Elements, and can, in fact, be described as non-communication. The tale is presented simply as part of the papers of N, addressed to no one in particular. Notably, there are no direct apostrophes to specific listeners or readers (like those to Aglaia or the dear friends), except the concluding apostrophes to 'the cold world', 'mad creatures, called men', and 'silent night – eternal peace – holy silence', the last of which in particular stresses non-communication rather than communication.

As for the past re-experience of the vicarious love story, N hears the Elvira–Alonzo story from Elvira herself and he re-narrates its main events and emotions in his text in his own words, inserted when his own N–Elvira story so requires, not strictly chronologically as a cohesive story. His performance as narratee goes far beyond Sentimentalist requirements for sympathetic involvement, and develops into a fullblown personal romance with the teller. Thus the vicarious love story develops organically into the narrator's personal love story. The main focus of 'Sierra-Morena' is his own love idyll *manqué*. As in most other Sentimental tales, the narrator is a traveller. But even his itinerary is determined by the love plot.

The structure of 'Sierra-Morena' is thus dominated by the continuous rising–falling curve of the narrator's moods from the immediate past to the present.[37] The tale's most interesting feature for the present analysis is the transformation of the idyll chronotope into its opposite.

Elvira's elegy takes place within the perfect idyllic setting of Southern Spain, in 'flowering Andalusia', with the rustle of palm trees, the fragrance of myrtle groves, the slow flowing waters of the Guadalquivir, and a rosemary-covered mountain, the Sierra-Morena. Elvira is introduced after her beloved Alonzo has perished at sea (outside the idyll), and she has erected a marble monument where she mourns his demise (we are particularly reminded of 'Palemon and Daphnis'). Elvira is introduced as the personification of beauty in sorrow (the de-adjectival noun *Prek-rasnaia* [Lovely one] is the first reference to her), standing in a typical sentimental pose next to the monument, leaning on it with her lily-white hand, her light-brown hair let down and falling on the black marble. The 'touching charms' of 'tender Elvira' are enhanced for the enraptured N by the morning sun. She has barely survived the blow, but now her extreme despair has turned into a 'quiet grief and languor', and N's sympathetic response further alleviates her sorrow and gradually leads to friendship and finally love. She benefits from the idyllic cure for outside evils, already advocated in most of the idylls and trifles. N reacts with the whole arsenal of Sentimentalist narratee responses: 'I mixed my tears with hers. She saw in my eyes a reflection of her grief, in the feelings of my heart she recognized her own feelings' (8).

He kisses her hand and performs as the sympathetic listener (secondary narratee) to her cathartic reminiscences about Alonzo and her own emotions. N's re-narration of her story is interesting in that it includes a summary of a typical Sentimental tale with its solipsistic focus on the teller and particularly on her inner states:

Elvira would speak to me about her unforgettable Alonzo, she would describe the beauty of his soul, her own love, her ecstasies, her bliss, and then her despair, pain, grief, and finally – the consolation, the comfort her heart found in dear friendship. (9)

Their friendship intensifies during typical Sentimental prom-enades along the shores of the river near Alonzo's monument, in silence, sighing in unison. 'Our hearts alone were speaking', against the background of the murmuring waters – an obvious reference to the eloquence of silence as opposed to human language, a variation on the inexpressibility topos. A night walk is particularly pleasant, in that the shadows of night 'drew our hearts together, they hid Elvira from all of Nature – and I delighted in her presence all the more vividly, in an all the more concentrated fashion' (11). The night experience can be seen as a variation on the Wieland-theme voiced already in 'A Promenade', and again in 'Liodor' and 'Bornholm Island', as we shall see. The first half of 'Sierra-Morena' ends in mutual love and wedding plans, and Elvira's elegy is transformed into a new love idyll.

The idyllic traits are obvious, but a closer reading reveals, I believe, a basically un-idyllic worldview. This can be seen already in the initial description of the setting, where many of the idyllic elements are characterized in terms usually linked to the outside world: *shumiat* (usually the sound of a hostile sea), *gordye* (pride is not a quality ranked high on the idyll scale) – both applied here to palm trees. The river is magnificent (*velikolepnyi*), and flows slowly – its majestic size and movement differ from the babbling brooks and small rivulets usually encountered. The Sierra-Morena is the largest mountain range in Southern Spain, and its color is stressed (the name is translated as *Black* Mountain in a footnote, drawing attention to its color and further enhancing the importance of the mountain, already conferred on it by the title). Neither aspect is typical of the miniaturization and the vivid color schemes of the idylls. The range of colors is much more restrained than was the case in the idylls and is more systematically integrated with the love plot than we have seen before.

The color scheme in 'Sierra-Morena' is black, white, and red, as well as nuances of these colors (light brown, rose, crimson, gray, dark, pale). One is struck particularly by the absence of greens and yellows, prominent in both idylls and Sentimental tales. Black is the dominant color, linked to the mountain, the marble monument to Alonzo, rock in general, Alonzo himself when he reappears, the sky at night, the monastery, and earth. Black and darkness recur throughout the tale. White is linked mainly to Alonzo's urn, Elvira's hands as she leans on his monument, and the lilies on the altar for the wedding ceremony – a symbol of Elvira's two commitments. Red is perhaps the most interesting color: it is part of the motif of Elvira's growing love for N, and is marked by its total absence in the second half of 'Sierra-Morena'. It occurs in conjunction with imagery of warmth and fire (N's and Elvira's love, heavenly fire, lightning and thunder), imagery which is also prominent in the first half and which is replaced by cold, dark, and death in the second. The image of blood is related to the red color and to warmth, and is linked to passionate feelings in each personage.

From the very first mention of the Guadalquivir, water imagery plays an important role, both as an elemental force and on a human level, as tears. Geographically the two halves of the tale contrast as the warm luscious South and the cold North, with a midpoint digression into the desert-like Middle East. Temporally, the contrast is expressed as morning (the rays of the morning sun enhancing Elvira's charms) and night, one of the objects of the narrator's final embraces. Cold, North, and night, we might note, also make up the narrator's present setting.

What is perhaps most striking about the imagery used, is that it all derives from the basic elements: earth, water, fire, and air. Elemental, infinite, chronotopics overshadow the miniature of the idyll, and determine the narrator's worldview. Everything in 'Sierra-Morena', including the innermost idyllic setting, the internal landscapes of the personages, is described in terms of large parameters. It is in this sense that 'Sierra-Morena' diametrically contrasts with the idylls and trifles and most of the Sentimental tales. In the idyll, everything was characterized in terms of the narrator's 'here' and 'now' with concentric ripple effects outwards. In 'Sierra-Morena' the outside has an inward directed effect: the general determines the particular, rather than vice versa.

A look at the development of the Elvira motif first, and the N motif next, will bear this out. Elvira's love idyll with Alonzo ends in tragedy because of the sea (outside world). Her initial shock and despair gradually develop into tender grief, languor, and warm tears – the idyll world (tender friendship, caresses, intimate walks, flowers, etc.), as it were, overcoming the elemental force of the sea, but only temporarily.

The line of extreme feelings and passions, as well as elemental outside forces, is gradually introduced as parallelling and overtaking the idyllic line: her vow of *eternal* and *exclusive* love for Alonzo is introduced early on as a *terrible* oath. The embraces and the surgings of her blood take place on the banks of the *magnificent* river to the accompaniment of the *sound* (*shum*) of its *waters*, and the echo of the *sound* (*shum*) *of waterfalls* between the *high cliffs of Sierra-Morena* and its *deep clefts and valleys*. The light Zephyrs which mix with their sighs develop into *strong winds* which agitate the *air*, accompanied by the *crimson strokes of lightning* on a *black* sky – all of which combines into the *terrors* of nature, beloved by Elvira. Thus one sees a gradually increasing force of water, air, and fire, and images of clefts and fissures in the rock of the mountain. Blacks and dark colors gradually become more frequent, and the rose color intensifies into crimson before its total disappearance. The image of rosy warmth turning into fiery currents of emotions within Elvira, is gradually overtaken by outside heavenly fire (lightning) and heavenly wrath (thunder) evoked as metaphors for the punishment of Elvira's breach of her 'terrible' vow to Alonzo. At first, the vow prevents N from expressing his love. Later, Elvira's expression of love is prefaced by her ominous words: 'May heavenly *thunder* strike the oath breaker.'[38]

The development of N's feelings is even more telling. His love (presumably at first sight) develops concurrently with Elvira's and his own grief for Alonzo. Out of respect for the deceased and Elvira's vow to him, N's passions are pent up within him under the guise of friendship, whereas in fact: 'Alas! in my breast raged an *Etna* of love. My heart *burned* from my feelings; my *blood* boiled like *a stormy sea.*' Finally 'Etna' erupts, as the metaphor is extended in an apologia for his love declaration to Elvira:

Ah! one can do battle with one's heart, long and persistently, but who is victorious over it? – the *stormy* surge of *furious waters* breaks down all dams and *stony mountains disintegrate* from the power of *fiery matter* pent up in their *depths*. The power of my feelings overcame all, and the long pent-up passion flowed out into a tender declaration! (11)

When the two are at the height of their love, *thunder* gathered over them and finally, Alonzo's passionate deed of love and vengeance culminates the development as (literally) '*blood* pours from his heart', and Elvira reacts (predictably) 'as struck by *thunder*'. The '*flame* of love was extinguished forever in her eyes and heart'. The tender flame of love is overpowered by heavenly wrath and the blood of passion. The fissures and valleys of the 'Black Mountain', the 'disintegration of mountains', have turned into a rent earth, an eternal abyss which separates the two lovers forever.

Elvira's elegy and subsequent idyll have turned into the grimmest tragedy, this time, without consolation. She takes strict monastic vows, and finally dies within the convent walls. N's thwarted idyll makes up the second half of 'Sierra-Morena'. In some respects it runs parallel to Elvira's, but even temporary human consolation is

entirely lacking. The elemental passions have killed all the sensitivities in both Elvira and N. Elvira refuses a farewell, a last
embrace, and even compassion – not to mention love. She is totally
isolated within the *black* towers and the *iron* locks which *gleam
black* on the gates, within the *eternal* silence of the convent, and
without any hints of a religious consolation. N in vain looks to his
own sensitive heart and the consolation of tears, but instead finds a
heart like *stone*, and he is incapable of weeping. He looks for traces
of 'his' Elvira in the locale of their courtship – also in vain: *cold and
darkness* is everywhere. He finally undertakes a Sentimental
journey of sorts, to the setting which most closely approximates his
mood: to the ancient ruins of Palmyra, the scene of a once
flourishing culture. He leans against the ruins in the 'eloquent
*silence*' of the *desert*, broken only by occasional peals of *thunder*.
He finds some consolation in the melancholy fact that his own fate
merely mirrors the ultimate life and death of nations, and that
human life lasts but a moment, its sorrows and joys equally
transient, and both fated for a similar end: to be covered with a
handful of *black earth*. He regains the ability to shed tears, but not
his vital capacity for love and friendship. After travelling for a while
and being the 'plaything of peoples' malice', after shedding tears on
Elvira's grave, he withdraws into total solitude in the cold, sad,
North, where the '*magnificent* Nature from the *depths* of insensitivity took me into its embraces and included me in the system of
*ephemeral* being'. The circular path back to 'insensitivity' is completed as he extends his embraces to 'quiet night – eternal peace –
sacred silence'. The idyllic cycle from birth to death to re-birth, is
here differently emphasized as death to birth to death. The void,
usually featured by Karamzin as the absence of life to set idyllic
pleasure into sharper relief, is here featured as the ultimate abyss of
tragic reality, present all around us.

    The image of narrator in 'Sierra-Morena' is that of an alienated
teller without an audience. The tone of his potentially idyllic story
is permeated from the beginning by his final (present) despair in the
gradual foregrounding of the darker elemental powers of water,
fire, and air, and, particularly, earth and rock, the inanimate,
insensitive elements of creation. 'Sierra-Morena' is thus a Sentimental tale about the spiritual death of the Sensitive Person, his
impotence brought about by elemental passions and impersonal
forces. It affirms the refrain of the dedication of the almanac

without including the 'sweet consolation' of love and friendship, that consolation depicted here as equally ephemeral as everything else.

'Sierra-Morena' can be seen as the end point of one particular line of aesthetic development in Karamzin's Sentimentalist paradigm. The beginning was represented by idylls expressing the pleasurable aesthetics of joyous nature or of tragic nature seen from a joyous vantage point of love and friendship. In the Sentimental tales, an increasing proportion of the text voices tragic aspects of reality. Yet, they, too, provide aesthetic pleasure for the narrators who can co-experience and co-create sympathetically from their idyllic vantage points, representing the consoling joyous whole of which the tragic love stories are fragments. Finally, in 'Sierra-Morena' that idyllic vantage point, even in its minimal, internal form, is conquered by an eternal anti-idyll. Hostile elements reign victoriously, while the narrator is depicted as a conquered victim on the brink of the eternal void. Similar sentiments are expressed in some of Karamzin's other works. Lotman quotes 'Athenian Life' and a programmatic epistle to Dmitriev, both of which conclude with the depiction of an alienated narrator who, like the narrator in 'Sierra-Morena', is completely alone and contemplates the horrors of the world.[39] The Sentimentalist proximities give way to a narrator, alienated from the entire human race, from the 'mad creatures, called men'. This, it seems to me, makes 'Sierra-Morena' more akin to the spirit of Romanticism than to that of Sentimentalism, and Karamzin here builds a bridge to the Romantic movement which was to emerge in early nineteenth-century Russia.

## INCOMPLETE FRAGMENTS

### 'Liodor'

'Liodor' is a peculiar compendium of Karamziniana.[40] It incorporates themes familiar from all the idylls and trifles: the idyllic setting in nature and at a country estate 'at the edge of Europe', night walks and daytime walks, a nocturnal love idyll, and the theme of spiritual communion of 'A Promenade' and 'The Countryside', the musical theme of 'The Bird of Paradise', the Aglaia addressee of the trifles, and the Agathon theme of 'Dedication of a Grove'.

'Liodor' also foreshadows later themes, such as the exotic Southern setting for love in 'Sierra-Morena', the Gothic and Ossianic tonalities as well as the air of mystery of 'Bornholm Island', the theme of a mother's death and the Actaeon motif of *Knight*, the theme of study and travel abroad of 'My Confession', historical and folkloric traits later developed, particularly in 'Natal'ia', 'Poor Liza', 'The Bird of Paradise', and *Knight*. 'Liodor' also echoes several of the topics dealt with in *Letters of a Russian Traveller* (Lavater, Kant, Provence, the traveller's staff, and, of course, the very theme of travel itself).

The tale has also been seen as autobiographical in certain respects: the Aglaia addressee referring once more to Pleshcheeva, Agathon to A. A. Petrov, readings of Kant and Lavater to Karamzin himself, and so on. Pogodin even went so far as to reconstruct the events in Karamzin's life during 1791 according to 'Liodor', much as Sipovskii and others were later to reconstruct Karamzin's childhood according to *Knight*. Foreign sources have been seen particularly in Goethe's *Werther* and in Ossian.[41]

'Liodor' ends with an editorial promise of a continuation to follow, which was never fulfilled, and it belongs among 'incomplete fragments', as defined above. Whether Karamzin ever intended to fulfill the promise of a sequel, is a question which can be answered only tentatively. There is some external evidence both of reader response and of Karamzin's intentions. In a letter written by A. A. Petrov to Karamzin at the end of 1792, the following remarks are made *à propos* 'Liodor': 'Your *Liodor* is not like other novel heroes; at least he does not suffer from insomnia, tossing and turning in his bed. He sleeps in a more than bogatyr like sleep. *Isn't it time to wake him up?*'[42] Petrov's reaction is all the more interesting, since he himself is recognized as the prototype for Agathon, twice prematurely pronounced dead and mourned (fictionally, of course) by Karamzin (or, rather, his narrators), as we saw in 'Dedication of a Grove' and now in 'Liodor'. He actually dies soon after his letter, in March, 1793. From this point of view, 'Liodor' can be seen as another sketch for Karamzin's actual eulogy, 'A Blossom on the Grave of My Agathon'. Petrov's response also exposes the fallacy of equating fiction with autobiography. This is particularly true in this era when, as we have repeatedly seen, the borders between life and art are extraordinarily fluid. It is interesting to note in this context that the real life relationship between Karamzin and Petrov was in many ways a peculiar literary game. Lotman quotes some of Petrov–Agathon's letters to Karamzin where the real world is described according to Wieland's satire *Die Abderiten*.[43] As we already mentioned, Petrov's nickname, Agathon, is based on another Wieland novel, *Agathon*. The device of premature mourning is in full accord with Sentimentalist poetics: full emotive involvement is best achieved by imagining the absence of the object or person, a tenet most elaborately explained, as we saw, in 'A Promenade'. Even the death of a dear one is thus aesthetically sublimated by Sentimentalist authors.

As for Karamzin's intentions to write and/or publish a sequel to 'Liodor', a letter from Karamzin to Dmitriev indicates that a sequel was indeed planned, and even planned for specific issues of *Moscow Journal* (October and November, 1792).[44] Whether is was actually written, and if so, why it never appeared in print, remains unknown.

Leaving aside the author's intentions, I will regard 'Liodor' as an incomplete fragment, briefly describe its triple utterance structure, and look closer at its sensitive narrators and narratees and the blatant trivialization of the core love plot left 'incomplete'.

The first 'layer' of narrative structure features the 'I' as narrator and Aglaia as narratee. The personages of the narrated event are 'I' and their mutual friends, Agathon, Izidor, and Liodor, its time a past autumn spent in the country. The actions are the typical country pleasures, expressions of friendship, and, most importantly, anticipating and finally listening to Liodor's story. The second narrative 'layer' features Liodor as narrator and Agathon, Izidor, and 'I' as narratees. The personages of the narrated event (Liodor's travels abroad, the death of his mother, and his love) are Liodor, his parents, his beloved, and various casual acquaintances in various settings, mostly abroad. In the third narrative 'layer' Liodor's mother (writer of a letter) and his beloved (singer of a song) are the narrators and Liodor is the narratee (reader and listener). The narrated events in the letter are non-events (expressions of love and longing) and the song consists of the blossoming, withering, and death of a violet. In each of these 'layers' the speech event, particularly its receptive side, is emphasized. 'Liodor' is a rich source for investigating the Sentimentalist devices of personalized, intimate, and friendly narration I listed in my typology, and a typology, and a particularly good illustration of the shifting roles between narrator, narratee, and personages since virtually everyone involved functions in all these capacities. All involved are also close friends or loved ones, and the cult of friendship–love (there is no great difference) is here for the first time expressed in great detail, perhaps more eloquently than anywhere else in Karamzin's fiction. Moreover, the Sentimentalist principles of solipsism, sympathy, and pleasure (here derived from grief) are interrelated and demonstrated by the very form of and the reasons for narrating.

'Liodor' is structured according to a solipsistically anchored multiplication principle: the I-narrator is the prime representative of the breed of Sensitive Person and his friends Aglaia, Agathon, and Izidor are just like him, and Liodor is just like Izidor. Even the violet is in some crucial respects a metaphor both for the 'delicacy' and the fates of the female personages and the excessive tenderness in the men as well. The participants in 'Liodor' are alike, not only as Sensitive Person multiples, but also as possessors of the primary characteristic of the Sensitive Person: his abilities both to narrate in a captivating, expressive way and to listen and perceive sympathetically. Each 'layer', by this token, demonstrates properties of the Sensitive Person (as narrator and narratee) and his sensitive friend/ beloved (as narratee and narrator) and each instance of narration serves as a kind of cathartic aesthetic sublimation of a tragic event (death) provoking pleasurable melancholy both in the tellers and their audiences (provoked by their innate sensitivities and by the acts of sharing tragic memories). Each 'layer' contrasts a present personal idyll of friendship between narrator and narratee to a past idyll *manqué*. As a corollary to these similarities, all the voices in this trivocal narration are in agreement, there is no verbal conflict, no verbal irony, no verbal parody, and the only way the voices can be distinguished at all is compositionally and by overt identification. The potentials for conflict between voices in such a structure (such as we already saw on a small scale in 'Poor Liza') were to be exploited by Karamzin later.

Let me demonstrate these claims selectively without going into the details of each 'layer' since many of the devices used are already familiar from Karamzin's earlier works and others will be further developed in more interesting ways in stories yet to follow.

The Sensitive Person (and thus all the participants in 'Liodor') is described early on (293–4) in one of the narrator's emotional digressions:

Happy is he who has a tender soul – a soul which notices all movements of Nature and together with it changes emotionally – blossoms and withers together with it! All that opens up before his eyes in the wide realm of creation, multiplies his being and is for him an object of delight; every tear shed by him engenders for him a new joy, sometimes secret, inexplicable, but all the deeper felt and therefore all the more blissful. But still a hundred times happier is this mortal when he finds a person like himself, whose soul is an equally pure mirror of Nature. What can be compared to the quickness of the move with which they at first glance throw themselves to embrace each other and in the sight of Heaven conclude for eternity a holy union of friendship, a union which is the strongest bond on earth. Who can describe that incomparable pleasure with which they express to each other their sympathetic feelings – sometimes without words, with a single glance – a single handshake.

Here we have all the essential attributes of the Sensitive Person: a tender soul, completely attuned to nature, the ability to take pleasure in all creation, the ability to feel joy in tears, and to sense the ineffable. The solipsistic aspects of the pleasure principle are articulated with unusual clarity: everything that appears before the eyes of the Sensitive Person 'multiplies his being and is always for him an object of pleasure'. Furthermore, the ideal friend is essential as an exact clone of the sensitive 'I'.

Although this passage is about the Sensitive Person and his sensitive friend in general terms, the immediately preceding context also makes it applicable to the narrator himself and his relationship to Aglaia (thereby complimented), and to his relationship (past and present) to Agathon and Izidor. It also foreshadows the narrator's meeting with Liodor. Karamzin's narrator here continues to congratulate himself and compliment his friends in ways we have already seen. 'Liodor' is doubly motivated by Aglaia's grief over the deaths of Agathon and Izidor (she has requested that the narrator speak of these mutual friends for cathartic reasons) and by the narrator's compliance and wish to 'express his sympathetic feelings to a person like himself', Aglaia, whose grief he shares, while also apologizing for renewing her grief and thanking her for the opportunity. It is overtly presented as a mixed speech act: a commissive, a directive, a condolence, an apology, etc. It is a *pleasurable* action against the background of *grief*: 'Gracious Heaven! . . . at this minute tears roll down on the

paper – tears of grief – ah, no! – tears of tenderness, gratitude!'
(294). This passage also reveals that the narration takes place in
writing – the tearstained pages were to become one of the most
shopworn topoi of Sentimentalism, particularly in its epistolary
form. 'Liodor' may indeed be seen as a letter (albeit without all the
formal epistolary trappings)[45], autobiographically–fictionally continuing Karamzin's *Letters of a Russian Traveller*, also addressed to
the Pleshcheevs. This connection is further borne out by the fact
that the narrator's travels are repeatedly referred to within the text
of 'Liodor'. Even more specifically, the second direct apostrophe to
Aglaia mentions the traveller's staff that Aglaia had given to the
narrator. Similar mentions are made in *Letters of a Russian
Traveller*, in 'Bornholm Island', and in the verse dedication to the
almanac *Aglaia*.

A more immediate parallel is suggested by Pogodin, who points
to another piece which had appeared in *Moscow Journal* two
months before 'Liodor', containing the following words addressed
to Aglaia in a New Year's greeting (a typical trifle): 'The coming
year will not return to you the one you lost during the past year. –. . .
I cannot resurrect Isidor. I can only weep with you . . . the thought
about immortality (in spring) will rekindle in your soul, and you
will see Isidor, extending his embraces to you from the land of our
fathers.'[46] Izidor (or Isidor) has not been identified 'bio-
graphically', but for our purposes such identification is not crucial.
In the larger context of Karamzin's oeuvres, 'Liodor' can be seen as
part of the ongoing conversation with Pleshcheeva, Petrov, and
other close friends, a conversation which includes this greeting, the
compliments, and dedications we have already seen, as well as
*Letters of a Russian Traveller*. Their extra-literary communication
has been transformed into several smaller literary works. The
personal letter format also justifies the lack of a formal introduction
of Agathon and Izidor (who were immediately named by first name
only in the first paragraph of 'Liodor'), as well as other personal
references understandable only to Aglaia (and more immediately
decipherable to Karamzin's contemporaries than to today's
reader).

The speech event between Aglaia and the narrator is curiously
extended to include the deceased friends, Agathon and Izidor, who
appear most distinctly *in presentia* as the narrator in an apostrophe
communicates with their spirits – and they with him – in words,

repeating almost verbatim the communion with the spirits in 'A Promenade'. Often the wind carries a consoling and beloved voice from the grave saying: *'only a thin curtain separates us; soon it too will be raised . . . '* (294).[47] In 'Liodor' the spirits are more specific than in 'A Promenade' due to the absence of the friendship theme in any concrete sense in the earlier work.

The autumn story further multiplies and defines the Sensitive Person, the friendship theme, and the duality of pleasure and grief: the autumnal landscape, the cold snowy weather, and the ancient dilapidated house, are contrasted to the warmth of friendship: no boredom, no emptiness in 'our' hearts, and togetherness during walks outside or during evenings in front of the warm fireplace.

An identical duality in imagery and tone characterizes the specific event of meeting Liodor, and the description of Liodor's house duplicates the description of the narrator's house, further developing the Gothic aspects of gloom: a large wooden house, built in the beginning of the century and close to its final ruin, mosses, grasses, and even trees growing on its roof, an overhang with windows jutting out like turrets, a once deep moat surrounding the house, small dark rooms, the wind howling, doors slamming, windows rattling, floor boards squeaking, and Liodor's room, the *terem* up high. This description is complemented by 'thousands of doves and jackdaws nesting below the roof', and their 'savage concert', so unlike pleasurable idyllic birdsong. Liodor's warm friendship and hospitality, and the intimate conversations between the four friends, contrast with this dismal autumnal setting.

The narrator's first encounter with Liodor and their instantaneous mutual attraction, are an elaboration on the Sensitive Person passage. It exemplifies it as a concrete instance of sensitive behavior, and complements it with a description of the external appearance of a specific Sensitive Person – Liodor. That Liodor is meant to be a multiple of the Sensitive Person–narrator–narratee–friends, is most explicitly laid bare in the third aside to Aglaia: 'Imagine a *second Izidor*, when he was twenty years old and when you saw him standing in the avenue of D\*\*\* *garden , after a serious ailment of the heart* '(297). Like other asides to Aglaia, this one serves to establish a feeling of privacy in the speech event, and like the reference to the traveller's staff, it can be fully understood only by Aglaia. We see the salon chronotope in full force.

The multiplication principle is also introduced as part of the second speech event for an ulterior narratological purpose: to build up suspense as to the Liodor-story. The narrator suffers from a deep grief, as does Aglaia. Izidor suffered from 'an ailment of the heart', and Liodor already from the first meeting shows signs of a similar predicament. The persistent mention of 'sorrows suffered', of Izidor's 'ailment of the heart' near a garden, of the ailments of lovelorn maidens of old weeping and sighing in the *terem* (now inhabited by Liodor), and of old-time landowners, nursing their wounds at their estates, serves as a gradual build-up of suspense as to Liodor's 'ailment of the heart', and many of the images (e.g., the garden) will later reappear as part of his story, which they foreshadow.

The narrator and his friends (as past personages and narratees) increasingly perceive that, despite Liodor's cheerful and happy external appearance, 'a dark melancholy was lodged deep inside him' (306). The introduction of this perceptual motif is interesting also in that it is explained by the narrator's present opinions as a partisan of Lavaterian physiognomy: 'a person cannot by any dissembling hide his internals from sharp eyes [ . . . ] Liodor against his will showed us what was hidden in his soul'.[48]

The suspense mounts as Liodor's lapses into melancholy are noted, and the friends' expectations for a resolution mount: 'We did not want to be indiscreet and were afraid of hurting him by showing our compassion (however sincere it was), *hoping that he himself would open his soul to us*' (306, emphasis added). These lines overtly convert the autumn story into a story about the quest for a story and the personages in the autumn story function mainly as prospective narratees. Coding motifs by this token, become increasingly important. The relief comes when the three friends one morning catch Liodor *in flagrante delicto*, in bed tearfully kissing a small medallion portrait, explained by Liodor as the portrait of his one and only true love, now dead. This, of course, relieves the suspense only partly, and Liodor's story, which follows, is to lead his friends into the 'sanctuary of my heart', and is to reveal to them the further details that led up to his 'eternal mourning', his 'incurable ailment'.

Interestingly enough, Liodor's telling of his story is motivated in almost exactly the same manner as the narrator's telling the autumn story, which proceeded from Aglaia's wish for catharsis for both of them. Not only does Liodor duplicate the narrator as Sensitive Person, but also as narrator. Their reasons for, and manner of, narration are similar. The narrator is thus also telling a story about himself as *narratee*, eager to hear Liodor's story. Both the narrator himself and Liodor perform all the functions described for narrative structure: they function as authors (reporting and control), as personages (action, interpretation, evaluation), and as readers (reception, co-reporting). Furthermore, they perform them for the same reasons, and in the same manner.

'Liodor' contains an excellent description of the ideal Sensitive Person as Sentimentalist author and reader (alias Liodor, alias the narrator):

Ah, dear Aglaia! how lovely he seemed to us in his every look, every word, and every movement! Everything, everything showed in him a tender soul, love, and sensitivity. Everything was exceedingly pleasant on his lips, even when he spoke about the most ordinary things: because his words always flowed from his heart, and being, so to say, warmed by the inner fire of his soul, moved his listeners and kindled the imagination of the coldest people. But Liodor could not only speak – he also *knew how to listen*, so that everyone loved to tell him things, to open up his soul to him, and everyone spoke with him more eloquently than with anyone else. His looks, his glances, his smile, his tears, had this amazing power to completely correspond to the thoughts and feelings of whoever was conversing with him or telling him things. Everyone saw that Liodor understood him, even when the topic was the nuances of Kant's Metaphysics; every tender heart found in him a brother, a like-minded person, and everyone – loved Liodor. (304–5)

The principles here expressed as part of a fiction, correspond entirely to non-fictional statements of Karamzin's poetic credo. This passage in particular, and the friendship theme of 'Liodor' as a whole, again remind us of Karamzin's biography and especially the German readings and orientation of Karamzin, Petrov, and their friends. Wieland's *Die Abderiten* contains a description of a meeting between two philosophers, Democritus and Hippocrates, whose mutual sympathy, previous solitude, intense friendship, and sympathetic 'brotherhood' is clearly one of Karamzin's models for 'Liodor'. Friendship in Wieland is described as a peculiar brotherhood where complete mutual understanding and sympathy is raised to a mystical–philosophical level. We have seen this reflected in other works by Karamzin as well ('A Promenade', for example). Lotman also links Wieland's work to Karamzin's later

*Knight*, citing a couple of lines from Wieland which are even more pertinent to the 'Liodor' passage I just cited: 'Their friendship [ . . . ] is based on the most essential of all natural laws: on the necessity to love *ourselves* in the person who is spiritually closest to us' (emphasis added).[49]

The act of Sentimentalist narration can be seen as the main topic of 'Liodor' as a whole. This contention is supported also by the fact that the plot of the Liodor story, his mysterious grief, is never really resolved, since he never gets to the 'main part' of the story. This fact would seem to indicate a markedly lesser interest in the love intrigue as such than in its telling, its teller, its audience, and the storytelling situation. All this information, as we have seen, is concentrated mainly in the first half of 'Liodor', the sixteen pages preceding Liodor's equally long story. This justifies labelling that section as an elaborate reporting clause to the Liodor story, a clause which most explicitly reveals the physical and emotive setting, the circumstances under which Liodor tells his story, the most important traits of its narrator, his gestures, his sensitive and aesthetic qualities, and his audience. If we recall, however, how Liodor was represented as a multiple of the narrator, we might view 'Liodor' as a rather roundabout way for the narrator to speak of himself.

This is not to say that Liodor's story is without interest, but that interest is, in itself, partly motivated by the fact that we already know the teller and the sad ending of the story. We know that the story is to include Liodor's love and its vicissitudes. We know that Liodor survived, and that his beloved died. We even know the basic skeleton of his story from his introduction of himself to his narratees: that he grew up in foreign parts, travelled widely, returned to Russia, and so on. We also know his likes and dislikes, and that he is both well-educated and sensitive. His story can only fill in certain lacunae, and more fully tell us the cause of Liodor's intense grief, the 'ailment of his heart'. His listeners expect to hear the *sad* story of his love. Yet, Liodor ends by telling about his *first* encounter with his beloved, on a *happy* note.

The fact that what Liodor tells is already familiar to a large extent to his listeners, is signalled by such asides as 'You yourselves can guess', 'You yourselves have travelled [ . . . ] and seen', 'You know'. These asides again stress the telling rather than the novelty of the plot. Only once is Liodor's story interrupted by the listeners, and that, significantly enough, to voice their *agreement* (reported parenthetically by the primary narrator: 'We agreed with Liodor, and he continued his tale', 314). Liodor's story contains no reported speech (in the narrow sense) by the other personages, with the important exceptions of a directly quoted, interpolated letter from his mother, and an Italian song, sung by his beloved.

Both setting and physical events serve mainly as background for Liodor's Sentimental education. Seven years at the university of Leipzig (from age twelve to nineteen) are described as a happy time of intellectual and physical growth: 'my soul received its first systematic understanding of things surrounding us and of me myself; there I learned to feel and to give myself account of my feelings' (308). Liodor's education conforms to the epistemological emphasis we have seen in Sentimentalist philosophy. His heart was at peace, he enjoyed learning, and amusements were equally pleasant. The death of his father, and particularly that of his mother shortly thereafter, jarred this harmonious equilibrium. The Leipzig years are interrupted by a surge of love brought on by his mother's letter, his belated return to Russia, and a period of intense grief over the lost loved ones.

His mother's death is the first blow of Fate, and one of the emotional peaks of the story. A subsequent three-year stay in Paris, described as a 'pleasant dream', returns his equilibrium and satisfies his love for the sciences and the arts. Paris comes to symbolize the positive fruits of Enlightenment. Soon, however, his 'soul demanded a change in pleasure', which resulted in a trip to Spain, the 'fatherland of novels (*romanov*)', which had always attracted his imagination, and which, no doubt, held promises of personal romance as well.

Liodor's tragedy can be seen in terms of lost idyll values: a lack of parent–child intimacy and love, an alienation from the native soil, an inability to enjoy idyllic nature due to social reality, and finally the loss of his beloved. In Spain, for instance, the nature and climate fully meet with his idyllic expectations. He enjoys a Southern *locus amoenus* with hot sunshine, cool translucent streams, the quiet Guadiana, and palm groves. The grim social reality is, however, a far cry from romance, and Spain comes to stand as a bad example of insufficient Enlightenment, of glorious potentials, stifled by ignorance, superstition, corruption, and social inequality. Liodor's response (here as elsewhere) is typical of the

impotent Sensitive Person: 'All this awakened in me pleasant feelings and I sighed for the poor Spaniards, the downtrodden amidst
riches, and the sad in the embraces of joyous Nature.' Similarly,
his forgotten childhood love for his mother is fated to be
unfulfilled, and is expressed in impotent tears shed on her grave.

In Marseille he experiences the perfect love idyll (316–23)
which is the emotive culmination of Liodor's story, and it is the
event described in greatest detail and in the most expressive
emotive language. It is a combination of a nocturnal promenade
and love idyll. It features both the aesthetic pleasures of nature
and poetry and the erotic pleasure of a lovers' rendezvous – albeit
as yet one-sided. A closer look at this section reveals its organic
links to both Karamzin's early idylls and trifles, and his later
fiction. Its Mediterranean setting aligns it prominently, not only
with the original homeland of the idyll, but also with 'Sierra-
Morena'.

Liodor walks away from the city, past flowering fields and
meadows, lies down on a hilltop with a view of the sea, a movement analogous to those of the narrators in 'A Promenade' and
'Poor Liza'. From there he moves to the most perfect *locus
amoenus:* a walled-in garden (we recall Izidor's connection to a
garden), with trees and a cool crystalline pool. The time of day is
equally familiar: sunset, a warm night with moon and stars, light
breezes and perfect silence, then a song and a gentle splashing of
waves in the pool. Liodor's emotions and experiences occur in a
familiar sequence: perception and enjoyment of nature, a state of
dreamy imagination ('my imagination was dreaming'), and then
complete oblivion to his surroundings ('I forgot all that sur-
rounded me and fell into an enthralling slumber'), which prepares
him for an aesthetic experience – the sequence identical to that in
'A Promenade'. Any overt reference to spiritual communion is
here lacking, and Karamzin downplays his earlier mystical inclinations. The poets and the song of Philomela in 'A Promenade'
here combine into human singing to the accompaniment of a
guitar. Liodor's aesthetic rapture is complete: 'Never had I felt
such pleasure from singing as I felt then; the voice (it was female)
flowed together with the tones of the strings, it penetrated straight
to my heart; my breast languished in tender emotions; I melted in
ecstasies and tears streamed from my eyes' (319–20). His mother's
letter had earlier called forth a somewhat weaker expression of

the identical aesthetic experience. It, too, became stained with his tears and its 'every word penetrated my heart'.

When the song suddenly ends, Liodor wants to see the 'heavenly' singer, for his heart tells him that she must be beautiful (to paraphrase Sentimentalist poetics, 'the singer is always reflected in her song'). The next scene bears out his intuitions: a beautiful young Turkish woman is sitting in the garden among trees on the edge of a pool. Her beauty is reflected in the surroundings. Using the typical method of personified foreshortening, Liodor describes how the moon from its heights kissed her with its rays and illuminated the snowy pallor of her face, and how the crystalline waters of the pool reflected her image so that it seemed as if they themselves fondled her charms. Her undressing and bathing mirrors the typical bathing shepherdesses and nymphs of idylls, and Liodor's surreptitious observing also coincides with the general eavesdropping topos. When her breasts (which could have served Phidias as a model for his *Venus di Medici*!) are bared, 'darkness covered my eyes – I saw nothing more, and after a few minutes, as if through a pleasant dream, I heard a quiet splashing in the pool' (322). His erotic experience corresponds to his earlier aesthetic one, and, as we also saw in 'Night', even the erotic is sublimated to the aesthetic.

The episode is completed as an Actaeon–Diana scene: Liodor is abruptly brought back to reality by a small yapping dog attacking him. Liodor escapes in the nick of time, returns to the city, and in great exhaustion throws himself on his bed. Thereby ends 'Liodor', and the narratees never find out the full reasons for Liodor's 'ailment of the heart', the very motivation for the telling of his story.

Nevertheless, from the very first revelation of Liodor's secret love ailment, the narratees already know that it is the death of the beloved (the end of the love idyll) that is at the root of Liodor's tragedy. Further details are, strictly speaking, not necessary. It is interesting to see just how much we know about the 'untold' part of the Liodor-story and how that information is conveyed. We have already followed the initial allusions to Liodor's predicament, and the mounting suspense and apprehensions on this score. Let us now follow that track to the end.

When Liodor shows the medallion and the three friends agree that she is indeed beautiful, Liodor reveals that 'she is no longer among the living'. He then goes on to reveal his 'secret': 'Know then! that I loved and in such a way as one can love only once in one's life. But Fate deprived me of that woman, who was dearer to me than anything and my heart was cloaked in eternal mourning' (307). These comments, as we saw, preface Liodor's story. A similar comment prefaces the bathing episode of the love idyll: 'here, my dear friends, I knew all the happiness Nature made me capable of – I knew it and delighted in it, and then I lost it forever' (315–16). Finally, the Turkish beauty is identified as the prototype for the medallion (321), and we thus know that Liodor–Actaeon was to meet his Turkish Diana on other occasions as well – or at least somehow come by her medallion.

In the Sensitive Person passage, and elsewhere in the early parts of the text, we have been apprised that sensitive narrators often reveal their innermost thoughts 'against their will', and that tender souls 'blossom and wither together with Nature'. Liodor, in fact, also reveals his tragedy – albeit by indirection, metaphorically, through the Italian song sung by the Turkish beauty (quoted in Russian in its entirety). It is clearly a parallel to Liodor's tragedy, and Violetta's fate can be seen as a metonymy for the singer's own fate, particularly if one remembers the larger context of the idyll tradition, where women were often likened to the shy violet. Karamzin himself was quite fond of that flower: the image is used both in 'Night' and in 'Eugene and Julia', and, as we shall see, it reappears in *Knight*. We recall the violet's links to death in Jakob Lenz's obituary which was echoed in Karamzin's more general 'blossom' (on Agathon's grave). The violet's beauty, its color, its fragrance, its hiding in the grass under shrubs, also evokes Liodor's perception of the singer. The last couplets extend the metaphorical link to the further fate of the beloved:

> What is the matter with the tender violet,
> What will happen in the end?

> Ah! the unhappy one languishes,
> dries, and suddenly disappears.

The first of these couplets metaphorically reiterates the narratees' main question, and the second couplet provides an answer to that question. Whatever the concrete causes, the young Turkish woman's fate is, no doubt, like that of the violet. She is like a tender plant and it is her sensitivities that make her both charming and shortlived, reminding us of Eugene's death from his 'delicate' sensitivity, and his epitaph which in botanical imagery is almost identical to this song. There is thus no real need to elaborate Liodor's story. The friends are in fact informed (albeit surreptitiously, in an oblique metaphorical way, almost 'against the narrator's will') of the causes for Liodor's 'eternal mourning'. Furthermore, by not hearing the concrete details directly and unambiguously, they (and we) are invited to think of all possible tragic events, and thereby further 'multiply' the tragedy to a greater degree than if we were directly told the missing sequel. One may speculate with Cross about Karamzin's intentions: 'It would seem that Karamzin had simply lost interest, or, more probably, they [works here referred to as incomplete fragments] were already finished in the sense that Karamzin had achieved his initial artistic intention.'[50] Perhaps, in the case of 'Liodor' Karamzin only subsequently realized the artistic potential of the incomplete fragment – which he was later to use intentionally in, for instance, 'Bornholm Island'. In that story, as I will show, he employs very similar techniques, including a revealing song, sung by one of the personages in a thwarted love idyll, and a similar display of mounting suspense to incorporate the mood, imagination, curiosity, and sensitivity, of narrators and narratees in a Sentimental tale. Co-creation is made a non-verbal, non-verbalizable, part of the plot at large.

Whether intentionally or not (I am rather inclined to think not), the abrupt ending with what amounts to a silly peeping-Tom episode, marks 'Liodor' with irony. Rothe notes the irony of 'Liodor' (similar to sections of *Letters of a Russian Traveller* prepared around the same time as 'Liodor' was written). He further observes that Karamzin's irony is often connected to erotic scenes.[51] This seems an acute observation, and irony is, certainly in the case of Karamzin's other works, too, frequently linked to erotic contexts. The irony of this Actaeon scene is later much more creatively developed in *Knight*.

'Liodor' has too long been ignored as an organic part of Karamzin's art, most probably due to its unfinished nature, which, ironically enough, is perhaps the feature of 'Liodor' that was most influential in shaping Karamzin's later works.

## 'Bornholm Island'

'Bornholm Island' was seen by Gukovskii as a model of Karamzin's Romanticism and 'perhaps his best tale'.[52] Equally favorable evaluations have led to several excellent studies of the tale – perhaps the least neglected of Karamzin's tales next to 'Poor Liza'.[53]

Most critics stress its Romantic features (e.g., Vatsuro, Neuhäuser, Gukovskii, Krestova, Anderson, and Cross), while some (Jensen and Titunik) see it as a prime example of Sentimentalist aesthetics. According to my definition of Sentimentalism, it is an organic link in Karamzin's Sentimentalist prose, developing certain themes and structures present already in the idylls and trifles. It is an 'incomplete fragment' and I will complement previous analyses with a closer look at the idyllic and the fragmentary implications in order to make its place within other Karamziniana and the Sentimentalist movement more explicit.

'Bornholm Island' and the other works of the *Aglaia* period (*ca.* 1793–1800), continue and further develop the solipsistic focus on narrator we have seen in all previous works. The predominant mood, emotions, and opinions described may be different. In the idylls and trifles, as well as the earlier Sentimental tales, there was an almost exclusive stress on joy, gratitude, contentment, and pleasure, despite some unpleasant aspects. In the *Aglaia* works, the mood is frequently elegiac despair, extreme grief, or Gothic horror, and the world is often depicted in its unidyllic aspects. But even during this period, this mood is most often a trait of the personages or of the narrator retrospectively co-experiencing their moods, and it is offset for the work as a whole by the positive Sentimental proximities between the present narrator and narratee (be it the 'dear friends', 'Aglaia', 'Dmitriev', or the 'Sensitive Person' in general). The major exceptions are, as we saw, 'Sierra-Morena', 'Athenian Life' and the epistle to Dmitriev mentioned above, where no such pleasurable whole emerges, and which were therefore provisionally labelled Romantic. In the Sentimentalist paradigm, the narrator finds an aesthetic refuge, shared with the like-minded, and although he speaks ultimately about himself, his self is, as 'A Promenade' and 'Liodor' most clearly demonstrated, multiplied outwards, in living humans, immortal poets, dear friends, God, or nature. In several of the idylls and trifles there were already some traces of existential despair. They were, however, featured as secondary phenomena, and were unfailingly counterbalanced by the narrator's joyous moods. The scales were tipped in favor of pure pleasure or pleasurable melancholy, the pleasure stemming from the morality of the narrator's own *aesthetic* vision.

In the Sentimental tales 'Eugene and Julia', 'Poor Liza', and 'Liodor', the ultimate meaning was similarly moral and pleasurable because of the aesthetic sublimation of tragedy in the narrator's present framework. Although vice or tragic fate is featured (or strongly alluded to) to a greater extent than in the idylls and trifles, on the level of the whole, positive idyllic values reign: the narrator's aesthetic pleasure from virtue in distress, from unidyllic aspects of nature or Gothic horrors, multiplied among his narratees, governs the paradigm. In discussions of 'Bornholm Island' the full significance of the 'framing' idyllic chronotope is usually overlooked.

'Bornholm Island' has a triple utterance structure similar to that of 'Poor Liza' and 'Liodor'. Its most salient feature is that the vicarious love plot is so demonstratively secondary to the story of the narrator's quest for, and perception of, it. The love story is, in fact, never overtly reported by the narrator as a complete story, although fragments of it are revealed *ex post facto* by each participant in turn. The main topic is, in typical solipsistic fashion, the narrator himself – his actions, perceptions, emotions, and opinions. The role of the narrator is twofold: he figures not only as narrator, but even more as narratee.[54] The main topic is thus the dialogical process of the aesthetic act, the narrator's present reporting function and, even more, his past reception function, i.e. his twofold participation in the aesthetic process as both primary narrator and secondary narratee.

In this respect 'Bornholm Island' differs only in degree from the works we have already looked at. In fact, one might well claim that most of them stress the *primacy* of artistic reception, which is viewed as a prerequisite for artistic creation. I shall first look at how the narrator as reporter is featured, and then turn to the topic of the narrator as perceiver.

'Bornholm Island' begins with a description of the present aesthetic event which consists of the narrator's oral narration to his friends as part of a larger winter time story-telling situation. The narrator and his friends are sitting in front of the warm fireplace, and will 'tell each other tales and stories and all sorts of true events'. The narrator, who takes the first turn, chooses to tell the 'truth, not fiction (*vydumku*)', related to his travels in foreign lands (parts of which his friends have already heard – an autobiographical reference to Karamzin's *Letters of a Russian Traveller*, encountered elsewhere in the tale as well). The present utterance situation is a typical winter idyll, and we are reminded of the fantasies of Palemon and Daphnis (the advantages of travel seen mainly in the subsequent intimacy of storytelling) as well as of the specific setting around the fireplace in 'Liodor'. Indeed, a winter idyll might be described as a situation of heightened intimacy, the idyll space reduced and intensified as a result of natural causes, as compared to the *locus amoenus* of the open fields, meadows, groves, and villages, of summer idylls. To substantiate my claim for an intimate winter story-telling situation as an idyllic topos, I shall once more have recourse to Gessner. His idyll 'Lycas oder die Erfindung der Gärten' opens with the following lines:

Now the stormy winter shuts us in the room, and whirlwinds churn up the silvery rain of flakes. Now imagination will open up for me the treasure of pictures gathered in the blossoming spring and in the cool summer and the bright fall; I will now choose the most beautiful of them and, for you lovely Daphne! arrange them into poems.[55]

The introductory exhortation by the narrator of 'Bornholm Island' to his friends differs little from that of Lycas to his Daphne:

Friends! Glorious summer has passed; golden autumn has parted; the greenery has withered; the trees stand fruitless and leafless; the hazy sky is stirring like the dark sea; a wintry down is sprinkling the cold earth – we will bid farewell to Nature until we see it again in joyous spring; we will take shelter from blizzards and snowstorms in our quiet study! Time must not oppress us; we know the cure for boredom. Friends! the oak and birch burn in our fireplace – let the wind rage, and cover the windows with white snow! We will sit down around the scarlet fire and tell each other tales and stories and all sorts of true events. (92)[56]

The narrator announces his topic as taken from his travels during which he 'saw many wonders, heard much surprising, told you much, but could not tell everything that had happened to me'. This use of discourse deixis already quite explicitly points out the solipsistic nature of his story: he will relate what *he saw, he heard,* and what happened to *him*. We are also apprehended that his story will contain marvellous and surprising things and, significantly, that much still remains *untold*. The introductory description of the world outside and within the idyllic setting, as is common in Karamzin's works, already contains most of the key images to be developed in the story of his past travels. The 'glorious summer' is the temporal setting of the story, the 'dark sea' and 'raging wind' is its spatial setting, and the reunion with friends is the goal of his Sentimental journey. The outside wintry imagery of fading, withering, cold, and death, foreshadows the predominant traits of the personages in his story, and much will again remain untold.

'Bornholm Island' can be viewed as a set of variations on the idyll theme, deriving from, and colored by, the narrator's present circumstances. The story as a whole affirms his present values and expresses his own gratitude for his fortunate situation by contrasting it to its absence – a typical Sentimentalist maneuver, as we have seen in, for instance, 'A Promenade' and 'Liodor'. His own past journey is, significantly, a *return* journey, a quest for recapturing the idyll of his childhood and youth. From this point of view the present speech event is a happy epilogue to his Sentimental journey. The speech event overture describing his winter idyll thus naturally leads to his story set in the near past, 'far, far from my fatherland, far from you, beloved of my heart'. The narrated events begin proleptically with an anticipation of what at the present is a *fait accompli*: 'Your fatherland and friends await you; it is time to rest in their embraces, it is time to dedicate your traveller's staff to the son of Maia; it is time to hang it on the thickest branch of the tree under which you used to play when you were young' (93).

The rest of the story develops as a description of his joyous feelings of anticipation mingled with fear that he may not reach his idyllic destination, and awe at the immensity and unidyllic properties of the outside world. Each feeling is, as it were, nourished by the events, personages, and settings that he encounters and experiences during his journey, and each feeling, in turn, determines to some extent those experiences. The sea which separates the narrator from his friends instills this fear, and the journey across the sea is one of the main plot lines. It is set in a hostile outside world which threatens his idyllic dreams, with interludes in idyllic settings on land when the ship is forced to anchor. The interludes are taken up by the narrator's walks and serve as setting for the second major plot line (the vicarious love story), which is an idyll *manqué*. Thus the narrated events of 'Bornholm Island' are developed as a quest for a personal idyll and, within that, another quest for hearing a vicarious love idyll *manqué*. I shall analyse each quest in turn, first the sea journey, and then the interludes and love idyll on land.

The first leg of the sea journey extends from London to Gravesend with the flowering shores of the Thames still in sight, and is interrupted by the unpredictable winds on the periphery of the idyll world. The threatening image of the boundless sea still lies ahead in the distance. The images of the unpredictable, of infinite dimensions, loud sounds, and agitated movement are diametrically opposed to the knowable, peaceful, small scale parameters of the idyll, and will recur throughout the story as a negative counterpoint to the narrator's idyll.

The same imagery is developed to its utmost in the description of the next leg of the journey from Gravesend to Bornholm.[57] As the ship leaves Gravesend, everything linked to the idyll gradually disappears in a sequence highly reminiscent of the onset of night in 'A Promenade'. A brief review of the sequence of events in the earlier work will convince us that the *aesthetic* experience described and the imagery used is the same in the two works, one set on dry land, and the other in the midst of the boundless sea, pointing to the ultimate insignificance of physical reality in a Sentimentalist journey. Such a comparison will also point to the difference between the two works and the intervening five-year evolution in artistic method. In 'A Promenade' we have the following sequence of events: as the sun sets, the mountains in the distance dissolve into darkness, the birds cease to sing, and finally all objects disappear, 'all except I, myself'. Complete silence reigns, except for the sounds of water. The narrator experiences his own 'sense of existence', and imagines the primeval lifeless void as the 'sound (*shum*) of rapid waters [which] is like the sound (*shum*) of the waves of the primeval ocean', before earth was created. Against this background he feels the immense power of Divine Creation, and against his own imagined future sickness (and the faraway sounding [*shumiashchie*] waves of the sea of eternity) and the terror (*uzhas*) of his own death, he feels the consolation of spiritual re-birth and immortality. Contemplating the infinitude of space and the absence of all surrounding matter, he relives creation of poetry and experiences a Wielandian affinity to the spirits, as if hidden by only 'a thin curtain'.[58]

In 'Bornholm Island' the English coast gradually recedes over the horizon and finally everything disappears, even the birds return to shore 'as if terrified (*ustrashennye*)' by the infinitude of the sea. The only remaining objects are the 'agitation of stirring (*shumnykh*) waves' and the 'misty sky', grandiose and terrible (*strashnyi*). An emotive apostrophe to the friends reiterates the Wieland theme of 'A Promenade' and 'Liodor':

My friends! in order to feel vividly all the daring of the human spirit, one must be on the open sea, *where only a thin small plank*, as Wieland says, *separates us from humid death*, but where a skilled navigator sets sail, flies, and in his thoughts already sees the glimmer of gold, whereby his enterprise will be rewarded, at the other end of the world. Nil mortalibus arduum est, – *for mortals nothing is impossible*, I thought with Horace, my glance losing itself in the infinity of Neptune's kingdom. (98)

The realia of his journey provoke an aesthetic metaphor affirming the power of Divine Creation over the deep and the power of man as part of Creation. The skillful navigator who masters the sea, with his visions of gold at the other end of the world, is mainly an image of man, life, and spiritual immortality – a metaphorical restatement of the metaphysical ideas in 'A Promenade'. The subsequent description of the narrator's actual seasickness and recovery, serves the same function as the imagined illness, death, and resurrection in 'A Promenade'. It lasts for six days (like Creation), and on the seventh day he re-emerges on deck from the womb of the ship and joyously beholds the sun in a clear sky, the sea illuminated by its golden rays (Light, the Firmament), the ship conquering the waves which in vain try to overwhelm it, and 'something like earth' (Land). While the narrator describes the actual events of his journey, he also describes the aesthetic act of Divine Creation. The awesome feelings of total void serve mainly to emphasize the power of Creation (by God) and co-creation (by Wieland, Horace, and the narrator himself). As in 'A Promenade', nature is viewed as the first aesthetic act, followed by poetry, and the chain is completed by the narrator's own creative perception. On a spiritual level, the sea journey describes the narrator's aesthetic pleasure derived from his emotions of fear and awe, a Gothic aesthetics of horror. One might also view this as a description of two parallel conquests of the elements (the narrator's aesthetic conquest and the captain's scientific conquest) – a fictional illustration of Karamzin's views of human progress in the arts and the sciences, as expressed in his article 'On the Sciences, Arts and Enlightenment'.[59] This article was written around the same time as 'Bornholm Island', and appeared in the same issue of *Aglaia*. It is in many respects a 'theoretical' companion piece to his fiction of this period.

As compared to 'A Promenade', the description of the sea journey serves a much more pronounced dual function, both advancing and developing the physical details of the journey plot line and describing its spiritual–aesthetic dimensions. In 'A Promenade', we recall, the physical plot for the most part 'stands still' during the metaphysical musings, and is hardly important or suspenseful in and of itself. The greater sophistication of the physical plot in 'Bornholm Island' results in a more balanced integration of the physical with the aesthetic dimensions of the journey. This is, I believe, one of the main results of Karamzin's intervening five-year literary evolution, and one of the features which distinguish his Sentimental tales from his idylls and trifles. Furthermore, as mentioned above, the tale as a whole is more complex than this dual physical–spiritual sea journey.

The aesthetics of horror at sea alternates with the aesthetics of joy experienced in a series of idyllic settings on land as the ship makes several stops during the journey. The theme of the beauty and goodness of Creation is developed in a rising line in the form of the narrator's successive idyllic stops on land, progressing from larger, more general, and less intensive, to smaller, more personal, and more intensive idylls: from the 'flowering coast' of England, to Gravesend (general, large, foreign) to Bornholm island and the fishermen's idyll on its peripheries (general, smaller, foreign, but with links to the Slavs) to the garden at the heart of the island (small, well-defined, personal, and intensely experienced), and, after a minimal description of the Bornholm–Russia leg, this rising line culminates in the idyllic goal of the narrator's present personal idyll around his native hearth which begins 'Bornholm Island' (a physically and spiritually internalized idyll of close friendship).

As in most Sentimental tales, a vicarious love plot is included. It develops on land during the breaks in the sea journey, as it were, within the idyllic interludes. Like the sea journey and the land interludes, it serves as an 'object' for the narrator's acts of aesthetic perception. Near the end of 'Bornholm Island' the entire vicarious love plot is told to the narrator by the old man, but the narrator himself chooses not to report it *at all* in his story, and merely provides a reporting clause without any reported message. He refuses to perform his main function with respect to the love story. In addition, he blatantly flaunts his refusal. This, of course, does not mean that he does not report at all, but what he reports is not the vicarious love plot as such (which was the case in 'Poor Liza', for instance), but his own extensive quest for the story, as it is revealed to him in fragments (much like Liodor's love story) through its three different epilogues. His performance as narratee in the telling of the love story is hereby developed into a second major personal plot. This second plot, furthermore, intertwines with and runs counterpoint to his quest for his personal idyll: the idyllic interludes on land, as we saw, served as a 'prologue' to his present idyll. Within these smaller 'journeys' on land the anti-idyllic 'epilogues' to the vicarious love idyll are revealed, and the three personages in turn mourn the loss of their idyll. Moreover, the love plot, temporally speaking, serves to retard the journey and endanger, or at least postpone, the narrator's realization of his own final Russian idyll. I shall now look more closely at the second plot: the narrator's role as a narratee in quest of a story.

This plot consists of four encounters with the personages (secondary narrators), separately and in different locations. It includes not only the inner actions so typical in most of the other works we have seen, but also the physical adventures and obstacles the narrator has to overcome to make contact with the secondary narrators. Each encounter develops out of a typical idyllic walk, which, however, in addition to the usual 'pleasures' of nature, reveals the tragic situations of the personages and, indirectly, their idyll *manqué*. At the first encounter the narrator unexpectedly overhears the elegiac song of the young man at Gravesend. After that the narrator's physical actions and walks are prompted not only by a quest for idyllic vistas, but also by a vague but irresistible urge to meet the other personages and to find out the full story behind the song, and by a certain amount of daring and of intuition as to where and how to go about it – aided by a great deal of chronotopical coincidence. The successful performance as narratee is the result of overcoming substantial physical obstacles: a special side trip to Bornholm island from the ship, despite the dangers and the captain's advice against such an enterprise; the walk to the interior of the island, despite the late hour; entering the castle, despite the natives' warnings and their fears of the locale; venturing out of the castle in the middle of the night, and entering the dungeon, obviously not meant to be a tourist attraction. These physical actions, in short, come close to an adventure plot.

Other obstacles have to do with the difficulty in obtaining information, in getting the personages to narrate. In fact, none of the secondary narrators intends to narrate. The young man simply sings a song not addressed to anyone in particular, but accidentally overheard by the narrator. There is no further communication between the two, owing to the sailing schedule. The old man on Bornholm (at their first encounter) carries on a conversation on the most general topics, skirting all direct reference to personal issues, and bids the narrator a good night after a mere half hour. His servant vanishes before the narrator has a chance to ask him the 'multitude of questions' he wanted to ask. The young woman in the dungeon rather hesitantly enters into conversation with the narrator, and by chance repeats some of the key elements of the song, and even explicitly forbids him to ask her about her story. The natives are equally reticent about the castle since 'God knows what is done there' – another oblique reference to the events of the love story. Only the old man finally, and after much hesitation, decides to tell the full story, *after* the narrator has seen too much. Nevertheless, all personages (before the final telling) inadvertently perform as narrators, providing some missing pieces to the puzzle of the love story from their respective retrospective points of view. In describing these encounters and the communicative events, the narrator reveals much of the story 'against his will', 'unknowingly', as was the case in 'Liodor'. Indeed, the skeleton of the plot is already included in the love song. Thus, by indirection, he in fact 'quotes' a story which he ostensibly refuses to tell.[60] 'Bornholm Island', as it were, poses as a fragment, while the reader in fact knows most of what there is to know. It seems clear that its fragmentary presentation is a conscious device to elicit reader response of the intense emotional kind that the Sentimentalists aimed for, stressing precisely all the varied aspects of becoming and being a narratee, and particularly sharing the narrator's own feelings of suspense, and the attraction that the horrible, the unspeakable, and the mysterious hold for him.[61]

From the very beginning of his quest (after hearing the song), the narrator knows, or must at least suspect, the incestuous plot (as do his narratees): the song refers to laws that condemn the object of the singer's love, not his love as such, a parental curse, his own punishment (exile), the separation of lovers, and even the name of his beloved (Lila) and the place he himself was exiled from (Bornholm). Thus the song contains the whole story in comparatively direct words (we might recall the song in 'Liodor', which, however, was entirely metaphorical). The other encounters fill in the rest, and answer the questions posed by the song. It is clear that the plot is presented as secondary to its aesthetic potential for the narrator himself, to be relived by his narratee. Furthermore, the very theme of incestuous love contains a paradox (as is most clearly felt by the young man and referred to in his song), not easily resolvable, and by not describing it in detail, and not overtly taking a stand on the issue, the narrator, as it were, passes on the paradox to be pondered by the narratee. The same is true of other equally difficult questions, such as the right to pass judgment on, and mete out punishment to, another human being, a problem to which I shall return shortly.

Another point that needs to be stressed in relation to the narrator's refusal to re-narrate what he heard, and to the question of 'Bornholm Island' as an 'incomplete fragment', is the promise of a continuation *at another time*. This sort of tactic may serve to prolong the narrator's idyll by assuring him that his friends will return – much like journal publishers will assure future sales by announcing a continuation at a particularly suspenseful moment in a story. We should also note that the promise is not made by Karamzin, nor even editorially, but by the narrator to his friends, i.e., within and as part of the fiction. As in the case of 'Liodor', at least some contemporary readers identified with the narratees to such a degree that they eagerly awaited a sequel. The Dowager Empress Maria Fedorovna was one such reader. According to a letter addressed to her by Karamzin (August 16, 1815, some twenty years after the publication of 'Bornholm Island'), her Imperial Highness 'took part in the sufferings of the unknown woman at Bornholm and thereby changed her fate'. The Empress, as it were, co-created together with Karamzin a happy ending to his story. Karamzin wrote the Empress that the suffering woman at Bornholm:

suddenly saw the light and the *Gravesend melancholic*, who threw himself in her embraces with the exclamation: you are not my *sister*, but my wife! They left the dungeon, were united in legal marriage and settled in the little house [the former huge, Gothic castle, transformed?] which now is unrecognizable! they fixed it up inside and out, mowed the wormwood and nettles in the yard. The old man – the host, delighted over the now legal love of his daughter and son-in-law, gives balls and himself dances the polonaise, and the dark cave where the pale, languorous beauty was imprisoned, is prepared for the imprisonment of the yellowish corpulent Napoleon, should the storms bring him to Bornholm.[62]

However, maintaining his game of historical truth and fiction, Karamzin adds that 'this is what they write me from Denmark', and promises to tell the Empress *the rest* in the rose-colored pavilion (i.e., at Pavlovsk). Thus, although he humors the Empress and provides her with a silly private non-incestuous epilogue, he still does not tell her the promised 'horrible' story and still leaves her to wait for the full details, just like the narrator left his friends in 'Bornholm Island'. Even the fuller story is thus left a fragment, and was obviously not seriously intended for publication. Other readers were not given further details nor an epilogue. A. T. Bolotov, that dependable barometer of contemporary reception, described the earlier reaction to the tale in the following words:

The continuation of Bornholm was eagerly awaited. Although the precise reasons why he [Karamzin] did not include it are unknown, there was a rumor according to which Mr Derzhavin had written him from Petersburg that he should not include it, which could be true; as to the content of this continuation, it could already be concluded that it would be contrary to good manners . . . ; it was to describe the love and illicit relationship between a brother and his own sister and accordingly it might even be good that he got a response and heeded the advice.[63]

No such letter from Derzhavin has been verified to exist, and it seems, in fact, quite unlikely that Derzhavin would have offered such advice to Karamzin.[64] He himself was the translator of an anonymous German adaptation of an Ovidian story dealing with the same topic of incestuous love. Derzhavin's work, quite possibly familiar to Karamzin, was entitled 'Iroida, ili Pis'mo Vivlidy k Kainu', and appeared in 1773 as Derzhavin's first published work.[65] It would seem most likely that 'Bornholm Island' is indeed meant to be a finished work of the 'incomplete fragment' form.

Another point to be made in this connection is that the promise of a sequel is not the end of 'Bornholm Island', which goes on for another two paragraphs describing the journey. Although the description does not follow the journey to its final destination, the conclusion symmetrically completes 'Bornholm Island' as a whole with the same idyllic frame it began with. I shall now look more closely at each idyllic interlude and each encounter with the personages in the love story, and in the process I hope to elucidate further the narrator as narratee, and to shed some light on the intricate ways in which the two plot lines are related as idyll and anti-idyll.

The ship is forced to anchor at Gravesend and the narrator goes ashore. With a peaceful heart and with an artist's eyes, he enjoys the idyllic setting and reposes in a typical *locus amoenus*, on the green grass, under a centenarian elm, by the sea shore. His view consists of the sea, outside his own idyllic vantage point, and is characterized by the usual superlative dimensions of infinite space. As opposed to the well-defined dimensions of the idyll, we have *beschislennye riady; mrachnaia otdalennost'; neobozrimye vody* and a *glukhoi rev; unylyi shum*, all of which, as we saw, recurs with slight variation in the subsequent description of the sea journey. The desolate sound and the boundless view lull him into 'that drowsiness, to that sweet idleness of the soul in which all ideas and all feelings stop and freeze like suddenly freezing spring waters, and which is the most striking and poetic image of death' (94). The narrator's poetic image of death suddenly comes to life in the male hero of the love story who abruptly intrudes in the idyllic setting, but whose reaction to it is antithetical to that of the narrator. His feelings are 'dead to the surrounding objects', and with one hand he tears off leaves from a tree (destruction of idyllic nature), as if unaware of what he is doing. He looks at the blue sea with immobile eyes in which 'shone the last ray of expiring life'. He sees nothing, hears nothing, and in fact, he is 'more like an apparition than a man' – an image literally, of living death. The narrator, who takes in all the sights and sounds, is profoundly moved by his obvious unhappiness. The young man sings an elegiac song in Danish (the language spoken on Bornholm, translated into Russian by the polyglot narrator), which elaborates his grief.

The song is an elegy which to a significant degree also reveals the reasons for the singer's present state, i.e., the love story. It provokes the narrator's immediate sensitive response and continues to haunt him. It is indeed the impetus for all his subsequent actions. He recalls it again when the captain announces their stop at Bornholm island. Its 'sad sounds and words' contain the 'secret of the young man's heart', and the narrator's thoughts revolve around questions of his identity and about the nature of the laws and the curse that resulted in his exile and separated him from his beloved. 'Who is he? What laws [ . . . ] what oath [ . . . ]?' (100) The main question is, however, none of the above, but the last in the sequence the narrator utters to himself: 'Will I ever find out his story?' The focal point of his tale becomes, not 'Who is he?' but *'Will I find out* who he is?' – i.e., the narrator's own quest for a story. His story about that quest has a happy ending: '*I found out* the secret of the unknown person at Gravesend' (118, emphasis added). The answers to the subordinate questions make up another story which, however, 'will be left for another time' (118).

The full poetic power of the elegy as an art form is more explicitly stated in 'On the Sciences', where Karamzin expresses a new (to him) idea of the elegy as man's first poetic expression:

I think that the first poetic creation was nothing but the out-pourings of a languorously sad heart, that is, that the first poetry was elegiac. [ . . . ] a sad friend, a sad lover, having lost the dear half of his soul, loves to think and speak of his sorrow, to pour out, describe his emotions; he chooses all nature as confidant for his sorrow; it seems to him that a babbling brook and a rustling tree sympathizes with his loss; the condition of his soul is already so to say poetry; he wants to soothe his heart and soothes it – with tears and song.[66]

In 'Bornholm Island' the narrator responds most effusively to both the 'soul' of the singer and his song, both equally poetic. The inclusion of the elegy, and the general elegiac tonalities in 'Bornholm Island' (and, as we saw, in 'Sierra-Morena') are indicative of Karamzin's artistic development. His early idylls (notably again 'A Promenade') and the poetic credo stated in the same period in other works, such as 'Poetry', feature joyous hymns as the original (human) poetry. Both his theory and practice seem to have evolved from the aesthetics of the joyous to that of the grievous – both emotions, however, equally pleasurable. Thus the pleasure principle still governs Karamzin's artistic paradigm. As the narrator of 'Bornholm Island' expresses this general principle with regard to birdsong: 'the little birds sing happily for the happy one, sadly for the sad one, pleasantly for everyone' (116).

The narrator's view of Bornholm from the sea is colored by his memory of the young man and his song and the images of death in Gravesend and at sea. The view of the island is aestheticized, and further develops the Biblical image of Creation, or rather the power of crea*ting* earth from the deep whose elemental force is powerless in its attempts to obliterate Creation: 'With terror I saw there an image of cold, silent eternity, inexorable death and that indescribable Creator's power, before which all that is mortal must tremble' (100). That this is meant as an image of Divine Creation of Earth, continuing the preceding experience, is made quite clear later, when the narrator's vantage point is reversed from sea to land and the island is described as a Northern idyll: 'Even here, where foamy waves *from the beginning of the world* struggle with granite cliffs, – even here did Your hand imprint the living signs of the Creator's love and bliss' (115–16). Once on land, and past the granite cliffs, there is a brief idyllic glimpse of the territory inhabited by the fishermen: a green plain, with *nizen'kie derevian-nye domiki, roshchitsy* among the huge rocks – the diminutive forms and the objects themselves already familiar. A simile further likens the scene to Alpine valleys, reminiscent of many of Gessner's idylls (and Karamzin's *Letters of a Russian Traveller*). The 'crude and savage' natives remind us of all the allusions to savage tribes, wild children of nature, the childhood of mankind, usually linked to an idyllic Arcadian age. The brief idyllic vision calls forth the narrator's wish to go further and 'for a little while longer delight in the pleasures of evening' – the idyllic preoccupation par excellence.

Within this idyll, the narrator encounters another anti-idyllic setting: a Gothic castle which seems as impenetrable as the island had seemed. The chronotope of the castle like that of the sea contrasts to the idyllic chronotope. It entails large dimensions and it encompasses an impersonal totality of human history: 'the castle is saturated with time'.[67] Everything about this castle is extreme (ancient castle, large building, deep moat, high walls, wide yard, huge house, tall peristyle, long passages, large room, ancient weaponry, tall bed, ancient basreliefs), even the people and their moods (a tall man in a long black garment, an old man, eternal grief). There is a particular emphasis on temporal infinitude. Historical time is linear, as opposed to cyclical idyllic time, and is here depicted as a declining line towards destruction, emptiness, winter, night, darkness, old age, and death, without the con-solation of creative renewal – another contrast to the rising line of the narrator's successive idylls.

Human historical accomplishments do not have the power to

withstand the onslaught of time and the elements that Divine
Creation possesses, and the castle is depicted as being on the brink
of the primeval void, symbolized previously by the ocean. There is
a lack of light and air, hollow metallic sounds echo in the dilapidated halls, and it is littered with the broken remnants of columns,
cornices, and pilasters. The uncanny atmosphere is rendered
through all the Gothic touches of a Radcliffe or a Lewis.[68]

The sights and sounds make a 'strange impression' on the
narrator, his mood is terror mixed with a 'mysterious inexplicable
pleasure' or, as he qualifies it for his listeners in retrospect, 'a
pleasant expectation of something extraordinary'. He sublimates
his fear according to the aesthetics of horror and the suspense of his
quest for a story.

Besides the deep moat and the high walls that protect the castle,
the ancient weaponry – armor, helmets, etc. – suggests a Medieval
knightly past of martial defense, and strengthens the impression of
a closed private territory, shielded at all cost from outside intrusion. Indeed, the incestuous love can be seen as the logical
consequence of this total seclusion, where now only the old man
and his servant live. The castle grounds instill uncanny fear in the
natives, and it is obvious that all communication with the outside
world is cut off.

The old man is described as 'distinguished' and 'greyhaired' and
he greets the narrator with a look of 'a certain sad kindness',
extending a 'weak hand'. In a quiet and pleasant voice he immediately qualifies his greeting with references to eternal grief and a
dying heart, reminiscent of the impression his young son had made
on the narrator at Gravesend. He wants to be cordial and entertain
his guest, but signs of heartfelt sorrow defeat his purpose. The
narrator's impression is that he is like a 'clear but cold autumn day
more like sad winter than joyous summer'.

The aftermath of this encounter is, for the narrator, a restless
night and nightmares in which his feeling of terror gains the upper
hand. He experiences 'the extraordinary' in his dreams of knights
punishing him for intruding in the castle and an indescribable
winged monster ready to attack him – both dreams with props
consisting of various objects and impressions from the day's experiences. His restless state is unconducive to aesthetic pleasure, which
requires internal peace. He needs fresh air and leaves the castle.

Although, as Vatsuro and others have pointed out, the old man is not depicted as the traditional, thoroughly evil, feudal lord, he is certainly the least appealing personage (the least sensitive one) in the love story. The narrator's response to his grief is not one of effusive compassion, but of horror as expressed subconsciously, in his dreams. The Sentimentalist narrator does not identify with the hand that metes out the punishment, but with the virtuous victim in distress. Before he falls asleep, it is the poetic image of the *victim* of the 'parental oath' that he sees when remembering the words 'here dwells eternal grief', pronounced by the father about *his own* state. In a way, his dreams are a sympathetic reliving of the young man's punishment for his, as yet, undefined 'crime'. The incommensurability between his own crime and the punishment in his dream (entering the castle grounds – death) can be seen as a subconscious evaluation of the punishment meted out to the Gravesend youth in relation to *his* crime, which, from the impression the narrator had formed of his externals and his song, could not possibly have been too serious.

Through a small door the narrator enters the garden for aesthetic relief and is immediately struck by the light, even at night. Still in the throes of terror from his nightmares, he hears the distant sound of the sea, sees the distant cliffs that border the island, and enters a dark avenue of oak trees, immersed in thoughts of pagan history – of Druids and their dread worship. The druidic image provoked by the oaks (the favored tree of Druids) continues the motif of the old man. The Druids meted out punishment to persons guilty of disobeying their decrees, and also presumably performed sacrifices of human victims, innocent ones if no criminals were at hand. Their rites were performed in forest clearings. The references to the 'secrets' and 'terrors of their worship' (after the nightmares and before the discovery of the dungeon) obliquely evaluate the severity of the punishment. The negative pagan and barbaric image of the old man is also strengthened by the immediately preceding reference to the sea as 'Neptune's kingdom', a fear-inspiring pagan kingdom as opposed to God's Creation.

The narrator's mood when outside the dark castle is one of 'reverential fear', but soon idyllic nature with its power to soothe, arouses a wish for an aesthetic view. Amidst rosemary bushes he sees a sandy hillock and selects it as a vantage point from which to contemplate the picture of sea and island illuminated by moonlight – the typical goal of idyllic night walks. The picturesque hillock, however, turns out to be a man-made dungeon, where the young heroine is held prisoner behind a huge iron door and iron grating with a huge lock (we recall the description of the convent where the young heroine ended her days in 'Sierra-Morena'). She is underground, shut out from the idyllic beauty of nature, as if buried alive. Her punishment seems as disproportionate to her crime as were the death sentence in the narrator's dream and the exile of the young man, especially when one considers her extreme weakness, her beauty (= goodness), her meek acceptance of her punishment, and her admission of the possibility of her guilt.

The picture of the young woman is the culmination of the theme of living death and the contrast between idyllic and outside reality which has been building up all along. She is described as pale, dressed in black (the color of mourning), she sleeps on a bed of yellow straw (dead stalks of grain), is barely breathing, and her white hand lying on the ground is 'withered'. At the present memory of this picture the narrator lapses into a highly emotive poetic digression to his friends, revealing its *aesthetic* potential:

If a painter wanted to depict languishing, endless, eternal grief, besprinkled with the poppy blossoms of Morpheus, then this woman could surely serve as a lovely model for his brush.

My friends! who is not moved by the sight of an unhappy person? But the sight of a young woman suffering in an underground prison – the sight of the weakest and loveliest of all beings oppressed by fate – could, like Orpheus's harp, make even stone come alive. (112)

The feeling of horror inside the castle after meeting the old man and hearing of his 'eternal grief', is renewed in the image of the young woman, an *aesthetic* analogue to the former image which was informed by terror. She is seen as a painter's image of 'eternal grief', and instead of being attacked by *winged monsters*, she reposes in the embraces of the *winged god* of dreams, besprinkled by soothing poppies. The pictorial image is presumably evoked because of the inability of words to convey the strong impression (the inexpressibility topos) and, as if that were not enough, the image is further synaesthesized by an appeal to music, Orpheus's art. Orpheus, we might note, was extolled already in Karamzin's 'Poetry' as one of the immortal poets. Orphic music is also well suited to the context of 'Bornholm Island' by virtue of its associations to the Argonauts' sea voyage in quest of the Golden Fleece and Orpheus's power to save the Argo from the Symplegades, the terrifying moving rocks. The Britannia, we recall, is lying at anchor, safe from the Bornholm cliffs, waiting to continue her quest for the 'gold at the other end of the world'.

The most compelling association is, however, to the Orpheus–Eurydice myth. The young woman underground is analogous to Eurydice in the nether world, and the young man at Gravesend is like a latter-day Orpheus, whose song (to another stringed instrument) contained an appeal to the 'loveliest shadow' – the superlative epithet repeated by the narrator in his reference to the young woman. The old man's part is also fitting: the 'human hands' which constructed the dungeon and keep Eurydice in the nether world belong to him, and it is fairly clear that the 'terrible parental oath' referred to by both lovers was also pronounced by him.

The aesthetically pleasing vision is once more the cause of the narrator's positive moral evaluation: the beautiful is identified with goodness and innocence. The cruel punishment and the terrible parental oath are endured in a meek Christian spirit by the victim. Although she does not rationally understand her guilt, she admits its possibility, and meekly accepts on faith a larger unfathomable Divine design where weakness is forgiven: 'my heart', she answered, 'could have erred. God forgives the weak one.'

The young woman submits both to human laws and Divine laws rather than questioning them rationally, and she finds at least some solace in religion and thoughts of afterlife. Her brother finds some solace in music and poetry and thoughts of a posthumous reunion with his beloved. Both can sublimate their grief to some extent. The old man finds no consolation and complains of his cruel lot and God's punishment, despite the fact that he has always loved virtue and lived by God's Commandments. He neither forgives nor hopes for forgiveness. He follows the Divine Commandments more to the letter than to the spirit – a procedure unacceptable to the Sentimental narrator.

The narrator himself finds both religious and aesthetic consolation for his own co-suffering in idyllic nature, and regrets that the same cure cannot take its course where the personages are concerned. He emerges from the dungeon into the fresh morning air, at dawn, when all nature is at its 'newborn' best, the setting stressing the idyllic cyclical renewal. In his thoughts he addresses a long panegyric apostrophe to the Creator and the work of his hand, contrasting it to the 'weak barbaric' hands of the father, the 'withered' hand of the daughter, and the 'destructive' hand of the son, and further developing the positive image of the protective hand of 'majestic nature':

My God! I thought – my God! how sad to be excluded from the society of living, free, joyous creatures which everywhere inhabit the boundless space of Nature! In the very North, among high mossy cliffs, terrible to behold, the creation of Your hand is beautiful – the creation of Your hand enraptures the spirit and heart. Even here where foamy waves since the beginning of the world struggle with granite cliffs – even here did Your hand imprint the living signs of the Creator's love and bliss; even here in the morning hours roses bloom on an azure sky; even here tender Zephyrs breathe with fragrance; even here green carpets spread out like soft velvet under human feet; even here little birds sing – sing happily for the happy one, sadly for the sad one, pleasantly for everyone; even here a grieving heart can find solace from the burden of its grievances in the embraces of sensitive Nature! (115–16)

The ecstatic affirmation of idyllic creation (with all the obligatory elements of the *locus amoenus*) comes as the culmination to the narrator's previous glimpses of peripheral idylls in Gravesend and on the outer reaches of the island. He is at the heart of the idyll world. More important, the apostrophe is pronounced after he has experienced and co-experienced its absence: he has re-lived the primeval void, the relics of Medieval barbarism, the downward trend of a once glorious state of the arts, human suffering and alienation. His own optimism and faith in Divine goodness remain undaunted and are even strengthened by the intermittent experiences of horror and grief.

In 'On the Sciences', Karamzin states: 'It seems as if nature, sometimes hiding the truth [ . . . ], wants only that we delight all the longer in the pleasant quest and feel its beauty all the more vividly'.[69] 'Bornholm Island' demonstrates mainly the pleasure in the aesthetic quest itself. The final garden idyll at the heart of the island provokes the narrator's most vivid sensation of nature's beauty, and permanence, despite adverse conditions and temporary aberrations. Nature consistently triumphs over the deep. Divine power is reflected in the human *physical* enterprises (the captain skillfully navigates the ship through treacherous waters), and *aesthetic* experience (the narrator's aesthetic co-creation after his seasickness). Even in the description of moral actions, I believe that Karamzin affirms virtue precisely by its absence.

The personages, each in his own way, ponder the 'plan of

nature', but its healing powers fail to cure them. The paradox between laws of the heart (nature) and human laws (the incest taboo), raised in the song, is in a way resolved by an appeal to a more encompassing Divine law which, however, cannot be comprehended by humans. Human limitations and weakness (the notorious 'delicacy') prevents nature's healing powers from taking effect. That is their tragedy. This does not mean that the narrator negates the morally renewing power of nature (and art and faith), nor that *his* view is pessimistic. On the contrary, although he admittedly does not comprehend the full design of Creation and its paradoxes, he nevertheless expresses his faith in the existence of such a design. He sees its beauty, and thus believes in its goodness. His apostrophe to the Creator concludes in a question: 'Creator! why did You give people the ruinous power to make each other and themselves unhappy?' (116). Yet, the continuation of 'Bornholm Island', the final leg of the sea journey from Bornholm to Russia, implies that the opposite power of making one another happy is also given to humans. It is that power which underlies the narrator's own subsequent life and which is stressed as the *optimistic* message of the tale as a whole.[70] The further events of the tale, *after* the narrator has heard the 'most terrible story', end on an upbeat: he stands on deck, immersed in sad thoughts, sighing, but 'finally I looked at the sky – and the wind blew away my tear into the sea' (118). The narrator finds new strength from above, and Nature dries his tears.

The account of the subsequent events in his own life (i.e., the beginning of 'Bornholm Island') is, to my mind, a final affirmation of the idyll as a cure for alienation, loneliness, and hopelessness, put into practice in the narrator's personal life. The oaks and birches that have provided shade during hot summer days 'now' provide heat as they burn in the fireplace. The pleasures provided by the *alaia zaria* and the dawn which *alela* in the summer idylls are now internalized as the *alaia ognia* of the hearth. The 'cloudy sky, agitated by the dark sea', as well as withering nature, strong winds, signs of death, and so on, are outside the bounds of the present idyll. The stress is on pleasant communion with close friends as the antidote to boredom, on the temporary nature of winter, the temporary farewell to external nature 'until joyous spring reunion'.

I believe that the narrator's own idyllic quest, his Sentimental journey, and especially its aesthetic dimension, are the focal points of the tale. The opposite movement of the love idyll to its tragic epilogue is used as a negative counterpoint to this quest in order to set the joyous idyllic view in sharper relief. 'Bornholm Island' is, by this token, an exploration of the aesthetics of horror and grief, affirming the *aesthetics* rather than the raw emotions themselves.

# 6

# Humorous Sentimental tales: narrator as parodist

Humor as a vital principle in Russian Sentimentalist prose fiction has, in general, been underestimated. The tendency has been to stress the serious (realistic, historical, moral, pedagogical, psychological) aspects even of the most humorous works. Sentimentalism has usually been described in terms of lachrymose melancholy, sadness, grief, pessimism, escape from grim (or progressive, depending on the point of view) social reality. As I have tried to show, such moods and topics were indeed prominent, although they were by no means exclusive, and they were furthermore almost always featured as subordinate to a pleasurable aesthetic sublimation through a narrator's perceptive apparatus. The perceptive–cognitive dimension was always more important as a topic, than the ontological.

Humor does not contradict Sentimentalist solipsism in principle. The *sine qua non* of the sensitive person is that he be moved by surrounding reality, personages, objects, and events. He may react to this environment with any of his inner faculties, the main point being that he react as fully as possible, with all his faculties engaged. Sentimentalism cannot be reduced to emotionalism as opposed to rationalism – both emotion and reason are stressed, although the former may be stressed more than the latter. Furthermore, when reason is stressed, the emphasis is on the individual's rational faculties and processes, rather than on a world organized by *a priori* rational principles or laws. For the Sentimentalist, 'to be moved' means to relate one's own person to objects and phenomena in the world, and, ultimately, to be aware of one's own self. The emotive part of this reaction cannot be reduced to tears, although, to be sure, tears (accompanied by sighs, exclamations, and appropriate gestures and motions) were frequently treated as the major emotional reaction – be they tears of sorrow or tears of joy – of personages and narrators in the works analyzed so far. Laughter is, however, as viable a response as are tears, and can be as pleasurable and infectious a response as are tears. Therefore it should not be surprising that humor enters the Sentimentalist paradigm.

The focus on emotion (more than reason) and tears (more than laughter) was, however, particularly prominent in some of the prose works written before the Sentimentalist period and the works of second-rate Sentimentalists, and prompted Karamzin to many statements (in his fiction as well as in his theoretical writings), such as the following, in his foreword to the second volume of *Aonidy*:

> It is also not necessary to speak constantly about tears, attaching to them various epithets, calling them shining or brilliant, – this *method of moving* is very undesirable: one ought to describe the reason for them in a striking way; represent grief not only with *general* characteristics, which being too ordinary, cannot have a strong effect on the heart of the reader, – but with specific characteristics which are related to the character and circumstances of the poet.[1]

Karamzin as editor of *Messenger of Europe*, chose to translate (presumably from an English original) and publish a 'letter to an English journalist' entitled 'The History of Tears', prominently featured as the second item.[2] The translation and the editorial decision to include the piece and include it so prominently, are in themselves indicative of Karamzin's attitude to excessive lachrymosity. The 'correspondent' announces his forthcoming ten-volume scientific work on the history of tears. It is a most outrageous parody of tearful Sentimentalist fiction: its topics, its manner, its form, and its structure. For example, the fourth volume is to consist of 'Great Britain. An Arithmetical Study of Lamentable News. The Increase in Tears in Families, with Some Digressions and Interpolated Tales, Surprisingly Pathetic.' The fifth volume will investigate the history of carriages, the increase in their number due to tears, anecdotes known to no one, the inception of hysterical attacks, and the curious habits of a certain dwarf. The sixth volume, among other topics, will describe the plan for a drama 'in which all actors and viewers are to cry themselves to death'. The tenth (and tentatively the final) volume will contain: 'A Division of Tears into Genera and Species, *Families and Kinds*, into Bitter, Sweet, Heartfelt, Insidious, Moving, and Others, Chemically Prepared in the Laboratories of the New Travellers and Novelists. Teary Waterfalls of Sensitivity. Conclusion.' Each volume will also have illustrations of ancient and modern female beauties in different tearful poses, such that anyone who takes a look at them will weep.

None of the most hallowed Sentimentalist topoi are exempt from parody. Many of them are, furthermore, quite specifically used in Karamzin's own works, and many of the same topoi also serve as the objects of Karamzin's humor and parody in the works we are about to discuss.

Laughter is as viable an emotive response as are tears, and it is also conducive to aesthetic pleasure in the perceiver. Laurence Sterne's prose provides perhaps the best illustration of Sentimentalist works where the two types of emotive response are in balance. His effusive humor does not contradict his Sentimentalism, but is part and parcel of the same phenomenon, of his focus on active reception and response. Thus I believe that it is utterly misleading to contrast the 'sensitive Sterne' with the 'humorous Sterne' as is frequently done, at least in Russian scholarship.[3] Gogol', who perhaps best deserves to be called the Russian Sterne, understood the connection between laughter and tears well: 'whoever frequently sheds heartfelt, sincere tears, that person, it seems, laughs more than anyone in the world'.[4]

Another point that should be stressed about Sentimentalist humor is that it is decidedly not of the 'loud', 'carnivalesque' kind described by Bakhtin. It is never allowed to transcend the bounds of propriety, and is always held in check by the all-powerful dictates of an educated refined taste – in language and in topic. The Sentimentalist, as it were, does not venture out onto the public square of the carnival, but stands with both feet in the salon parlor. The refined humor of the non-serious works is thus operative within the same idyll and salon chronotope as we saw in the serious works, although the distance between narrator/narratee on the one hand, and personages on the other hand, tends to be greater.

The structure of humorous Sentimental tales is similar to that of the serious tales we analyzed: a core story (with a vicarious love plot) is told by a primary narrator who has usually heard the story (or some variant of it) previously from someone else. A primary narrator also serves as secondary narratee. The reporting is bivocal or multivocal and the voices of previous tellers are more or less distinctly heard 'through' the primary narrator's voice. In the serious Sentimental tales the successive tellers were more or less in agreement in terms of their attitudes to the story and their manner of telling. These tales can be seen as representing Bakhtin's 'unidirectional bivocal speech'.

The humorous Sentimental tales differ from the serious tales with respect to agreement. Clashes between the different voices are much more prominent, and the voices of previous storytellers may differ in significant ways from that of the primary narrator. There is a greater axiological and literary distance between the different levels of the works, and the humor is indeed usually generated precisely through the clashes in voices between narrators, narratees, and personages. The humorous Sentimental tales can be said to demonstrate Bakhtin's 'heterodirectional bivocal speech'. The narrator engages in polemics with, or parody of, various other storytellers. Storytelling itself remains a major topic and frequently it is featured as a professional activity so that the primary narrator comes across as a literary critic of sorts. He mocks and parodies and jests with other ways of storytelling.

Other ways of telling may be extra-literary or literary, and the enterprise of literature itself is often one of the topics. Extra-literary telling (notably folklore and history writing), quasi-literary telling (the older lowly literature, Petrine tales by anonymous authors or a collective), and literary telling (the older Neoclassicist novels, the older adventure tales or earlier literary adaptations of former non-literature) are frequent targets of the Sentimentalist humorist. The Sentimentalist narrator contrasts his own superior manner of telling in a humorous and playful way to that of other narrators. One could say that the old controversy over prose fiction, its status as literature, and the proper characteristics of the new prose, is still continued under the cover of fiction.

A good-natured critique of alternative approaches to literature is thus given to highlight the superiority of the Sentimentalist approach. A similar critique is directed at the epigones of Sentimentalism itself, and particularly the excesses in their various expressions of sensitivity are humorously revealed. Furthermore, even admired 'good' Sentimentalists (notably Rousseau) and Karamzin himself are not exempt from these kinds of 'attacks' by his own humorous narrators. Indeed, the present narrator's own present telling is frequently the object of his own mockery, and some of these works are hilarious self-parodies, in which case the narrator provides a kind of running critical commentary on his own work in progress, his own literary method, his own formal devices, the philosophy he himself espouses, his own sources, and so on.

Kanunova makes an important point about Karamzin's humor in

'Natal'ia' which can be generalized for all humorous Sentimental tales. She points out that Karamzin's humor often takes the form of a 'laying bare of the device' (*obnazhenie priema*) and is directed not against sensitivity in general but against extreme representations of sensitivity.[5] This laying bare of the device is part of the discourse-deictic apparatus which serves to mark the speech event. It is one of the prime means for focusing on the narrator in his authorial function and an important device within the general solipsistic stress on narrator–narratee that characterizes all Sentimental tales – humorous, as well as serious ones. Indeed, one could see the humorous Sentimental tales as 'laying bare' Sentimentalism itself as a literary movement. The kind of solipsistic parody and self-parody these tales represent, is ultimately a sign that Sentimentalism as a literary movement had matured, since a parody is effective only if the readers recognize what is parodied, can hear the voice which the present narrator's voice clashes with. Parody of Sentimentalism and Sentimentalist forms, when it becomes critical in tone, may also be a sign of the imminent demise of the movement, a kind of disintegration from within. Once the premises of a literary movement are no longer taken entirely seriously, the time has usually come for literary renewal. Thus it is not perhaps surprising that the humorous Sentimental tales are much more frequent in the later part of Karamzin's literary career, and indeed that his last works of prose fiction before he finally turned away from literature to history writing were humorous Sentimental tales. The humorous tales thus have several metaliterary effects: they criticize the older literary currents and genres and extoll Sentimentalism, they criticize Sentimentalist excesses, and, finally, they criticize the very movement they themselves are part of. Oscar Wilde is reputed to have commented that one would have to have a heart of stone to read about the death of Little Nell without laughing. It seems that Karamzin may have come to the same conclusion about poor Liza.

## A HUMOROUS SENTIMENTAL FAIRY TALE

### 'The Beautiful Princess and the Fortunate Dwarf'

During the second part of the eighteenth century there was a marked increase in the interest in folklore. The folk song had attracted some attention already in the seventeenth century, and was later imitated even by such sophisticated Neoclassicist writers as Trediakovskii and Sumarokov as a bona fide literary genre – albeit through the veil of their own ideas on versification and style. From roughly the 1760s on, other folklore genres besides the song came to the fore, notably the fairy tale and the *bylina*. Numerous foreign collections of fairy tales were translated and/or adapted, Russian imitations appeared, and the native oral and written folk tradition was tapped.[6]

The fairy tales usually entered the book market not *in puris naturalibus*, but modified, adapted, and embellished to be acceptable as literary fact in the same way as other lowly prose was made respectable. For the generation before Karamzin (and for some of his contemporaries), this meant the introduction of an authoritative, didactic, moralizing, chivalric–elegant (or mock-authoritative, mock-didactic, etc.) narrator–narratee framework. The fairy tales were frequently couched in an excessively 'poetic' diction or enveloped in an interpretative and evaluative framework which explicitly stressed the allegorical meaning of the tale (such as Perrault's collections), or its moral level (like Marmontel's *Contes moraux*).[7] Eighteenth-century versions of the fairy tale included in their topic, besides the narrated events themselves, the speech event (or events) of the telling. The narrative structure of an eighteenth-century fairy tale was bivocal.

That this was perceived at the time, is clear from statements by contemporary theoreticians of the fairy tale, such as the following: 'The author of a fairy tale [ . . . ] may add his own arguments and feelings; but all that belongs to him, should be natural and well-planned, and, moreover, the narration becomes boring if the arguments are very long and very frequent'.[8]

The narrated event in a fairy tale is 'ontologically' different from the speech event. In the fairy tale, the narrated events take place in a world of their own, where the 'natural' laws of the 'present' world of the speech event need not be in force, or even ought not be in force. Magic talismans are real, animals speak, people move freely in magic boots, huts are erected on chicken legs, all sorts of beasts and monsters inhabit the world, spells of various kinds are normal, people sleep for a hundred years without aging, metamorphoses take place so that people turn into frogs and frogs into people, and so on and so forth. The speech event contrasts to the narrated event 'ontologically' as real to magic ('magic' will henceforth be used as shorthand for magic proper, the improbable, the impossible, the surreal, the supernatural).

The basic structure of a Sentimentalist fairy tale consists of a more or less magic narrated event, enveloped in the speech event of a folk story-teller, which is retold by the Sentimentalist narrator at the present time. The voice of the original teller is usually heard as an unidentified voice of 'the folk', or sometimes identified as the voice of a nanny or a granny. In no case is the language authentic folk speech, let alone dialect, but traces of that voice are heard mostly in formulaic or 'poetic' turns of phrase, perceivable as part of the folk tradition. All that is coarse or vulgar or incomprehensibly dialectal is eschewed according to the dictates of the refined taste of the Sentimentalist narrator and narratee. The narrator's presence penetrates the original narration both as the source of poetic selection and as a minus device, purifying the original account for the benefit of sensitive and refined ears. In Karamzin's humorous Sentimental fairy tales, modern tellers' voices are heard (in addition to the folk voice): the voices of excessively learned or didactic or elegant adaptors which add a touch of the chivalric romance or an excessive emotionalism to the original material.

As would be expected, it is the primary narrator's present voice that dominates the structure. The features of his voice penetrate all other voices, and he uses all the other voices for his own humorous, mocking, or parodic purposes. It is important to stress that all the different narrative voices are, to some degree, perceptible, despite the transformation and lack of formal attribution. Together with the original fairy tale and the various eighteenth-century voices, one always perceives the Sentimentalist transformation, but even though the latter voice speaks more loudly, the other voices do not totally disappear. We perceive both the magic world and the Sentimentalist interpretation, evaluation, and experience of that world and of its previous interpretations. Perhaps the most striking feature of the Sentimentalist re-interpretation is the profound transformation of the magic elements. For the most part, the status of the magic is transformed from the realm of ontology to that of epistemology – it is no longer featured as a 'real' property of the fairy world, but is seen as a property of the sensitive perceiver. It is part of the ability to give oneself up to the 'magic of beautiful fantasies', as the narrator of 'Il'ia Muromets' expresses it. The ability to fantasize is, as we have seen, a vital requirement in

Sentimentalist poetics, an aspect of the gift of seeing the extra-ordinary in the ordinary.

The major personages, despite their stylized fairy tale externals, are often transformed into heroes like the idyllic heroes in *any* Sentimentalist work – replicas of the narrator in all important respects. Often some of their main actions consist in the sensitive perception of nature and beauty, and the perception and creation of art. They subscribe to the same basic idyllic values as do all Sentimentalist personages – be they rulers, *bogatyrs*, monks, dwarfs, or ordinary mortals. Despite this 'serious' stress on Senti-mentalist ideas, the humorous fairy tales are rife with irony, parody, satire, and caricature. Although the humor is to some extent oriented towards the narrated events, it is frequently of a more literary kind, oriented towards previous and contemporary narrative methods. There is a constant tension between the magic and the real, between simple or poetic folk voices and erudite eighteenth-century voices, and between both these voices and Sentimentalist excesses.

All of Karamzin's fairy tales are fairy tales and something else simultaneously. In all cases, this dual focus is revealed explicitly in the title, subtitle, or footnotes. 'The Bird of Paradise', as we recall, was originally supplied with a footnote indicating the author's source as a 'Russian folk tale', demonstrative of 'the won-drous effect of harmony on the human heart' – the Sentimentalist motif of the 'magic' that inheres in the reception of beauty. The fairy tale was then transformed into a compliment trifle. 'The Deep Forest' was both a fairy tale for children and a parlor game. The fairy epic in verse 'Il'ia Muromets' is subtitled a '*bogatyr* fairy tale', with a footnote which indicates another 'incomplete frag-ment' trifle.

'The Beautiful Princess and the Fortunate Dwarf' is loosely based on the traditional international fairy tale motif of the beauty and the beast.[9] As pointed out already by Sipovskii, the motif was included in several written versions widely circulating in Russia during the late eighteenth century: primarily Perrault's 'Riquet à la Houppe', tales by H. Pajon, Mme Le Prince-de-Beaumont, A. F. E. Langbein, and others.[10] Brang mentions more moderniz-ed versions by Anton Wall and Marmontel, as well as Karamzin's own 'Julia'.[11] These versions are important for us, together with the non-Sentimentalist 'new prose', as voices pitted against that of the present narrator or even adopted by him for his new parodic purposes.

In Karamzin's humorous Sentimental tale a core fairy tale is definitely discernible, but the narrator also plays a game with the topoi of the fairy tale. It is both 'an olden fairy tale' and a 'new caricature', as its subtitle tells us. Furthermore, it is as if Karamzin incorporated all the devices representative of contemporary fairy tale adaptations, both the older ones and the Sentimentalist ones: a serious moralistic, didactic voice; a voice that lays bare the allegory as Perrault was wont to do; an authoritative voice based on 'scholarly' sources (old poets, chronicles, and history); a chivalric, elegant voice reminiscent of the 'new' Prévost-type prose fiction; and his own Sentimental–idyllic voice. The narrator uses all these voices tongue in cheek, adopting them as his own and pitting them against each other for silly clashes and humorous effects. The result is not only a 'caricature' of a fairy tale, but also, and perhaps primarily, a caricature of non-Sentimentalist eighteenth-century prose – the 'new' in the subtitle is as significant as the 'caricature'. There is also a fair amount of self-irony directed at both Senti-mentalism and the present utterance itself.

As has been pointed out, the folkloric voice in 'The Beautiful Princess' consists mainly of certain typical fairy tale formulae (*V nekotorom tsarstve, v nekotorom gosudarstve zhil*; *iz-za trideviati zemel', tridesiatogo tsarstva*) constant epithets (*stol dubovyi; skatert' branaia; vysokie terema; med sladkii*), extended negative metaphors (*Ne tak priiatna polnaia luna, voskhodiashchaia na nebe mezhdu beschislennymi zvezdami, kak priiatna nasha milaia tsarevna*), folk similes (*kak gordyi lebed'*), folk sayings (*negde bylo past' iabloku*), and some perceptibly archaic diction.[12] To this we may add many instances of folk intonations in the trochaic-dactylic meter of 'Il'ia Muromets', described by Karamzin as 'completely Russian' (*za skatert'iu branoiu, vmeste s Tsarem i Tsarevnoiu*).[13] Most of these features are present in both the reported speech of the personages and the speech of the narrator. As noted by Brang, this folkloric archaic coloration is significantly increased in the later editions of the tale.[14]

The cast of personages is schematic according to the traditional fairy tale pattern: a good king (sitting on a high throne, attired in a crown studded with sapphires and rubies, holding a golden scepter), his only daughter (a princess of unspeakable beauty), numerous royal suitors, a wizard (attired in a tall hat decorated with moon and stars), and finally, an ugly but wise dwarf who marries the princess and lives happily ever after. The setting is also the traditional castle with the hospitable oaken 'round table', as typical of Vladimir's Old Russia as of Arthurian tales, and the princess's high tower (*terem*), where she sits by her sewing frame.[15]

If we now turn to the adaptation of this basic fairy tale skeleton, quite an amazing picture emerges. The fairy tale is presented not, as one would expect, as a story orally told by a nanny or a granny, but as the result of the serious and erudite narrator's scholarly research. The princess's beauty is documented by a 'true translation' of the words used by eyewitness poets of the olden days, which the studious narrator has succeeded in finding in the 'ancient archives'. A page-long passage is devoted to the princess's beauty, where, as pointed out by Anderson, the folkloric alternates with the most favored Sentimentalist expressions.[16] It is, one might add, quite an exaggerated version of similar descriptions of beauty in 'Innocence' and 'Liodor'. It too ends (elliptically) at breast level, with the ancient poet's use of the inexpressibility topos (familiar from all of Karamzin's works): 'But who can describe all her beauties?' The passage is introduced by the narrator's evaluation of the ancient poet and his peers, which makes the narrator's own game quite obvious: 'For poets were then not such flatterers as nowadays; they did not call black white, a dwarf a giant, and ugliness an example of harmony.' The narrator's irony is directed against eighteenth-century writers' tendency to flatter, but no less against his own utterance in progress, which sets out precisely to depict a dwarf as a giant and ugliness as true beauty.

A similar playful mixture of incompatible voices is revealed in all the narrator's further references to his authoritative sources. The description of the hapless suitors is interrupted by a kind of postpositive reporting clause which implies that the foregoing description was taken from the chronicles: 'But what the sixth one, the seventh one, and the rest were doing at that minute, about that the chronicles are silent' (223). The implication is of course absurd, since the description of the suitors is far removed from the type of information contained in any known chronicles. It relates to the suitors' reactions to being rejected by the princess: 'One dried himself with a white cloth, another gazed at the ground, the third covered his eyes with his hand, the fourth pinched his garb, the fifth stood leaning against the stove and hung his head like an Indian Bramide contemplating the nature of the human soul, the sixth . . . ' (223). This description, absurd in itself, is doubly absurd both because of the attribution to the chronicles and the selection of exaggerated 'sensitive' gestures of response. The description of the entire courtship is clearly not a chronicle account, nor a fairy tale account, but a tongue-in-cheek parody of the chivalric and pathetic traits of the older novels and fairy tale adaptations still popular in Russia at the time. It begins with the narrator expressing his regret that lovers are no longer as coy as they used to be, and that the 'eloquence of glances' is lost in modern times. Next he points to another part of the courtship ritual 'no longer fashionable', namely the tradition of serenading the beloved. However, the description of the princes' serenades (which went on for days, weeks, and months!) is such that the narrator's regret cannot be taken entirely seriously. Their songs are described as 'pathetic love songs', each couplet of which ends with deep sighs which could have moved even hearts of stone to tears. Sighing seems to be one of their main activities, and at the final rejection, they all sigh again 'so strongly, that the stone walls nearly shook' (223). In the first scene, the sighs and tears occur successively (for days, weeks, etc.); in the latter scene, it seems as if they all sighed in unison (twenty or so strong). Not only are the suitors thereby caricatured, but so is the method of those Sentimentalists whose main approach to any subject was to add an impressive number of sighs and tears. The romantic serenading is described as follows: 'When five, six, ten, twenty suitors gathered there simultaneously, they cast lots about who was to sing first and each in turn began to sing of his heartfelt torment; the others meanwhile, wringing their hands, would pace back and forth and kept their eyes on the Princess's window' (219). A sound sleep not only makes them forget their love pangs, but seems extremely well deserved. The princess's lack of response comes as a surprise only if taken as part of the narrator's game.

The humorous enumerations of the suitors both at the beginning and the end of their courtship, can also be seen as narratorial play with one of the most basic features of fairy tale narration, namely, the device of incremental ternary repetition. Instead of going through the more or less similar motions of unsuccessful courtship of first one, then a second, and finally a third suitor, the narrator humorously summarizes and playfully exaggerates both the

number of suitors and the events themselves. He chooses to dwell
at length on speech acts, gestures, and states most typical of
Sentimentalist fiction. In addition to the humor, the effect is a
profound transformation of the traditional rhythm of the fairy tale.

We might also note how the king's dialogues with the suitors and
with his daughter further develop the theme of folktales in chivalric
and Sentimentalist clothing in an absurd direction. The foreign
princes speak in a surprisingly homespun 'Russian' folk-voice
("'Dovol'no pozhili my v kamennom dvortse tvoem", govorili oni:
"poeli khleba i soli tvoei, i popili medu sladkago; pora nam
vozvratit'sia vo svoi strany, k ottsam, k mamushkam i k rodnym
sestram"', 220), quite incongruous to their 'elegant' serenading.
The king, on the other hand, uses all the gallant politesse of a
chivalric knight. His language is also deferential to an absurd
degree (regardless of addressee), and entirely alien to anything
even remotely resembling the 'royal we'. It is also studded with all
manner of late eighteenth-century jargon, particularly that pertaining to the upbringing of children, as found in novels from Rousseau
to Richardson to Karamzin. Occasionally he speaks in a *bavardage
de la fièvre* more like the heroes of Fedor Emin than any of
Karamzin's serious heroes. Highly emotional phrases such as
'Beloved guests! even if you stayed for a few years at my court, you
certainly would not bore the host' (220–1) and 'Dear, intelligent
daughter of mine, *beautiful Princess!* you know that I have no
children except you, light of mine eyes' (221), are juxtaposed with
Sentimentalist pedagogical jargon, spoken by the same royal
personage, such as 'I am your tender father and not your tyrant
[ . . . ] sensible parents can *guide* their children's inclinations; but
they cannot instigate nor change them' (222), and yet others in the
folk voice. All of this, we recall, alternates with the absurd descriptions of the suitors, and is presumably gleaned from the chronicles.

Similar appeals to authoritative sources mixed with Sentimentalist topoi are maintained to the very end. The princess's fondness for
the dwarf is 'psychologically' explained by the 'chronicle account'
of the dwarf's background. The king's heart-to-heart talks, first
with his daughter and then with the dwarf, are not described in
detail, for on this score 'History is silent' – the same History which
presumably revealed how the king caught the two *in flagrante
delicto*, and the details of his reaction (falling down in armchairs,
slamming doors, incoherent speech, and other decidedly unroyal

behavior), and the detailed actions of the lovers. Finally, the happy conclusion of the tale is reported in accord with the same 'impartial History'. The narrator's references to Shakespeare, psychologists, Demosthenes, Orpheus, and other indications of his own erudition, are as absurd in their respective contexts, and it is clear that what is featured is not an authoritative erudite narrator, but one who caricatures that particular mode of transforming folk literature into 'respectable', 'sophisticated' art.

The description of the wizard is perhaps the high point of the parody directed against the Emin-type fiction. The picture is a most explicit caricature of the traditional personification of wisdom – traditional, that is, in fairy tales and adventure novels. As in the case of the suitors' appearance, that of the wizard interrupts the 'difficult but sacred and pleasant' duty of the king, namely that of governing his subjects 'as a father governs his children'. The humorous implication is that this, in all respects ideal, ruler is quite easily distracted from 'governing'. The wizard is introduced as an *Astrolog, Gimnosofist, Mag, Khaldei*, and is attired appropriately. During the course of his stay (which lasts for several weeks) he is further referred to as a 'courteous cavalier', an 'itinerant knight', and a 'wise man'. His chivalric attendance upon the princess at table, his amiable conversation, his knowledge of people, his gracious leave-taking, his great wisdom, and his great service to the king are good-naturedly mocked by the narrator, who punctuates his description with parenthetical serious and mock-serious commentary. The wizard's philosophy and his table manners are equated in the narrator's parenthetical gloss: '[he] drank and ate philosophically, that is, for five, and constantly spoke of moderation and abstention' (225). When he thanks the king for his 'kindnesses', the narrator parenthetically points out what he should have thanked the king for: '*and for your good table*, he could have added'. As for his wisdom, the narrator 'does him justice' and ventures his own 'positive' opinion: 'With all respect for this itinerant knight, it must be said, that he had much historical, physical, and philosophical knowledge, and that the human heart was not entirely *gibberish* (*tarabarskoiu gramotoiu*) to him – that is, he knew people and often would guess from their eyes their most secret feelings and thoughts' (225). He applies his 'great wisdom' (more or less reduced to guesswork by such an introduction) to perform his 'great' service to the king: a modest hint that the

princess is in love and hides it from her father. His hint is couched in
the appropriate metaphorical trappings of 'wisdom'. Not only is
'wisdom' completely relativized on an implicit level, but the narrator himself poses as properly awed by the concept as conceived in
the superior olden days: 'Nowadays he [the wizard] would be called
– I do not know what; but in those days he was called a wise man.
True, every century brings with it a new understanding of this word'
(225). The narrator has by now called him a sponger and glutton, a
cavalier, an itinerant knight, and a philosopher, in addition to the
impressive titles he was introduced by.

The humorous presentation of both suitors and wizard is motivated partly by the literary tradition (which is here mocked), and
partly by internal narrative structure. They are used as foils for the
dwarf's superior qualities: the suitors and their serenading are
contrasted to the dwarf's literary abilities, the wizard's sham
wisdom is contrasted to the dwarf's true wisdom.

One prime feature of this Sentimentalist transformation is the
complete lack of villains. The suitors and the wizard represent only
slightly negative personages and are by no means evil. There are no
evil fairies or other villains that traditionally provide the major
obstacles for the ultimate triumph of goodness and beauty in the
fairy tale. The positive personages are equally sentimentalized –
besides the fact that there are no bounds to the goodness, beauty,
and wisdom depicted, these qualities themselves are personified as
arch-sentimental heroes – also exaggerated and caricatured to the
most absurd and even grotesque proportions. It is all the more
surprising that this particular Sentimental and 'mock-Sentimental'
aspect of the tale has gone practically unnoticed in Karamzin
scholarship.

A look at the Sentimentalist voice of the narrator will clarify
what I mean. The main aspect of the Sentimentalist transformation
is the total lack of magic, or more properly speaking, the redefin-
ition of magic from the level of ontology to that of epistemology.
The fairy tale is introduced in a speech event overture as an
exemplum, or in more properly Sentimentalist terms, as a consolation to the unfortunate 'ugly sons of mankind' who do not
believe that they can be liked or loved because of their ugly
appearance. The narrator's message to his unfortunate 'friends' is
clearly spelled out in the conclusion to a lengthy and extremely
pathetic apostrophe, reminiscent of that to the goddess Fantasy.

The consoling words are: 'Believe me, you can still be lovely and beloved; accommodating Zephyrs today or tomorrow might bring you some charming little Psyche, who ecstatically will throw herself in your embraces and will tell you that there is nothing dearer than you in the whole world' (214).[17] Thus the fairy tale magic is presented as less important than the allegorical meaning, the purpose of the telling. One could view 'The Beautiful Princess' as another Sentimentalist trifle, as an extra-literary consolation turned into a literary work.

We have already seen that the magic is lacking in the wizard who had no supernatural powers, although one is led to expect some such powers from the impressive titles whereby he was introduced. Even his 'natural' wisdom, his sensitivity to the princess's predicament, is undercut by the narrator's whimsical double talk.

The next instance of magic unmasked is equally playful, and occurs when the king confronts his daughter with her secret (half-revealed to him by the wizard). This is done not directly, but in the form of a fairy tale concocted *ad hoc* by the king, but presented 'naturally' as his dream. The king's pathetic conclusion of his dream is, however, indistinguishable from his 'actual' reality, as is his daughter's reaction – depicted by the typical Sentimentalist gestures that say more than words. One cannot but suspect that this is part of the narrator's caricature, exaggerating to absurd proportions the favored Sentimentalist device of periphrastic expression. This play with periphrasis may be seen on a smaller scale elsewhere in the tale as well, in sentences such as the following: 'When *King good person*, after an active life, ended his days with blessed death, that is fell asleep like a weary wanderer falls asleep to the babbling of a brooklet on a green meadow' (239). The king's tirade to his daughter is carried on in the arch-Sentimental diction of the ideal parent: 'Will the father be an enemy to his lovely daughter? Can I oppose your heart's choice dear Princess. Were not your desires always law to me?' (228). The subsequent description of how he even in his old age would chase after a butterfly that had captured her fancy and water her favorite flower, completes the narrator's play both with royal behavior and Sentimentalist topoi.

The irony becomes apparent when the king's suspicions about the identity of the beloved are revealed in the description of his subsequent thoughts. He assumes (and the narratee is thereby encouraged to do the same) that his daughter has chosen one of the

lesser royal suitors. He stresses that there is no need for riches and
fame, and that he himself would have nothing against such a match.
Therefore, in his view, there is no need for secrecy. When the
object of the Princess's love turns out to be the dwarf, the king's
initial reaction is not all that approving of her 'heart's choice'. Thus
even this supersensitive, ideal parent has some difficulty in accepting ugliness (that, too, exaggerated to grotesque proportions: 'with
a hump in front and a hump in back'). The greater irony is, of
course, that the parental obstacle to a love match often found in
fairy tales, is here transformed into sensitive concern.

The narrator's debunking of magic culminates when, in spite of
the princess's fiery kisses, the dwarf remains a dwarf. He does not
undergo the magic transformation into a handsome prince, nor is
an unsuspected royal parentage revealed, as one would expect in a
fairy tale. The Sentimentalist (and mock-Sentimentalist) narrator is
most clearly revealed in this lack of magic, and in the ensuing
'psychological' explanation for why the dwarf was attractive to the
princess. While the narrator is clearly toying with fairy tale magic
topoi, this explanation is also the most pronounced part of the
caricature of Sentimentalist topoi, parodying both the typical
images of narrators, narratees, and personages, and the most
sacred precepts of Sentimentalist poetics, seriously presented in
Karamzin's other works so far discussed. The 'psychological'
explanation is introduced by a frivolous reporting clause, attributing the explanation to the olden chronicles. First the narratee's
voice is revealed: '"How, how could the *Beautiful Princess* fall in
love with a humpbacked dwarf?", – the reader asks or does not ask'
(230). The ideal of a sensitive narratee, fully involved and interested in the telling, is thereby relativized. Next the explanation of
the 'great Shakespeare', although his words are 'well said for a
Poet', is faulted as lacking in psychological acuity.[18] The psycho-
logist–reader demands a more detailed explanation for the
princess's love than Shakespeare can provide, and the mock-
serious narrator turns to the chronicles for a 'true' description of
such a curious 'moral phenomenon'.

The chronicle account of the dwarf's background reveals his
superior inner qualities: his great wisdom and his artistic talents –
the two are more or less equated. In terms of wisdom he is
contrasted to the wizard, and in terms of artistic performance, to
the suitors.

The description of the dwarf's talents amounts to a typical Sentimentalist image of a (secondary) narrator (the dwarf) and a (secondary) narratee (the princess) presented through the narrator's continued double talk. The dwarf's artistic training begins when he as a 'little freaklet' decided to compensate for his external deficiencies with 'spiritual beauty' and to emulate Demosthenes by declaiming 'pathetic speeches of his own composition' to the waves. Soon he acquired:

this great, this precious art, which wins the heart of people, and which makes even the most insensitive person weep and laugh – that gift and that art whereby the Thracian Orpheus captivated both beasts and birds, both forests and stones, both rivers and winds – *eloquence*. (231)

Here the narrator expresses the Sentimentalist aim of art, and emphasizes both tears and laughter in the response. Orpheus, as we have seen, was repeatedly extolled (earlier and later) by a more serious Karamzin. As if this were not enough, the pathetic exaggeration continues: the dwarf also plays nicely on the harp and guitar and sings 'moving songs of his own composition'. We recall the suitors who, without Orphic effects on the princess, played their banduras and sang 'pathetic love songs, composed by the poets of their lands' – the contrast, besides enhancing the dwarf's personal abilities, also extolls original 'native' poetry over foreign poetry. Furthermore, the dwarf is an accomplished painter, who could bring to life on canvas among other objects, 'crystalline brooklets, shaded by tall willows and lulling to sweet drowsiness the shepherd with his shepherdess' – the typical idyllist's picture, as we have seen. Not without irony the narrator (or the chronicler?) points out that because of these accomplishments the wise dwarf 'became the latest fashion'.

His romance with the princess begins when she is ten to twelve years old and the dwarf begins to frequent her tower as a story-teller. The stories he tells are described in detail. They are tales about good fairies and evil wizards, symbolizing virtue and vice, and about adventures of princes and princesses with happy endings, the heroes embellished with 'moving traits of dear sensitivity'. The plots sound suspiciously like the Prévost-type 'new prose' or the corresponding native Russian works by Fedor Emin.[19] It is, however, the dwarf's manner of telling and the effects of his telling on the princess that are Sentimentalist, not the plots as such. In other words, what the dwarf is telling the princess is surprisingly like the eighteenth-century 'new' prose – Emin-type adventure plots with a multitude of interpolated tales and exaggerated pathetic diction. The way he is telling it and the way it is received, on the other hand, is surprisingly like the methods of Sentimentalist narrators and the behavior of Sentimentalist narratees.

The pathetic love declarations between dwarf and princess, and the blissful ending are not unlike scenes from the dwarf's tales; the parodic tone is maintained by the primary narrator, however.

In 'The Beautiful Princess' a physical transformation is lacking and it is here that Sentimentalist precepts are most obviously caricatured. The princess's love is the result not of magic but of her own sensitivities and the dwarf's art. Like the ideal Sentimentalist narrator, the dwarf is exactly like the good heroes of his own stories, or conversely, the teller is reflected in his stories to the extent that his heroes are just like him. Like the ideal Sentimentalist narratee, the princess projects herself into the vicarious experiences of the stories to the extent that her own life becomes a replica of that of the heroes: 'Loving the tales of the eloquent dwarf, she imperceptibly fell in love with the teller and her penetrating eyes uncovered in the dwarf himself the moving traits of dear sensitivity which adorned his fictional Heroes' (233).

Furthermore, the dwarf's art has such a beneficial effect on her that she begins to see the rest of the world in terms of his goodness (and therefore beauty): 'soon it seemed to the Princess that whoever is taller than twenty-five *vershki* and whoever does not have a hump in front and a hump in back cannot be a beauty' – a rather silly exaggeration of the moral.

In addition to the dwarf's good qualities (as if they were not sufficient!), his great service to the state (contrasted to the wizard's modest service), helps to gain both the king's approval and that of the people. It turns out that the dwarf is also a hero, who, like the folkloric *bogatyrs*, saved his homeland when the 'barbarians under the rule of their gigantic King', were at the point of attacking the kingdom. When the 'scythe fell from the hands of the terrified villager and the pale shepherd in terror left his flock', the courageous dwarf single-handedly saved the kingdom. The means whereby he did it are, however, singularly out of character for a *bogatyr's* superhuman prowess in battle, his superhuman strength with the sword, and are part of the extended grotesque double caricature of fairy tales and Sentimentalist aspirations to move the reader. Unarmed, carrying an olive branch, the dwarf approaches the enemy lines and sings a 'sweet song of peace' whereby he literally disarms the barbarians.

Significantly, physical heroism has been transformed into artistic power, and the artist becomes ruler. Thus the moral, in addition to the fairy tale moral stressing the superiority of spiritual beauty over physical beauty, defines spiritual beauty aesthetically. The present humorous narrator, through exaggeration and caricature of traditional forms and motifs, nevertheless conveys the main 'serious' message of all Sentimentalist narrators, namely the equation of artistic sensitivity with moral goodness. Beauty is goodness and goodness is beauty, and art will lead not only individuals but also nations to peace and happiness. Not for nothing is the king named simply 'King, good person', the princess named 'Beautiful Princess', and the dwarf depicted as artist. From such a lineage there can only issue descendants, 'beautiful like their mother and intelligent like their father'. Whether this demonstration of goodness and beauty in ugliness will actually console those 'unfortunate sons of mankind' the narrator chose to address at the onset, would seem to depend on whether they have the appropriate sense of humor and are sufficiently well-read to appreciate the narrator's literary games. It seems that Karamzin here advocates consolation by laughter.

### A HUMOROUS SENTIMENTAL HISTORICAL TALE

## 'Natal'ia, the Boyar's Daughter'

'Natal'ia, the Boyar's Daughter' is a game with fact and fiction, 'lies and truth', with stories told by ancestors and more contemporary storytelling, with the 'genuinely' Russian olden days and the contemporary storyteller's reality.[20] It is decidedly not, or not only, a 'historical tale', a misleading label which has unfortunately persisted in Karamzin scholarship since the days of Sipovskii. Before turning more specifically to 'Natal'ia', let us look briefly at the various views of history in 'Natal'ia' expressed by critics and by Karamzin himself.

Sipovskii's discussion stresses 'Natal'ia's' originality, its correspondence to Russian reality (whether inspired by older original tales, such as 'Frol Skobeev' – also regarded as realistic – or family chronicles), and its historicity.[21] Despite reservations voiced about the generic label – not to speak of the variations in definitions of such a genre – the label persists, as evinced by, for instance, Kanunova.[22] Despite the fact that she points out the Sentimentalist psychological subordination of the historical facts, and perceptively analyses its psychological dimensions and Karamzin's lack of true historical verisimilitude, due to his 'more important task' of depicting 'human personality', she nevertheless discusses the tale under the rubric 'The First Attempt at a Historical Tale'. The demands of 'realism', 'objectivity', and the 'superior' endeavors of Pushkin loom large in the background of her discussion, and, therefore, no doubt, 'Natal'ia' is seen as a mere 'attempt' and not particularly successful, to boot.

Orlov also finds the label justified, with the reservation that Karamzin's 'approach to history in it is unique'. His discussion of the tale is, however, more or less limited to the actual historical sources, summarizing data presented since Starchevskii.[23] Even discussions where the label is rejected are, for the most part, carried out 'negatively' in terms of criteria which define that genre as it was to develop later, and, not surprisingly, Karamzin is faulted for not quite succeeding. Fedorov comes to the following rather typical conclusion: 'In his solution to the problem of historicism in the tale "Natal'ia, the Boyar's Daughter," Karamzin achieved rather modest results.'[24] Other scholars tend to find fault in the fact that the personages in 'Natal'ia' speak out of character. Belozerskaia is one of the first to take this tack: 'the flowery tender speech of the gifted author poorly fits in with the depiction of the patriarchal everyday life of old Muscovite boyars and the simple language of the olden days'.[25]

'Historical', as a term in literary scholarship, tends to become as imprecise as the term 'realistic', which it is often paired with, since each era, each school, each group of speakers, and even individual speakers tend to have their own concept of 'history' and 'realism'.[26] One may speak of Pushkin's historical works, Tolstoi's historical works, and Karamzin's historical works, but, since the respective literary systems are different and the respective meanings of 'historical' are operative only within these systems, the works are not directly comparable in terms of the same criteria. A more relevant question with respect to Karamzin's works is how the historical data function within the work and the Sentimentalist artistic canon. The general answer to that question is a simple one: historical personages, events, and phenomena, function precisely like *any* personages, events, and phenomena. They are selected for their power to induce a maximally active (emotive and intellectual) response in the perceiver (first the narrator and subsequently the narratee). Their ability to move the perceiver determines both the selection of personages and events and their description, and the perceiver should always be reflected in the description of the 'historical' data.

History was for Karamzin always a subjective venture, and this is true of tales such as 'Martha, The Mayoress' and even of *History of the Russian State*.[27] This does not, of course, mean that the latter is any less serious or less professional history; it simply reflects the changing views of what professional history ought to be like. Karamzin himself wrote what amounts to a Sentimentalist manifesto on the role of history in works of art, 'On Incidents and Characters in Russian History, which May Provide Subjects for the Arts'.[28] It is mainly a study of what to select and how to embellish historical material to make it moving, picturesque, or morally enlightening. Karamzin concentrates on potential effects on the perceiver, be that perceiver one of the personages, the narrator himself, or the narratee. He suggests that the writer of fiction add facial expressions, expressive gestures, emotive phrases, auxiliary events and personages, to the chronicle accounts, and that he select particularly emotional or expressive events. Statements such as the following indicate the tenor of the article: 'None of the ancient Russian princes affects my imagination as strongly as Sviatoslav'; 'Who can imagine the beautiful and unhappy Rogneda without a feeling of pity'; 'It seems to me that this subject is moving and picturesque'; 'This is interesting for the imagination and moving for the heart'; 'Here sensitivity ought to be the artist's inspiration.' The point of the Sentimentalist concept of history in art is not only, nor even mainly, to give a credible psychological description of the historical personages with attention to their inner stirrings (which *was* an innovation, one perceptively analyzed by Kanunova),[29] but to make the psychology of the narrator and narratee part of the topic. This effected a more profound change in narrative structure.[30]

'Natal'ia' is historical only in a narrow Sentimentalist sense.[31]

The historical sources uncovered by scholars are interesting in the present context mainly for the manner in which the data were previously presented, as previous narrations, voices from an earlier era which the present narrator engages dialogically. The sources are also interesting for what they do not tell of 'Natal'ia', or for what they tell of in addition to 'Natal'ia' – both indicative of Karamzin's selection and emphasis and part of the dialogue between his present narrator and the previous narrators of the 'same story'. Earlier literary accounts of a similar abduction motif are particularly interesting, and Karamzin's (or his narrator's) polemical stand with respect to the earlier versions are an important part of the topic of 'Natal'ia'. In this sense, the topic of the tale is not only history, but also literary history.

The most likely historical sources for 'Natal'ia' are family chronicles, such as A.[P.] S[umarok]ov's 'Notes of an Old-Fashioned Person' ('Zapiski otzhivshego cheloveka'),[32] which included most of the major plot elements of 'Natal'ia', or the oral family chronicle of the Rumiantsevs, whose forefather, A. S. Matveev, presumably brought up Peter the Great's mother, Natal'ia Naryshkina. Her romance with tsar Aleksei Mikhailovich is, in some respects analogous to Karamzin's 'Natal'ia'.[33] Some of the major differences between these chronicles and 'Natal'ia' are indicative of Karamzin's literary method.

In Sumarokov's 'Notes', the abduction (or, more properly, elopement, since both parties agree) is necessitated by the fact that Natal'ia's father, boyar Nikita Ivanovich Zinov'ev, had arranged Natal'ia's betrothal to another 'almost at birth'. Thus the elopement and secret marriage are clearly undertaken in defiance of her father's wishes and previous commitments. Similarly, Aleksei Mikhailovich's marriage to Natal'ia Naryshkina in the Rumiantsev chronicles is said to have taken place despite their social differences and against the wishes of the boyars. In 'Natal'ia', there are no such obstacles; Karamzin's Natal'ia never really sees the necessity for eloping at all, and all indications are that her sensitive and loving father would have agreed to the marriage. Moreover, the very figure of the father is transformed according to all the Sentimentalist ideals concerning parent–child relationships. Boyar Matvei is hurt because his sensitivities are underestimated, and concerned about his daughter's safety and the fact that no one will be there to console him in his old age. Boyar Nikita in Sumarokov, is angered because he has been disobeyed, and his anger abates only because the tsar forgives the couple and promotes Pankratii, not because of any fatherly sympathy.

The picture of the good tsar in Karamzin is also more like the model sensitive person – or, for that matter King Good Person in 'The Beautiful Princess' – than any concrete ruler. Even the nurse is more a reflection of the narrator's own sensitivities than of 'history'. Aleksei is similarly transformed in the Karamzinian mold – we might note the following specifics: his exile is spent 'where the Sviiaga flows into the Volga', among non-Russian tribes (compare Leon's childhood in *Knight*, and also 'The Countryside' and 'Liodor'), he is a 'natural' artist in accord with Karamzin's views of imitation of nature (as set forth, for instance, in 'On the Sciences' and also in 'The Beautiful Princess'). He is also a ternary narrator who tells his life story much like the primary narrator later tells the story of Aleksei and Natal'ia. His narration, furthermore, reflects some specifics of other Karamzinian descriptions of childhood innocence, and solitude away from the city.

A most interesting transformation of history is Karamzin's development of the usual ancestral source for such chronicles. In Sumarokov's account, the description of Pankratii's appearance is done 'according to the words of grandmother, who had heard about him from her mother'.[34] A similar elderly lady, the ninety-year-old granddaughter of A. S. Matveev, served as source for L. P. Ségur's later account of the marriage between the tsar and Natal'ia Naryshkina.[35] This type of source is developed by Karamzin into a most playfully absurd (secondary) narrator in 'Natal'ia': grand-father's grandmother – of whom more shall be said later. This play with the 'serious' historical sources gives at least some reason to suspect parodic intent on the part of Karamzin.

It seems likely that Karamzin was familiar with the 'genre' and probably some variants of the specific accounts discussed above, and that 'Natal'ia' was a humorous reaction against such serious genealogical documents.[36] We have in 'Natal'ia' another illustration of how an extra-literary genre was transformed into a literary work during this era.

Brang points to some rather interesting data which indicate that two earlier literary accounts of the motif may have been inspired by the same historical incidents related by Sumarokov. The works in question are the early eighteenth-century 'The Tale of Frol

Skobeev' ('Povest' o Frole Skobeeve') and Ivan Novikov's 1785 tale 'The Novgorod Girls' Yuletide Evening . . . ' ('Novgorodskikh devushek sviatochnyi vecher').[37] The similarities between these two works and Karamzin's 'Natal'ia' have long been noted by scholars.[38] I believe that it is safe to assume that Karamzin was familiar with some such works, and indeed assumed the same of his readers. The mode of narration in the three works can be seen as representative of three different stages of eighteenth-century prose evolution. In particular, three entirely different images of narrator emerge.[39]

The narrator of 'Frol Skobeev' performs almost exclusively the authorial function of reporting. The textual features that mark speech event are conspicuous in their absence from the narrator's speech. The narrator's speech lacks personal, evaluative, and expressive features. He reports the events as facts, in the past tense in a simple paratactical fashion and introduces the personages neutrally by rank, title, or family relationship. Their speech is transmitted without comments, without elaboration, and without analysis beyond what is needed for information about his story, mostly in the form of direct discourse, with the speakers clearly and unambiguously identified. No transformation of personage speech is discernible. There is no strongly marked image of narrator (or narratee), besides that which emerges more indirectly through the selection of the material.

The narrative structure of Novikov's later adaptation is different. The basic events of 'Frol Skobeev' and their sequence are retained, but the events and personages themselves are, for the most part, vastly embellished and provided with elaborate pathetic motivations and commentary. An image of narrator is delineated whose evaluative, interpretive, didactic, analytic, and pretentious presence is constantly felt. In other words, speech event features abound within the reporting context, ranging from simple epithets and variations in the forms of personal names used, to brief parenthetical remarks, to extended asides and flowery sententiae, and the overall evaluation is shifted so that the blame is placed not only on the personages but even more on their social circumstances. Particularly interesting are the 'literary' personifications of evil (serpents) and love (cupids). A more educated narratee is also assumed, to whom such sinful deeds as are told are unknown (hence some elaborate motivations), as are folk customs (which need to be explained by the narrator). Many overly naturalistic features of the narrator's description are removed, but by far not all. The major aspect of the transformation is the introduction of a respectable, erudite, and analytical image of narrator. The reporting utterance contrasts to the personage utterance (especially the speech of the auxiliary personages), which retains and further enhances and varies the colloquial, vulgar aspects of personage speech in 'Frol Skobeev'. The 'literate' narrator stands in sharp contrast to the coarse uneducated personages. 'Novgorod Girls'' is, I think, an excellent example of how lowly literature was adapted by the early proponents for the legitimacy of prose fiction.

Karamzin's Sentimentalist version carries the transformation of 'Frol Skobeev' one step further. *All* that is coarse, vulgar, improper, uneducated, in topic, as well as in language, is removed, *even* from the personage utterance. Everyone acts and speaks as would the narrator himself: according to the dictates of the narrator's refined taste, the pleasure principle, and the idyllic and salon proximities and values. All personages are ideals, whereas in 'Frol Skobeev' and 'Novgorod Girls'' no one is ideal in any sense. In 'Natal'ia', love is mutual from the very beginning. The elopement takes place after much concern for boyar Matvei, and is precipitated not by evil cunning, carnal lust, or tempting riches, but by the unjust accusations against Aleksei's father. There is no seduction, only innocent glances, kisses, and embraces, and the wedding night occurs lawfully – after the wedding. Thus, for example, the event of the Yuletide party during which the seduction takes place in the two other works, is retained, but the stress is (polemically?) on innocent girlish pleasure, and no men in girls' clothing are present:

They frolicked without breaking decorum and laughed without derision, so that the modest and chaste daughter of Fauna, dear Dryada, could always have participated in these parties. Deep midnight separated the girls, and charming Natal'ia in the embraces of darkness enjoyed a quiet sleep, which young innocence always enjoys. (34)

The male transvestite exploits in the boudoir are replaced by Natal'ia's transvestite feats on the battle field. The apartment to which the seducers transported their 'beloveds' is replaced by an idyllic forest hideout. The meetings in church are also retained, but occur as the first (non-verbal) contact between the two, whereas in the other tales they occur with the help of much scheming by nurses and lovers. The gypsy woman, versed in folk remedies, who in

Novikov is called in after Grushin'ka's disappearance to find her
(but serves mainly to cure her mother), is recreated as Matvei's
wise hundred-year-old aunt in the Murom forests, called in to
advise about Natal'ia's love ailments. This scene is clearly a
caricature of Novikov's account, and its conclusion is characteristic
of Karamzin's humorous approach to folk topoi: 'The success of
this embassy remains in obscurity; however, there is no great need
to know about it. Now we must get down to the description of the
most important adventures' (42). The nurse who aided in the
seduction in the two earlier works, is transformed into a guardian of
Natal'ia's virtue: she was the faithful nurse of Natal'ia's mother
before, she carefully locks the doors when they leave for church to
keep 'evil men' out, she signs the cross over Natal'ia, pronounces
pious sayings, and curses the same 'evil men' because she is sure
that they eye her ward. Her only 'bad' deed is that she is blinded by
Aleksei's gifts (as are all old people, according to the apologetic
narrator), although even that blindness is perhaps due to Aleksei's
resemblance to her own son. The reactions of the parents are also
differently described. In 'Frol Skobeev', Annushka's parents' reaction is to 'weep bitterly' – the standard reaction of grief for all
personages in the tale – and they turn to the tsar, who takes the
appropriate measures. In Novikov's tale, the scene is developed
into a heated dialogue, first between Grushin'ka's father and aunt,
and then between father and mother, with shouting, screaming,
tears, threats, rustic domestic descriptions, police searches, and so
on – perhaps best describable as unintentional slapstick. In contrast, boyar Matvei's reaction is a typical Sentimentalist faint, an
inability to speak coherently, tears, and a meeting with the tsar, his
close friend, who consoles him as only a friend can. Matvei
apostrophizes his daughter (and the tsar): 'God sees – he said
having glanced at the sky – God sees, how I loved you, ungrateful,
cruel, *dear* Natal'ia! . . . Yes Sir! she is even now dear to me, more
than anything in the world!' (257, emphasis added).

   The list of parallel scenes could be expanded. The most striking
structural difference between Novikov and Karamzin is the further
'personalization' of the narrator. Karamzin's narrator refers to
himself as 'I', and vastly elaborates the description of his own
speech event, its setting, its participants, his own writing activity,
and his sources, by introducing features similar to what we have
seen in Karamzin's other works, but with some important differ-

ences to which I shall return later. Although 'Natal'ia' is essentially
a different story, and one can hardly speak of it literally as a
transformation of 'Frol Skobeev' or 'Novgorod Girls" in any
specific direct sense, the parallels are sufficient, and I believe,
intentionally included in order that the two other stories may be
heard as voices (a simple folk voice and a presumptious literary
adaptor) with which the Sentimentalist narrator polemicizes and
plays games. In this respect, 'Natal'ia' has a structure similar to the
humorous Sentimental fairy tales. It is as if the Sentimentalist
narrator agreed with the adaptor–narrator in excluding the coarse
naturalistic details of the illiterate folk narrator in his own speech
(but, as opposed to the adaptor, he substitutes a 'poetic' more
pleasing folk voice). He is also in agreement regarding the necessity
to include his own 'educated' voice for the benefit of the narratee.
He disagrees about the specifics of that voice (which he, to some
extent, laughs at), and especially about allowing the personages to
act and speak in their unrefined manner, contrary to true sensitivities and good taste.

A brief comparison of the 'seduction' scenes from the three
works will illustrate some of these claims, and will serve as a point
of departure for our further discussion of 'Natal'ia'. In 'Frol
Skobeev', the factually reported, undetailed rape of Annushka
(whose initial reaction of fear quickly gives way not to love, but to a
rational and practical assessment of her situation and an unemotional acceptance of her lost virtue), reveals nothing about a
narrator, but is neutrally reported without evaluation, emotion, or
reference to the reporting situation or the report itself.

In Novikov's version, the scene is described first in ample (not to
say excessive) physical detail as the lustful mutual (after Grushin'-
ka's fleeting thoughts of honor) satisfaction of physical desire. The
language is heavily evaluative (*skvernoiu rukoiu; nezhnogo tela*),
and it is a good illustration of the kind of stylistic mixture which was
characteristic of pre-Karamzinian prose: chancery style (*vo
pervykh; po prikaznomu poriadku*) is mixed with 'sensitive' diction
(*nezhnyi; liubovnye priiatnosti; prelesti*). The phrase structure is
characterized by complex subordination, participial constructions,
and clumsy inversions (*prebyvaniia liubovnykh priiatnostei mesta*),
and present tense alternates with past tense without any apparent
rhyme or reason. Erudition is added by the inclusion of a lengthy
figurative description of the *same* physical actions – personifications

of love (a typical rococo-cupid) and shame (the Biblical serpent and his wisdom). The whole scene is finally endorsed (!!) by the narrator's *sententiae*, extolling virginity, with, however, the cautious addition of the 'even more precious phenomenon' of infecting a heart with love.

'Natal'ia's' narrator (besides the rearrangement of the amorous events into a more proper sequence) clearly is against the 'serpent's wisdom'. Carnal passions are condemned (even after marriage), as is overt description of such private events. In fact, very little of the narrated event is directly reported. Instead, we have the characteristic Karamzinian emotively suggestive prose, a description of the *narrator's* Muse, of a figurative 'sacred curtain' shielding the lovers from curious glances, and, finally an apostrophe to the personages and/or narratees. Not only does the narrator show his own emotive involvement (almost entirely lacking in either of the two other accounts) and describe his own opinions (diametrically opposed to those voiced by Novikov's narrator), but a more imaginatively active narratee is assumed. The preferences for 'chaste love' and 'passions of the heart' are voiced as directives (optative or imperative forms) expressing both the narrator's own wishes and his advice to the personages (and/or married narratees), that is, the kind of muted didacticism we have seen in Karamzin's other works as well. We might also note, besides the Karamzinian 'new style' lexicon and syntax, the typical idyllic reference to Diana and Endymion (used also in 'Night'), and the botanical metaphor for love, which is equally characteristic and which will later be further extended and parodied in *Knight*.

The humorous play with the cupid topos, used seriously in Novikov, is indicative of the type of play with literary tradition which takes place throughout 'Natal'ia'. The winged youngster with his arrows (holding a picked flower) is, significantly, attributed to the nurse's feeble vision. The reader is advised against believing in such nonsense. This is particularly humorous, since the nurse's way of thinking is characteristic also of the narrator and his Muse. We recall, for instance, the description of Natal'ia's dimples as a sign of Cupid's kisses at birth (35). Another similar instance is the description of the curious ailment that disrupts Natal'ia's calm and contented girlhood:

– What happened to her? Modest Muse, tell me! – from the azure vault of heaven or maybe from somewhere higher still, flew, like the little bird

Colibri, fluttered and fluttered in the pure spring air, flew into Natal'ia's tender heart – the need to love, to love, to love!!! (37)

The reader is asked to believe this description, and if he still does not understand, he is asked to turn to his favorite eighteen-year-old girl friend for further detail. It would seem that this passage, too, is part of the play with fanciful literary devices as they were used 'seriously' by writers such as Ivan Novikov – and by Karamzin and even his present narrator.

'Natal'ia's' narrator engages in a dialogue not only with Novikov specifically, but also with the preceding literary tradition in a wider sense. He also reacts to the writers of old-fashioned adventure novels (Fedor Emin comes to mind). The most obvious case in point is the description of the late night trip from Moscow to Alexei's forest hideout (the destination as yet unknown to Natal'ia and her nurse and to the narratee – as is Alexei's true identity). The mysterious circumstances in general, the late hour, the strong winds, cold and darkness, the desolate forest, the nurse's fears and tears, and, finally, the armed men who meet them, build up expectations for some extraordinary adventure. The nurse's screams ('woe is me! we are ruined! we are in the hands – of robbers!' 73) express this sort of expectation. Next the narrator himself exposes his intentions precisely to build up and to frustrate these expectations, by means of praeteritio:

Now I could present a terrifying picture to the readers' eyes – enticed innocence, deceived love, the unfortunate beauty in the power of barbarians, murderers – as the wife of the robber *ataman*, and the witness of terrible evil deeds, and finally after a torturous life, expiring on the scaffold under the axe of justice, before the eyes of an unhappy parent; I could present all this as credible, natural, and a sensitive person would shed tears of grief and sorrow – but in that case I would move away from the historical truth on which my narration is based. No, dear reader, no! this time, hold your tears – calm down – the old nanny was mistaken – Natal'ia is not with robbers! (73–4)

This passage foreshadows a technique which was later to be much exploited in *Knight*. The sequence of setting up and frustrating expectations, and subsequently laying bare the device is similar to what we saw in 'The Deep Forest'. The digressive nature of this passage also serves to create suspense – a function which was more strongly motivated in the original serial publication, where the passage concluded the first installment. The suspense is, of course, only partly alleviated by the narrator's indications of where Natal'ia was not, and the original readers had to wait another month to find out where she, in fact, was.

While thus laying bare his rejection of the topoi of adventure novels, the narrator in his own story is not altogether hostile to that tradition. The dramatic abduction (and its happy ending), Natal'ia's masquerading in knightly garb as Aleksei's younger brother, the glorious deeds in battle where both prove themselves, an interpolated tale (but only one!), fall within that tradition. Thus, as in the case of the cupid topos, the narrator, while laughing at the older tradition, also laughs at himself. Similar points can be made with regard to the tradition of historical novels, such as those by Kheraskov (which shared some traits of the adventure novels). Compare the presentation of the 'true Russian' ideal ruler to those in, for instance, *Numa*.[40]

The Sentimentalist–idyllic topoi in 'Natal'ia' are particularly illustrative of this double game with traditional narration and the present narration as well. When applied to idyll topoi, the humorous, light self-parody is all the more effective (for the real reader), since a substantial part of Karamzin's own works falls within that tradition. Besides the obvious prevalence of intimate familial idyllic proximities on all levels of the work, there are several overt references to Zephyrs, shepherds and shepherdesses, birds, flowers, butterflies, natural cycles, as well as the typical crafts and the gatherings around the table, walks in nature, storytelling, and the like, familiar from all of Karamzin's works.

Zephyrs, for instance, are introduced to stress Natal'ia's beauty and modesty. Her beauty is first described in traditional idyllic terms: her tender blushing cheeks, her pale face on which the rays of the sun play, her hair, which like velvet falls down on her shoulders and her marble breast, 'uncovered (but not quite) to the cool kiss of the Zephyr'. The Zephyrs on occasion venture even further, but Natal'ia's modesty prevents such liberties. We note the foreshortening and personification of meteorological phenomena and the playful erotic exploits of the Zephyrs – the exploits are, however, less typical of Karamzin's serious idylls than, for example, Sumarokov's eclogues and Bogdanovich's 'Dushen'ka'.

The most developed idyllic cliché occurs à propos Natal'ia's first subconscious longings for the opposite sex (39–41). It is expressed as an extended apostrophe to beauties (including both beautiful readers and Natal'ia, thus generalizing Natal'ia's condition to speech event chronotopics): 'So beauties! your life from a certain age on cannot be happy if it flows like a solitary river in the desert; and without a dear shepherd the whole world is for you a desert.' The apostrophe continues with an elaboration on how Daphne and Chloe have ceased to satisfy 'you', and how in a myrtle bower 'a golden-haired youth is sitting in languor, and in sad songs complains of your outward cruelty'. The apostrophe concludes discourse-deictically, laying bare the device: 'Dear reader! forgive me this digression! Not only Sterne was a slave to his pen. – Let us again return to our tale' (41). Despite the concluding statement of intent, the narrator does not, in fact, return to his story, but continues to speak of his own literary method for another paragraph.

On another occasion, the reader is asked to imagine Natal'ia's beauty with some idyllic comparisons, none of which, however, does her justice. Next, the narrator expresses his own professional opinion of using such idyllic clichés: 'I am afraid to continue this simile in order not to bore the reader with the repetition of what is well-known; for in our luxurious time the storehouse of poetic comparisons for beauty is quite depleted, and not just one writer chews on his pen in vexation, searching and not finding new ones' (24). He goes on to add to his own description precisely such an old cliché, pointing out that Natal'ia could serve a painter as a model for Dione (Dione, we note, was seduced by Chronos, at least according to one myth!), or as the fourth Grace – the type of comparison abundantly used by Karamzin elsewhere, yet another instance of both laughing at the tradition and implementing it. The narrator is not afraid to extend his description of Natal'ia's charms, by whimsical appeals to Socrates, tongue-in-cheek comparisons to Anton Wall trifles, and play with contemporary authorities (Locke on education, Rousseau's *Emile*, Campe, Weisse, and Moritz, i.e., the leading eighteenth-century authorities on 'natural' pedagogy). Natal'ia is praised as a most excellent product of natural education despite the fact that these authorities were not read, first because they were not yet born, and, second, because people in those days were not literate. After this anachronistic play and display of erudition, the narrator continues in the same 'erudite' manner and in the process, reveals his own literary strategy and hints at the desired interpretation of his story.

Obvious toying with arch-Sentimentalist topoi can be seen, for instance, in the extended apostrophe to tears (239–40), or the detailed 'slow-motion' description of Natal'ia's tears and sighs (35), or ordinary language glosses to periphrastic expressions, such as the following: 'the year turned on its axis: the green carpets of spring and summer were covered by downy snow; the awesome tsaritsa of cold sat down on her icy throne and breathed blizzards on the Russian tsardom; that is, winter came' (43).

Different aspects of literary tradition are thus heard in the form of voices recognizable as those of a previous tradition (adaptors, such as Ivan Novikov, native 'literati', such as Fedor Emin and Kheraskov) and the present Sentimentalist–idyllic tradition (Sterne, Rousseau, Locke, Campe, Weisse, Moritz, as well as Karamzin and his epigones) which the narrator on occasion adopts as his own, on occasion polemicizes with, and on occasion both uses and abuses in various absurd ways. Whatever the case may be, the narrator's more or less hidden dialogue with them is part of the topic of 'Natal'ia'. The narrator is depicted as narratee or active perceiver and responder, and he responds more professionally than we have seen before as a literary critic, frequently objects to other voices, laughs at them or exposes their absurdities and re-creates their reality according to his own tastes and whims.

This more or less hidden polemic and parody takes place in 'Natal'ia' on the peripheries of, and counterpoint to, a more open dialogue with his acknowledged source for 'Natal'ia': his grand-father's grandmother. 'Natal'ia' begins with a variant of the familiar Sentimentalist overture, which is mainly concerned with coding motifs: the narrator's reasons for telling the story, his personal preferences, where, when, and how he first heard it, his inspiration, his present telling, the generic and stylistic nature of the original story, and his own present re-narration. The narrator first describes the original oral speech event where he performs as listener, and then the present written speech event where he performs as writer. By this token, 'Natal'ia' is as solipsistically anchored as any of Karamzin's works.

Like the singer of 'Il'ia Muromets', the narrator of 'Natal'ia' immediately states his preference for that which is authentically Russian. The epic singer vociferously rejects the Greco-Roman epic tradition in favor of a homespun epic as told by his nannies. The narrator of 'Natal'ia' speaks up for tales of yore told by ancestors about old Rus', and against all that is 'Franco-Albian'. In both cases, this is done tongue in cheek, and each narrator 'slips' in his intentions, and cannot completely free himself from the respective rejected traditions and his own contemporary reality. The narrator of 'Natal'ia' assumes the same fondness for the olden days on the part of his narratees, but, as in the overture of 'Poor Liza', he stresses his own exceptional qualifications. In 'Poor Liza', the narrator took an aesthetic walk to an idyllic spot outside Moscow. In 'Il'ia Muromets', the narratees are invited to join the narrator in his homespun *locus amoenus*, where, in the shade of ancient trees, they will hear his 'tale', 'a mixture of true events with fictitious ones' (*povest', smes' bylei s nebylitsami*), free to doze off, should it become boring. 'Natal'ia's' narrator describes how he 'on the wings of his imagination' transports himself to the 'distant darkness', and, in the shade of long since decayed elm trees, chats with his bearded ancestors about ancient adventures and the character of the glorious Russian People, kisses the hands of his great-grandmothers (a somewhat eighteenth-century touch, it would seem), flatters them, and thus gains their admiration and hears their stories. He considers himself a connoisseur of Old Rus'. His head is crammed with all sorts of anecdotes and tales (*anekdoty i povesti*) thus acquired. His grandfather's grandmother, famed for telling fairy tales (*skazki*) to a certain tsaritsa, has told him a true event or history (*byl' ili istoriiu*) which periodical composition (*periodicheskoe sochinenie*) he now intends to communicate to periodical readers (*periodicheskie chitateli*), punning on the fact that 'Natal'ia' originally appeared in installments in *Moscow Journal*, presumably as a period piece. He confesses, however, to a certain apprehension that he might 'disfigure her tale (*povest'*)'. Russian history here serves the same function as do, for instance, spring and nature in 'A Promenade', the environs of Moscow in 'Poor Liza', the trip to the country in 'The Countryside' – namely that of stimulating the narrator's sensitivities and his imagination. It is no more meant to be factual history than Moscow in 'Poor Liza' is meant to be factual geography. It originates entirely in the narrator's own imagination, as does the original narrator herself.

The 'genre' of 'Natal'ia' is, from the outset, laid bare as imaginary history of an imaginary Old Rus', told by an imaginary old Russian. It is a 'true story' or 'history' which originated in imaginary 'conversations' with imaginary ancestors, part of the narrator's accumulated 'anecdotes and tales' told by his ancestor, illustrious for her talent to 'tell fairy tales' and a 'periodical composition' in both a historical and journalistic sense. The tale is generically as anomalous and as contradictory as are the generic labels openly connected with it by the narrator. The narrator goes on to describe his present professional activity as a writer as the 'praiseworthy craft of scribbling on paper, to spin yarns about living and dead (*vzvodit' nebylitsy na zhivykh i mertvykh*)', and, like the singer of 'Il'ia Muromets', he envisions the effect of his art on his readers as testing their patience and finally inducing them to Morphic sleep.

The setting of the present speech event is also different from that of the original oral telling under the elms: the narrator is now sitting at his desk and struggling with his writing. The readers repose on soft couches. His own style is referred to as 'poor rhetoric' (*khudoe ritorstvo*), as something presumptuous on his part with deference to grandfather's grandmother's superior eloquence, which he is afraid that he might not be able to reproduce.

Grandfather's grandmother is present in spirit at the present speech event, too. Her function is somewhat like that of the goddess Fantasy in 'Dedication of a Grove' – she appears in different guises. First, she appears as a critic in the shape of an old woman who threatens to punish her presumptuous great-great-grandson with her crutch for destroying her story. The next minute, however, the narrator sees her as a 'magnanimous shadow' in the 'sea of undescribable bliss' who, even in her earthly hypostasis, is the image of benevolence (even butterflies would peacefully perch on her nose), and who could not possibly now raise her hand against her submissive descendant. Her next guise is more like those mentioned for Fantasy: she appears 'this very minute' as the narrator's Muse, miraculously lighting up the dark corridor. The ecstatic narrator apostrophizes her as the image of youth and beauty, deferentially praising her eyes which 'shine like the sun', her lips which 'are crimson like dawn, like peaks of snowy mountains at the setting of the luminary of daytime', her smile like that of a 'young creation at its first day of being' – similes familiar from many of Karamzin's descriptions of ideal female beauty, and not altogether unlike those which later will be linked to Natal'ia. In this context, the effect of juxtaposing this image of youth with the immediately preceding image of an old woman armed with a crutch, butterflies on her nose, etc., is, to say the least, grotesque.

Her 'sweetly roaring' voice (*sladkogremiashchii*, set off in italics) maintains the dual image.

She has the power possessed by *all* Muses to transport the narrator into a state of rapture, and to inspire him to continue 'Natal'ia, the Boyar's Daughter' – thus referred to discourse-deictically within 'Natal'ia, the Boyar's Daughter'. Such, we might recall, was also the power of Nature, other artists, and female singers in 'A Promenade', 'The Countryside', and 'Liodor'. In these works, the rapture gave rise to a sweet state of oblivion and to spontaneous artistic co-creation. In 'Natal'ia', the image of the Muse/granny literally exhausts the narrator's 'spiritual strength'. He lays his pen aside and proclaims (discourse-deictically) 'these' lines 'now' being written an 'Introduction' or 'Foreword' – not very conventional as introductions or forewords go. Thus, from the very beginning, the tone is set as a frivolous play with 'truth' and 'fiction', 'now' and 'then', and with the most sacred Sentimentalist topoi and artistic precepts (the function, aim, effect, and creative process of art).

Granny's original telling is heard throughout 'Natal'ia' together with the voice of the narrator who tries to imitate it, but who fears that he might spoil her native eloquence (we recall that in the olden days Russians presumably spoke their own language, 'according to their own hearts, that is, spoke as they thought') by a more contemporary eighteenth-century jargon (by implication, not a truly Russian language, not according to one's heart, not what one thinks). Such fears are expressed not only in the introduction, but keep recurring during the course of the telling. For example, as digressions: 'Grandfather's grandmother described the grief of the tender boyar's daughter with great eloquence, maybe because she knew it from her own experience; but I, her humble great-great-grandson, totally weakened the copy of this description – I feel – but what's to be done – and so forth!' (41). Such expressions of his fears are certainly vastly understated for humorous effect, and there is relatively little left of the original telling. The narrator, as we have seen, tends to adopt (partly to affirm, partly to expose) more contemporary manners of narration. Furthermore, he most explicitly manifests his own control of the telling by overtly rearranging the temporal sequence, partly to create suspense, (e.g., revealing Aleksei's home in the forest), partly for humorous effect (such as the bribing of the nurse revealed only gradually and

with ample apologies from the narrator), partly simply to reveal
his authorial privileges or literary method. The switch from the
description of the decisive battle to Moscow is one of the more
fanciful examples of overt digression–resumption:

> But we will abandon our spouses for a while in the hope that Heaven will
> not abandon them [ . . . ]. Let us return to Moscow – there our story
> began, and there it must end. For the last time I ask the reader to sit
> down with me in a Montgolfier balloon – to fly and to descend from the
> crystal mountains of the air on the wide square of the capital. (269–70)

His contemporary eighteenth-century voice is also heard as he
addresses a great variety of narratees for a variety of purposes:
explanatory (quaint old customs, now out of fashion), emphatic,
emotive, didactic, moralistic, satirical (the good old days are contrasted to a less admirable present), orientational ('where nowadays tower the *beautiful gates with trumpeting Glory*'), and so on,
ranging from the strictly factual to the absurd. 'Natal'ia' differs
from the other works discussed in the great variety of narratees it
addresses. Sometimes they are simply called 'reader', sometimes
the narratee is included in 'everyone', and often in the inclusive
plural 'we'. Sometimes more specific narratees are singled out
(beauties, parents, gardeners, married readers, sensitive readers,
incredulous readers). This variety is correlated with the narrated
events so that beauties are addressed à propos Natal'ia's beauty,
parents when Matvei's feelings are the topic, lovers when love is
discussed, 'we' when common principles are elucidated. The narrator's relationship to the narratees is thereby established, and it is
also much more varied than we have seen so far. There is room for
differences in opinion, polemics, and even advice not to read on.
Thus, for example, in a playful anticipation of objections to the
idea of love at first sight, the dialogue between narrator and narratee is developed:

> At dinner she did not eat, as is common for all who are in love – for why
> not tell you straight out that Natal'ia fell in love with the stranger? 'In one
> minute?' (says the reader:) 'having seen him for the first time and not
> having heard a single word from him?' Gentlemen! I am telling you how
> this thing really happened: do not doubt the truth! do not doubt the
> power of that mutual attraction felt by two hearts created for each other!
> And whoever does not believe in sympathy, leave us, and do not read our
> story which is told solely for sensitive souls, who hold this sweet belief!
> (46–7)

A similar playful tone characterizes the (indirect) reporting of Alexei's love declaration. He spoke 'not in the language of novels, but in the language of true sensitivity; he spoke in simple, but tender, passionate words'. The directly reported speech of the personages (presumably reported first by grandfather's grandmother and re-narrated by this narrator) sounds suspiciously like that of Liodor or Erast or any other Sentimentalist personage. The narrator is aware of this, and on one occasion provides a humorously self-contradictory apologia in a footnote: 'The reader figures, that olden lovers did not speak exactly like they do here, but then, we could not now even understand the language of those days. It was necessary only to *somehow* fake an ancient *coloration*' (59–60). In other cases the narrator uses asides to point out facts he does not know or cannot describe, or to corroborate or contradict his ancestor's account (which, we recall, took place in the realm of imagination) by appeals to various authorities, from Socrates to his own personal experience, to faded gravestones and accounts by old people and other literary accounts. Or he might simply refer to various contemporary phenomena, such as Mesmer's magnetism, Muscovite landmarks, and the like. The mixture of eighteenth-century reality with the days of yore often creates absurdly humorous anachronisms, such as landing a balloon on an old Muscovite square at the time of the Lithuanian wars. We saw that the mixture of styles was equally anachronistic: Montgolfier balloons versus the wide square of the capital (*tsarstvuiushchego grada*) – the latter in lofty Church Slavic form.

The voice of grandfather's grandmother is rendered as a highly poeticized folk voice, and has little in common with such simple native storytelling as 'Frol Skobeev', or any actually spoken language, for that matter. Often her voice coincides with that of the narrator, and, in particular, the border between eighteenth-century idyllic diction and 'authentic' folk diction is not clearcut. The devices whereby her voice is set off from that of the narrator (so that the effect is one of quoting) are the same as described above for the fairy tales. The archaic–folkloric elements have been thoroughly investigated by Karamzin scholars, and need not concern us here.[41] What is usually not sufficiently stressed is the fact that the mixture of folk elements and archaic diction, with various forms of eighteenth-century jargon, is clearly motivated by the aims of multiple, simultaneous narration. Karamzin did not, it seems to me, try to create an authentic-sounding Old Russian, nor did he strive for historical verisimilitude. As an accomplished linguist, he could no doubt have done so, had he wished. What he did want to render was both Old Rus' and an eighteenth-century perception of that era. He chose a multivocal narration precisely because such a manner could convey both the historical 'facts' and various opinions about them by the participants, by grandfather's grandmother, by family chroniclers, by older and contemporary literati, and by the narrator himself. Neither these voices themselves, nor the silly clashes between them, are taken entirely seriously. The only entirely 'serious' statement, I believe, is the generic conundrum the narrator proposes in his introduction: he intends to tell both a true story and to spin yarns about the living and the dead. Neither history nor contemporary reality is taken at all seriously, and, taken together, all the voices incorporated suggest that there is no preferred 'correct' way of storytelling either.

## A HUMOROUS SENTIMENTAL CONFESSION

### 'My Confession'

'My Confession' is, as pointed out by Eikhenbaum, 'not at all a simple satire'.[42] It has since been seen as a 'peculiar anti-Emile' and an expression of Karamzin's view that human nature is inherently evil (Lotman),[43] as the last stage in Karamzin's 'strivings to free himself from the path of extreme subjectivism' (Kanunova),[44] as a parody of the didactic–satirical novels of the era (Kupreianova),[45] and as 'a game of philosophical hermeneutics' (Page).[46]

It seems to me that Lotman's conclusion is too categorical in that he assigns such a crucial role to one work. Furthermore, he tends to ignore Karamzin's humor. Kanunova's objections to Lotman are well taken, but her conclusions about the objectivity of Karamzin's method are, to say the least, surprising. 'My Confession' is, on the contrary, thoroughly subjective and no less Sentimentalist than other works by Karamzin. In it Karamzin demonstrates the danger of carrying the solipsistic, sympathetic, and pleasure principles of Sentimentalism to their logical limits. It is Sentimentalist in its subjectivism, and simultaneously exposes some fundamental problems embedded in the Sentimentalist world view. It is the same kind of humorous double game of implementation and simultaneous debunking of Sentimentalist topoi as the other humorous tales we have analyzed.

'My Confession' can best be understood within the context of the three Sentimentalist principles. In general structure and outlook it adheres to the solipsistic principle and it is similar to Karamzin's other tales of personal experience, where the 'I' refers both to 'I' as present narrator and 'I' as past personage, and where the two are frequently fused. The confession begins and ends with the typical present tense overture and epilogue and the narrator's past tense story is interrupted by, or reported concurrently with, his retrospective and introspective evaluations, opinions and interpretations. The bivocal method is familiar from all of Karamzin's works.

The major difference between 'My Confession' and the other works discussed, is that the narrator, NN, rejects the principle of sympathy. In this sense the work is solipsistic in a more extreme sense than the other works, in all of which solipsism is held in check by a certain sympathetic 'moral sense' with which any sensitive person could identify. For the most part, the idyllic and salon chronotope prevailed both within the speech event and the narrated event, and between the two. The narrators, although self-preoccupied, were not self-sufficient, and depended on 'another', a close friend, Nature, the Divinity, with whom they could communicate. If we label that kind of solipsism 'moral solipsism', 'My Confession' can be seen as an example of 'amoral solipsism', demonstrating something like the 'bleak and anarchic nihilism' of the Marquis de Sade – or, for that matter, expressing thoughts that foreshadow some of the later 'underground men' in Dostoevskii.[47] The pleasure principle is in force, but in an exclusively physical sense. From this follows that the very make-up of the narrated events is different: the focus is almost exclusively on 'external' aspects of events, 'adventures', rather than the typical Karamzinian focus on inner events (thoughts, emotions, sensitivities, perceptions). 'My Confession' demonstrates how Sentimentalists viewed corruption.

As we have repeatedly seen from Karamzin's other works, an excessive sensitivity led to both the highest rapture and the deepest sorrow. Most Sensitive Persons derived the highest pleasure from satisfying all their senses (both spiritual and physical senses, aesthetically sublimated) in perceiving the Creator, Nature, or art, in experiencing friendship or love. For some hypersensitive personages, the intense pleasure became fatal and others plunged into the deepest despair through their realization of their own impotence. Other cases of suffering or co-suffering occurred through despair at not being able to understand the greater divine plan, but was alleviated by beholding the beauty in Nature (a more understandable expression of that plan) which demonstrated the ultimate, if incomprehensible goodness. In other words, they all derived pleasure from a heightened consciousness, and a clear conscience kept them from feeling pain. They were all thoroughly moral beings, even though some might have erred temporarily. The same strivings to satisfy one's own sensitivities for personal pleasure were, ironically, also held by Sentimentalists to be at the roots of corruption. Sensitivity usually implied weakness (physical or spiritual), and was held to be 'delicate' in both senses of the word. A delicate (in the sense of sickly) sensitivity was one of the dangers. Another danger was sensuality, a purely physical gratification of the senses. As Albrecht von Haller expressed it:

The body, by its intimate union with the soul, draws towards it the pleasure of the senses . . . The soul too weak to govern the passions yields to their empire. The means for our preservation become poison to us: our natural inclinations exceed their due bounds, so that at length all our heavenly qualities are debased . . . This is the origin of the corruption of man.[48]

Count NN of 'My Confession' is an example of a thoroughly corrupted man who has lost all awareness of the 'great Sensorium' within him and has no conscience. He is the thoroughly 'malicious and spiteful creature', the 'freak outside Nature', referred to by Hume and Karamzin. All his sentiments are 'inverted, and directly opposite to those which prevail in the human species'. His senses and sensibilities have degenerated into 'outer' sensuality without the 'inner' guidance of conscience.[49] He takes advantage of many women in his life, capitalizing on their 'delicacy' and 'weakness' which make them corruptible. Furthermore, he sees the rest of society in the same light, solipsistically relying on his own skewed values in his description. He is, in other words, an example of Sentimentalist principles 'gone wrong'.

What is particularly interesting about 'My Confession' is that the voice of 'correct', 'moral' Sentimentalism is distinctly heard in the bivocal narration as the voice of the Sentimentalist 'norm' author, and, moreover, that this norm voice is in many cases specifically identifiable as that of Karamzin or a Karamzinian narrator. Another twist is that the narrator, Count NN, formulates his confession as a letter to the editor of *Messenger of Europe*, i.e., Karamzin. In a sense then, Count NN carries on a polemical dialogue with Karamzin the Sentimentalist writer and Karamzin the editor, on Karamzin's own terms, inverting or putting his own (mis)interpretation on Karamzin's 'true' voice. To add to the complexity, Count NN is, of course, Karamzin's creature, and is, as such, in some respects like many of his other creatures. Much of the humor is generated precisely by the inversions or (mis)interpretations of a serious Karamzinian voice. To demonstrate these claims more concretely, let us now turn to the text itself for a closer analysis.

The first surprising fact about the overture is the preponderance of un-Karamzinian negative assertions. The narrator states that: he does not read the journal; he wants his letter printed but he does not know why; he has never given himself an account of his wishes and actions; he intends to speak of himself and does not care whether it will be pleasant (we note the arch-Sentimental *priiatna*) to the readers; his generic choice is made because a confession does not demand any special effort; he does not wish to seem a slavish imitator; and his confessions have no moral aim.

His relationship to the editor (and, later in the text, to the other readers) is strictly formal and impersonal (*vy, Gosudar', Chitatel'*), in striking contrast to Karamzin's other narrators' effusively emotional relationships to their 'dear friends', 'dearest Aglaia', who were always assumed to take a genuine interest in the stories, being themselves of the same sensitive and impressionable nature as the narrators. NN also assumes a narratee cut to his own measure, one who is as apathetic as NN himself and who reads out of boredom simply to pass the time. Although the reader is, occasionally, perceived by NN as reacting incredulously or with surprise, such reactions are either forestalled or discouraged by unemotional, 'factual' explanations or elaborations ('I inform the Reader, that [ . . . ] usurers know', [158–9]; 'If the Reader is surprised that [ . . . ] then he, no doubt knows' [159–60]). For the most part, he is assumed to be in a rather apathetic mood and not imaginatively, actively involved. As if he was not quite convinced that imagining is even worth the effort, NN turns to some narratees with the following suggestions: 'Whoever feels like it, may imagine' (160). Thus both the narrator and the narratee are described as diametrically opposite to other Karamzinian narrators and narratees. That does not, however, change the basic solipsistic structure: the narrator speaks of himself as personage and as narrator (the two being philosophically identical), and the narratee is depicted as a replica of the narrator's phlegmatic self, that self being further mirrored in the world.

NN writes according to his 'motto', the 'great word *so*' (*tak*) and the narratees are assumed to read 'just so' (*prosto tak*). The narratee is assumed to co-experience, or more aptly nonexperience, apathy. *Tak* as a word is a typical empty 'filler' word, devoid of any inherent meaning, and takes on meaning only through the specific context where it occurs. It is perfectly fitting for an opportunist such as NN, and as empty of inner essence as NN himself professes to be. We are reminded, once again, of Karamzin's aphorisms in 'Various Fragments', the ninth one of which concludes: 'beyond pleasure, there is a limit for utility – there begins *for no good reason* (*ne dlia chego*) harm, vice'.[50] The words, italicized by Karamzin are analogous to NN's *tak* and *prosto tak* and serve as NN's motto of evil for the sake of evil, 'just because'. From the very beginning we hear Karamzin's voice in addition to NN's. This is even more specific if we recall Karamzin's vocabulary in the conclusion to his article 'On Love of One's Country and National Pride', which appeared in an earlier issue of *Messenger of Europe* for the same year: 'Our symbol is an ardent youth; his heart is full of life, he loves activity; his motto is *works and hope*!' – this motto (*deviz*) is the very opposite of NN's.[51]

The second paragraph of the overture to 'My Confession' comments on the present century, 'the century of *openness* in a physical and moral sense', with an appeal to observe 'our dear beauties' for evidence. The passage summarizes Karamzin's pronouncements about Parisian fashions in *Letters of a Russian Traveller*, but also more specifically his article 'On the Light Dress of Fashionable Beauties of the Nineteenth Century' which appeared in the following issue of the *Messenger of Europe*. While NN uses fashions (rather approvingly) as a parallel to and a justification for his own confessional 'openness', his 'art', Karamzin is fervent in stressing the adverse effects of such 'openness' on art: 'imagination is the most flattering artist: it feeds passions; but the eyes already weaken its effect; I cannot imagine what I see; and seeing [it] today and tomorrow, I will get used to [it] and from hour to hour I will look [at it] more and more indifferently'.[52] Karamzin, as we have seen, was an early proponent for telling by indirection, or telling by not telling (drawing attention to what is normally seen as trifling, ellipsis, 'drawing the curtain', fragmentary form, and suggestive hints). NN, on the contrary, is for laying all the cards on the table, and leaves little for the imagination. NN also sees 'openness' as characteristic of the literature of the era: people travel not to find out and faithfully transmit information about foreign lands, but, in his opinion, to speak of themselves; novelists convey their own thoughts about important and unimportant objects; works appear under titles such as 'My Experiences', 'Secret Journal of My Heart'; and authors in general go on endlessly about the most trifling things (*samoe nichto*). We could hardly wish for a more explicit laying bare of the solipsistic and trifling basis of Karamzin's works, particularly his *Letters of a Russian Traveller*, his promenades, and *My Trifles*. Here NN acts tongue in cheek like many other hostile critics of Sentimentalism.

To be a modern author of a confession, according to NN, is the easiest thing in the world: all one has to do is to remember one's own past escapades and abandon 'old-fashioned barbaric shame (*styd*)', and the work is finished. NN, however, will not be a 'slavish imitator', and his own work will differ in that it has no moral aim. Instead of speaking at length about trivia, NN will put down all the most important events in his life on the trifling space of 'a single sheet'. This is a clear example of implementing one feature of trifles (size) and reversing another feature (important events will substitute for trivia). NN is curiously similar in many respects to the 'Author' in a pamphlet by Ivan Elagin published in 1755 as part of the earliest phases of the polemic surrounding the new personalized image of author. Elagin sarcastically shows his Author as an ignorant, lazy, self-promoting braggart who praises stupidity and 'likes everything he jots down and jots down everything he likes, everything he likes being in the best taste'. Being an Author is for him too the easiest thing in the world.[53]

In his *cri de cœur*, NN follows Karamzin in focusing on the self, but he does so for wholly un-Karamzinian reasons: he does so from laziness. Karamzin repeatedly stressed the laborious aspects of art. Like Karamzin, NN also rejects length and the didactic, moralizing tendencies in the new literature, but for opposite reasons. While Karamzin did not reject the morals expressed, he did reject moralizing by means of pathetic exaggeration. NN rejects both moralizing and morals. Furthermore, what makes up 'important' events for NN are his escapades and pranks, while for Karamzin it is the reactions to events that are important by the very fact that they are trifling. In addition, Karamzin's events themselves are, for the most part, quite innocuous, and it is precisely 'old-fashioned shame (*styd*)' or, in more Karamzinian diction, 'bashfulness, modesty (*stydlivost', skromnost'*)', that frequently compels his narrators to 'draw the curtain' or leave off elliptically – particularly in erotic scenes. NN openly flaunts precisely his erotic conquests. Not to be a 'slavish imitator' is another Karamzinian principle, to which NN adheres in a naively simplistic manner.[54] In a sense, then, NN is a caricatured version of Karamzin and follows the main tenets of the leading literary current by vulgarizing them.

The confession is also partly a parody of didactic–satirical novels such as A. E. Izmailov's *Eugene, or Ruinous Consequences of Poor Upbringing and Companionship* (*Evgenii, ili Pagubnye sledstvii durnogo vospitaniia i soobshchestva*), as pointed out by Kupreianova.[55] Its links to Rousseau's *Les Confessions* have also repeatedly been pointed out by scholars. For instance, Anderson views the tale in the following way:

> The tale's title refers specifically to Rousseau's own *Les Confessions* (published 1781–1888) (Karamzin originally subtitled his piece 'A Response to J. J. Rousseau's *Confessions*'). The fact that Count N. N. indulges in the memory of past sins brings to mind the Frenchman's [*sic*] own self-castigation for milder offenses against God and decency. The master confessionist extolled virtue directly while Karamzin indirectly sought the same end by the rhetorical device of negative example.[56]

This is evident from the very beginning of NN's story proper (which clearly paraphrases the beginning of Rousseau's confessions): 'I begin with the conviction that Nature created me as a completely unique person, and that Fate imprinted all the events of my life with a certain seal of excellence' (148–9).

The way he continues the passage makes it abundantly clear that, while utilizing the solipsistic principle, his picture of himself is utterly devoid of all the values most treasured by Karamzin and other 'moral' Sentimentalists. Key values such as sympathy are stressed by Karamzin through NN's *reductio ad absurdum* of their absence, and the presence of evil sensuality is also subject to absurd exaggeration.

NN's professed uniqueness resides in all the qualities of contemporary noblemen that Karamzin elsewhere deplores: despite his birth of rich and famous parents he has turned out a good-for-nothing, despite his sins he has not been punished, he has learned French and does not know his native language, and at age fifteen he does not have the faintest idea of the duties of a man and a citizen. Given NN's professed talents for caricature ('the only talent given me by Nature!') 'My Confession' can be seen as a self-caricature, inverting and exaggerating all the qualities that Karamzin held most sacred.

The specifics of NN's biography correspond to a significant degree to Karamzin's actual biography, as well as to those of some of his narrators (particularly the narrator of *Letters of a Russian Traveller*), or his personages: Eugene, Liodor, the recluse in the work of that title ('Pustynnik'),[57] and more directly, Prince NN in 'Julia', the main personage in 'Anecdote' (also named Liodor and with a fiancée named Emilia, as is this NN's wife) and, perhaps, an adult version of Leon, whose childhood is described in *Knight*. Of the characters in this gallery of namesakes, only Prince NN ('Julia') and Liodor ('Anecdote') correspond to Count NN of 'My Confession' in terms of 'philosophy'. Significantly, though, Prince NN in 'Julia' acts mainly as a foil for the virtuous Aris, and virtue triumphs over the Prince's vice. In 'Anecdote', Liodor is initially a normal sensitive person and turns to 'improper escapades' only after several tragic incidents, and his indecent exploits are such 'which I cannot describe' with the tale left as an incomplete fragment. The narrator instead goes on to advise his young readers in the proper ways of avoiding Liodor's fate. All the other characters mentioned are depicted in situations similar to those in 'My Confession', but the specifics are polemically reversed.

Let us look closer at a few specific instances where Karamzin's serious voice from various works is heard in a hidden polemic with NN's voice.

NN tells us that he 'learned French and did not know his own native language'. Karamzin, although he himself was often accused of Gallomania, speaks out against the neglect of the Russian language, and on improving education in Russia in numerous works which appeared in *Messenger of Europe* in 1802–3, the same years as did 'My Confession'.

NN describes how he is sent to Leipzig University to study at the age of fifteen, 'got acquainted with all famous Professors – and Nymphs', slept during lectures 'and could not hear enough of them, because [he] never listened'. Numerous of Karamzin's works are devoted to gentry education and, in general, he speaks out against the lack of parental involvement and the custom of hiring foreign tutors. The articles 'Why are there Few Authors of Talent' and 'On a Sure Means to Have Enough Teachers in Russia' address the same topic, and 'An Aberration' describes education by foreigners at its most absurd: a Frenchman has founded a 'pension' for Russian youth where, among other subjects, he offers to teach them Russian. The traveller in *Letters of a Russian Traveller* speaks seriously about studies in Leipzig as a fond childhood dream, and later speaks with disdain about Parisian 'nymphs of joy'. Liodor and Eugene, among his fictional heroes, study seriously in Leipzig.

NN tells us how he, during his travels, 'jumping in contredanses with important ladies [ . . . ] on purpose dropped them on the ground in the most unseemly manner', and 'with the good catholics, kissing the Pope's shoes, bit him in the foot and made the poor old man scream with all his might' (151). Such sacrilegious slapstick runs diametrically counter to the serious religious tolerance which is reflected in other works by Karamzin. In 'On the Light Dress', similar dancing is censured in similar vocabulary when performed by young French post-revolutionary women, and Karamzin disparagingly notes that young Russian women imitate the fashions of such models.[58]

In Paris, Count NN learns the language of social dandies, is received in some good families, gets to know some of the 'most famous French wits', attends a reading of La Harpe's *Mélanie*, flatters its author, is introduced to the duke of Orleans, and shares his and his company's amusements, 'worthy of the brush of a new Petronius' – as NN remarks, using a characteristic Karamzinian topos. In *Letters of a Russian Traveller* and 'Liodor', the narrators also meet with the foremost scholars and artists in Paris, are also received cordially into the best families, and also attend various artistic events. La Harpe, the neighbor of the Sentimental traveller in Paris, was described as a perceptive scholar and literary critic and 'the best tragedian after Voltaire' – the qualities usually still stressed in accounts of La Harpe.[59] Count NN, characteristically, flatters La Harpe for *Mélanie*, an anticlerical comedy which was ultimately to be forbidden in France. The allusion to *Satyricon* is equally in character. Of the same nature is the reference to Richardson – of all his personages, only Lovelace is mentioned by NN, who in his own behavior imitates and vastly surpasses even Lovelace.

From his sickbed (due to too much drinking) in England, Count NN amuses himself by drawing caricatures of the royal family. It is tempting to see this as a humorous allusion of sorts to Karamzin's own caricature of another royal family, 'The Beautiful Princess', subtitled, as we recall, an 'olden fairy tale or a new caricature'. When Count NN returns home, he displays various 'aberrations', and is aped by all the young people, to his great amusement.

One of the digressions to the narratees in the Count's confession, consists of lengthy 'philosophical discussions about *Being in love* (*Vliublennost'*), – forgive the new word'. This is a good example of the most overt form of play on Karamzinian language that characterizes NN's speech throughout his confessions. The word *vliublennost'* is one of Karamzin's most debated neologistic coinages, and NN humorously reverses any serious definition of the word.[60] Furthermore, the same passage plays on the overture to 'Julia'.

The positive Sentimentalist attitude to women is particularly profaned in NN's description of his vile behavior towards women. To NN they are nothing but sex objects who, because of their weakness, can easily be exploited for his amusement. And exploit them he does: using all the tricks of a dandy, he creates jealousies between some women, makes other women leave their husbands, finally marries Emilia, totally subjugating and corrupting her. He turns her into the ideal hostess of extravagant domestic entertainments above their means, and finally agrees to give her up to a rich old Prince (to escape debtors' prison), only to move in with them after they marry, after which he seduces his own ex-wife, persuades her to elope with him, and immediately takes new mistresses. Indeed by his behavior he causes the death of both his mother and his ex-wife–mistress. I hardly need to point out that this is an absolute perversion of some of the mild, innocent forms of dandyism expressed by Karamzin in both his life and his works, and Count NN certainly reverses the evaluation of gender roles elsewhere professed by the Sentimentalists.

Count NN describes his path to financial ruin and back to prosperity, with lengthy digressions on 'clever usurers', the needs and assets of rich dandies (158–9), and the 'multiplicatory power of debts' (159–60), seeing spendthrifts as benefactors to the nation. He of course speaks from experience, and ends his days content with his lot as 'an usurer and moreover an entertainer, a jester and confidant of men and women in their small weaknesses' (166). A contrary view of all these 'professions' is expressed in Karamzin's 'Pleasing Prospects', which, as a whole, can be seen as a serious answer to Count NN, and is one of Karamzin's most explicit statements about the duties of young noblemen.

The whole text of NN is studded with other less extended Karamzinian formulae voiced both earlier and later, and particularly in the works of 1802–3. Other bivocal utterances evoke Karamzin's *Letters of a Russian Traveller*, with its 'Chinese shadows', mirror imagery, optical illusions of other kinds, and particularly the famous concluding lines expressing the solipsistic principle of the work.[61] Other instances of bivocality could be added, but suffice this to show how pervasively Karamzin's serious works and his other humorous works, both earlier ones and ones contemporary to 'My Confession', are humorously turned into their opposites by NN. NN's opening assertion about not reading *Messenger of Europe* is clearly an understatement.

NN's voice in 'My Confession' is a parody of Karamzin, but also of Rousseau (especially his *Emile* and *Les Confessions*), who in many respects was Karamzin's teacher. Rousseau, as Karamzin's Swiss mentor, also has a parallel personage in 'My Confession': NN's Genevan tutor, Mendel, 'Genevan, I beg to note, and not a Frenchman because at this time French tutors in our famous houses had already gone out of fashion' – as NN muses in his typical Karamzinian/un-Karamzinian manner. This 'republican' who hates 'tyranny' is, like his pupil, the ultimate travesty of everything the Sentimentalists held sacred in terms of individual liberty and duties. He embodies the Sentimentalist paradox of liberty turned into its extreme: libertinism – a streak that Rousseau also to a certain extent exposes in himself in his confessions.

His name, Mendel, is somewhat of a puzzle, but it was possibly chosen for its rich sound connotations to various currents of eighteenth-century philosophy, and I will use it as my final example of multivocalism in 'My Confession'. The name evokes associations to Bernard Mandeville. NN's discourse on the social utility of spendthrifts, his opinions about rich dandies, usurers, and creditors, are practically paraphrases of Mandeville's most famous works, 'The Fable of the Bees' and 'The Grumbling Hive'. Mandeville was one of de Sade's acknowledged authorities. That Karamzin was familiar with Mandeville is beyond any doubt. Haller's 'Über den Ursprung des Übels' (translated by Karamzin), for instance, was directed specifically against Mandeville and Bayle.

The name Mendel also evokes Moses Mendelssohn, closer to a serious Karamzin than was Mandeville. Mendelssohn's subjectivist philosophy and aesthetics cannot but have influenced a serious Karamzin directly or indirectly through Lavater, Bonnet, Lessing, and other German thinkers close to Mendelssohn and revered by Karamzin.[62]

Finally, the sound of the name Mendel, coupled with Mendel's profession as a tutor to a young nobleman travelling in the world, particularly in the eighteenth-century literary context, cannot but call forth associations to all the ideal 'Mentors' which populated Neoclassicist novels in Russia (such as those of Kheraskov), written on the model of Fénelon's *Télémaque*. The brevity, the lack of moralizing, and the whole educational path without any moral aims or results in the pupil, would seem to indicate that 'My Confession' is, at least partly a hidden parody of Kheraskov's novels.

One may interpret the name Mendel as a microcosm of the ingeniously complex structure of voices and meanings in 'My Confession' as a whole – which is indeed 'no simple satire'.

## A SENTIMENTAL NOVEL

### A Knight of our Time

*A Knight of our Time*, Karamzin's only novel, appeared in three installments in his last journal, *Messenger of Europe,* in 1802 and 1803 .[63] The last installment was preceded by the following editorial note:

The continuation of a Novel, the beginning of which was printed in nos. 13 and 18 of *Messenger of Europe* for last year. If the readers have forgotten it, then the following chapters will be *a fragment* for them. This Novel is in general based on *recollections* of youth, which the Author was engaged in during a time of spiritual and physical illness: so at least he told us, when, with a low bow, he gave it to us for printing in the Journal. (14, 121)

The playful note is indicative of the novel itself. It is based on personal recollections – or so the author (Karamzin) told the editor (Karamzin). While Karamzin as author states that his novel consists of recollections, Karamzin as editor chooses to remain noncommittal as to the veracity of the sources. This is, of course, a typical literary 'editorial' device, 'author' referring to the narrator in *Knight*, and 'editor' referring to what might be seen as the narrator of the journal. The note, by itself, can obviously not be taken as absolute proof of the novel's autobiographical nature. There are, however, other indications that corroborate the note on this score, and many scholars view it as a fictional autobiography.[64]

The novel contains youthful recollections in another sense, as well. As in the case of 'My Confession', Karamzin humorously re-evaluates the latter part of the eighteenth century – both the ideas of Sentimentalist philosophy (on human nature, politics, education, etc.) and the literature of the era, his own works included.

The prose fiction in *Messenger of Europe* has in general received much less scholarly attention than Karamzin's other prose works. *Knight*, until recently, was not afforded more than the most summary mention in more general contexts of either eighteenth-century literature or Karamzin biography, and was often not mentioned at all, even where Karamzin's other prose works were discussed.[65] Recently, *Knight* has fared somewhat better in more specialized works on Karamzin's prose. The works of Brang, Lotman, Kanunova, Cross, and Anderson include particularly valuable sections on the novel, and *Knight* has recently even been translated into English for the first time.[66]

Most critics tend to stress the thematic aspects of the novel (Karamzin's new philosophy, his views of Rousseau's or Locke's works on education), and usually *Knight* is seen as an important stage in Karamzin's development toward a more 'objective' historical fiction. His new emphasis on psychological characterization is generally also stressed by scholars, and *Knight* has been hailed as the first psychological depiction of a child in Russian literature.[67] No major work has so far been devoted exclusively to the novel or even to the *Messenger of Europe* prose fiction as a group.[68]

The events in *Knight* can be summarized as the psychological biography of a child, Leon, from birth to age eleven. The following main stages are depicted: his birth and infancy under the loving care of his mother, his mother's untimely death, his early education by the village priest and his first exposure to literature, his early religious experiences through his mother and through his encounter with a ferocious bear, the influence of his father and the male provincial gentry, his acquaintance with Countess Emilia Mirova and her subsequent influence on him as his 'second mummy' and teacher, and, finally, his growing sexual awareness as he watches Emilia bathe. The focus of the narrated events is on Leon's personality as seen against the different external stimuli. It is this aspect of the novel that has been most emphasized in the scholarly literature. The tendency among scholars has been to see the narrated events proper as the main theme, while sections of speech event (the subjective part) are viewed, at best, as serving to objectify the narrated event, at worst, as failures on Karamzin's part.[69] The humor of the novel has largely been neglected. I am not disputing the merits of previous scholarly works, all of which do treat, in more or less detail, the various aspects of subjectivism with many astute observations. I merely wish to disagree with their ranking of the subjective elements as somehow inferior or subordinate to the objective ones. It seems to me that Karamzin uses subjectivity, fully aware of what he is doing. The subjective pronouncements, rather than being subordinated to the objective ones, on the contrary subordinate the narrated events to Karamzin's main aim, which is not social or even psychological, but *literary*: to parody the novels of his time, as well as Sentimentalism in general, including his own earlier works. Thus, *Knight*, in my view should be seen mainly as a sustained work of metafiction, as a fictional work about fiction, or an extended exercise in discourse-deictic techniques. *Knight* possesses much greater complexity than it has been credited with, and laughter is one of our most legitimate responses to the novel. The 'true' story of Leon is but one of its levels, and, furthermore, a level which serves as a mere pretext for the author's airing of what are essentially *literary* questions. In the following I will show how the objective 'then and there' of Leon's story is subordinated to the 'here and now' of the narrator – how the speech event overtly subordinates the narrated event to its own aim.

As the title indicates, the narrator's main protagonist is his own contemporary. The setting is also the narrator's (and narratee's) own environment – in fact, one might meet the (now adult) hero in the street and even recognize him. The main difference between the narrator's 'here and now' and the personage's 'there and then' is that the narrator is the adult, 'professional' chronicler of the hero's childhood. The narrator's mature point of view is contrasted to the hero's innocent one, and the speech event is distanced from the narrated event, not so much temporally or spatially as axiologically. This is laid bare in several speech event sections; for instance, the attentions Leon gets from his 'second mummy' have quite different potentials for the mature narrator than for the child: 'Fortunate child! had you been eight years older, – who wouldn't have envied your good fortune?' (14, 135). Sometimes, however, the narrator plays with the relative temporal proximity (often for satirical purposes). The countess's 'strict morals', for example, are footnoted by a whimsical 'one ought to remember that this was in the olden days; at least very long ago' (14, 130). Such satire is, however, much more prominent in, for example, 'Natal'ia', where it is motivated by the 'real' temporal distance between the narrator and his tale, by the presumably historical content. The difference between maturity and innocence also, to some extent, colors the narrator's relationship to Leon. An exaggeration of endearing diminutives and child language (*malen'kie ruchenki; malen'kaia krovat'ka*), reveals the narrator's paternalistic attitude to his hero. The description of Leon at birth (done, as it were, jointly by narrator and narratee–parent-to-be) is the most extreme case in point: 'belen'kim, polnen'kim, s rosovymi gubkami, s Grecheskim nosikom, s chernymy glazkami, s kofeinymi voloskami na kruglen'koi golovke' (13, 40). Here all nouns and most adjectives are diminutives – an extravagance unusual even in Russian. Overall, however, the direct emotional involvement of the narrator with his personages, as pointed out by the critics referred to above, is significantly toned down as compared with Karamzin's earlier works. The image of narrator emerges mostly in his relationship to the narratee, to other literary voices, and his focus on authorial function, his own manipulation of the narrated event.

Let us first look at the narrator–narratee relationship. The allocutional means are utilized to the utmost: imperatives, vocatives, and interrogatives abound. The explicit dialogue between the narrator and the narratee is especially prominent. In fact, a large part of the work consists precisely of narrator–narratee dialogue as a kind of on-going discussion of the narrated events. The narrator constantly plays with the narratee's expectations, confirms them, frustrates them, poses riddles and refuses to give the solutions, takes the narratee into his confidence ('be it said between us'), and so on. He involves the narratee in a literary discussion – after naming Leon's favorite books, he parenthetically asks whether the reader is familiar with the works. He puts words into the narratee's mouth – for example, all of Chapter II consists of the narratee's description of his ideal baby – which turns out to be the 'exact' description of Leon ('such was Leon', the narrator affirms). There are, however, some differences between the narratee's description of Leon (as anticipated by the narrator) and the narrator's own. In the narratee's imagination, Leon has black little eyes (*chernye glazki*) and coffee-colored hair (*kofeinye voloski*), while the narrator himself later describes Leon's hair as light brown (*rusye* ) and his eyes as pale blue (*golubye*). This subtly humorous play on voices was not appreciated by Sipovskii, who saw these 'curious minor details' as careless inconsistencies.[70]

The narrator quite obviously makes the narratee aware of his own authorial privileges and, in turn, has the narratee's expectations and reactions to his tale in mind. For example, in Chapter III the narratee is teased: '"End of chapter!" – says the reader', whereupon the narrator 'spites' him, goes on for another page, and finally reverses the situation 'I have much more to describe; I'll save the paper, the reader's attention and . . . end of chapter!' Chapter IV begins with a similarly capricious truth-claim directed to the narratees:

My dear Sirs! you are reading not a novel, but a true story: accordingly, the Author is not obliged to give an account of the events. *So it was exactly!* . . . and I won't say another word. Is it to the point? relevant? that's none of my business. I only follow fate, with my pen, and describe what she decrees in her omnipotence – why? ask her; but I tell you in advance that you won't get an answer. (13, 46; the rest of the chapter goes on in the same vein)

This passage can be seen as a good demonstration of how Karamzin ultimately came to play with his old devices. We recall how the narrator in 'Poor Liza' completely seriously is ready to curse Erast's base behavior, but instead can only weep and bemoan his own calling as re-narrator of a true story. In 'Natal'ia', the same device is developed into a somewhat more extended and lighter dialogue with the narratee *à propos* the latter's doubts about love at first sight. In *Knight*, this dialogue makes up a whole chapter (rife with

philosophizing on history, Fate, Nature, the afterworld, and other
favorite Karamzinian topics), and refers back to the preceding
chapter which ended in various absurd speculations about how the
narrator *could* tell his story. Thus an initially serious device for
expressing mainly emotive involvement with the personages has
been developed to its utmost absurd limits to expostulating on
narrative method and the story in progress – a story, we might add,
which was elsewhere overtly labelled a novel (*roman*). I shall return
to the generic aspects below.

There are numerous other twists to the narrator's truth-claim.
After the description of Leon's miraculous escape from the attacking bear (struck dead by lightning), the narrator turns to his
narratee: 'Reader! believe it or not: but this incident is not a
fiction.' However, in the next lines he reveals that he is not, in
principle, adverse to changing the 'truth' – within the limits of
verisimilitude, of course: 'I would transform the bear into a most
noble lion or tiger if only they . . . existed here in Russia' (18, 120).
This, no doubt, is an allusion to the novels of the time with their
exoticism – his own miraculous tale, however, is not entirely free
from the same trait! There are many other hints of this nature, and
the 'objective truth' must always be taken with a grain of salt.
Moreover, the passage can also be seen as another curious allusion
to Karamzin's more youthful literary endeavors. We recall that
'The Countryside' contained the following flashback to the narrator's youth:

> There [in the country, 'at the edge of Europe', as in *Knight*] my soul was
> brought up in natural simplicity; the great phenomena of Nature were the
> first objects of its attention. A clap of thunder, rolling from the heavenly
> vault above my head, gave me my first notion of the greatness of the
> Creator (*Miropravitel'*); and this thunder clap was the basis of my
> Religion.[71]

The narrator of *Knight* expresses the same serious idea and uses
much of the same lexicon ('Leon's heart experienced a vivid sense
of the Creator (*Miropravitel'*) [ . . . ] The notion of the Divinity was
one of his first ideas', 18, 117–18), but elaborates the event of the
thunder (itself an impressive phenomenon) with the more impressive bear aspect, and comments tongue in cheek that he could
introduce even more impressive beasts were it not geographically
impossible. Both these instances of playful dialogue with the
narratee are thus also indicative of the frivolous dialogue with

Karamzin, the Sentimentalist author – as pervasive in *Knight* as it was in 'My Confession'.

Different types of narratees are addressed, depending on the context, as in Karamzin's earlier works. New types of narratees appear: cruel people, phlegmatics, and egoists – all contrasted tongue in cheek with the innocent child, who will never be like them.

From the very outset, the narrator makes his aim explicit – he wants to entertain his narratees and keep them from yawning, and therefore will tell them the 'romantic (hi)story' (*romanicheskaia istoriia*) of a friend of his. Romance is to be his main means for keeping the narratee awake. The narrator 'fills in' the narratee's anticipated excitement: already in Chapter I he, the narratee, is immensely curious about the true identity of the protagonist – whom he might even know. The narrator refuses, however, to reveal his identity, but promises such a true-to-life depiction that the narratee might well recognize him in the street. In Chapter III, the narrator reveals his intention to spice up an otherwise yawn-inspiring story about the Arcadia of childhood innocence – imputing to his narratee a salacious interest in the passions of life. We need hardly point out that the story of Leon's childhood has all the makings of a family/love idyll, culminating in the most typical idyll motif of a 'shepherd' watching a bathing nymph. The *malaia forma* of the idyll has, as it were, been transformed into the *bol'shaia forma* of the novel by stringing together several idylls within a single narrator–narratee framework. In the process, the idyll becomes the object of the narrator's none too flattering evaluation (yawn-inspiring, boring). Instead of the idyll (a boring description of childhood innocence) the narrator secures his narratee's attention with a promise of 'something completely **contrary to this innocence**, this happiness' (13, 41).[72] The balance between the innocent and the risqué is skillfully maintained. On the one hand, the narrator explicitly promises the romantically inclined narratee something to keep him from yawning, and continues to hint at upcoming topics:

Now I must relate certain **oddities** (*strannosti*) . . . . It is no wonder that one could love our Hero, beautiful in appearance, handsome, sensitive, intelligent; but to become attached to him head over heels, with all signs of deepest passion, to an innocent child: that is what I call an **inexplicable oddity**! (14, 125–6)

On the other hand, when the narratee is (presumably) prepared to interpret the events described with the narrator's promises in mind, the narrator discourages or overtly frustrates such interpretations by telling the narratee something seemingly innocent – clinging, as it were, to the 'old' idyll. Thus, after the above promise about some **inexplicable oddity**, and after reinforcing the expectations by referring to women's stories as *toujours un roman* ('in a sense that is obvious to everyone'), the narrator goes on to tell Emilia's 'touching story'. On the surface, it is the story of a beautiful, virtuous woman and her loveless marriage to an older man, who cannot fulfill her natural inclinations for a deeper relationship. Rather than taking a lover, she distances herself from the social whirl, and all her pent-up romantic propensities are transformed into maternal feelings for Leon, her 'adopted son'. Meanwhile, her story is full of innuendos of not so strict morals and rumors of '*coquettishness from absentmindedness*'. The introduction of her letter to a friend similarly ostensibly reaffirms her strict morals, but, coupled with the narrator's remarks, also hints at her amorous disposition.

The education Leon receives from his 'second mummy' is explicitly called the 'explanation' for the **inexplicable oddity**, promised in the above quote. It consists of French (mostly lovers' phrases), the ways of the world (which leads her to dress up Leon *à la mode*, and leads Leon into her boudoir – when her husband is absent – to assist in her toilette, even helping her on with her shoes!), geography (which leads the two to secluded spots in the environs), etc., all of which has quite erotic overtones, and amounts to nothing but a protracted seduction process by an experienced coquette.[73] The description ends with an apostrophe to the Countess: 'The heart of your loved one matures together with his mind, and the **flower of innocence has the fate of other flowers**' (14, 138). This is followed by the narratee's anticipated response: 'The reader will think that by this rhetorical figure we are preparing him for something **contrary to innocence**: no! . . . that time is still ahead! Our Hero had only just turned eleven years old . . . ' (14, 138). The words I have emphasized point to the identity between the narrator's promise and the narratee's presumed expectations. The narrator's negation must also be seen in an ironical light: if the hero were not eleven, but older, the whole relationship would certainly be less strange and less contrary to innocence.

The 'botany of the text' can serve to illustrate the tightly knit structure of the novel, as well as the intricate relationship between speech event and narrated event. On the one hand, the flora is used as an extended metaphor for the relationship between Leon and the female protagonists, and for Leon himself in his development from innocence to sexual receptiveness. On the other hand, the flora is purely rhetorical. We might recall the various 'shy violets' in Karamzin's idylls and Sentimental tales and note, once more, how an earlier device is exaggerated, embellished, and infused with humor in *Knight*.

The first flower image is used with reference to Leon's mother: 'She knew the cruel one (*zhestokuiu*, feminine); the cruel one (*zhestokaia*, feminine) put her imprint upon her – and the mother of our Hero would never have been married to his father, if the cruel one (*zhestokii*, masculine) **in the month of April** had plucked the **first violet on the banks** of the Sviiaga! . . . ' (13, 39).[74] She did not succumb to seduction (the violet was not plucked), and she remained **'innocent** in soul and body' until her marriage to Leon's father. The seduction site, as well as the other vocabulary, here emphasized, is significant, as we shall see later.

The second flower connected to her is picked when she teaches Leon religion: 'picking for him a **spring field flower**', she teaches him that 'God gives us **flowers**' (18, 118). Thus the botanical imagery is used to show her virtuous and deeply religious nature, and her good influence on Leon.

Leon's childhood innocence is also described in botanical terms. In his total devotion to his mother he is likened to a **sunflower**, always turning towards the **sun**, even when the sun is hidden behind clouds, and even when it itself begins to '**wither and dry**', as the narrator rather ominously adds (13, 44). He spends his days reading **on the banks of the Volga river**, amidst **field flowers**, and 'he himself seemed the most beautiful, animated **flower**', with his **rosy** cheeks. Significantly, his '**cap** served him as a little table: on it he placed his book' (18, 116). The description of his reading ends with the narrator's ecstatic exclamation: 'The Homeland, **April** of life, the **first flowers of the spring** of the soul!' (18, 117), using the same vocabulary that was connected with Leon's virtuous mother.

The narrator uses similar botanical imagery to philosophize over the stages of human life. In so doing, he simultaneously foreshadows events to come. Chapter IV consists of a lengthy philo-

sophical digression on the mysteries of time passing, part of which
reads: 'everywhere there are Sphinx-like **riddles**, which even
**Oedipus** himself cannot guess. – **The rose withers**, the thorns
remain [ . . . ] A fortunate young man whose life could be called the
smile of **Fate and Nature, fades in a minute**, like a meteor' (13,
46–7). Here we should note that the first violet too was connected
with a riddle. The 'minute' is subsequently stressed in connection
with passions ('coquettishness **for a minute**') and '*ardent passions*
have heavenly **minutes** – but *minutes*!' in connection with the
Countess's wishful thinking (14, 127–8). The reference to Oedipus
is also ominous.

In Chapter V, the floral imagery serves as a transition between
what has been and what is to come. The narrator apostrophizes
time: 'And you, like Morpheus, scatter the **poppy flowers** of
oblivion: throw a few **little flowers** on my young Hero' (13, 50). This
is followed by a foreshadowing of more grievous things in store for
Leon.

The discussion of Leon's readings further extends the botanical
metaphor in an ominous direction: the narrator describes Leon's
readings as a '**hothouse** for a young soul who **ripens ahead of time**
from this reading' (14, 122). This ostensibly positive metaphor is, in
the wider context, an artificial environment (as opposed to the field
flowers and the sunflower, nurtured by the sun), which accelerates
our 'plant's' path to withering.[75]

This becomes obvious when the same floral imagery is used to
describe Leon's relationship to his 'second mummy'. Leon's story
turns into an Oedipus myth with a new twist – the 'mother' is two
different persons. After describing the growing familiarity between
Emilia and Leon, in the erotically loaded section referred to above,
the narrator apostrophizes Emilia: 'The dawn of sensitivity is quiet
and beautiful, but storms are nearby. The heart of your loved one
**matures** together with his mind, and **the flower of innocence has the
fate of other flowers!**' (14, 138). This is literally what happens. In
the last chapter, the botanical metaphor is further extended: after
Leon has watched Emilia bathe, Emilia, significantly places a **rose**
on Leon's **cap**, acknowledging her forgiveness and also her ultimate
victory over Leon's innocence – the rose is (to continue the
narrator's metaphor) plucked, her seduction a *fait accompli*.

To summarize: the floral euphemism is accompanied by the same
imagery in the three main stages of Leon's innocence:

(1) his mother's virtue was affirmed and passed on to Leon on the riverbank, in spring, in April (innocence).

(2) his reading (accelerating his fall from innocence) took place on the riverbank, in the spring of life, April, his cap serving to prop up his books.

(3) his transgression (fall from innocence) took place on a riverbank, and the plucked rose was placed on the same cap which previously held his books.

By this detailed analysis I wish to stress the striking structural unity of the novel.

These instances of metaphorical flora are, at the same time, accompanied by the narrator's laying bare his own metaphor as **rhetorical flowers**. He is thereby flaunting his authorial privilege of manipulating the narrated event. Utilizing the device of praeteritio, he tells his narratee: 'I could gather enough **flowers to adorn this chapter**' (13, 41). This, as we have seen, is precisely what he does, and it must be taken seriously. The sunflower is directly followed by a playful pun on the 'life of **plants**' (*rastitel'noe bytie*) and his own 'striking comparison' (*razitel'noe sravnenie*), and he hopes that his dear female readers might sigh from the bottom of their hearts (both at Leon's innocence and his own striking literary techniques), and that they 'would have this **flower engraved** (*vyrezat'* = engrave and cut) on their seals' (13, 44). The words contain a light metaphorical hint at what will, in fact, later take on a darker significance with the cut rose image. The reference to the fate of the 'flower of innocence' is directly followed by an address to the narratee: 'The reader will think that we with this **rhetorical figure** are preparing him for something **contrary to innocence**' (14, 138), referring, as we have seen, to his own promises. He does, in fact, fulfill his promises, and, despite his protestations, he finally must admit that 'the love for truth forces us to describe a small incident, which can be interpreted this way and that . . . ' (14, 138). Here, too, the narrator lays bare his techniques, and finally (more or less) sanctions the narratee's salacious interpretation of the Actaeon scene which follows. In all these instances of revealing his own literary devices (and more could be added), the narrator uses the language of a professional critic, which indicates the metafictional nature of the novel as a whole. While giving an 'objective' description of Leon's development (the 'blank slate' of his soul, which is subjected to both good and bad external stimuli), the description is, at the same time, subjected to the narrator's own literary analysis. I shall return to the subject below.

The same 'tampering' with the 'objective' educational aspects of Leon's development can be seen in the narrator's presentations of the other influences in Leon's life. The profound religious teachings of Leon's mother are juxtaposed to the miraculous escape from the bear and the narrator's absurd tongue-in-cheek comments about lions and tigers.

The male influence is represented by Leon's father and the male provincial gentry. Their influence, although basically positive, is not exempt from the narrator's irony and humor. The 'neutral' document and the personages' own speech is contrasted to the narrator's ironical speech event statements. The latter reveal that Bacchus had a hand in drafting and signing the friendship pact, and the 'enlightenment' of the men is unmasked as arguments and loud discussions about trivia or matters they know nothing about. Their prosaic old age is incongruously commented on in the narrator's mock-solemn apostrophes to his *'bogatyrs'* and 'matadors of the province', with their weak legs, walking sticks, prosaic dress, and more or less senile or drunken deliberations. Nevertheless, their influence on Leon is positive – or at least not harmful.[76]

These prosaic old men are contrasted to the more glorious *bogatyrs* and matadors which fill the pages of Leon's books: *Daira, an Eastern Tale, Selim and Damasina, Inconstant Fortune, or the Voyage of Miramond,* and *The History of Lord N.*[77] In juxtaposition to the prosaic company of his father, Leon's readings must be seen as a harmful influence on the young child. Although initially extolled as a 'hothouse' for the receptive youngster, the narrator, either by indirection or in explicit asides to the narratee, lays bare their harmful effects. The narrator describes how Leon was fascinated by the dangerous adventures and heroic friendships depicted in the novels (18, 14). This stands in sharp contrast to the more down-to-earth 'adventures' and more domestic friendships in Leon's provincial environment. Leon also, according to the narrator, always saw himself as the 'deliverer' (*izbavitel'*) rather than the 'delivered' (*izbavlennyi*) when imagining himself as the protagonist of similar adventures (14, 122). Ironically, in the only adventures that befall him in the novel describing his own life, the opposite is true: he is *izbavlennyi* by God (or Divine Providence) from the bear, and later he is *izbavlennyi* by the Countess from the dogs which threaten him in the conclusion to *Knight*.

In an aside to the narratee, the narrator ironically remarks that, according to the 'philosophical medicos', reading can at most hurt the physical well-being of young readers (14, 122). Later, *à propos* the 'beneficial' education Leon receives from the Countess, the narrator remarks 'confidentially' to the narratee (whimsically laying bare the separation between speech event and narrated event): 'Leon (be it said between us!) up till now knew nothing except Aesop's fables, *Daira* and the great works of Fedor Emin' (14, 134), the latter two elsewhere 'professionally' referred to as 'nonsense' (*neskladitsa*) (18, 113).

In addition to adventures and heroic friendship, the topic of all of Leon's books is love, and the Eastern tales in particular were famed for their somewhat *risqué* content. When Leon's reading is first mentioned, however, a great deal of stress is placed on what the youngster found so interesting in the works – not the amorous matters, but the adventures themselves, as the narrator remarks in a lengthy ironical aside to the narratee (18, 113). This is followed by another digression on the natural curiosity of children as the basis for their later knowledge and experiences. The digression ends on an ominous note of warning: 'but whenever the object of our curiosity ceases to be a true need and turns into a trivial pursuit, then our flight turns pedestrian and our steps become heavier by the hour' (18, 114). Curiosity is regarded as a source of learning unless directed toward useless objects. Leon's curiosity is consistently stressed in *Knight*, this quality often being used as an epithet describing him, and it is, ostensibly, one of the sources of his learning. The books (including, of course, the amorous parts), coupled with his inherent curiosity, are an integral part of the novel plot – it is the same curiosity that ultimately leads him to the river where Emilia bathes (the same vocabulary that is used in the above quote is repeated in the latter scene). Thus, any ideas about virtuous love, that should ideally have been instilled in Leon by his books, in fact, left him an ill-prepared victim of the mature seductress, and the narrator's warnings come true.

Such foreshadowings by the narrator are of extreme importance in *Knight*. We have already seen that Leon's reading often took place on the riverbank, where he was later to witness the bathing. From the very beginning, water imagery is important; for example, the reference to the impact of 'noisy rivers' on a vivid imagination in Chapter III also foreshadows the later event – the imagined is, so to speak, reenacted in real life. In Chapter IV, Leon's soul 'was sailing in the world of books like Christopher Columbus on the Atlantic ocean, to discover . . . the undiscovered' (*dlia otkrytiia . . . sokrytogo*, a pun emerges in Russian, since these words can also mean 'uncover, open' . . . 'covered, hidden') (18, 114). Here both the water imagery and the '*otkrytie sokrytogo*' can again be seen as the narrator's metaphorical foreshadowing of Leon's subsequent 'discovery' of the 'uncovered' Countess. A variation of water imagery used as a foreshadowing to the final scene can also be seen in the narrator's comparison of childhood to 'a beautiful pool', good to glance at but not interesting to dwell on. This rhetorical figure also becomes quite literal with Leon 'glancing at' Emilia in a sort of 'pool'.

Thus, what many critics have viewed as 'unwarranted' narratorial digressions, are intimately tied to the central romantic thread of *Knight*. The novel polemic carried out in *Knight* is, however, more complex. As in the case of 'My Confession', the narrator of *Knight* also playfully engages in an 'external' dialogue with a more serious Karamzin. Such play can be heard throughout the discussion of Leon's reading. Karamzin early became a staunch defender of learning through both arts and sciences (most notably in his article 'On the Sciences', where questions, such as curiosity being a source of learning, and the development of sensitivities and morals through arts and sciences, were discussed). In 1802, when *Knight* began to appear, several works by Karamzin endorse even the Emin-type 'new' prose fiction. In a 'Letter to the Editor' (unsigned, but written by the 'editor' himself, Karamzin) of *Messenger of Europe*, introducing the section 'Literature and Varia' in the first issue of the journal, the writer has the following to say about that type of prose: 'I do not know what others think; but I would not want to blame a person even for "Milord George", printed five or six times. A stupid book is no great evil in the world.'[78] 'Milord George' is footnoted (by Karamzin, the editor) as 'perhaps the most stupid of Russian novels'.[79] Matvei Komarov, its author, fares no better (or worse?) in another article by Karamzin, 'On Booktrade and Love for Reading in Russia' which also appeared in 1802 in *Messenger of Europe*, Karamzin expresses his joy at the increase in reading among all classes, and fervently endorses the reading even of 'the most average' novels.[80]

In the discussion of Leon's reading in *Knight*, the narrator, for the most part, explicitly agrees with Karamzin and the Emin–Komarov–Novikov camp, and endorses, and even extolls, Leon's reading. Yet, as in the two works cited above, while on the one hand praising the 'new' prose, on the other hand he slyly introduces disparaging remarks about the quality of this prose. *Knight* as a whole, as it were, proves both the Emin camp and Karamzin wrong in their assessments of the positive moral influence of this type of prose. If we recall the beginning of the debate in Russia over the 'new' prose, the Elagin camp (including also Emin and Co.) was opposed by the Classicist proponents for, and practitioners of, a different kind of 'serious' prose, such as Kheraskov's historical novels (or non-novels?). Kheraskov, in 1760, had the following to say about the 'new' prose fiction:

Novels are read in order to love more artfully and often have the most tender passages set off in red marks; philosophy, moral content, books on sciences and the like – are not novels and are not read for the sake of love declarations.[81]

*Knight* as a whole, in a sense, proves Kheraskov's fears well-founded (and Karamzin and Emin wrong) in terms of the harmful influence the amorous parts have on Leon. At the same time, however, Kheraskov's own historical novels are, as we shall see, quite mercilessly parodied. *Knight* is a curious double parody, pitting the different camps of the novel controversy against each other, and updating that controversy to include later Sentimentalist fiction, Karamzin, and even the work in progress.[82]

As for Karamzin's works referred to in *Knight*, we might point to the specific reference to 'Natal'ia' in Chapter I ('on the Volga [ ... ] as you know from the tale of Natal'ia, the boyar's daughter, lived and died boyar Liuboslavskii as an innocent exile'), the already mentioned development of the childhood passage from 'The Countryside', many similarities to 'Il'ia Muromets' in the overture, to 'Liodor' in the concluding scene, and, by implication, to all his fiction with a 'romantic' content. Furthermore, a stanza from his poem 'To Virtue' ('K dobrodeteli'), which appeared in *Messenger of Europe* between the second and the third installments of *Knight*, is included in Chapter VI.[83] This poem is a most fervent expression of the traditional Sentimentalist belief that vice cannot triumph in the world, and its message is thus also undercut by the none too virtuous ending of *Knight*. The irony of the novel as a whole, we should perhaps stress, is nevertheless of the light and humorous kind, and Leon's 'vice' is by no means made into the worst of sins. Two of the most popular themes in Sentimentalist works are parodied in *Knight*: childhood and friendship. We have already seen how the theme of friendship is made light of in the section concerning the male provincial gentry and their Bacchic friendship pact. The Sentimentalist fondness for idyllic childhood is even more mercilessly toyed with. In the beginning of Chapter II, the 'Arcadia of childhood' is laid bare in the following words:

[Childhood] is too simple, too innocent and therefore completely uninteresting for us corrupt people. I do not dispute the fact that in some sense it can be called a happy time, the true Arcadia of life; but precisely therefore there is nothing to be written about it [ . . . ]. Let us call childhood a beautiful pool which is good to glance at, good to praise in two or three words, but which I do not advise any poet to describe in detail. (13, 40–1)

The narrator contends that it needs to be spiced up with passions, 'with something contrary to innocence', in order to make an interesting theme. Nevertheless, his own novel does precisely what he advises against. He describes childhood not just in 'two or three words', but for an entire novel and *ends* precisely when 'passions' are about to appear, with Emilia literally stirring up the ' beautiful pool'. *Knight* is also a parody of the exaggerated Sentimentalist idyllic diction. This aspect is most prominently revealed in the narrator's laying bare of the style he himself uses in the Leon story, i.e., by the explicit attention to his authorial function. The narrator has total control over the narrated event, an aspect consistently stressed in speech event sections, and most overtly laid bare in the use of praeteritio (which we saw on a more limited scale in 'Natal'ia'), which begins the description of Leon's childhood. After a lengthy discussion with the narratee about how to spice up the topic of childhood, the narrator goes on to describe what he **could** do:

I **could** gather enough flowers to adorn this chapter; I **could** without deviating from historical truth, describe [ . . . ] I **could** without breaking either Aristotelian or Horatian rules, vary my style ten times over, soaring rapidly upwards and smoothly plunging down – now, drawing with a pencil, now painting with a brush – mixing important ideas for the mind with moving strokes for the heart, I **could for example say**: '[ . . . ]. (13, 41–2)

He **could**, and does, in fact, proceed to do precisely that. Using literary terminology, he talks about his own story, which is, in fact placed in quotation marks as an example of what he **could** do. In his example, he uses precisely the exaggerated diction he describes in his 'professional' assessments of his own potential work. The Leon story is used explicitly as an example of the Sentimentalist style of which Karamzin and his epigones were 'guilty'.

After a page-long section of the Leon story, the narrator again intrudes and comments on his own tale in progress: 'Is it not true that this **could** appeal to someone or other? Here we have painting, antitheses, and pleasant punning' (13, 43). By such 'professionally' worded commentary on his own story, he simultaneously mocks other writers who use the devices mentioned. After his comment on style, the narrator goes on in the same vein to discuss the already mentioned sunflower image, again resorting to 'professional' jargon (Zoilus is mentioned, and he points to his 'striking simile', the botanical metaphor). The praeteritio device is employed to the end of Chapter III, at which point he refuses to do what he **could do** (and, of course, already did!) and puts a decisive end to the chapter. The whole narrated event gathers momentum as a story the narrator **could** write, a story, which from the beginning is subjected to discussion between the narrator and narratee. *Knight* as a whole is thus both the story about Leon and the story about the story about Leon. The use of praeteritio is not sustained to the end; it is as if the narrator forgot that he is merely giving an example, and as if the story continued of its own inertia ('I only follow fate with my pen and describe what she decrees in her omnipotence' 13, 46). The narrator 'forgets' to end his example with the quotation mark which should properly be there. The discussions with the narratee continue, and the first part (ending with Chapter V, marked by the date 1799 in later editions), ends with another discourse-deictic reference to the Leon story as a 'small notebook', which the narrator will, at some time, present to his narratee, and which will, he hopes, call forth the narratee's proper response – tears ('or I am . . . no Author', 13, 51) – another ironical comment on the Sentimental author's main aim: to move his reader.

The second part is also continuously interrupted by the narrator's commentary on his own story. He introduces his 'documentary' evidence – only to use it as another butt for his irony. *Knight* is metafictional to the core: a Sentimental tale, written in a typical

Sentimentalist manner, is simultaneously being mockingly and parodically scrutinized by its less serious Sentimental narrator.

Not only is *Knight* a parody of serious Sentimentalist writing, but, as indicated earlier, it is metafictional in another sense as well: it is a novel about the novel as it was represented in Russia during the latter part of the eighteenth century. This is, perhaps, the most carefully worked out aspect of *Knight* – and the aspect which has been least explored by scholars. Lotman in his 'Puti razvitiia russkoi prozy', mentions this aspect, but does not further investigate the specifics. *Knight* can, in fact, be seen as a parody of historical novels, and specifically, of those written by Kheraskov: *Numa, or Flourishing Rome, Cadmus and Harmonia*, and *Polydorus, Son of Cadmus and Harmonia*. It might seem odd that Karamzin should parody Kheraskov who was generally respected as the grand old man of Russian letters and who, furthermore, was one of the few old Masonic friends who had seen Karamzin's plans for publishing *Moscow Journal* in a positive light. In the first issue of that journal Karamzin had also included a positive review of *Cadmus and Harmonia*. As Lotman points out, however, the contents of that review was contradicted by another review in the same issue so that in the wider context the *Cadmus* review seemed less positive.[84] Karamzin's 'critique' in this instance was indirect and gentle so as not to offend Kheraskov. One could say the same thing of *Knight* – the parody is lighthearted and playful. Novels like Kheraskov's were written with the serious aim of educating as well as entertaining the reader, with a stress on the former (the Classicist *utile* and *dulce*). The author's aim was to propagate the ideas of the Enlightenment by showing ideal heroes, who, although they might err temporarily, were always led back to the path of virtue by various Mentors. The heroes were taken from the distant past, often semi-historical, semi-mythological figures, and were always of the highest social standing, often rulers or knights. The Mentors were often goddesses in disguise. Fénelon's *Les Aventures de Télémaque* was the prototype *par excellence*, and Kheraskov his most ardent Russian follower, with the three above mentioned novels to his name.[85] These novels tended to be of enormous dimensions (several volumes), and the tone was unfailingly one of lofty didactic advice. This is the image that Karamzin parodies in his *Knight*. The title itself is indicative: 'knight' was a most frequent rank in the historical novels. For example, according to Sipovskii:

In both novels by Kheraskov the influence of knightly novels shows in the use of the words 'knight', 'knightly' – applied to personages set in mythical times; thus in the novel 'Cadmus' Babylonian youths are called 'knights'; 'knightly art' is mentioned; in 'Polydorus' the personages are also 'knights' and 'knightly exploits', 'knightly garb', are mentioned.[86]

By applying the title to an eleven-year-old boy, the narrator of *Knight* makes the whole concept absurd. The term is also as anachronistic as in Kheraskov's novels, although the events are moved to the present era – another break with the tradition. In the narrator's introduction, his opinion of the traditional novels (*Numa* is mentioned) is made quite explicit: they are far from truthful, and can, at best, be characterized as 'beautiful puppet comedies', which make the reader yawn. Instead of Numa's toga, the narrator, in order to create more interest, dresses his knight in contemporary garb. Instead of the traditional unrounded, virtuous or evil, personages, he sets out to create a psychologically rounded cast of characters. Instead of writing a 'historical novel' (*istoricheskii roman*), he sets out to write a 'romantic/novelistic history' (*romani-cheskaia istoriia*).[87] The narrator's choice of generic label is interesting, in that it shows his triple aim:

(1) To write a *romantic* (in the sense of amorous) *istoriia*, a play on the term as it was often used at the time to signify an 'escapade' of a slightly scabrous nature, such as a duel or an amorous adventure, but also 'history' as he refers to himself as Leon's 'Historian' (*Istorik*).
(2) To write a story *about the novel* (i.e., *roman-icheskaia*)
(3) To write a work in the *novel genre*.

We have already seen that the narrator's story is a rococo-like romance about the seduction of Leon – the ultimate result of all his so-called education.[88]

As for the novel format, *Knight* consists of an introduction and thirteen chapters – all in *ca.* sixty pages (twenty-two in the 1984 edition). The very brevity can be seen as a device mocking the inordinate length of the traditional novels about knights, also mocked, as we saw, in 'My Confession'. After all, the narrator points out as one of the things he could do: 'I could invent and color much more [followed by a page-long list of possibilities consisting mostly of Sentimentalist idyllic topoi]. My words would flow like a river, if only I wished to go into detail; but I don't want to, I don't!

There is much more for me to describe; I'm saving paper, the reader's attention and . . . end of chapter!' (13, 45–6). His brevity thus parodies those who were not as thrifty with their paper, nor as concerned about their readers' attention span. The fact that a continuation is promised by the narrator (or editor) need not mean that Karamzin ever intended the novel to continue. Fragments, as we have seen, had gained the status of bona fide literary form, and it seems more likely that *Knight* is another variant on that form. Indeed, the editorial note to the third installment, sanctions a reading of that installment as a fragment: 'If the readers have forgotten it [the beginning of *Knight* which had appeared a good while ago], then the following chapters will be a *fragment* for them.' The irony is that the whole novel is a fragment for all readers, and the last installment is, by the same token, elliptical at both ends for forgetful readers – yet another variation on the 'incomplete fragment'. Karamzin lived for another twenty-three years after the publication of *Knight*, and, to my knowledge, there are no indications that he ever returned to his novel. It seems to me very unlikely indeed, that he ever intended a continuation. The tightly knit structure of the novel as it stands supports such an assumption. As we have seen, the first twelve chapters lead up to the culminating Chapter XIII (the similarity in imagery, the very development of the imagery, foreshadowings, hints, promises, etc.). Compositionally, the novel is symmetrical: the initial 'good' stimulus from Leon's virtuous mother, the intermediate stimuli from the men in his life ('good') and from books ('bad'), and the last, 'bad' stimulus from his 'second mummy', who is not so virtuous. One can only speculate, of course, but the fact remains that the novel, as it stands, is structured as a unit, complete in itself. Furthermore, a more overt elaboration of the presumably erotic topic to come, was taboo from a Sentimentalist point of view, as we have repeatedly seen in other works as well. Perhaps, by promising a continuation, Karamzin intended to mock the traditional novel with its potentially open structure: any number of events could be added (and was) within the structure of the historical novels, without essentially changing the hero's unfailing path to virtue – the path merely being made longer.

The chapter headings in *Knight* parody those in the traditional novels in a Sternian fashion (Chapter IV, for example, is called 'Written Only for the Sake of the Fifth'), which requires no comment. The contents of the different chapters fulfill the same objective: Chapter II, for instance, consists of one fourteen-line chat with the narratee.

As a novel about the novel, we can point to the metafictional nature of the work as analyzed above. This aspect is, however, most blatantly laid bare in the choice of hero and plot. In most of the Neoclassicist novels (all of Kheraskov's, mentioned above), the knight hero encounters, or is accompanied by, one or more Mentors (virtuous nymphs, wise old hermits, etc.). He is also subjected to various temptations, often in the form of seductive women or nymphs. Numa has his Mentor, the nymph Eger, who teaches him virtue, and initiates him into the secrets of a good ruler. Cadmus' Mentors are many, his virtuous and faithful wife, Harmonia, being perhaps the main one. His temptations are also many. The seductive nymph, Taksila, for example, leads to his initial downfall. Despite numerous other 'downfalls', Cadmus is ultimately led to true virtue. Polydorus encounters both Mentors and seductive nymphs. One of the nymphs on his path, the 'false' Teandra, has some affinities to Emilia in *Knight*. Polydorus is quite taken with her beauty, and, despite her admonitions, tries to lift her veil – with disastrous results: he is severely punished. Soon, however, he realizes his faults, finds the 'true' Teandra (who, like Fénelon's Mentor, is the human embodiment of the goddess Minerva), and ends up another paragon of virtue. Thus Kheraskov's heroes develop either within the realm of virtue (Numa), or on a complex path which always ends in the realm of virtue. They share this pattern with most other novel heroes of the era, including those of the novels Leon read. The narrator comments ironically: 'In all the novels in the yellow cupboard the Heroes and Heroines, despite numerous temptations of fate, remain virtuous, all the villains are depicted in the blackest colors, the former triumph in the end, the latter finally disappear like dust' (18, 115).

His own novel reverses this pattern. The knight, Leon, also has his nymph, Diana–Emilia, who quite successfully seduces her unrepentant charge. The Mentors are represented by the various educational influences in Leon's life. These representatives of virtue are, however, in one way or another treated with irony or even mocked, rather than seriously extolled as in Kheraskov.

Most interestingly, the knightly lineage of Leon is revealed in the last chapter, where the narrator calls him the 'New Actaeon'. Both parts of the sobriquet are significant. Actaeon is an Ovidian figure, the grandson of Cadmus! Thus *Knight* could be seen as a sequel to Kheraskov's two novels: *Cadmus and Harmonia, Polydorus, Son of Cadmus and Harmonia,* and, (*Knight*), '*Actaeon, Grandson of Cadmus and Harmonia*'. Leon is, however, a *new* Actaeon, as his story clearly shows. Ovid's Actaeon, after watching Diana bathe in her stream, is punished for his transgression (as were his grandfather and uncle in Kheraskov): Diana turns him into a stag. Later, hunting dogs tear him to pieces, as Diana acts in keeping with her strict chastity. The new Actaeon re-enacts his mythical prototype's transgression. The imagery is quite in accordance with that of Ovid, replete with references (in a humorous narratorial aside) to Diana (also foreshadowed in this role in Chapter XI where Emilia's figure is referred to as 'Diana-like') and nymphs, hunting dogs, and the 'correct' idyllic setting. Interestingly enough, the narrator has already made a reference to 'horns' in Chapter I, in the old crone's 'accurate' prediction of Leon's future (13, 38). Only in the last chapter does their full significance become apparent: Actaeon's metamorphosis into a stag began with horns sprouting on his forehead. The new Actaeon's horns, however, remain solely symbolical: he is not punished for his transgression. Although the hunting dogs threaten him for a while, they are called back by Diana–Emilia, and instead of Actaeon–Leon being physically transformed, the innocent boy has been mentally and emotionally transformed into a sexually receptive eleven-year-old. Thus Karamzin's 'knight' reverses the fate of both his Ovidian prototype and his Russian ancestors: Leon is led from virtue and innocence into a less virtuous relationship. We also recall that there is another, closer, prototype for Leon: Liodor in the tale by that name. 'Liodor' ended with a similar scene, which cast a veil of irony over the whole, otherwise serious, tale – whether intentionally or not. And Liodor in 'Anecdote' also turns to mysterious 'improper escapades'. *Knight* fully exploits all the humorous and ironical potentials latent in the earlier tales and, I would venture to say, quite intentionally.

I think we are fully justified in considering *Knight*, Karamzin's last work of prose fiction, first and foremost, a parody on the eighteenth-century Russian novel in all its aspects. The prominent image of the narrator is that of a Sternian mocker who parodies the preceding Sentimentalist–idyllic writings, the *utile* of the Emin-type adventure novels, Eastern tales, and romances, both the *utile* and *dulce* of the Kheraskovian historical novels, his own novel in progress, and, finally, the very novel genre itself. With this work, Karamzin's prose fiction has come full circle, and appropriately, I think, Karamzin moved on to write professional history.

# Notes

## 1 THE LITERARY AND INTELLECTUAL CONTEXT

1 I. Z. Serman, 'Zarozhdenie romana v russkoi literature XVIII veka', *Istoriia russkogo romana v dvukh tomakh*, ed. A. S. Bushmin et al (Moscow, 1962), vol. I, 40–64 and J. D. Goodliffe, 'Some Comments on Narrative Prose Fiction in Eighteenth Century Russian Literature, with Special Reference to Čulkov', *Melbourne Slavonic Studies*, 5-6 (1971), 124–36 are good concise outlines of the development of prose fiction during the period under consideration. Gary Marker, *Publishing, Printing, and the Origins of Intellectual Life in Russia, 1700–1800* (Princeton, 1985), 201–11 shows the prominence of this 'Grub Street' literature as 'leisure books'. Marker also points out that precisely such books were particularly profitable for publishers (118–20).

2 See Marker for an excellent account of book printing and publishing in eighteenth-century Russia.

3 For details about the journal, see D. D. Shamrai, 'Ob izdateliakh pervogo chastnogo russkogo zhurnala', *XVIII vek*, 1 (1935), 377–85.

4 See L. V. Pumpianskii, 'Trediakovskii', *Istoriia russkoi literatury* (Moscow, 1941), vol. I, 238–45 on the full significance of Trediakovskii's translations, the importance of the works in their country and period of origin, and in the development of the Russian novel. See also B. A. Uspenskii, *Iz istorii russkogo literaturnogo iazyka XVIII – nachala XIX veka* (Moscow, 1985) where Trediakovskii and Adodurov are viewed as precursors to Karamzin's ideas on style.

5 V. V. Sipovskii, *Ocherki iz istorii russkogo romana* (S.-Peterburg, 1909), vol. I, 1, 508–63 classifies these novels as 'pseudoclassicist novels of the *Télémaque* type'; G. A. Gukovskii, *Russkaia literatura XVIII veka* (Moscow, 1939), 187–9 describes *Numa* as a utopian political novel, written on the model of Marmontel's *Bélisaire*. Cf. also C. L. Drage, *Russian Literature in the Eighteenth Century* (London, 1978), 190–2; William Edward Brown, *A History of 18th Century Russian Literature* (Ann Arbor, 1980), 255–6.

6 See Sipovskii, *Ocherki*, vol. I, 1, 497–508; Gukovskii, *Russkaia literatura*, 207; Brown, 184–5; Drage, 189–90.

7 See I. R. Titunik, 'The Problem of *Skaz* in Russian Literature of the Eighteenth Century', *Forum at Iowa on Russian Literature*, 2 (1977)

87–103 for an analysis of image of author in the tale adaptations and in works by Emin and Chulkov; in his 'Matvej Komarov's *Vanka Kain* and Eighteenth-Century Russian Prose Fiction', *Slavic and East European Journal*, 18, 4 (1974), 351–66 he provides an analysis of the 'Vanka Kain' tale; and in 'Mikhail Chulkov's "Double-Talk" Narrative (Skazka o rozhdenii taftianoi mushki)', *Canadian-American Slavic Studies*, 9, 1 (1975), 30–42 Titunik gives an analysis of Chulkov's works from this angle.

8 Serman, 'Zarozhdenie romana', 62–3.

9 G. A. Gukovskii, *Ocherki po istorii russkoi literatury i obshchestvennoi mysli XVIII veka* (Leningrad, 1938), 235–314.

10 R. F. Brissenden, *Virtue in Distress* (London, 1974), 11–64.

11 Gukovskii, *Ocherki po istorii*, 270–1.

12 Ibid., 266.

13 Brissenden, 26.

14 David Hume, *Enquiry Concerning the Principles of Morals,* in *Enquiry Concerning Human Understanding and Concerning the Principles and Morals* (1777), 3rd rev. edn, ed. L. A. Selby-Biggs (Oxford, 1975), V, ii, 184.

15 The first quote stems from Karamzin's 'What Does an Author Need?' ('Chto nuzhno avtoru?' K1984b, vol. II, 62), the second from 'On the Book Trade and Love for Reading in Russia' ('O knizhnoi torgovle i liubvi ko chteniiu v Rossii', K1984b, vol. II, 120).

16 K1803, vol. VII, 268.

17 Brissenden, 29.

18 Laurence Sterne, *A Sentimental Journey through France and Italy by Mr. Yorick* (2 vols., London, 1786), vol. II, 182–3.

19 K1984b, vol. II, 58.

20 See Brissenden, 53–64 for a most interesting treatment of the Sentimentalist implications of the French Revolution – an account which can also help us understand some of the seeming paradoxes in Karamzin's much discussed attitudes to, and descriptions of, that event. Iu. M. Lotman, *Sotvorenie Karamzina* (Moscow, 1987) contains an enlightened analysis of Karamzin's activities during the French Revolution and his evolving attitudes to that event as part of his development as a person.

21 See Iu. M. Lotman, 'Evoliutsiia mirovozzreniia Karamzina (1789–1803)', *Uchenye zapiski Tartuskogo gosudarstvennogo universiteta*, 51 (1957), 155–8; his 'Puti razvitiia russkoi prozy 1800-kh – 1810-kh godov', *Uchenye zapiski Tartuskogo gosudarstvennogo universiteta*, 104 (1961), 31–4; and his 'Russo i russkaia kult'ura XVIII veka', *Epokha prosveshcheniia*, ed. M. P. Alekseev (Leningrad, 1967), 275–7 where the emphasis is on Karamzin's view of human nature as evil at this period of his life. Compare F. Z. Kanunova, *Iz istorii russkoi povesti* (Tomsk, 1967), 140 where Lotman's views are rejected. Lotman's latest and most balanced views on this topic are presented in

great detail in his *Sotvorenie Karamzina* where he traces the vacillations in, and evolution of, Karamzin's views on human nature from the most varied perspectives. He stresses in particular that despite intermittent periods of pessimism and disillusion, Karamzin was a firm believer in progress, defined as the perfectibility of individual behavior as well as of society at large. This Lotman sees reflected both in Karamzin's literary and social activities, and in his life-long quest for his own self-renewal.

22 The growth in distance between authors and their readers was a very gradual process that continued well into the nineteenth century. For an account of the tendency, see William Mills Todd, III, *Fiction and Society in the Age of Pushkin* (Cambridge, MA, 1986), especially 45–105.

23 G. A. Gukovskii addresses these issues in two works: 'O russkom klassitsizme. Sotiazaniia i perevody', *Poetika. Vremennik otdela slovesnykh iskusstv*, 4 (1928), 126–48; 'O russkom klassitsizme', *Poetika. Vremennik otdela slovesnykh iskusstv*, 4 (1929), 21–65. See Tynianov, *Arkhaisty i novatory* (Leningrad, 1929; rpt., Munich, 1967), 5–29 where the term 'literary fact' is defined.

24 Lotman, *Sotvorenie Karamzina*, 15–17.

25 Ibid., 256–8.

26 VE, 12, 23–4 (1803), 282–5.

27 The publishers' opening statement in the first issue of the journal is interesting: 'Works in verse and prose, imitations and translations by the publishers, will be printed with their names. What need is there to be bashful about one's name if the aim of the work is not contrary to good behavior and does not disturb anyone's peace? – Persons who have done us the honor of sending in their works, imitations, or translations have their rights.' (*St:Petersburgskii Merkurii,* 1793, I, v).

28 See Lotman, *Sotvorenie Karamzina*, 192–221 and 242–55.

29 VE, 8, 5 (1803), 49–61; K1984b, vol. II, 123–6; K1984b, vol. II, 44–60.

30 K1984b, vol. II, 117–20.

31 Lotman, *Sotvorenie Karamzina,* 227–37. See Sipovskii, *Ocherki*, vol. I, 1, 1–21, 32–43; Rudolf Neuhäuser, *Towards the Romantic Age* (The Hague, 1974), 53 for a concise listing of numbers of books published between 1750 and 1780. Marker provides the most systematic and detailed treatment of the eighteenth-century book market. See especially pp. 184–211 on book sales and reading during this period.

32 Bertrand Harris Bronson, *Facets of the Enlightenment* (Berkeley, 1968), 309–10.

33 Gukovskii, *Ocherki po istorii,* 276–98.

## 2 THEORY OF SENTIMENTALISM

1 I am labelling my approach 'Bakhtinian' as a matter of convenience and do not thereby mean to belittle the distinct contributions by the other

scholars mentioned, nor do I subscribe to the notion that Bakhtin is the real author of works published under Voloshinov's name. For a recent discussion of the Bakhtin-school controversy, see Gary Saul Morson and Caryl Emerson, eds., *Rethinking Bakhtin* (Evanston, 1989), 1–60. I use Voloshinov's insights about 'speech reporting' ('chuzhaia rech'') and its subsequent development by Titunik in particular, as the most coherent conceptual framework for organizing Bakhtin's rich ideas on dialogue and genre. Jakobson's ideas on shifters (deixis) and the complexities of speech event/narrated event/narrated speech event, are akin to Voloshinov's framework and germane to my theory. I am in other words focusing on what I perceive as a common theoretical core among these scholars and intentionally ignoring their differences (as to Formalism, Marxism, theology, etc.) as peripheral to my specific argument. The most important works for my purposes are: M. M. Bakhtin, *Problemy poetiki Dostoevskogo* (3rd edn, Moscow, 1972); his *Voprosy literatury i estetiki* (Moscow, 1975); his *Estetika slovesnogo tvorchestva* (Moscow, 1979); V. N. Voloshinov, 'Slovo v zhizni i slovo v poezii', *Zvezda*, 6 (1926), 244–67; his *Marksizm i filosofiia iazyka* (2nd edn, Leningrad, 1930); his 'Stilistika khudozhestvennoi rechi', *Literaturnaia ucheba*, 2 (1930), 3–66; 3 (1930), 65–87; 5 (1930), 43–59; Lubomir Doležel, 'The Typology of the Narrator', *To Honor Roman Jakobson* (The Hague, 1967), 541–52; his *Narrative Modes in Czech Literature* (Toronto, 1973); I. R. Titunik, 'The Problem of *Skaz* in Russian Literature' (Berkeley, 1963); his 'The Problem of *Skaz* (Critique and Theory)', *Papers in Slavic Philology*, 1 (1977), 276–301; Roman Jakobson, 'Closing Statement: Linguistics and Poetics', *Style in Language*, ed. Thomas Sebeok (Cambridge, MA, 1960), 350–77; and his 'Shifters, Verbal Categories, and the Russian Verb', *Selected Writings* (The Hague, 1971), vol. II, 130–47. The fact that the Bakhtin–Voloshinov theory is designed for and specifically appropriate to literature, sets it apart both from Vinogradov and SA theory. V. V. Vinogradov establishes 'image of author' (*obraz avtora*) as a literary term in works such as *O poezii Anny Akhmatovoi* (Leningrad, 1925, rpt. Munich, 1970), 'O iazyke Tolstogo (50 – 60-e gody)', *Literaturnoe nasledstvo*, 35–36 (1939), 117–220, and *O teorii khudozhestvennoi rechi* (Moscow, 1971). Despite some similarities to the Bakhtinian approach, Vinogradov's theories of author are limited by their basically Saussurean linguistic framework. His literary categories are in fact peculiar transpositions of linguistic *langue/parole* distinctions. SA theory was developed in, e.g.: J. L. Austin, *How to Do Things with Words* (New York, 1962); John R. Searle, *Speech Acts* (London, 1969); his 'The Logical Status of Fictional Discourse', *New Literary History*, 6, 2 (1975), 319–32; and H. P. Grice, 'Logic and Conversation', *Syntax and Semantics*, vol. III: *Speech Acts*, eds. P. Cole and J. Morgan (New York, 1975), 41–58. It has been applied to literature ever since the early 1970s and culminated in Mary L. Pratt's monograph on the topic

(*Towards a Speech Act Theory of Literary Discourse*, Bloomington, IN, 1977). Robert Meyer and Karen Hopkins, 'A Speech-Act Theory Bibliography', *Centrum*, 5, 2 (1977), 73–108 contains representative works on SA theory as applied to literature. For a critique of literary applications of SA theory, see James A. Fanto, 'Speech Act Theory and its Applications to the Study of Literature', *The Sign: Semiotics around the World*, eds. R. W. Bailey, L. Matejka, and P. Steiner (Ann Arbor, 1978), 280–304; Lubomir Doležel, 'In Defense of Structural Poetics', *Poetics*, 8 (1979), 521–30; and Jürgen Streeck, 'Speech Acts in Interaction', *Discourse Processes*, 3, 2 (1980), 133–54. The crucial advantage of the Bakhtinian framework in comparison to SA theory is the focus on interaction (dialogue, 'how to do things with other's words'), while SA theory mainly emphasizes description and classification of 'how to do things with words'. SA theory is thus not suited for analyzing complex speech acts such as literature – nor was it designed for this purpose (see e.g., Austin, 22, 92; Searle, *Speech Acts*, 20, 57, 98; Grice, 74). I find, however, that some of the systematic taxonomies of speech acts (John Searle, 'A Taxonomy of Illocutionary Acts', *Minnesota Studies in the Philosophy of Science*, 7 [1975], 344–69) are useful once viewed within Voloshinov's 'speech reporting' structure.

2 Bakhtin, *Estetika*, 237–80; Voloshinov, *Marksizm*, 109–57, the specific quote appears on p. 113.

3 Voloshinov, 'Slovo v zhizni', 249.

4 Pratt, 143–51 has an interesting discussion of what she calls 'display texts', somewhat similar to the Bakhtinian view of literary teleology. Pratt's approach, however, is in other respects different from that of the Bakhtin school.

5 I am here and henceforth using the term 'chronotopical' (and its derivatives) in Bakhtin's sense, as discussed mainly in his 'Forms of Time and Chronotope in the Novel' ('Formy vremeni i khronotopa v romane', in his *Voprosy literatury*, 234–407).

6 Bakhtin, *Voprosy literatury*, 72–233.

7 Ibid., 111.

8 The problem of 'author' preoccupied Bakhtin from the 1920s to the 1970s. See Bakhtin, *Estetika*, 163–80 and 353–7; *Voprosy literatury*, 72–234 and 400–6; *Problemy poetiki*, 270 – to name just the most explicit discussions and critiques of 'image of author'.

9 He plays with different wordings of these dicta in *Estetika*, 287–9, 352–4, 362–3 and explains his theological sources on p. 408.

10 For a more detailed discussion of the ontological question, see Bakhtin, *Voprosy literatury*, 400–6.

11 See e.g., *Estetika*, 354.

12 These problems are extensively discussed in terms of the author's extraposition (*vnenakhodimost'*) to his hero and the different typical forms for constructing a whole that result from changes in this inter-relationship, in a work written in the 1920s, 'The Author and the Hero

in Aesthetic Activity' ('Avtor i geroi v esteticheskoi deiatel'nosti', Bakhtin, *Estetika*, 7–180).

13 Narratee as a literary term was coined by Prince in 1971, and has subsequently gained wide acceptance. See for instance, Gerald Prince, 'Notes toward a Categorization of Fictional "Narratees"', *Genre*, 4, 1 (1971), 100–6; his 'On Readers and Listeners in Narrative', *Neophilologus*, 55, 2 (1971), 117–22; his 'Introduction to the Study of the Narratee', *Poétique*, 14 (1973), 177–96; and Seymour Chatman, *Story and Discourse* (Ithaca, NY, 1978). The term as used in these works is somewhat similar to Booth's 'implied reader', also widely used in the so-called reader-response criticism. See Jane Tompkins, *Reader-Response Criticism* (Baltimore, 1980) for a survey of the most recent developments in that current of literary studies. I must stress, however, that my definition of the term is different from all the above.

14 See Doležel, 'Typology of Narrator', and *Narrative Modes*; Titunik, 'Problem of *Skaz*' and '*Skaz* (Critique and Theory)'; Jakobson, 'Shifters'.

15 This, it must be stressed, is a purely theoretical norm, an abstract model which is never perfectly realized in actual texts. It must also be stressed that it does not model a text without a speaker, but it simply means that there is nothing in the text which explicitly draws attention to speaker, listener, or their communicative situation, and an image of author (narrator) is not part of the author's referent. In Bakhtin's system, it is as inadmissible to view the author as someone who silently pares his fingernails as it is to view him as a behind-the-scenes puppeteer or stage manager. The author is always the utterer of the work as a whole, he always speaks, although he often speaks by indirection. The Bakhtinian approach allows us to distinguish between nuanced forms of open and hidden dialogue and between absent author and unmarked author.

16 See Searle, 'Taxonomy'.

17 See Voloshinov, *Marksizm*, 122–57 and Ladislav Matejka, 'Reported Speech in Contemporary Standard Russian' (Harvard, 1960).

18 Indeed, the actual, explicit presence of direct author's speech which serves to set the norms (in terms of contents as well as style) is by no means mandatory, and has in fact during the history of the novel become more and more negligible. The total absence of explicit, direct author's speech is a commonplace in the modern novel, but its implicit presence as a norm is mandatory. Thus, to proclaim the disappearance of the author, or to divide up a text into speech by author, narrator *or* personage, as is frequently done in traditional point-of-view approaches, is to oversimplify and even misrepresent the structure of narrative texts. For a concise survey of earlier point-of-view approaches, see Norman Friedman, *Form and Meaning in Fiction* (Athens, GA, 1975), 134–42, an updated version of one of the classics in point of view theory Norman Friedman, 'Point of View in Fiction' *PMLA*, 70 (1955), 1160–84. Bertil Romberg, *Studies in the Narrative*

*Technique of the First-Person Novel* (Stockholm, 1962), 11–30 surveys the parallel developments in Anglo-American, Germanic, and Romance criticism. See also Wayne C. Booth, *The Rhetoric of Fiction* (Chicago, 1961), 3–144 for a more detailed analysis and critique of the earlier approaches. Interesting in the present context of Karamzin's prose fiction, is Roger B. Anderson, *N. M. Karamzin's Prose: The Teller in the Tale* (Houston, 1974), a point-of-view approach to Karamzin's major non-historical fiction according to principles outlined in Friedman, 'Point of View in Fiction'.

19  Titunik, 'Problem of *Skaz*', 38.

20  Preface to Fedor Emin, *Nepostoiannaia Fortuna, ili Pokhozhdenie Miramonda* (3 vols., Sanktpeterburg, 1763), n. p. I. Z. Serman, 'Stanovlenie i razvitie romana v russkoi literature serediny XVIII veka', *Iz istorii russkikh literaturnykh otnoshenii XVIII–XX vekov* (Moscow, 1959), 89–90 notes the indignation expressed by Bolotov at this unheard of breach of the Neoclassicist anonymity etiquette. Indicative of the same phenomenon is also the fact that Emin's own accounts of his real life are no less fanciful than his fiction, and attempts to establish the real autobiography of Fedor Emin continue to this day (see E. B. Beshenkovskii, 'Zhizn' Fedora Emina', *XVIII vek*, 11 (1976), 186–203. This can be compared to Karamzin creating Karamzin both in life and in his texts, emphasized in Lotman, *Sotvorenie Karamzina*.

21  VE, 9, 12 (1803), 283–91. Karamzin's comments about the women's letters read exactly like any of his book reviews.

22  See Lotman, *Sotvorenie Karamzina*, 17–29 and 227–37 on Karamzin's systematic creation of Karamzin and the relationship between autobiography and the formation of one's own self. Indeed the title of Lotman's work (taken from a Chaadaev letter), indicates his emphasis.

23  Jakobson, 'Closing Statement', 354.

24  K1984b, vol. II, 60–2.

25  K1984b, vol. II, 62.

26  It is beyond my scope to discuss all the intricacies of the linguistic situation during the era. V. D. Levin, *Ocherk stilistiki russkogo literaturnogo iazyka kontsa XVIII v. (Leksika)* (Moscow, 1964) offers one of the best discussions of the late eighteenth-century developments and Karamzin's part in them. See also N. I. Mordovchenko, *Russkaia kritika pervoi chetverti XIX veka* (Moscow, 1959), 17–99; and Uspenskii, *Iz istorii*.

27  Searle, 'Taxonomy'.

28  Charles J. Fillmore, *Santa Cruz Lectures on Deixis 1971* (Bloomington, IN, 1975) is the most extensive discussion of this topic that I have come across. The specific quote occurs on p. 38. Other classics on deixis are Jakobson, 'Shifters', Emile Benveniste, *Problèmes de linguistique générale* (Paris, 1966), and Henri Frei, 'Systèmes de déictiques', *Acta Linguistica*, 4, 3 (1944), 111–29. Numerous other discussions of deixis

by linguists, philosophers, psychologists, and others are cited in the works mentioned.

29 See Doležel, 'Typology of Narrator', 545; Titunik, 'Problem of *Skaz*', 48–59.

30 G. G. Elizavetina, 'Stanovlenie zhanrov avtobiografii i memuarov', *Russkii i zapadnoevropeiskii klassitsizm*, eds. A. S. Kurilov et al. (Moscow, 1982), 248 observes a curious phenomenon: while the 'autobiographical' first person became increasingly popular in prose fiction (the novel), autobiographies themselves often came to be written in third person form for various reasons.

31 Bakhtin, *Voprosy literatury*, 447–83.

32 Fillmore, 41.

33 Paul Friedrich, 'Structural Implications of Russian Pronominal Usage', *Socioloinguistics*, ed. William Bright (The Hague, 1966), 214–59.

34 Excellent discussions on this topic can be found in Vinogradov, 'O iazyke Tolstogo' on the language of Tolstoi's works, subsequently utilized and amplified in B. A. Uspenskii, *A Poetics of Composition*, tr. V. Zavarin and Susan Wittig (Berkeley, 1973), 20–56, particularly with regard to the different names used for Napoleon and the use of French versus Russian. Voloshinov, 'Stilistika khudozhestvennoi rechi', 3, 77–83 briefly discusses the differences in language used by Gogol''s Chichikov with different interlocutors, which reveals a great range of speech levels.

35 Levin, *Ocherk stilistiki* provides ample material from the writings by Karamzin and Makarov as well as the opposing camp. See in particular, pp. 130–4. Uspenskii, *Iz istorii*, 57–60 and 154–5 shows that Karamzin's gender orientation and his style in general, has its native roots in Trediakovskii's approach to literary style.

36 Walter Ong, 'The Writer's Audience is Always a Fiction', *PMLA*, 90, 1 (1975), 9–21.

37 Jakobson, 'Closing Statement', 355.

38 See Fillmore, 70–2.

39 See Titunik, 'Problem of *Skaz*', 68–70.

40 Doležel, *Narrative Modes*, 60–5.

41 See Levin, *Ocherk stilistiki*, 149–53, 237–41, 260–2; Uspenskii, *Iz istorii*, 92–100.

42 See Iu. M. Lotman, 'Poeziia Karamzina', introduction to N. M. Karamzin, *Polnoe sobranie sochinenii*, ed. Iu. M. Lotman (2nd edn, Moscow, 1966), 5–52.

43 K1984b, vol. II, 89.

44 Compare similar statements about poetic deceit in Karamzin's article 'Why are there Few Writers of Talent in Russia?' (K1984b, vol. II, 123–6).

45 V. V. Vinogradov, *Problema avtorstva i teoriia stilei*, (Moscow, 1961), 311–23.

46 See Bakhtin, *Voprosy literatury*, 447–81.

47 Ibid., 460.
48 Ibid., 457–61.
49 For the most thorough investigation of this phenomenon as it applies to Russian, see Matejka, 'Reported Speech', which contains an extensive bibliography for further reference. As for reported speech in eighteenth-century Russia, see also V. I. Kodukhov, 'Sposoby peredachi chuzhoi rechi v russkom iazyke vtoroi poloviny XVII–XVIII vv', (Moscow, 1953) and I. I. Kovtunova, 'Nesobstvenno priamaia rech' v iazyke russkoi literatury kontsa XVIII–pervoi poloviny XIX v', (Moscow, 1956). Voloshinov, *Marksizm*, 109–57 sketches a synchronic as well as diachronic development of the phenomenon, including remarks on eighteenth-century Russian.

### 3 THE LITERARY MODEL: IDYLL

1 K1966, 58–63.
2 The roots of Sentimentalism are discussed in Gukovskii, *Ocherki po istorii*; G. N. Pospelov, 'U istokov russkogo sentimentalizma', *Vestnik Moskovskogo universiteta. Seriia filologii*, 1 (Moscow, 1948); his *Problemy literaturnogo stilia* (Moscow, 1970); K. A. Nazaretskaia, 'Ob istokakh russkogo sentimentalizma', *Uchenye zapiski Kazanskogo universiteta*, 123, 8 (1963), 3–34; her 'Poeziia i proza v moskovskikh zhurnalakh 60-kx godov XVIII v', *Uchenye zapiski Kazanskogo universiteta*, 124, 5 (1964), 3–25; and her 'Literaturno-khudozhestvennye vzgliady i tvorchestvo Masonov i ikh znachenie dlia formirovaniia sentimentalizma i predromantizma', *Uchenye zapiski Kazanskogo universiteta*, 128, 4 (1969), 79–95; Rudolf Neuhäuser, 'Periodization and Classification of Sentimental and Preromantic trends in Russian Literature between 1750 and 1815', *Canadian Contributions to the Seventh International Congress of Slavists*, (The Hague, 1973), 11–39; his *Towards the Romantic Age*; and P. A. Orlov, *Russkii sentimentalizm* (Moscow, 1977).
3 Orlov, *Russkii sentimentalizm*, 50–1. See A. P. Sumarokov, *Polnoe sobranie sochinenii v stikhakh i v proze* (Moscow, 1781), vol. I, 360–1.
4 See, for example K1984b, vol. II, 60–2.
5 Ernst Robert Curtius, *European Literature and the Latin Middle Ages* (Princeton, 1973), 195.
6 Heidemarie Kesselmann, *Die Idyllen Salomon Gessners im Beziehungsfeld von Ästhetik und Geschichte im 18. Jahrhundert* (Kronberg/Ts, 1976), 29–30.
7 Bakhtin, *Voprosy literatury*, 373.
8 One such handbook is called *Osnovatel'noe i iasnoe nastavlenie v miniaturnoi zhivopisi* (*A Basic and Clear Guide to Miniature Painting*), translated from German by Mikhail Agentov and published in Moscow in 1765.
9 A. N. Brukhanskii, 'M. N. Murav'ev i "legkoe stikhotvorstvo"', *XVIII*

*vek*, 4 (1959), 71 applies the term as a new fullfledged unit of Murav'ev's light verse.

10 This is evident in for instance Karamzin's 'Poetry' and in several works by Murav'ev: 'On Virgil' ('O Virgilii'), 'On Pastoral Poetry' ('O pastusheskoi poezii'), 'Emile's Letters' ('Emilievy pis'ma') and 'A Suburban Dweller' ('Obitatel' predmest'ia'), all of which are republished in M. N. Murav'ev, *Sochineniia* (2 vols., Sanktpeterburg, 1847).

11 Murav'ev, vol. I, 142.

12 K. Skipina, 'O chuvstvitel'noi povesti', *Russkaia proza*, ed. B. Eikhenbaum and Iu. Tynianov (Leningrad, 1926), 13–41 and Anthony. G. Cross, 'Karamzin's Versions of the Idyll', *Essays on Karamzin*, ed. J. L. Black (The Hague, 1975), 75–90.

13 See Salomon Gessner, *Schriften* (Mess, 1824), vol. II, 'An den Leser', n.p., for his own view of the genre. For more detail on Gessner's idylls as they relate to the tradition, see Kesselmann, and also John Hibberd, *Salomon Gessner* (Cambridge, 1976), 29–43.

14 Hibberd, 49–50.

15 The works mentioned can be found in K1783; DCha, 18 (1789), 110–12; and K1796a, 22–4, respectively.

16 DCha, 17 (1789), 198–9, emotion ellipsis original.

17 Another interesting demonstration of this, and a good illustration of the genre as perceived in Russia at the time, is a work entitled 'Idyll. About the Nature of the Idyll' ('Idilliia. O svoistve idillii') written by an English writer, Richard Steele[?], and published in *Priiatnoe i poleznoe preprovozhdenie vremeni*, 7 (1795), 89–102, with comments on the idyll topic by the editor.

18 Kanunova , *Iz istorii;* Henry M. Nebel, *N. M. Karamzin* (The Hague, 1967); Hans Rothe, *N. M. Karamzins europäische Reise* (Bad Homburg v. d. H., 1968); Anthony G. Cross, *N. M. Karamzin* (Carbondale, IL., 1971); Anderson, *N. M. Karamzin's Prose;* N. D. Kochetkova, *Nikolay Karamzin* (Boston, 1975); and S. E. Pavlovich, *Puti razvitiia russkoi sentimental'noi prozy XVIII veka* (Saratov, 1974).

19 It is significant that the two most recent Soviet collections of Karamzin's works (K1964 and K1984b) do not contain a single one of the works mentioned. In the 1803–04 edition, supervised by Karamzin himself, only 'The Countryside' was included.

20 Cross, 'Karamzin's Versions of the Idyll'.

21 N. M. Karamzin, 'Palemon i Dafnis', MZha, 4 (1791), 278–86. Gessner's idyll appears in his *Schriften*, vol. II, 161–5.

22 G. A. Gukovskii, 'Elegiia v XVIII veke', *Russkaia poeziia XVIII veka* (Leningrad, 1927, rpt. Munich 1971), 48–102.

23 Cross, 'Karamzin's Versions of the Idyll', 83.

24 Lotman, *Sotvorenie Karamzina*, 22–3, 31.

25 I shall not analyse *Letters of a Russian Traveller* except in passing, due to considerations of space, and to the fact that this work has received a

great deal of attention ever since V. V. Sipovskii's thorough study *N. M. Karamzin, avtor 'Pisem russkogo puteshestvennika'* (S.-Peterburg, 1899). The most detailed recent study is Rothe, *N. M. Karamzins europäische Reise*, where Karamzin's work is viewed as a novel about the author's development (literary, spiritual, ideological), pointing out properties which I would include under the rubric 'narrator'. The main part of Lotman, *Sotvorenie Karamzina*, (29–201), is devoted to *Letters of a Russian Traveller*, their preparation, and aftermath, and Lotman reconstructs Karamzin's intellectual and spiritual life as well as the narrator–traveller as revealed in the work. Lotman analyzes Karamzin's actual journey, and the rich intellectual and ideological climate in Europe on the eve of the French Revolution in great detail. He also compares Karamzin's literary letters to his actual letters to friends. It is interesting that Lotman adopts the travel metaphor (following Karamzin himself) even when describing Karamzin as a historian (293–308). See also Pavlovich, 60–125, and Roger B. Anderson, 'Karamzin's *Letters of a Russian Traveller*, An Education in Western Sentimentalism', *Essays on Karamzin*, ed. J. L. Black (The Hague, 1975), 22–39. The most recent scholarly edition of *Letters of a Russian Traveller* includes among many relevant appendices an article by Lotman and Uspenskii, '"Pis'ma russkogo puteshestvennika" Karamzina i ikh mesto v razvitii russkoi kul'tury' (K1984a, 525–606).

26 N. M. Karamzin, 'Navodnenie. Otryvok', MZha, 4 (1791), 235–40. Cross, 'Karamzin's Versions of the Idyll', attributes it 'very probably' to Karamzin and points out that it echoes Gessner's 'Ein Gemälde aus der Sündflut' (Gessner, vol. II, 179–84). It also bears some resemblance to Gessner's 'Der Sturm', particularly its opening scene with the onset of a storm, and its moral which stresses the transience of material riches and the permanence of spiritual ones against the background of a natural disaster, this time a flood. Cross's attribution is supported by the style, which is characteristic of Karamzin in the early 90s.

27 K1984b, vol. II, 61.

28 'Progulka', DCha, 18 (1789), 161–75; 'Derevnia. Otryvok', MZhb, 7 (1792, 2nd ed. 1803), 58–69; and 'Noch'', MZhb, 5 (1792, 2nd ed. 1803), 271–7. Henceforth these editions are referred to by page numbers within my text.

29 Sipovskii, *N. M. Karamzin*, 133–4.

30 See Bakhtin, *Voprosy literatury*, 373.

31 'Nature as a poetic text' is an old topos, very much alive during the eighteenth century. It forms an integral part of the poetic theory of both English Preromanticism and the German Sturm-und-Drang movement, both of which influenced Karamzin's poetics. Of particular interest in the present context is Edward Young's 'Conjectures on Original Composition', published in 1759 (*The Complete Works, Poetry and Prose*, ed. James Nichols [2 vols., London, 1854, rpt. Hildesheim, 1968], vol. II, 547–86). This text extolls originality over imitation,

making many points made by Karamzin in 'A Promenade' and elsewhere. Young extolls Shakespeare (Karamzin's admiration for Shakespeare is also well known) not for his learning, but for his mastery of
'two books, unknown to many of the profoundly read, though books
which the last conflagration alone can destroy, – the book of nature and
that of man. These he had by heart, and has transcribed many
admirable pages of them into his immortal works. These are the
fountainhead, where the Castilian streams of original composition flow'
(Young, 'Conjectures', 574). Curtius, when discussing the topos in
eighteenth-century theories of poetry, mentions (in addition to Young)
Robert Wood's 'Essay on the Original Genius and Writings of Homer',
where Homer (also praised in 'A Promenade') is praised as a student of
'the great book of nature'. Goethe uses the topos in his 'Sendschreiben'
(1774): 'Sieh, so ist Natur ein Buch lebendig' (Curtius, 319–26).
Karamzin may also have been exposed to this topos already in his
youthful reading of and correspondence with Lavater (see Lavater's
*Brüderliche Schreiben,* Winterthur, 1767, 79, cited in Sipovskii, *N. M.
Karamzin,* 57). In a contemporary Russian context, one might mention
Murav'ev's references to the 'great book of nature' (*Sochineniia,* vol.
II, 186). 'A Promenade' in general reflects ideas much discussed among
the Moscow Masons at the time when Karamzin was a member of one
of their lodges. See Sipovskii, *N. M. Karamzin,* 16–134 for these and
other influences on Karamzin's early works. 'A Promenade' specifically
is discussed briefly on pp. 132–4. Aage A. Hansen-Löve, 'Die Entfaltung des "Welt-Text"-Paradigmus in der Poesie V. Chlebnikovs',
*Velemir Chlebnikov,* ed. Nils Åke Nilsson (Stockholm, 1985), 68–9
surveys the literature on the semiotic significance of the 'World–Book'
topos as it pertains to literary periodization. According to this literature, 'secondary styles', such as Romanticism, are typically characterized by the 'semiotization of reality' (as opposed to 'primary
styles', such as Classicism or Realism, characterized by the 'realization
of semiotic signs'). In the topos 'Nature as text' this means that reality
('nature') is viewed as a semiotic system or signs ('poem') during
Romanticism. This is Karamzin's view in 'A Promenade'. The work,
modest as it is, could thus also be cited in support of the view that
Sentimentalism is part of the Romantic paradigm, and more properly
ought to be called 'Preromanticism' (on this problem, see G. S. Smith,
'Sentimentalism and Pre-Romanticism as Terms and Concepts',
*Russian Literature in the Age of Catherine the Great,* ed. Anthony G.
Cross [Oxford, 1976], 173–84).

32 Similar 'promenades' were quite popular among Karamzin's European
predecessors and contemporaries. Rousseau's *Les Rêveries du promeneur solitaire,* structured as a series of chapters or 'promenades', may
be the most famous example. A few other examples will indicate the
lasting popularity as well as the flexibility of the genre: Schiller's 'Der
Spaziergang' (1795, first published under this title in 1800), K. N.

Batiushkov's 1814 epistolary 'Progulka v Akademiiu khudozhestv', *Opity v stikhakh i proze* (Moscow, 1977), 71–94, Andrei Siniavskii's [Abram Terts's] *Progulki s Pushkinym* (London, 1975). The question of the 'promenade' as a genre is a complex one and requires special investigation. It would seem, however, that in most of the variants, and throughout its long history, its dual scope (physical and spiritual–artistic) is one of its permanent generic markers. Many promenades, among them Batiushkov's can also be read as statements of artistic credo and are thus akin to Karamzin's 'A Promenade'. A single walk, such as 'A Promenade' might also be regarded as a *malaia forma* variant of the travelogue or 'journey'. As such, its importance during Sentimentalism is no surprise: both journeys and all sorts of trifles, as we have seen, were immensely popular. For suggestions about, and discussions of, the 'walk' genre, I am particularly grateful to Nils Åke Nilsson, David Sanford, and I. R. Titunik.

33 It is interesting to recall how Karamzin later announced the forth-coming publication of his *Letters of a Russian Traveller*: 'A friend of mine [ . . . ] jotted down what he saw, heard, felt, thought, and dreamt' (cited in M. Pogodin, *Nikolai Mikhailovich Karamzin, po ego sochine-niiam, pis'mam i otzyvam sovremennikov* [Moscow, 1866], part I, 170). The fact that the two works (one, an insignificant trifle of a mere 15 pages, the other a *magnum opus* of hundreds of pages) are summarized in such similar terms, can be seen as an indication that the egocentric principles guiding each work remained unchanged, regardless of genre or scope.

34 Peter Brang, *Studien zu Theorie und Praxis der Russischen Erzählung 1770–1811* (Wiesbaden, 1960), 130 states that 'the usage of tenses is consistent: all narrative parts are given in the past, the contemplations in present tense'. This is somewhat of an oversimplification. It ignores contemplative narration and narrative contemplation, so important in this work.

35 Cf. Karamzin's *Letters of a Russian Traveller* (K1984a: 43, 233, 361, and note, p. 621) where Marchesi and Todi, two opera singers, are unfavorably reviewed because they do not move the heart and they sing without soul. We might note that 'A Promenade' was written before Karamzin's journey.

36 Cf. John C. O'Neal, *Seeing and Observing* (Saratoga, 1985) on the role of perception in Rousseau's works.

37 Extreme solipsism and narcissism was equally characteristic of English Preromantic poetics. Karamzin's poet seems to be following and expanding on Edward Young's two golden rules for budding authors, whose genius may never be known due to a lack of selfconfidence: '1."Know thyself" 2. "Reverence thyself," [ . . . ] Therefore dive deep into thy bosom; learn the depth extent, bias, and full fort of thy mind; contract full intimacy with the stranger within thee; excite and cherish every spark of intellectual light and heat, however smothered under

former negligence, or scattered through the dull dark mass of common thoughts; and, collecting them into a body, let the genius rise (if a genius thou hast) as the sun from chaos; and if I should then say, like an Indian, "Worship it," [cf. Karamzin's Indian sage and his use of sunrise] (though too bold), yet should I say little more than my second rule enjoins; namely "Reverence thyself!"' (Young, 'Conjectures', 564). Karamzin's familiarity with Rousseau's work is amply documented. Rousseau's *Rêveries* illustrate the same solipsistic, narcissistic principles. Renato Poggioli, *The Oaten Flute* (Cambridge, MA, 1975), 22–3 contains a pithy description of the *Rêveries* which also reads as a good synopsis of Karamzin's 'A Promenade': '[In Rousseau's *Rêveries*] the ego idly and indifferently enjoys "le sentiment de l'existence . . . sans prendre le peine de penser" [. . . ] [Karamzin's 'chuvstvo sushchestvovaniia']. What Rousseau terms "rêverie" is a state of passive introspection, by which the pastoral psyche reflects its shadow in nature's mirror, fondly and blissfully losing its being within the image of itself. Here sensibility and selfhood merge, and man ceases to distinguish between conscience and consciousness, wish and will. The individual seems to achieve perfection through the sense of a happiness untouched by doubt, of an innocence unblemished by sin.' Cf. also O'Neal, 115–38 on promenades, solitude, and Rousseau's *sentiment de l'existence*.

38  It is interesting to compare this passage to the concluding lines of Karamzin's poem, 'Poetry':

> Kogda zh umru, zasnu i snova probuzhus', –
> Togda, v vostorgakh pogruzhaius',
> I vechno, vechno naslazhdaius',
> Ja budu gimnu pet' tvortsu,
> Tebe, liubvi istochnik dinvyi,
> Uzrev tam vse litsem k litsu! (K1966, 23).

39  Similar preferences were frequently stated by, for instance, Kheraskov and Murav'ev, and in Karamzin's own 'The Countryside', for nature to gardens, for the English garden to the artificially shaped French garden, for the natural rivulet to the artificial fountain. This tendency was typical for all the arts during the era. This is not to say that Karamzin or his narrator falls into the trap of denying the value of art as such. As is abundantly clear from the present context of 'A Promenade', and corroborated in other contexts as well, he merely denies 'artificial' art, whereas he always extolls 'natural' art. Indeed, good art is in a sense preferable to nature, because it is doubly art – or doubly nature. In the poem 'Gifts' ('Darovaniia') this attitude to nature and art is most explicitly spelled out:

> I chasto prelest' v podrazhan'i
> Milee, chem v Prirode, nam:
> Lesok, tsvetochek v opisan'i
> Eshche priiatnee ocham.

In a footnote to this passage Karamzin further elaborates: 'All the charms of the *beaux arts* are nothing but imitation of Nature; but the copy is sometimes better than the original, at least it always makes the original more interesting for us: we have the pleasure of comparing them' (K1966, 219). In 'A Promenade' the poet states that nature *is* art and art *is* nature. What he seems to object to is empty artifice, blind imitation of forms, repetition of clichés without the poet's personal experiential involvement. The advantage of good art over nature lies in the fact that it is, so to speak, art to the second power – or nature to the second power. Art further intensifies our response by compounding our pleasure in nature by the added pleasure of comparison.

40 Karamzin's view of imitation reminds us once more of Young's 'Conjectures': '"Must we then," you say, "not imitate ancient authors?" Imitate them by all means; but imitate aright. He that imitates the divine Iliad does not imitate Homer; but he who takes the same method which Homer took for arriving at a capacity of accomplishing a work so great. Tread in his steps to the sole fountain of immortality; drink where he drank, at the true Helicon, that is, at the breast of nature. Imitate; but imitate not the composition, but the man' (Young, 'Conjectures', 554–5).

41 Cf. Karamzin's infamous announcement in the *Moscow News* (*Moskovskie Vedomosti*) a year after 'A Promenade' was published which explicitly states that various 'mystical' works are not to be accepted for his new journal *Moscow Journal* (*Moskovskie Vedomosti*, 89 [1790, Nov.6], quoted in full in Pogodin, part I: 169–72). Vinogradov, *Problema avtorstva*, 246–9 also partly quotes and discusses the announcement and the reactions to it. Lotman, *Sotvorenie Karamzina* discusses the Masonic connections extensively and also mentions the reactions to Karamzin's announcement and other reactions from his friends after his return from abroad. See especially pp. 192–209.

42 Gresset wrote verse novels and novellas of the *précieuse* kind, such as a humorous description of the adventures of a parrot, brought up in a nunnery, freely mocking the monastic orders. For such writing he was in fact expelled from the Jesuit order. He also wrote a novel, *La Chartreuse*, which praises the solitary life of the poet – a more likely kind of summer reading for Karamzin's country dweller. LaFontaine, in addition to his fables, is famed for his light *précieuse* verse (elegies, madrigals, epistles), *contes*, and novellas in verse, and perhaps most important in the present context, his adaptation of Longus' pastoral novel *Les amours de Psyche et de Cupidon*. Karamzin's familiarity with the latter is well attested in his piece on Bogdanovich, whose main claim to fame was based on the same work.

43 Cf. Cross (*N. M. Karamzin*, 15, 111, and 119) who points out the bipartite composition and also mentions its fragmentary nature, which it shares with a number of works by Karamzin. Cross also points to Sturm's 'Contemplation on a Meadow' (a 'typical Sentimentalist "bot-

anizing" piece') as a possible antecedent for 'The Countryside'. In his article about the idyll, he does not mention the piece, although it could be included as one of Karamzin's 'versions of the idyll'. Kanunova, *Iz istorii* 43–4 mentions it in passing as one of Karamzin's lyrical and metaphysical poems in prose. Neither Kochetkova, *Nikolay Karamzin* nor Anderson, *N. M. Karamzin's Prose* mentions the piece. Rothe, 224, 237–8 briefly describes the work as it relates to *Letters of a Russian Traveller*, and Brang, 147–9 compares and contrasts it to previous Classicist idealizations of country life: works by Trediakovskii, Petr Rychkov, and anonymous pieces – mainly in terms of theme, and with a hint that Karamzin was more 'realistic', a claim which, in my opinion, could be questioned.

44 Bakhtin, *Voprosy literatury*, 374.
45 This passage may serve as an example of the Thomsonian influence on 'The Countryside'. Thomson's description of the same phenomenon reads:

> Low walks the sun, and broadens by degrees,
> Just o'er the verge of day. The rising clouds,
> That shift perpetual in his vivid train,
> Their watry mirrors, numberless, oppos'd,
> Unfold the hidden riches of his ray;
> And chafe a change of colours round the sky.
> 'Tis all one blush from east to west! and now,
> Behind the dusky earth, he dips his orb;
> Now half immers'd; and now a golden curve
> Gives one faint glimmer, and then disappears.
> (James Thomson, *The Seasons* [London, 1730, rpt. Menston], 1970, 113).

Thomson's summary of 'Summer' ('The Argument') indicates that Karamzin's work was indeed heavily indebted to Thomson's: '[ . . . ] Morning. A view of the sun rising. Hymn to the sun. Forenoon. Rural prospects. Summer insects described. Noon-day. A woodland retreat. A groupe of flocks and herds. A solemn grove. How it affects a contemplative mind. Transition to the prospect of a rich well-cultivated country; [ . . . ] Storm of thunder and lightning. A tale. The storm over; a serene afternoon. Bathing. Sun set. Evening. The whole concluding with the Praise of Philosophy' (Thomson, 58). One could find similar echoes of Young and others – Karamzin's imagery is by no means new.
46 Botanizing was a prime Sentimentalist activity, made famous in, for instance, Rousseau's *Lettres sur la botanique*, and, fictionally, in *Les Rêveries*, where the Fifth and Seventh Promenades are devoted to this activity. See O'Neal, 122–31 for an analysis of Rousseau's botanizing in light of Sentimentalist perception.
47 Cf. Brang, 147–49.
48 Murav'ev, vol. I, 71–111 and 112–71.

4 THE EXTRA-LITERARY MODEL: SALON TRIFLES

1 See William Mills Todd, III, *The Familiar Letter as a Literary Genre in the Age of Pushkin* (Princeton, 1976) for a most interesting account of how the familiar letter developed as a literary genre and flourished later in the early nineteenth century.

2 See 'Literaturnyi fakt', in Tynianov, *Arkhaisty i novatory*, 21 and, in the same collection, 'O literaturnoi evoliutsii', esp. 42–7.

3 Lotman, *Sotvorenie Karamzina*, 104–68.

4 N. M. Karamzin, 'Samoubiitsa', MZha, 1 (1791), 56–62.

5 That Lotman may have overemphasized Karamzin's cold attitude towards salons is indicated by his own footnote in that section (140) and also by the emphasis he himself places on lightheartedness, play, and wit, in a later chapter devoted to Karamzin's life at the Pleshcheev estate (see especially 242–65). In the later chapter Lotman emphasizes precisely those qualities that left Karamzin cold in Paris: lightheartedness and the spirit of art as play and play as art. In the Paris section (140) Lotman quotes Mme de Staël and an earlier study of French salons to the effect that salon conversation is a 'free art', 'an instrument on which they [the French] like to play and which inspires the mind' and which gives artistic form to its theme. The pleasure derived from conversation is more due to the manner in which it is carried out than to its topic. Karamzin may have seemed cold towards these aspects of salon life while in Paris, but they certainly became important properties of his own works.

6 See Lotman, *Sotvorenie Karamzina*, 242–55.

7 See Elizavetina, 243–63. Estelle C. Jelinek, 'Women's Autobiography and the Male Tradition', introduction to *Women's Autobiography* (Bloomington, IN, 1980), 1–20 makes a similar point in her survey comparing a wide range of women's autobiographies to the male tradition. In stressing personal, as opposed to professional, aspects, women's autobiographies contradict the male-defined canon for the genre. Her observations that women more frequently than men include children in their autobiographies and tend to write 'episodically and fragmentedly' and be proportionally more fond than men of the lesser autobiographical genres (notebooks, diaries, journals, as compared to autobiographies proper) are also interesting in the Sentimentalist context.

8 Uspenskii, *Iz istorii*, 57–67.

9 K1984b, vol. II, 124.

10 Lotman, *Sotvorenie Karamzina*, 270–1.

11 The gender question in late eighteenth-century life and literature is a complicated question which requires further study. For some interesting points about women in literature and literary style, see Uspenskii, *Iz istorii*, 30–4; 55–67; Lotman, *Sotvorenie Karamzina*, 227–37 and 265–77.

12 See N. A. Marchenko, 'Istoriia teksta "Pisem russkogo puteshestvennika"', K1984a, 607–12. Lotman, *Sotvorenie Karamzina* emphatically

stresses the *literariness* of all Karamzin's works, even those that are seemingly the most autobiographical (like *Letters of a Russian Traveller*). His most concise statement of this occurs on p. 32.

13 By its very nature the invective forms were less 'refined' and less proper to polite society than the compliment forms. The pamphlet was by this token less important within the Sentimentalist canon, but the literary development of this genre is nevertheless symptomatic of the era. On the history and development of the pamphlet in eighteenth-century Russia, see E. L. Afanas'ev, 'Pamflet', *Russkii i zapadnoevropeiskii klassitsizm* (Moscow, 1982), 263–97.

14 Quoted in V. V. Sipovskii, *Iz istorii russkogo romana i povesti* (Sanktpeterburg, 1903), vol. I, 214.

15 Ibid., vol. I, 215.

16 Ibid., vol. I, 226.

17 W. Gareth Jones, 'Biography in Eighteenth-Century Russia', *Oxford Slavonic Papers*, 22 (1989), 68.

18 Cf. also Elizavetina.

19 K1866, 61.

20 Quoted in Sipovskii, *Iz istorii*, vol. I, 223.

21 VE, 2, 6 (1802), 147–8.

22 Quoted in Sipovskii, *Iz istorii*, vol. I, 259–60.

23 Lotman, *Sotvorenie Karamzina*, 294.

24 Italics original, as quoted in Lotman, *Sotvorenie Karamzina*, 293.

25 N. M. Karamzin, 'Posviashchenie kushchi', MZha, 3 (1791), 323–36.

26 Fedor Emin's dedication of *Miramond* (vol. I, n.p., following title page) is a good example of the elaborate kind.

27 See, for instance, Chulkov's prose and verse dedication of *The Comely Cook* (*Prigozhaia povarikha*), reprinted in *Russkaia proza XVIII veka*, ed. G. Makogonenko (Moscow, 1971), 41–2.

28 See also Sumarokov's dedication of his eclogues – an elaborate address 'to the lovely female sex of the Russian nation', which, besides dedicating the eclogues, also sets forth his poetics of the genre, which is close to Sentimentalist ideas, as were the parts of his *Nastavlenie*, mentioned earlier. Sumarokov, vol. III, 3–4.

29 The name Fantaziia is appropriately feminine in Russian.

30 See, for instance, Karamzin's foreword to the second volume of *Aonidy* where it is stated that the poet ought not to be a tyrant over his imagination but its slave (here a constant worshipper in the temple). In 'What does an Author Need?' a vivid imagination is seen as a desirable quality (here the poet vows to sit with trembling heart and await his goddess's arrival). In 'A Promenade', a vivid imagination is seen as a prerequisite to the ability to co-create, crucial in a poet. Other instances could be added.

31 K1803, vol. VII, 1–19.

32 Lotman, *Sotvorenie Karamzina*, 55.

33 Cited in Cross, *N. M. Karamzin*, 120.

34 Karamzin's own description of Herder's *Paramythien* is particularly apt

in this context. He calls them 'tender works of flowering fantasy, which breathe Greek air and are lovely as a morning rose' and describes how he read them just before his meeting with Herder. In the same letter, he also cites Goethe's poem 'Meine Göttin', which is perhaps an even more obvious inspiration for Karamzin's own 'Goddess', down to identical description and epithets (K1984a, 72).

35 N. M. Karamzin, 'Nevinnost'', MZha, 2 (1791), 63–5; Cross, *N. M. Karamzin*, 120–1.

36 For details about Karamzin's relationship to Pleshcheeva, see L. V. Krestova, 'A. I. Pleshcheeva v zhizni i tvorchestve Karamzina', *XVIII vek*, 10 (1975), 146–75. Lotman, *Sotvorenie Karamzina*, 242–55 and 264–71, especially, provides numerous interesting insights about the relationship and its literary expression.

37 N. M. Karamzin, 'Raiskaia ptichka', MZhb, 3 (1791, 2nd edn 1803), 206–8.

38 For an account of Karamzin's sources, see L. V. Krestova, 'Drevne-russkaia povest' kak odin iz istokov povestei N. M. Karamzina "Raiskaia ptichka", "Ostrov Borngol'm", "Marfa Posadnitsa"', *Issledovaniia i materialy po drevnerusskoi literature* (Moscow, 1961), 193–226.

39 MZha, 3 (1791), 201.

40 Cited in Mark Al'tshuller, *Predtechi slavianofil'stva v russkoi literature* (Ann Arbor, 1984), 282. It might be pointed out in this context that the artistic value of folklore in and of itself was particularly highly treasured and analyzed by the Shishkovites in the first decades of the nineteenth century. Shishkov in his important speech at the opening of the *Beseda* circle stressed folklore as the second most important source for Russian literature (next to the sacred texts of old). For further details, see Al'tshuller, 273–95.

41 Lotman, *Sotvorenie Karamzina*, 242–55.

42 N. M. Karamzin, 'Dremuchii les', *Aglaia,* vol. II, 102–19. Further references to this edition will be made parenthetically within my text.

43 Sipovskii, *Ocherki*, vol. I, 2, 332.

44 Lotman, *Sotvorenie Karamzina*, 242–55.

45 Ibid., 246–7. To my knowledge this particular kind of word game has not survived in other published texts (besides the already mentioned Znamenskoe brochure), but similar games did gain some popularity. For instance, so-called *bouts-rimés*, a verse counterpart to Karamzin's game, were popular in the salons. Here the task was to compose verses on given rhyme words. Todd, *Fiction and Society*, 56 mentions this game as an example of the co-authorial relationship between addressers and addressees which was characteristic of an era when literature was still to a large extent practiced in intimate settings among friends.

46 K1803, vol. VI, 122–41.

47 Lotman, *Sotvorenie Karamzina*, 249–50.

48 N. M. Karamzin, 'Frol Silin, blagodetel'nyi chelovek', MZha, 3 (1791), 31–7. References to this edition will henceforth appear parenthetically within my text.

49 Sipovskii, *Ocherki*, vol. I, 2, 738–9 provides an impressive listing of similar works in the journals. See also V. P. Stepanov, 'Povest' Karamzina "Frol Silin"', *XVIII vek*, 8 (1969), 241.

50 Cf. Stepanov, 242–3.

51 K1797, 98.

52 M. A. Dmitriev, *Melochi iz zapasa moei pamiati* (2nd ed., Moscow, 1869), 68–70.

53 VE, 7, 3 (1803), 231.

54 N. I. Grech, *Izbrannye mesta iz russkikh sochinenii i perevodov v proze* (Sanktpeterburg, 1812); Sipovskii, *Ocherki*, vol. I, 2, 736; D. D. Blagoi, *Istoriia russkoi literatury XVIII veka* (4th edn, Moscow, 1960), 540; Stepanov, 'Povest' Karamzina'; Cross, *N. M. Karamzin*, 105, 108; P. A. Orlov, 'Zhanr proizvedeniia N. M. Karamzina "Frol Silin, blagodetel'nyi chelovek"', *Russkaia literatura*, 4 (1976), 189–91. A tri-partite composition such as Orlov describes (itself an oversimplification of the work's structure) is by no means the unique property of panegyric orations. Furthermore, as Orlov himself points out, it was not perceived as a 'lowering' of the panegyric oration by the contemporary imitators. Finally, the reception does not prove that the panegyric oration was perceived as a *reliktnoe iavlenie*, as Orlov maintains, thus contradicting his own earlier statements about the fact that Karamzin himself wrote precisely in that genre as well – his 'Historical Panegyric Oration to Catherine II' ('Istoricheskoe pokhvalnoe slovo Ekaterine II'), in 1802, eleven years after 'Frol Silin' appeared.

55 Cf. N. Bulich, *Biograficheskii ocherk N. M. Karamzina i razvitie ego literaturnoi deiatel'nosti* (Kazan, 1866), 1–18.

56 Gessner, vol. II, i.

57 The stress on universal brotherhood is one of the main tenets in Karamzin's idylls. It is most clearly stated as the eleventh aphorism in his 'Various Fragments (from the Notes of a Young Russian)' ('Raznye otryvki [iz zapisok odnogo molodogo Rossianina]'), which appeared in *Moscow Journal* (MZha, 6 (1791), 65–73). Karamzin's authorship has been conclusively proven by Vinogradov, *Problema avtorstva*, 246–324. Vinogradov also reproduces the work in its entirety (265–7). The belief in this ideal was clearly seen in, for example, 'The Flood' and 'A Promenade'. In other works it is questioned and/or seen as an aesthetic vision, a beautiful dream. This is the case in 'Various Fragments'. Lotman, *Sotvorenie Karamzina*, 170–5 also places Karamzin's emphasis on brotherhood and friendship in the context of Schiller, Wieland, Lessing, and Klopstock as these authors were discussed by the young Karamzin and his friends. His observations about Karamzin's pose as a traveller–pupil (61–3) link the theme of brotherhood to Karamzin's wishes to see his fellow authors (the works of whom he had already read widely before his journey) as *persons* behind the texts. This is another aspect of the personalization of 'author' that I noted as typical of the era.

5 SERIOUS SENTIMENTAL TALES: NARRATOR AS NARRATEE

1 Predecessors, such as F. Emin's *Letters of Ernest and Doravra* (1766–68), N. Emin's *Roza* (1786) and *The Game of Fate* (*Igra sud'by*, 1789), V. Lazarevich's *Virtuous Rozana* (*Dobrodetel'naia Rozana*, 1782), the works by P. L'vov, and the like. See also Klaus Städtke, *Die Entwicklung der russischen Erzählung (1800–1825)*, (Berlin, 1971), 29–38.

2 See, for example Städtke, 63–80.

3 See Lotman and Uspenskii 'Tekstologicheskie printsipy izdaniia' (K1984a, 516–24), where an anonymous 1803 work 'My Cousin's Journey in [his] Pockets' ('Puteshestvie moego dvoiurodnogo brata v karmany') is cited for containing the following verse parody on Karamzinian orthography:

$$!! -- \ldots \ldots -- !!$$
$$? \ldots ? \ldots ? \ldots ? \ldots ? \ldots$$
$$------$$
$$\ldots \ldots \ldots \ldots$$
$$/?//\backslash //\backslash //\backslash //\backslash /$$
$$!! -- \ldots \ldots -- !!$$

This is a good example of telling by not telling (ellipsis) and of telling by purely expressive means, as well as the typically cyclical structure of Karamzin's works.

4 Similar trends in Murav'ev's poetry are described in Brukhanskii.

5 N. M. Karamzin, 'Evgenii i Iuliia, russkaia istinnaia povest'', DChb, 17 (1789, 3rd edn 1819), 146–62. References to this edition will henceforth be made parenthetically within my text. See Brang, 131 and Sipovskii, *N. M. Karamzin*, 134–9.

6 Cross, *N. M. Karamzin*, 99–100.

7 See also Brang, 130–3; Kanunova, *Iz istorii*, 42–3; and Kochetkova, *Nikolay Karamzin*, 26–8.

8 For influences on works other than Karamzin's, see Brang, 213–15, 231.

9 The reference is probably to the famous 'Willkommen silberner Mond', as pointed out by Cross, *N. M. Karamzin*, 99–100.

10 We recall the idyll on Gessner's death, the grave of Frol Silin, the interpolated Phillida idyll in 'Night', the epitaph in 'Bird of Paradise' with very similar graveside imagery.

11 N. M. Karamzin, 'Bednaia Liza', MZhb, 6 (1792, 2nd edn 1803), 225–64. This edition will henceforth be referred to parenthetically within my text. Bulich, 75; Bulich's reference is to a section in Karamzin's *Letters of a Russian Traveller* (K1984a, 243), where the traveller meets a destitute old woman who relates to him the tragic fate of her daughter, Luiza, described somewhat like Liza, but without any other details reminiscent of 'Poor Liza'. Other sources for the tale have been seen in Goethe's *Werther*, where an interpolated story features a

female suicide by drowning after the heroine was abandoned by her lover. See Sipovskii, *Ocherki*, vol. I, 2, 519. Brang, 142 points out marked similarities to one of Anton Wall's *Bagatellen*, which relates the fate of a Leipzig student and a poor girl, indeed quite close to 'Poor Liza'. The tale has also been compared to Richardson's novels (L. V. Pumpianskii, 'Sentimentalizm', *Istoriia russkoi literatury* [Moscow, 1947], vol. IV, 440), Rousseau's *La Nouvelle Héloïse* (Z. G. Rozova, '"Novaia Eloiza" Russo i "Bednaia Liza" Karamzina', *XVIII vek*, 8 [1969], 259–68), and various native sources. Brang, 142–3, names works particularly by I. B. Kniazhnin, and V. Pukhov, 'Pervaia russkaia povest' o bednoi Lize', *Russkaia literatura*, 1 (1965), 120–2 is specifically devoted to this topic, suggesting additional works by Kniazhnin. The unavoidable comparison to Radishchev has been carried out by N. K. Piksanov, '"Bednaia Aniuta" Radishcheva i "Bednaia Liza" Karamzina', *XVIII vek*, 3 (1958), 309–25. The list of potential sources could be multiplied – all of which goes to show that 'Poor Liza' was a product of the era, not necessarily that any single work was the source.

12 See, for example, Rothe, 132–5, who shows that the same myth was also questioned in Karamzin's other works of the same period, particularly *Letters of a Russian Traveller*. Cross, 'Karamzin's Versions of the Idyll', and his *N. M. Karamzin*, 102–3 point to similar ideas. A most detailed account of Karamzin's expressions of his doubts can also be found in Vinogradov, *Problema avtorstva*, 246–323, where Karamzin's 'Various Fragments', aphorism 11, serves as the point of departure for an investigation of philosophical, thematic, lexical, and syntactic aspects of Karamzin's idyllic views – in numerous other works, as well. Various views of 'Poor Liza' and its relationship to the idyll have also been voiced by Pavlovich, 155; Kanunova, *Iz istorii*, 55–8; Skipina, 37–8; and J. G. Garrard, 'Poor Erast, or Point of View in Karamzin', *Essays on Karamzin*, ed. J. L. Black (The Hague, 1975), 40–55.

13 Cf. Karamzin's 'Letter from a Country Dweller' ('Pis'mo sel'skogo zhitelia'), where such a peasant idyll is more fully developed (VE, 11, 17 [1803], 42–59).

14 Cf., for example, Karamzin's description of Swiss peasants in *Letters of a Russian Traveller* and the children's ministrations to the distressed stranger in 'Eugene and Julia'.

15 Sumarokov, vol. VIII, 7–8.

16 Orlov, *Russkii sentimentalizm*, 211 mistakenly reads this as the narrator's comments on the idyll world. The words are clearly attributed to Liza – the narrator only quotes them.

17 P. A. Orlov, 'Ideinyi smysl povesti Karamzina "Bednaia Liza"', *Uchenye zapiski Riazanskogo gosudarstvennogo pedagogicheskogo instituta*, 10, (1955).

18 P. N. Berkov, 'Derzhavin i Karamzin v istorii russkoi literatury kontsa XVIII–nachala XIX veka', *XVIII vek*, 8 (1969), 5–17.

19 There is no reason to interpret Karamzin's wording in the epilogue to the effect that Erast, 'although Karamzin does not say that directly – will die soon after', as does Rudolf Neuhäuser, 'Karamzin's Spiritual Crisis of 1793 and 1794', *Essays on Karamzin*, ed. J. L. Black (The Hague, 1975), 63. All we know from the story is that the events took place thirty years before the narrator's 'now', and that the narrator met Erast one year before Erast's death, which could have occurred at any time within the thirty year span (minus the summer of the story) which separates the narrator from the story. Indeed, the words 'Erast was unhappy to the end of his life' may indicate a *long* life of suffering for Erast, which would make his punishment more just. Garrard is equally incorrect in stating that Erast told the narrator the story 'shortly before he died *one year previously*' (Garrard, 48, emphasis added). Erast told the story to the narrator some time within the last year of his life, during their acquaintance, which does not necessarily mean one year before 'now'. In fact, quite the contrary is indicated in the narrator's overture: he is in the habit of visiting the Si-nov monastery *frequently*, in spring and fall, and most frequently he visits the site to relive Liza's tragic story – i.e., many a spring and fall, in all likelihood.

20 Garrard, 46, 48–9.

21 Here and further on in this section I use bold face type for my own emphasis in order to highlight developments of specific vocabulary and sound texture in Karamzin's work.

22 To this end, Karamzin elsewhere most explicitly suggests that the readers turn to works such as Büsching's *Geography*. See Karamzin's foreword to a new edition of *Letters of a Russian Traveller* (K1984a, 393). See also Kanunova, *Iz istorii*, 55–6, who maintains that Karamzin's subjectivist limitations reveal themselves in the idyllic tone that colors 'Poor Liza' as a whole. The pastoral idyllic motifs, in her opinion, are clearly present despite the author's striving to describe real life and to create an illusion of verisimilitude. The sweet pastoral tone is particularly noticeable where Liza is concerned, but it is to Karamzin's credit in Kanunova's view, that where Erast is concerned, the idyllic mode does not fully satisfy Karamzin. That Karamzin was dissatisfied with the overly idyllic tone is true – and I will return to the topic later – but his use of the idyllic tone does not necessarily indicate a lack of skill or a striving for realism, as Kanunova implies. Kanunova ignores the trivocal structure of the tale. That Karamzin would have striven towards a realistic description (in any modern sense) is an utterly anachronistic notion, which contradicts all we know about Karamzin's own statements on poetics. Yet, that notion is to some extent discernible throughout Kanunova's work, in many other respects excellent.

23 Iu. M. Lotman, 'The Stage and Painting as Code Mechanisms for Cultural Behavior in the Early Nineteenth Century', *The Semiotics of Russian Culture*, Iu. M. Lotman and B. A. Uspenskii, ed. Ann Shukman (Ann Arbor, 1984), 165–76, notes that the stage and painting

were especially important in the cultural code of the early nineteenth century. This passage from 'Poor Liza' suggests that the same areas of art were important already in the late eighteenth century. Many other works demonstrate the same code, for instance Karamzin's 'Bornholm Island', where the narrator is struck by the *mesta redkie i zhivopisnye* at Gravesend. One also frequently sees references to the 'brush of Raphael' and similar metaphors for the writer's craft, and we recall that, for instance, Gessner was a painter as well as a writer.

24 Rothe, 239–40.

25 Brang, 145–7; see also Kanunova, *Iz istorii*, 51–2 and Orlov, *Russkii sentimentalizm*, 214–16. V. V. Vinogradov, 'O stile Karamzina i ego razvitii (ispravleniia teksta povestei)', *Protsessy formirovaniia leksiki russkogo literaturnogo iazyka* (Moscow, 1966), 237–41 provides an interesting analysis of stylistic changes made in different editions of the tale, and in the process gives a good analysis of the most prevalent stylistic means.

26 Garrard, 48.

27 Ibid., 48.

28 I am grateful to the anonymous referee of the *Slavic and East European Journal* version of my analysis for this example.

29 Alexander Zholkovsky (private communication) drew my attention to Erast's reaction. Zholkovsky cleverly uses it as a pedagogical device in the classroom, asking students to identify 'the most absurd sentence' in 'Poor Liza'.

30 See Kanunova's (*Iz istorii*, 47–50) excellent analysis of the means whereby Karamzin attains a psychologically sensitive description.

31 Bakhtin, *Estetika*, 7–162, especially 82–8.

32 See Kanunova, *Iz istorii*, 59 for a more detailed discussion.

33 Brang, 145 stresses the narrator's wish to create an illusion of reality by distancing his own 'sad true story' from the unreal idylls and romances. For other treatments of irony in 'Poor Liza', see Kanunova, *Iz istorii*, 55–6; Anderson, *N. M. Karamzin's Prose*, 84; Rothe, 242.

34 N. M. Karamzin, 'Sierra-Morena', *Aglaia*, vol. II, 7–18. Further references to this edition will be made parenthetically within my text.

35 *Aglaia*, vol. II, n.p., also in K1966, 135. As has been pointed out by Lotman, the refrain 'We live' was later included in new editions of the poem 'Veselyi chas' – a very life-affirming poem (K1966, 100–1). Much has been written about Karamzin's crisis in the early 1790s, and almost any account of the works from the *Aglaia* period (1793–1800) includes some information about it. See, for example, Lotman, 'Evoliutsiia mirovozzreniia Karamzina', and *Sotvorenie Karamzina*; L. I. Kulakova, 'Esteticheskie vzgliady N. M. Karamzina', *XVIII vek*, 6 (1964), 146–75; A. V. Predtechenskii, 'Obshchestvenno–politicheskie vzgliady N. M. Karamzina v 1790-kh godakh', *Problemy russkogo Prosveshcheniia v literature XVIII veka*, ed. P. Berkov (Leningrad, 1961), 63–78; and Orlov, *Russkii sentimentalizm*, 225–34.

298 Notes to pages 160–73

36 See Neuhäuser, *Towards the Romantic Age*, 183 for an excellent discussion of the problem of guilt in 'Sierra-Morena'.
37 See B. M. Eikhenbaum, 'Karamzin', *Skvoz' literaturu*, (Leningrad, 1924, rpt. 1969), 212 for an interesting brief analysis of its lyrical–musical qualities, and Lotman, 'Evoliutsiia mirovozzreniia Karamzina', 142–4, who complements Eikhenbaum's analysis of its lyrical elements, and who sees the tale as a forerunner to the Romantic poetry of Zhukovskii. Its affinities to other works by Karamzin have been analyzed by, e.g., Rothe, 292–3, who links it to 'Liodor'. Most scholars point to its affinities to the other works of the *Aglaia* period, especially 'Bornholm Island'. Anderson, *N. M. Karamzin's Prose*, 143–50 also sees it as a prefiguration of things to come in 'My Confession'. See also Kanunova, *Iz istorii*, 119–20; Pavlovich, 180–7; Neuhäuser, *Towards the Romantic Age*, 182–4. Among foreign sources, many candidates have been suggested: a work by Mme de Genlis, translated by Karamzin for *Children's Reading* in 1787 (Cross, *N. M. Karamzin*, 115–16), Petronius, and J. de LaFontaine, who among others used the motif of the Ephesian widow (Brang, 166), and perhaps the closest foreign model, a ballad by M. G. Lewis 'Brave Alonso and Beautiful Imogene', which appeared in the seventh chapter of his novel *The Monk*, as well as other Scottish and German ballads. See also L. V. Krestova, 'Povest' N. M. Karamzina "Sierra-Morena"', *XVIII vek*, 7 (1966), 262–4, who brings in autobiographical themes. The questions of influence and autobiographical elements are amply analyzed, and shall not directly concern us here.
38 The emphasis here and for the rest of my discussion of 'Sierra-Morena' is mine, even within quotes of Karamzin.
39 Lotman, *Sotvorenie Karamzina*, 251–2.
40 N. M. Karamzin, 'Liodor', MZhb, 5 (1792, 2nd edn 1803), 292–323. References to this edition will henceforth be made parenthetically within my text.
41 Pogodin, *Nikolai Mikhailovich Karamzin*, 135–9. See Sipovskii, *Ocherki*, part I, 2, 520–4, in particular; Brang, 135–9; Rothe, 221–3; all of which further elucidate these connections.
42 Cited in Pogodin, 206; italics in Pogodin.
43 Lotman, *Sotvorenie Karamzina*, 62–3.
44 K1866, 31.
45 See Rothe, 221 who without exploiting epistolary poetics labels 'Liodor' as a 'Briefform an Aglaja dabei häufige autobiografische Beglaubigungen'.
46 Pogodin, 193–4, footnote. The reference is to 'Novyi God', MZhb, 5 (1792, 2nd ed. 1803), 88–90.
47 Cf. 'A Promenade': 'Then it seems to him as if a quite thin curtain hides from him the incorporeal world [ . . . ] impressions of spiritual objects, the rays of which penetrate through this curtain', followed by an account of how the narrator will soon be united with the spirits. A similar idea will later reappear in 'Bornholm Island'.

48 Karamzin was, as is well known, early attracted to Lavater and even corresponded with him before the two actually met during Karamzin's journey. This is another 'autobiographical' reference to *Letters of a Russian Traveller*, where Lavater is visited, his teachings a frequent topic, and so on. This particular Lavaterian insight might well be at the roots of Sentimentalist poetics as well. Consider, for example, the description of author in Karamzin's 'What does an Author Need?': 'The creator is always depicted in his creation and often – against his will', and Karamzin's numerous protestations against any form of dissembling in art.

49 Lotman, *Sotvorenie Karamzina*, 62.

50 Cross, *N. M. Karamzin*, 111.

51 Rothe, 242.

52 N. M. Karamzin, 'Ostrov Borngol'm', *Aglaia*, vol. I, 92–118. Gukovskii, *Russkaia literatura*, 508.

53 Krestova, 'Drevnerusskaia povest'' is devoted to its native sources, and V. E. Vatsuro, 'Literaturno–filosoficheskaia problematika povesti Karamzina "Ostrov Borngol'm"', *XVIII vek*, 8 (1969), 190–209 is a study of its similarities to and differences from foreign and native Gothic works, stressing also its compositional and structural links to the later Byronic *poema* in Russia. Three recent articles focus on the role of the narrator: Roger B. Anderson, 'Karamzin's "Bornholm Island": Its Narrator and its Meaning', *Orbis Litterarum*, 28 (1973), 204–15; Kjeld Bjørnager Jensen, 'The Fruits of Curiosity. On the Composition of N. M. Karamzin's *Ostrov Borngol'm*', *Svantevit*, 4 (1978), 51–9; and I. R. Titunik, 'Russian Sentimentalist Rhetoric of Fiction', *Semiosis. Semiotics of Culture*, ed. M. Halle et al (Ann Arbor, 1984), 228–39. Lotman, 'Evoliutsiia mirovozzreniia Karamzina' places the tale in the context of Karamzin's philosophical and aesthetic evolution, as does Neuhäuser, *Towards the Romantic Age*.

54 Titunik, 'Russian Sentimentalist Rhetoric of Fiction', 235–6, stresses the role of the Sentimentalist author as model responder and addressee. Lotman, 'Evoliutsiia mirovozzreniia Karamzina', 141 describes the tale as a 'lyrical narrative' which emphasizes the author's moods connected with the objective events, rather than those events themselves, and he points out that the central episode remains untold. Anderson, 'Karamzin's "Bornholm Island"' similarly stresses the centrality of the narrator's moods, and Jensen, 53 emphasizes the fact that the 'narrator's curiosity, its awakening, titillation and finally satisfaction' is the main topic of the tale. These scholars each highlight what seem to me aspects of a more encompassing main topic (the dialogical nature of the aesthetic act), without, however, fully elucidating that topic itself.

55 Gessner, vol. II, 32.

56 Compare 'Liodor' (MZhb, 5 [1792, 2nd edn 1803], 295): 'Often stormy winds shook the eaves in our ancient house, and howled sadly in the chimney of the fireplace, before which we were sitting in the evenings;

often the fields were covered by snow but we still wandered in the fields, fearing neither blizzards nor snowstorms', continuing with a description of the cure for boredom (and even cold) through friendly communication as in 'Bornholm Island'.

57 One wonders whether Karamzin (who knew English) consciously used the implications of the English onomastics, which, conjures up the images of death and birth, so pervasively developed in the text, as well as the concrete situation of the young man, born on Bornholm and awaiting his grave at Gravesend. Whether used intentionally or not, the names make for an interesting excursus over the language barrier.

58 DCha, 18 (1789), 162–8.

59 K1984b, vol. II, 44–60.

60 That the song, as such, is a 'complete story', can be seen in the fact that the song itself independently became immensely popular. See Iu. M. Lotman and B. A. Uspenskii, 'Spory o iazyke v nachale XIX v. kak fakt russkoi kul'tury', *Trudy po russkoi i slavianskoi filologii*, 24 (1975), 318, footnote No. 200.

61 Clearly some of Karamzin's contemporaries did not see the aesthetic potential of the incest theme and objected strongly to the young man's 'natural' justification for his love (usually read as Karamzin's justification, to boot). Semen Bobrov's parody of the Karamzinists' new style, called 'Proisshestvie v tsarstve tenei, ili Sud'bina rossiiskogo iazyka' has the personage 'Lomonosov' read the Gravesend song and condemn its ideas and sentiments after having complimented its language and poetic features. He condemns the author as a sensualist indulging in improper weakness and poisoning young minds by justifying such voluptuousness (1805, rpt. in Lotman and Uspenskii, 'Spory o iazyke', 276). See also Krestova, 'Drevnerusskaia povest'', 209. Lotman, *Sotvorenie Karamzina*, 18–21 quotes a most interesting parody on Karamzin written by A. S. Kaisarov, 'Karamzin's Wedding' ('Svad'ba Karamzina') on the occasion of Karamzin's real first marriage (to Pleshcheeva's sister). This parody is a compilation of lines from various poems by Karamzin and many lines of the Bornholm elegy are included. This is another instance when contemporaries equated Karamzin's literary images with his personal life, as Lotman points out.

62 K1898, 36.

63 Cited in Krestova, 'Drevnerusskaia povest'', 209.

64 See Brang, 163.

65 See Neuhäuser, *Towards the Romantic Age*, 180–1 for a description of the work. There are clear similarities in theme between 'Bornholm Island' and Derzhavin's translation, but it was not the first nor by far the only work circulating in Russia at the time dealing with incest, as has been demonstrated by Krestova, 'Drevnerusskaia povest'' and Vatsuro.

66 K1984b, vol. II, 47–8, footnote.

67 See Bakhtin, *Voprosy literatury*, 394.

68 See Vatsuro, for an excellent study of the Gothic elements in 'Bornholm Island'.

69 K1984b, vol. II, 55–6.

70 See Anderson, 'Karamzin's "Bornholm Island"' for a diametrically opposite view.

6 HUMOROUS SENTIMENTAL TALES: NARRATOR AS PARODIST

1 K1984b, vol. II, 89.

2 VE, 9, 9 (1803), 18–22.

3 See, for example, F. Z. Kanunova, 'Karamzin i Stern', *XVIII vek*, 10 (1975), 258–64.

4 N. V. Gogol', 'Teatral'nyi raz"ezd posle predstavleniia novoi komedii', *Sochineniia v dvukh tomakh*, (Moscow, 1971), vol. II, 252.

5 Kanunova, 'Karamzin i Stern'.

6 See Sipovskii, *Ocherki*, vol. I, 2, 1–374; I. P. Lupanova, *Russkaia narodnaia skazka v tvorchestve pisatelei pervoi poloviny XIX veka* (Petrozavodsk, 1959), 7–56; Neuhäuser, *Towards the Romantic Age*, 127–42, for discussions of the status of folklore in Russia at the time.

7 Cf. Tzvetan Todorov, *The Fantastic* (Ithaca, 1975), 64–5, who excludes Perrault's fairy tales from the 'fantastic' on the grounds that the allegory is made explicit within the text itself.

8 Ostolopov; as quoted in Sipovskii, *Iz istorii*, 264.

9 N. M. Karamzin, 'Prekrasnaia tsarevna i shchastlivyi karla', MZhb, 7 (1792, 2nd edn 1803), 213–40. References to this edition will henceforth be made parenthetically within my text.

10 Sipovskii, *Ocherki*, vol. I, 2, 316–21.

11 Brang, 150–1.

12 See especially A. I. Efimov, 'Frazeologicheskii sostav povesti Karamzina "Natal'ia, boiarskaia doch'"', *Materialy i issledovaniia po istorii russkogo literaturnogo iazyka*, (Moscow, 1949), vol. I, 69–94; Brang, 151–2; and Anderson, *N. M. Karamzin's Prose*, 104.

13 K1966, 149.

14 Brang, 151.

15 The image of a hospitable oaken table is also used by Karamzin in 'Natal'ia' and 'Letter from a Country Dweller', where it is described in the following words: 'we give dinners, such as described in olden Russian fairy tales and Homeric epics, we seat the villagers with their families at *oaken tables*' (VE, 11, 17 [1803], 57). The *terem* image is also used in 'Liodor' to evoke the olden days and recurs in 'Natal'ia'.

16 Anderson, *N. M. Karamzin's Prose*, 104.

17 Compare the conclusion to Bogdanovich's 'Dushen'ka'. Karamzin's analysis of that work (K1984b, vol. II, 128–54) contains many interesting general comments about the fairy tale, the caricature, and the light fantastic. A comparison of the two works is beyond my present scope, but it seems that 'Dushen'ka' should be included as one of

Karamzin's sources for 'The Beautiful Princess', particularly since he himself paid so much attention to Bogdanovich's work.

18 We recall that Karamzin was one of the first to translate and introduce Shakespeare to Russia, and had nothing but praise for him, despite some prestigious contemporary differences in opinion (e.g., Voltaire, whom Karamzin quotes in his discussion of Shakespeare). As for his psychological depth, a serious Karamzin has the following to say: 'Few writers penetrated human nature as deeply as Shakespeare; few knew as well as this amazing artist all the most secret springs of a human being, his most hidden motives, the distinct nature of every passion, every temperament and every kind of life' (K1984b, vol. II, 8).

19 On this point I cannot agree with Anderson's (*N. M. Karamzin's Prose*, 108) assessment of some of the dwarf's stories as 'capsulized versions of *Pamela* and *Clarissa*'. In Richardson's novels there were no fairies, no princes or princesses, no *pokhozhdeniia* nor *mnogchislennye iskusheniia roka*. The fairy or royal personages, the adventures, the vicissitudes of an abstract 'Fate', the happy endings, and the overt allegorizing are much more typical of chivalric romances and adventure novels. 'Sentimentalist' behavior entered such works as exaggerated pathetic *bavardage de la fièvre*, and the endings were unfailingly happy. Even the vocabulary used by the narrator to describe the dwarf's stories is reminiscent of the Emin-type literature rather than Richardson – one need only think of titles such as *Nepostoiannaia Fortuna, ili Pokhozhdenie Miramonda; Pokhozhdenie nekotorogo Rossiianina; Torzhestvuiushchaia dobrodetel', ili zhizn' i prikliucheniia gonimago fortunoiu Selima; Leinard i Tamira, ili Zloshchastnaia sud'ba dvukh liubovnikov; chudnye pokhozhdeniia Izrada*, or any of the fairy tales in the collections of the time. Karamzin elsewhere uses similar vocabulary to describe the older didactic–chivalric adventure novels. The narrator of *Knight*, for instance, describes *Daira, Miramond,* and *Selim i Damasina* in the following words: 'Geroi i geroini, ne smotria na mnogochislennye iskusheniia roka, ostaiutsia dobrodetel'nymi; vse zlodei opisyvaiutsia samymi chernymi kraskami; pervye nakonets torzhestvuiut, poslednie nakonets kak prakh ischezaiut' (VE, 5, 18 [1802], 115). Yet Anderson is right in that Sentimentalism too is parodied.

20 N. M. Karamzin, 'Natal'ia, boiarskaia doch'', MZhb, 8 (1792, 2nd ed. 1803), 15–74 and 238–79. References to this edition will henceforth be made parenthetically within my text.

21 Sipovskii, *Ocherki*, vol. I, 2, 721–34.

22 Kanunova, *Iz istorii*, 72–100. Cf., e.g., Pavlovich, 159–72 for a discussion of the arguments for and against the label, as well as for her own reasons for why it is not applicable.

23 Orlov, *Russkii Sentimentalizm*, 222–5. A. Starchevskii, *Nikolai Mikhailovich Karamzin* (S.-Peterburg, 1849), 91.

24 V. I. Fedorov, 'Povest' Karamzina "Natal'ia - boiarskaia doch'"', *Uchenye zapiski Moskovskogo pedagogicheskogo instituta imeni Potemkina*, 48, 5 (1955), 141.

25 N. A. Belozerskaia, *Vasilii Trofimovich Narezhnyi* (2nd. edn, S. Peterburg, 1896), 64.

26 See Roman Jakobson, 'O khudozhestvennoi realizme' (Prague, rpt. Ann Arbor, 1962), 30–6 for the most convincing demonstration of the elusiveness of the term 'realism'. Similar points could be made against a careless application of the term 'historical'.

27 For a similar view, see T. S. Karlova, 'Esteticheskii smysl istorii v tvorcheskom vospriiatii Karamzina', *XVIII vek*, 8 (1969), 281–9. Cf. also Horace W. Dewey, 'Sentimentalism in the Historical Writings of N. M. Karamzin', *American Contributions to the Fourth International Congress of Slavists* (The Hague, 1958), 41–50.

28 K1984b, vol. II, 154–62.

29 Kanunova, *Iz istorii*.

30 See Lotman, *Sotvorenie Karamzina,* 293–308 for an interesting discussion of Karamzin as a historian.

31 As has been convincingly demonstrated by Vinogradov, 'O stile Karamzina', Karamzin's views of historical narration changed somewhat over time. Later editions of 'Natal'ia' differ sharply from the first edition. Vinogradov compares the first edition with the 1820 edition, and comes to the conclusion that many of the references to the contemporary literary context are lacking in the later edition. Whether this makes 'Natal'ia' any more historical, as Vinogradov contends, seems to me an open question. Although it is less subjective in a literary sense, it is still by no means 'pure' history. As in the first edition, the tale still originates in the narrator's imagination, and the whimsical overture is still retained. In my discussion I will refer solely to the second *Moscow Journal* edition, which differs insignificantly from the first edition.

32 See Sipovskii, *Ocherki*, vol. I, 2, 731–2 for an excerpt and Brang, 158–9 for a further discussion of similarities and differences.

33 See L. V. Krestova, 'Romanicheskaia povest' N. M. Karamzina "Natal'ia, boiarskaia doch'" i russkie semeinye predaniia XVIII veka', *Drevnerusskaia literatura i ee sviazi s novym vremenem* (Moscow, 1967), 237–59 for more detail.

34 Sipovskii, *Ocherki*, vol. I, 2, 731.

35 Cf. Krestova, 'Drevnerusskaia povest'', 241.

36 See Brang, 158–9 and Krestova, 'Drevnerusskaia povest'' for discussions of Karamzin's familiarity with specific chronicles.

37 N. A. Baklanova, 'K voprosu o datirovke "Povesti o Frole Skobeeve"', *Trudy otdela drevnerusskoi literatury*, 13 (1957), 517 establishes the 1720s as the most likely date of origin of 'Frol Skobeev'. In the following, I will refer to 'Povest' o Frole Skobeeve', *Russkaia povest' XVII veka*, comp. M. O. Skripil', ed. I. P. Eremin (Leningrad, 1954), 155–66. The full title of Novikov's tale is: 'Novgorodskikh devushek sviatochnyi vecher sygrannyi v Moskve svadebnoi', and the tale appeared in Novikov's 1785 collection *Pokhozhdenie Ivana gosti-*

*nogo syna*. References in my text are to this edition. The tale has been reprinted only once to my knowledge, in *Russkie povesti XVII–XVIII vv.*, ed. V. V. Sipovskii (S.-Peterburg, 1905), 73–89.

38  See Sipovskii, *Ocherki*, vol. I, 2, 643–8; N. Apostolov, *Karamzin kak romanist–istorik* (Petrograd, 1916), 15–16; Kanunova, *Iz istorii*, 86–8. Kanunova attributes 'Novgorod Girls" incorrectly to N. I. Novikov.

39  See Gitta Hammarberg, 'Eighteenth Century Narrative Variations on "Frol Skobeev"', *Slavic Review*, 46, 3/4 (1987), 529–39 for a more detailed analysis of the different modes of narration.

40  See Kanunova, *Iz istorii*, 88–9, where the links to Kheraskov are discussed from a different angle.

41  See Efimov, and Kanunova, *Iz istorii*, 91–4. It is interesting to note that Karamzin quite widely used selected folkloric language here and elsewhere (e.g., in the fairy tales), thus anticipating the somewhat later emphasis on folklore 'to depict the inner world of a human being, the tender stirrings of the soul' among the Shishkovites. Shishkov of course advocates a language and literature based on native Russian folklore which he *opposes* to the Sentimentalist literature based, as he sees it, on European traditions. Karamzin's works amply show that such an opposition is false – although, to be sure, their ideas about folklore differed. On the Shishkovite ideas about folklore, see Al'tshuller, 273–95.

42  N. M. Karamzin, 'Moia Ispoved'', VE, 2, 6 (1802), 147–67. I will hereafter refer to this edition parenthetically within my text. See Eikhenbaum, 201–10.

43  Lotman, 'Evoliutsiia mirovozzreniia Karamzina', 155–8; his 'Puti razvitiia russkoi prozy', 31–4; and his 'Russo i russkaia kul'tura', 275–7.

44  Kanunova, *Iz istorii*, 140, where Lotman's view is rejected.

45  E. N. Kupreianova, 'Russkii roman pervoi chetverti XIX veka', *Istoriia russkogo romana*, (Moscow, 1962), vol. I, 72–3.

46  Tanya Page, 'Karamzin's Immoralist Count NN or Three Hermeneutical Games of "Chinese Shadows"', *Slavic and East European Journal*, 29, 2 (1985), 144–56.

47  Lotman, in 'Puti razvitiia russkoi prozy', 33–4 and in his 'Russo i russkaia kul'tura', 266, points out some rather specific textual correspondencies between the narrator of 'My Confession' and Dostoevskii's novel *The Devils* (*Besy*) and similarities to Dostoevskii's other works as well.

48  Quoted in Brissenden, 40.

49  See O'Neal, 19–31; 55–72; 82–103 for especially interesting discussions (in terms of perception) of similar phenomena in Rousseau.

50  K1961, 266.

51  K1984b, vol. II, 230.

52  VE, 2, 7 (1802), 254–5. See O'Neal, 35–54 for similar ideas about different ways of 'seeing' and imagination in Rousseau. Imagination is, for instance, one of the capabilities that saves Julie in *La Nouvelle*

*Héloise* and Rousseau himself in his confessions, from the vice of sensuality.

53 See Afanas'ev, 266–72. Afanas'ev perceptively sees Elagin's Author as a worthy ancestor both of Krylov's Karamzin-parody, 'Panegyric speech to Ermalafid' and of Koz'ma Prutkov – the latter, an interesting example of how a fictitious 'author' gained real life status in the literary life of nineteenth-century Russia.

54 See my discussion of 'A Promenade' above and also works, more contemporary to 'My Confession', where imitation is discussed, such as 'On Love for One's Country' and 'On the Light Dress', both serious statements against slavish imitation. See 'Notes of an Old Moscow Dweller' for a mock-serious treatment of the same topic. Imitation was also part of the topic of Karamzin's later (1818) speech at the Imperial Academy (K1984b, vol. II, 169–76).

55 Page, 144 mentions several other West European and Russian works with immoral heroes like NN in 'My Confession' – 'an immoral hero of a different order'.

56 Anderson, *N. M. Karamzin's Prose*, 156–7. The subtitle did not appear in the first *Messenger of Europe* edition of the tale. See Lotman, 'Russo i russkaia kul'tura' for an extensive analysis of Karamzin's vacillating attitudes toward Rousseau.

57 'The Recluse' has been claimed as Karamzin's earliest piece of original fiction by Anthony G. Cross ('Karamzin's First Short Story?', *Russia: Essays in History and Literature*, ed. Lyman H. Legters [Leiden, 1972], 38–55). He points out numerous links between the recluse and some of the narrators and personages I mentioned – not Count NN, however. See especially pp. 44–6.

58 VE, 2, 7 (1802), 251.

59 K1984a, 255.

60 See e.g., Vinogradov, *Problema avtorstva*, 313–14.

61 See Page for further discussion of the game of Chinese shadows. We are also again reminded of Rousseau's use of *chambre obscure* and other optical illusions in *Les Confessions*. Lotman, *Sotvorenie Karamzina*, 144, mentions a little known Paris theater of Chinese shadows that attracted Karamzin's attention as a likely source for his later symbolic use of 'Chinese shadows' in his works.

62 Karamzin's familiarity with Mendelssohn's ideas has been amply documented by Rothe (66–9), who also gives further references on the subject.

63 N. M. Karamzin, *Rytsar' nashego vremeni*, VE, 4, 13 (1802), 35–51; VE, 5, 18 (1802), 111–25; VE, 10, 14 (1803), 121–42. References will be made to this edition, citing page number preceded by issue number, e.g., '13, 36' refers to page 36 in issue 13, volume 4 (1802) of the journal.

64 Starchevskii, 11–12 briefly discusses *Knight*, and comes to the following conclusion: 'This whole story is for the most part fiction, but there are

people, who in the simplicity of their hearts, taking this tale for the most credible description of Karamzin's childhood, use it as a basis for his biography. What is one to do with such gullible biographers? But it seems sinful to base Karamzin's biography on these kinds of data.' Sipovskii, *N. M. Karamzin*, 16–31, is one of these biographers, although he is aware of the problem of *Dichtung und Wahrheit*. In Note 1 in the Appendix, he defends his position against Starchevskii, and points to some correspondences between the historical facts of Karamzin's biography and *Knight*, and to Karamzin's models in fictionalizing autobiographical data (Rousseau's confessions, for instance). See also Gukovskii, *Russkaia literatura*, 511; Kupreianova, 73; P. N. Berkov and G. Makogonenko, 'Zhizn' i tvorchestvo N. M. Karamzina', Introduction to K1964, vol. I, 49; Nebel, *N. M. Karamzin*, 117; Cross, *N. M. Karamzin*, 1 and 125; Kochetkova, *Nikolay Karamzin*, 107. All these scholars view the novel as autobiographical, some do so solely on the basis of the note, others proceed with more caution and introduce added evidence.

65 It is revealing that Lotman in his most recent work, *Sotvorenie Karamzina*, discusses *Messenger of Europe* almost exclusively as a political journal, with very little attention to the fiction. To be sure, it is largely a political journal (and as a private political journal, it was also innovatory), and its appearance a major cultural event, the implications of which Lotman places in an entirely new light. Nevertheless the title of the literary section, 'Literature and Varia' and the fact that mostly minor works are included does not necessarily mean that that section is qualitatively inferior. In fact, as we have seen, and as Lotman himself points out repeatedly, trifles were especially important during this era. Furthermore, most of Karamzin's finest humorous works are contained in this journal. Lotman in general pays surprisingly little attention to humor in Karamzin.

66 See Brang, 180–7; Lotman, 'Puti razvitiia russkoi prozy', 30–6; Kanunova, *Iz istorii*, 144–56; Cross, *N. M. Karamzin*, 123–6; Anderson, *N. M. Karamzin's Prose*, 170–83; Kanunova, 'Karamzin i Stern', 258–64. The English translation by Cross appeared in *Russian Literature Triquarterly*, 20 (1987), 139–58.

67 Kupreianova, 73; see also Berkov and Makogonenko, 49; Gukovskii, *Russkaia literatura*, 511; Brang, 181.

68 See Anthony G. Cross, 'Karamzin Studies', *The Slavonic and East European Review*, 45, 104 (1967), 8–9 and his 'N. M. Karamzin's "Messenger of Europe"', *Forum for Modern Language Studies*, 5, 1 (1969), 4, where the fictional works of the journal are mentioned, but not analyzed. Pertinent references are also given.

69 Lotman, 'Puti razvitiia russkoi prozy', 34–5 views the novel as a depiction of the inherent contradictions and complexities of one individual. He sees the image of Leon as more objective than Karamzin's previous heroes, although Karamzin's subjective method is, in his

opinion, still to be felt. The subjectivism, Lotman correctly argues, is transformed – it is no longer of the lyrical, emotionally intensive kind, nor does it, in his opinion, lie in the Sternian digressions, but rather in the fact that 'the character of the central hero as before exists outside the influence of external circumstances'. Lotman goes on to state that Karamzin at the time was deeply interested in the politics of the day, but that the task of describing one single individual was not conducive to the [greater?] task of creating a prose style by which he could illustrate his growing political concerns, and which would replace the Classicist 'political novels', which he, according to Lotman, responds to in this text. In his *Sotvorenie Karamzina*, Lotman labels Karamzin, of his *Messenger of Europe* period, 'the politician' (280). Kanunova, *Iz istorii* also stresses Karamzin's increased interest in social and environmental motivations for psychological character development. There are in her work traces of the typical Soviet tendency to spot predecessors to Realism which we have noted in her analyses of Karamzin's other works as well. She hails Karamzin's growing objectivity, and points out that the narrative manner in the second part of the novel is more objective, and that there are less subjective authorial intrusions, which themselves are now better motivated. While her statements are partly correct, I would object to the fact that she imputes the aim of greater objectivity to Karamzin himself, and considers the 'unwarranted' remnants of subjectivism a flaw that he was unable to overcome, although he presumably tried. Anderson, *N. M. Karamzin's Prose* similarly stresses the objectivity of the narrated events (what he calls neutral omniscience). Others see *Knight* as Karamzin's 'attempt to write a *Bildungsroman*, to portray the youthful development of his hero Leon' (Cross, *N. M. Karamzin*, 124–6).

70  Sipovskii, *N. M. Karamzin*, Notes, 47.
71  MZhb, 7 (1792, 2nd edn 1803), 59.
72  Here and henceforth expressions in bold face are mine, even within Karamzin's texts. I am highlighting repeated vocabulary in order to emphasize the development of similar topics and style.
73  Many scholars, e.g., Kupreianova, 74, point to affinities between Leon/Emilia and Rousseau/Mme de Warens, particularly as described in *Les Confessions*. As has been pointed out by many scholars, one could also compare Leon/Emilia to Karamzin/Pleshcheeva.
74  This passage is intentionally and overtly ambiguous in Russian, and Cross translates this sentence differently ('if the *cruel man* had **not** plucked the first violet' [K1987: 141, bold face added]). The Russian reads: 'i mat' Geroia nashego nikogda ne byla by suprugoiu ottsa ego, est'li by *zhestokii* v Aprele mesiatse sorval pervuiu fiialku na beregu Sviiagi'(39). Grammatically, native informants have confirmed my translation; logically either one could be supported. The mother's other actions seem to support my more innocent interpretation, although a good case could also be made for Cross's less innocent one.

75 A similar view is expressed by Rousseau, who stresses that education, especially during the formative years, the 'age of Nature' (birth to age twelve – also Leon's age here), should be a slow and natural process, not to be accelerated by overzealous adults. The first two books of *Emile* are devoted to this period in a child's life.

76 Lotman, *Sotvorenie Karamzina*, 34 sees the description of the male gentry and their friendship pact as an autobiographical allusion to the provincial gentry environment where Karamzin grew up. *Knight* is clearly autobiographical on some level (one could further point to the library of novels left by Karamzin's own mother who also died early, Karamzin's own friendship with older women, etc.). Lotman (22) makes the interesting observation that Karamzin in his early relationship with Pleshcheeva played the role of 'little boy', and that Pleshcheeva was to him both a 'tender friend' and a mother figure. Lotman links this to Karamzin's later traveller–pupil pose. However, it seems to me that Lotman takes the autobiographical elements in *Knight* a bit too seriously and tends to ignore the lighthearted irony in the novel. To be sure, the irony here as elsewhere is not blatant but of the gentle Sentimentalist variety.

77 Sipovskii, *Iz istorii* includes all these works. *Daira* (Nos. 180 and 1548) is identified as an Eastern tale in four volumes by J. de la Pepelinière [?], translated from the French by N. Dan[ilovskii] in 1766–8, with a second edition in 1794. *Selim and Damasina* (Nos. 77 and 1279) is an African tale, translated from the French in 1761 with a second edition in 1791. The Rare Book Collection at the Library of Congress holds a copy and attributes the original, *Aventures de Zéline et Damasine*, to Mme de Givre de Richebourg (LC: PQ 1995.L47A98). *Miramond* (Nos. 106, 534, and 1352) is a more familiar work by Fedor Emin in three volumes, published in 1763, with a second edition in 1781 and a third in 1792. See Sipovskii's discussion of the work (*Ocherki*, vol. I, 1, 649–70). *The History of Lord N* is identified by Berkov (K1964, vol. I, Notes, 808–9) as *Prikliucheniia milorda, ili zhizn' mladogo cheloveka, byvshego igralishchem liubvi* (Sipovskii *Iz istorii*, No. 263) an English original, translated into Russian from the French in 1771. See also Sipovskii, *N. M. Karamzin*, 22–6 and Kanunova, *Iz istorii*, 90–1, where these works are briefly discussed in connection with *Knight*.

78 K1984b, vol. II, 116.

79 The reference is to Matvei Komarov's three-volume *Povest' o prikliuchenii Anglinskago Milorda Georga i Brandenburgskoi Markgrafinii Frideriki Luizi* which appeared in five editions between 1782 and 1800 (see Sipovskii, *Iz istorii*: Nos. 628, 762, 1266, 1969, and 2027).

80 K1984b, vol. II, 119–20. The reference here is to Matvei Komarov's *Neshchastnyi Nikanor, ili prikliucheniia Rossiiskogo Dvorianina G*, the first part of which appeared in 1775. The second edition appeared in 1787 in two parts, and in three parts in 1787–9 (Sipovskii, *Iz istorii*: Nos. 317 and 869). Komarov was one of the most prolific 'literary'

adaptors of popular prose, as well as a writer of original prose in the same vein (see Titunik, 'Matvej Komarov's *Vanka Kain*'). In other words, he is part of the same camp as Fedor Emin and Ivan Novikov. Karamzin's reactions against these authors was expressed, as we have seen, in several of his earlier works, particularly 'Natal'ia' and 'My Confession'.

81 Quoted in Sipovskii, *Iz istorii*, 234.

82 The 'updating' of the old controversy seems less curious if we recall more contemporary reactions to Karamzin's own 'amorous' works, for instance, Bolotov's comments on 'Bornholm Island' and Bobrov's parody of the same work. We might also note that certain more prudish readers reacted negatively even to the amorous escapades in 'Natal'ia'. Shishkov reputedly declared that he would tear the work out of his daughter's hands, for 'tlat obychai blagi besedy zly' (See Brang, 163, footnote).

83 VE, 6, 23 (1802), 206–11.

84 Lotman, *Sotvorenie Karamzina*, 211–12.

85 Sipovskii, *Ocherki*, vol. I, 1, 333–4 refers to this type of novel as 'psevdoklassicheskii roman tipa "Telemak"'. Kheraskov's three novels are discussed by Sipovskii on pp. 508–63. See also Brown, 255–6 and 544–5, where this type of prose is referred to as 'pseudohistorical didactic narrative'.

86 Sipovskii, *Ocherki*, vol. I, 2, 364.

87 See Dan E. Davidson, 'N. M. Karamzin and the New Critical Vocabulary', *Mnemosina*, ed. J. T. Baer and Norman W. Ingham (Munich, 1974), 88–94 for an interesting discussion of the word *romanicheskii* in eighteenth-century Russia, particularly as it was used by Karamzin. Davidson does not mention the playful use of the word in *Knight*, and, in general, neglects to account for Karamzin's fondness for punning and playing with language. In *Knight*, it would seem that the combination of *romanicheskaia* and *istoriia*, usually seen as opposites, is done in a spirit of play. We recall that *Knight* is labelled both a 'novel' and 'not a novel'. Davidson quotes from Karamzin's 'On Book Trade': 'indisputably, novels (*romany*) make the heart and imagination . . . *romantic* (*romanicheskimi*)'. Davidson's serious interpretation, it would seem, does not account for playful (intentional) *non sequiturs* in Karamzin's works. As we have seen, his praise for novels tended to be of a bivocal nature, one voice praising them, while another deplored their style. In light of Karamzin's playful tone, it is not at all to be taken for granted that he here intended the word *romanicheskii* in a complimentary sense.

88 Cross, *N. M. Karamzin*, 126 describes *Knight*: 'In the elaboration of the relationship between Leon and Countess Mirova, Karamzin still pays tribute to the unfortunate tradition of rococo sensualism with his suggestive innuendo and ultimate Acteon–Diana set piece.'

# Bibliography

WORKS BY N. M. KARAMZIN

(Listed chronologically, each entry beginning with the reference code used
in the notes to the text)

K1783.    *Dereviannaia noga, shveitsarskaia idilliia gos. Gesnera.* Tr. N.
          M. Karamzin. S.-Peterburg, 1783.
DCha.     *Detskoe chtenie dlia serdtsa i razuma.* (Vols. for 1787–9 ed. by
          Karamzin). 20 vols. Moscow, V Univ. tip., u N. Novikova,
          1785–9.
K1786.    *O proiskhozhdenii zla, poema velikago Gallera.* Tr. N. M.
          Karamzin. Moscow, V Tip. kompanii tipograficheskoi, 1786.
MZha.     *Moskovskii Zhurnal.* Ed. N. M. Karamzin. 8 vols. Moscow, V
          Univ. tip., u V. Okorokova, 1791–2.
Aglaia.   *Aglaia, almanakh.* 2 vols. Moscow, V Univ. tip., u Ridigera i
          Klaudiia, 1794–5.
K1796.    'Juliia'. Moscow, V Univ. tip., u Ridigera i Klaudiia, 1796.
K1796a.   'Idilliia: Zefiry (iz Gesnera)'. Tr. N. M. Karamzin. *Priiatnoe i
          poleznoe preprovozhdenie vremeni* 12 (1796), 22–4.
Aonidy.   *Aonidy, ili sobranie raznykh novykh stikhotvorenii.* 3 vols.
          Moscow, V Univ. tip., u Ridigera i Klaudiia, 1796–9.
K1797.    *Moi bezdelki.* 2 vols. 2nd edn. Moscow, V Univ. tip., u
          Ridigera i Klaudiia, 1797.
K1801.    *Panteon rossiiskikh avtorov.* Izd. Platona Beketova. Moscow,
          V Senatskoi tip. u Selivanovskago, 1801.
VE.       *Vestnik Evropy.* Ed. N. M. Karamzin. 12 vols. Moscow, V
          Univ. tip., u Liubi Gariia i Popova, 1802–3.
MZhb.     *Moskovskii Zhurnal.* 2nd edn. Moscow, V tipografii S. Seliva-
          novskago, 1803.
K1803.    *Sochineniia.* 8 vols. Moscow, V tipografii S. Selivanovskago,
          1803–4.
DChb.     *Detskoe chtenie dlia serdtsa i razuma.* 18 vols. 3rd edn
          Moscow, 1819.
K1848.    *Sochineniia.* (Polnoe sobranie sochinenii russkikh avtorov). 3
          vols. Sanktpeterburg, Izd. A. Smirdina, 1848.
K1866.    *Pis'ma N. M. Karamzina k I. I. Dmitrievu.* Ed. Ia. Grot and P.
          Pekarskii. Sanktpeterburg, Imperatorskaia Akademiia Nauk,
          1866.

K1898.  'N. M. Karamzin v perepiske s imperatritsei Mariei Fedorovnoi'. *Russkaia starina*, 96 (1898), 31–40.
K1961.  'Raznye otryvki (iz zapisok odnogo molodogo Rossiianina)'. *Moskovskii Zhurnal*, 6 (1792), 65–73. Rpt. V. V. Vinogradov. *Problema avtorstva i teoriia stilei*. Moscow, Gosudarstvennoe izdatel'stvo khudozhestvennoi literatury, 1961, pp. 265–7.
K1964.  *Izbrannye sochineniia*. Ed. P. Berkov. 2 vols. Moscow, Izdatel'stvo Khudozhestvennaia literatura, 1964.
K1966.  *Polnoe sobranie stikhotvorenii*. (Biblioteka poeta. Bol'shaia seriia). Ed. Iu. M. Lotman. 2nd edn Moscow, Sovetskii pisatel', 1966.
K1980.  *Pis'ma russkogo puteshestvennika*. *Povesti*. Ed. N. N. Akopova; G. P. Makogonenko; and M. V. Ivanov. Moscow, Pravda, 1980.
K1983.  *Pis'ma russkogo puteshest vennika*. Ed. V. A. Grikhin. Moscow, Sovetskaia Rossiia, 1983.
K1984a.  *Pis'ma russkogo puteshestvennika*. (Literaturnye pamiatniki). Ed. Iu. M. Lotman; N. A. Marchenko; and B. A. Uspenskii. Leningrad, Nauka, 1984.
K1984b.  *Sochineniia*. Ed. G. P. Makogonenko. 2 vols. Leningrad, Khudozhestvennaia literatura, 1984.
K1987.  *A Knight of Our Time*. Tr. A. G. Cross. *Russian Literature Triquarterly*, 20 (1987), 139–58.

OTHER WORKS

Afanas'ev, E. L. 'Pamflet'. *Russkii i zapadnoevropeiskii klassitsizm. Proza*. Ed. A. S. Kurilov; K. V. Pigarev; and B. I. Purishev. Moscow, Izdatel'stvo 'Nauka', 1982, pp. 263–97.
Al'tshuller, Mark. *Predtechi slavianofil'stva v russkoi literature. (Obshchestvo 'Beseda liubitelei russkogo slova')*. Ann Arbor, Ardis, 1984.
Anderson, Roger B. 'Karamzin's "Bornholm Island": Its Narrator and its Meaning'. *Orbis Litterarum*, 28 (1973), 204–15.
—— *N. M. Karamzin's Prose: The Teller in the Tale. A Study in Narrative Technique*. Houston, Cordovan Press, 1974.
—— 'Karamzin's *Letters of a Russian Traveller*: An Education in Western Sentimentalism'. *Essays on Karamzin: Russian Man-of-Letters, Political Thinker, Historian, 1766–1826*. Ed. J. L. Black. (Slavistic Printings and Reprintings, 309). The Hague, Mouton, 1975, pp. 22–39.
Apostolov, N. *Karamzin kak romanist–istorik.(Ocherk iz istorii russkago "istoricheskago" romana)*. Petrograd, Senatskaia tipografiia, 1916.
Arzumanova, M. A. 'Russkii sentimentalizm v kritike 90-kh godov XVIII v'. *XVIII vek*, 6 (1964), 511–18.
Austin, J. L. *How to Do Things with Words*. New York, Oxford University Press, 1962.
Bakhtin, M. M. *Problemy poetiki Dostoevskogo*. 3rd edn. Moscow, Izdatel'stvo khudozhestvennoi literatury, 1972.

*Voprosy literatury i estetiki. Issledovaniia raznykh let.* Moscow, Izdatel'stvo Khudozhestvennaia literatura, 1975.

*Estetika slovesnogo tvorchestva.* Moscow, Izdatel'stvo Iskusstvo, 1979.

Baklanova, N. A. 'K voprosu o dativirovke "Povesti o Frole Skobeeve"'. *Trudy otdela drevnerusskoi literatury,* 13 (1957), 511–18.

Banfield, Ann. 'Narrative Style and the Grammar of Direct and Indirect Speech'. *Foundations of Language,* 10, 1 (1973), 1–39.

Batiushkov, K. N. 'Progulka v Akademiiu khudozhestv'. *Opity v stikhakh i proze.* Moscow, Nauka, 1977, pp. 71–94.

Belozerskaia, N. A. *Vasilii Trofimovich Narezhnyi. Istoriko–literaturnyi ocherk.* 2nd edn. S. Peterburg, Izdatel'stvo L. F. Panteleva, 1896.

Benveniste, Emile. *Problèmes de linguistique générale.* Paris, Editions Gallimard, 1966.

Berkov, P. N. 'Derzhavin i Karamzin v istorii russkoi literatury kontsa XVIII–nachala XIX veka'. *XVIII vek,* 8 (1969), 5–17.

Berkov, P. N. and Makogonenko, G. 'Zhizn' i tvorchestvo N. M. Karamzina'. Introduction to Karamzin, N. M. *Izbrannye proizvedeniia.* Ed. P. Berkov. Vol. I. Moscow, Izdatel'stvo Khudozhestvennaia literatura, 1964, pp. 5–76.

Beshenkovskii, E. B. 'Zhizn' Fedora Emina'. *XVIII vek,* 11 (1976), 186–203.

Black, J. L., ed. *Essays on Karamzin: Russian Man-of-Letters, Political Thinker, Historian, 1766–1826.* (Slavistic Printings and Reprintings, 309). The Hague, Mouton, 1975.

Blagoi, D. D. *Istoriia russkoi literatury XVIII veka.* 4th edn. Moscow, Uchpedgiz, 1960.

Bobrov, Semen. 'Proisshestvie v tsarstve tenei, ili sud'bina rossiiskogo iazyka'. 1805. Rpt. in Iu. M. Lotman and B. A. Uspenskii. 'Spory o iazyke v nachale XIX v. kak fakt russkoi kul'tury. (Proisshestvie v tsarstve tenei, ili sud'bina rossiiskogo iazyka' – neizvestnoe sochinenie Semena Bobrova)'. *Trudy po russkoi i slavianskoi filologii,* 24 (1975), 168–335, pp. 255–80.

Booth, Wayne C. *The Rhetoric of Fiction.* Chicago, University of Chicago Press, 1961.

Brang, Peter. *Studien zu Theorie und Praxis der russischen Erzählung 1770–1811.* (Bibliotheca Slavica). Wiesbaden, Otto Harrassowitz, 1960.

Brissenden, R. F. *Virtue in Distress: Studies in the Novel of Sentiment from Richardson to Sade.* London, The Macmillan Press, 1974.

Bronson, Bertrand Harris. *Facets of the Enlightenment: Studies in English Literature and its Contexts.* Berkeley, University of California Press, 1968.

Brown, William Edward. *A History of 18th Century Russian Literature.* Ann Arbor, Ardis, 1980.

Brukhanskii, A. N. 'M. N. Murav'ev i "legkoe stikhotvorstvo"'. *XVIII vek,* 4 (1959), 157–71.

Bulich, N. *Biograficheskii ocherk N. M. Karamzina i razvitie ego literaturnoi deiatel'nosti*. Kazan, V universitetskoi tipografii, 1866.

Chatman, Seymour. *Story and Discourse: Narrative Structure in Fiction
and Film*. Ithaca, NY, Cornell University Press, 1978.

Cross, Anthony G. 'Karamzin Studies: For the Bicentenary of the Birth of
N. M. Karamzin (1766–1966)'. *The Slavonic and East European
Review*, 45, 104 (1967), 1–11.

'N. M. Karamzin's "Messenger of Europe" (Vestnik Evropy), 1802–3'.
*Forum for Modern Language Studies*, 5, 1 (1969), 1–25.

*N. M. Karamzin: A Study of his Literary Career 1783–1803*. Carbondale,
IL, Southern Illinois University Press, 1971.

'Karamzin's First Short Story?' *Russia: Essays in History and Literature*.
Ed. Lyman H. Legters. Leiden, E. J. Brill, 1972, pp. 38–55.

'Karamzin's Versions of the Idyll'. *Essays on Karamzin: Russian Man-
of-Letters, Political Thinker, Historian, 1766–1826*. Ed. J. L. Black.
(Slavistic Printings and Reprintings, 309) The Hague, Mouton, 1975,
pp. 75–90.

Cross, Anthony G., ed. *Russian Literature in the Age of Catherine the
Great: A Collection of Essays*. Oxford, Meeuws, 1976.

Curtius, Ernst Robert. *European Literature and the Latin Middle Ages*. Tr.
Willard R. Trask. (Bollingen Series, 36). Princeton, NJ, Princeton
University Press, 1973.

Davidson, Dan E. 'N. M. Karamzin and the New Critical Vocabulary:
Toward a Semantic History of the Term *romantic* in Russia'. *Mnemo-
zina. Studia litteraria russica in honorem Vsevolod Setchkarev*. Ed. J.
T. Baer and Norman W. Ingham. (Centrifuga Russian Reprintings
and Printings, 15). Munich, Wilhelm Fink Verlag, 1974, pp. 88–94.

Dewey, Horace W. 'Sentimentalism in the Historical Writings of N. M.
Karamzin'. *American Contributions to the Fourth International Con-
gress of Slavists, Moscow, September, 1958*. (Slavistic Printings and
Reprintings, 21). The Hague, Mouton, 1958, pp. 41–50.

Dmitriev, I. I. *I moi bezdelki*. Moscow, V universitetskoi Tipografii u
Ridigera i Klaudiia, 1795.

Dmitriev, M. A. *Melochi iz zapasa moei pamiati*. 2nd edn. Moscow,
Tipografiia Gracheva i Koni, 1869.

Doležel, Lubomir. 'The Typology of the Narrator: Point of View in
Fiction'. *To Honor Roman Jakobson: Essays on the Occasion of his
Seventeenth Birthday 11 October 1966*. (Janua Linguarum. Series
maior, 31). The Hague, Mouton, 1967, pp. 541–52.

*Narrative Modes in Czech Literature*. Toronto, University of Toronto
Press, 1973.

'Commentary'. *New Literary History*, 6, 2 (1975), 463–8.

'In Defense of Structural Poetics'. *Poetics*, 8 (1979), 521–30.

Drage, C. L. *Russian Literature in the Eighteenth Century: An Introduction
for University Courses*. London, By the Author, 1978.

Efimov, A. I. 'Frazeologicheskii sostav povesti Karamzina "Natal'ia, *boiarskaia doch'"'*. *Materialy i issledovaniia po istorii russkogo litera-turnogo iazyka*. Vol. I. Ed. V. V. Vinogradov. Moscow, Izdatel'stvo AN SSSR, 1949, pp. 69–94.

Eidel'man, N. *Poslednii letopisets*. Moscow, Kniga, 1983.

Eikhenbaum, B. M. 'Karamzin'. *Skvoz' literaturu*. Leningrad, Izdatel'stvo Academia, 1924. Rpt. *O proze*. *Sbornik statei*. Leningrad, Izdatel'-stvo Khudozhestvennaia literatura, 1969, pp. 203–13.

Elizavetina, G. G. 'Stanovlenie zhanrov avtobiografii i memuarov'. *Russkii i zapadnoevropeiskii klassitsizm*. *Proza*. Ed. A. S. Kurilov; K. V. Pigarev; and B. I. Purishev. Moscow, Izdatel'stvo 'Nauka', 1982, pp. 235–63.

Emin, Fedor. *Nepostoiannaia Fortuna, ili Pokhozhdenie Miramonda*. 3 vols. V Sanktpeterburge, 1763.

Fanto, James A. 'Speech Act Theory and its Applications to the Study of Literature'. *The Sign: Semiotics around the World*. Ed. R. W. Bailey; L. Matejka; and P. Steiner. (Michigan Slavic Contributions, 9). Ann Arbor, Michigan Slavic Publications, 1978, pp. 280–304.

Fedorov, V. I. 'Povest' Karamzina "Natal'ia – boiarskaia doch'"'. *Uchenye zapiski Moskovskogo pedagogicheskogo instituta imeni Pot-emkina*, 48, 5 (1955), 109–141.

Fillmore, Charles J. *Santa Cruz Lectures on Deixis 1971*. Lectures given at the 1971 Summer Linguistics Program at the University of California, Santa Cruz. Bloomington, IN, The Indiana University Linguistics Club, 1975.

Fish, Stanley E. 'How to Do Things with Austin and Searle: Speech Act Theory and Literary Criticism'. *Modern Language Notes*, 91 (1976), 983–1025.

Frei, Henri. 'Systèmes de déictiques'. *Acta Linguistica*, 4, 3 (1944), 111–29.

Friedman, Norman. 'Point of View in Fiction: The Development of a Critical Concept'. *PMLA*, 70 (1955), 1160–84.

*Form and Meaning in Fiction*. Athens, GA, University of Georgia Press, 1975.

Friedrich, Paul. 'Structural Implications of Russian Pronominal Usage'. *Sociolinguistics*. Proceedings of the UCLA Sociolinguistics Confer-ence, Los Angeles and Lake Arrowhead, California, 1964. Ed. William Bright. The Hague, Mouton, 1966, pp. 214–59.

Garrard, J. G. 'Poor Erast, or Point of View in Karamzin'. *Essays on Karamzin: Russian Man-of-Letters, Political Thinker, Historian, 1766–1826*. Ed. J. L. Black. (Slavistic Printings and Reprintings, 309). The Hague, Mouton, 1975, pp. 40–55.

Gessner, Salomon. *Schriften*. New edn. Mess, In der Buchdruckerey von G. Hadamord, 1824.

Gogol', N. V. 'Teatral'nyi raŽezd posle predstavleniia novoi komedii'. *Sochineniia v dvukh tomakh*. Moscow, Izdatel'stvo 'Khudozhestven-naia literatura', 1971, vol. II, pp. 219–52.

Golovchiner, V. D. 'Iz istorii stanovleniia iazyka russkoi literaturnoi prozy 50–60kh godov XVIII veka. (Roman abbata Prevo "Prikliucheniia Markiza G\*\*\*, ili Zhizn' blagorodnogo cheloveka, ostavivshego svet", v perevode I. P. Elagina i V. I. Lukina)'. *XVIII vek*, 4 (1959), 66–84.

Goodliffe, J. D. 'Some Comments on Narrative Prose Fiction in Eighteenth Century Russian Literature, with Special Reference to Čulkov'. *Melbourne Slavonic Studies*, 5–6 (1971), 124–36.

Grech, N. I. *Izbrannye mesta iz russkikh sochinenii i perevodov v proze.* Izdany N. Grechem. Sanktpeterburg, 1812.

Grice, H. P. 'Logic and Conversation'. *Syntax and Semantics*, vol. III: *Speech Acts.* Ed. P. Cole and J. Morgan. New York, Academic Press, 1975, pp. 41–58.

Grot, Ia. and Pekarskii, P. eds. *Pis'ma N. M. Karamzina k I. I. Dmitrievu.* Sanktpeterburg, V Tipografii Imperatorskoi Akademii Nauk, 1866.

Gukovskii, G. A. *Russkaia poeziia XVIII veka.* (Voprosy Poetiki, 10). Leningrad, Academia, 1927. Rpt. (Slavische Propyläen, 136). Munich, Wilhelm Fink Verlag, 1971.

'O russkom klassitsizme. Sotiazaniia i perevody'. *Poetika. Vremennik otdela slovesnykh iskusstv*, 4 (1928), 126–48.

'O russkom klassitsizme'. *Poetika. Vremennik otdela slovesnykh iskusstv*, 4 (1929), 21–65.

*Ocherki po istorii russkoi literatury i obshchestvennoi mysli XVIII veka.* Leningrad, Gosudarstvennoe izdatel'stvo Khudozhestvennaia literatura, 1938.

*Russkaia literatura XVIII veka. Uchebnik dlia vysshikh uchebnykh zavedenii.* Moscow, Gosudarstvennoe uchebno–pedagogicheskoe izdatel'stvo narkomprosa RSFSR, 1939.

'Emin i Sumarokov'. *XVIII vek*, 2 (1940), 77–94.

Halle, M.; Pomorska, K.; Matejka, L.; and Uspenskii, B., eds. *Semiosis. Semiotics and the History of Culture. In Honorem Georgii Lotman.* (Michigan Slavic Contributions, 10). Ann Arbor, The University of Michigan, 1984.

Hammarberg, Gitta. 'Metafiction in Russian 18th Century Prose: Karamzin's *Rycar' našego vremeni* or *Novyj Akteon, vnuk Kadma i Garmonii'. Scando–Slavica*, 27 (1981), 27–46.

'Eighteenth Century Narrative Variations on "Frol Skobeev"'. *Slavic Review*, 46, 3/4 (1987), 529–39.

'Poor Liza, Poor Èrast, Lucky Narrator'. *Slavic and East European Journal*, 31, 3 (1987), 305–21.

'Karamzin's "Progulka" as Sentimentalist Manifesto'. *Russian Literature*, 26 (1989), 249–66.

Hansen-Löve, Aage A. 'Die Entfaltung des "Welt–Text"-Paradigmus in der Poesie V. Chlebnikovs'. *Velemir Chlebnikov: A Stockholm Symposium.* Ed. Nils Åke Nilsson. (Stockholm Studies in Russian Literature, 20). Stockholm, Almquist & Wiksell, 1985, pp. 27–87.

Hibberd, John. *Salomon Gessner: His Creative Achievement*. (Anglica Germanica series, 2). Cambridge, Cambridge University Press, 1976.

Hume, David. *Enquiry Concerning the Principles of Morals*. In *Enquiries Concerning Human Understanding and Concerning the Principles and Morals*. 1777, 3rd rev. edn. Ed. L. A. Selby-Biggs. Oxford, Clarendon Press, 1975, pp. 170–323.

Jakobson, Roman. 'Closing Statement: Linguistics and Poetics'. *Style in Language*. Ed. Thomas Sebeok. Cambridge, MA, The M. I. T. Press, 1960, pp. 350–77.

'O khudozhestvennom realizme'. Prague. Rpt. *Readings in Russian Poetics*. Comp. L. Matejka. (Michigan Slavic Materials, 2). Ann Arbor, 1962, pp. 30–6.

'Shifters, Verbal Categories, and the Russian Verb'. *Selected Writings*, Vol. II: *Word and Language*. The Hague, Mouton, 1971, pp. 130–47.

Jelinek, Estelle C. 'Women's Autobiography and the Male Tradition'. Introduction to *Women's Autobiography: Essays in Criticism*. Ed. Estelle C. Jelinek. Bloomington, IN, Indiana University Press, 1980, pp. 1–20.

Jensen, Kjeld Bjørnager. 'The Fruits of Curiosity. On the Composition of N. M. Karamzin's *Ostrov Borngol'm*'. *Svantevit. Dansk Tidskrift for Slavistik*, 4 (1978), 51–9.

Jones, W. Gareth. 'Biography in Eighteenth-Century Russia', *Oxford Slavonic Papers*, 22 (1989), 58–80.

Kanunova, F. Z. 'Evoliutsiia sentimentalizma Karamzina. ("Moia ispoved'")'. *XVIII vek*, 7 (1966), 286–90.

*Iz istorii russkoi povesti (Istoriko–literaturnoe znachenie N. M. Karamzina)*. Tomsk, Izdatel'stvo Tomskogo universiteta, 1967.

'Karamzin i Stern'. *XVIII vek*, 10 (1975), 258–64.

Karlova, T. S. 'Esteticheskii smysl istorii v tvorcheskom vospriiatii Karamzina'. *XVIII vek*, 8 (1969), 281–9.

Kesselmann, Heidemarie. *Die Idyllen Salomon Gessners im Beziehungsfeld von Ästhetik und Geschichte im 18. Jahrhundert. Ein Beitrag zur Gattungsgeschichte der Idylle*. (Scriptor–Hochschulschriften, Literaturwissenschaft, 18). Kronberg/Ts., Scriptor Verlag, 1976.

Kheraskov, M. M. *Numa, ili protsvetaiushchii Rim*. Moscow, Pechatano pri Imperatorskom Moskovskom Universitete, 1768.

*Kadm i Garmoniia, drevnee povestvovanie*. 2 vols. 2nd edn Moscow, V Tipografii I. Zelennikova, 1786.

*Polidor, syn Kadma i Garmonii*. 3 vols. Moscow, V Tipografii I. Zelennikova, 1794.

Kochetkova, N. D. *Nikolay Karamzin*. (Twayne's World Author Series, TWAS, 250: Russia). Boston, G. K. Hall–Twayne, 1975.

'Sentimentalizm. Karamzin'. *Istoriia russkoi literatury v chetyrekh tomakh*, Vol. I: *Literatura XVIII veka*. Ed. D. S. Likhachev and G. P. Makogonenko. Leningrad, Nauka, Leningradskoe otdelenie, 1980. pp. 726–64.

Kodukhov, V. I. 'Sposoby peredachi chuzhoi rechi v russkom iazyke vtoroi poloviny XVII–XVIII vv'. Avtoreferat dissertatsii. Leningrad, Leningradskii gosudarstvennyi pedagogicheskii institut imeni A. I. Gertsena, 1953.

Kovtunova, I. I. 'Nesobstvenno priamaia rech' v iazyke russkoi literatury kontsa XVIII–pervoi poloviny XIX v'. Avtoreferat dissertatsii. Moscow, Institut iazykoznaniia, AN SSSR, 1956.

Krestova, L. V. 'Drevnerusskaia povest' kak odin iz istokov povestei N. M. Karamzina "Raiskaia ptichka", "Ostrov Borngol'm", "Marfa Posadnitsa"'. *Issledovaniia i materialy po drevnerusskoi literature.* Moscow, Izdatel'stvo AN SSSR, 1961, pp. 193–226.

'Povest' N. M. Karamzina "Sierra-Morena"'. *XVIII vek*, 7 (1966), 261–6.

'Romanicheskaia povest' N. M. Karamzina "Natal'ia, boiarskaia doch'" i russkie semeinye predaniia XVII veka'. *Drevnerusskaia literatura i ee sviazi s novym vremenem. Issledovaniia i materialy po drevnerusskoi literature.* Moscow, Izdatel'stvo Nauka, 1967, pp. 237–59.

'A. I. Pleshcheeva v zhizni i tvorchestve Karamzina'. *XVIII vek*, 10 (1975), 265–70.

Kulakova, L. I. 'Esteticheskie vzgliady N. M. Karamzina'. *XVIII vek* 6 (1964), 146–75.

'Poeziia M. N. Murav'eva'. Introduction to M. N. Murav'ev. *Stikhot-voreniia.* (Biblioteka Poeta, Bol'shaia seriia). 2nd edn. Leningrad, Izdatel'stvo Sovetskii pisatel', 1967, pp. 5–49.

Kupreianova, E. N. 'Russkii roman pervoi chetverti XIX veka. Ot sentimental'noi povesti k romanu'. *Istoriia russkogo romana.* Vol. I. Ed. G. M. Fridlender. Moscow, Izdatel'stvo AN SSSR, 1962, pp. 66–85.

Levin, V. D. *Ocherk stilistiki russkogo literaturnogo iazyka kontsa XVIII v. (Leksika).* Moscow, Izdatel'stvo Nauka, 1964.

Lotman, Iu. M. 'Evoliutsiia mirovozzreniia Karamzina (1789–1803)'. *Trudy istoriko–filologicheskogo fakul'teta.* (Uchenye zapiski Tartuskogo gosudarstvennogo universiteta, 51), Tartu, 1957, pp. 122–62.

'Puti razvitiia russkoi prozy 1800-kh – 1810-kh godov'. *Trudy po russkoi i slavianskoi filologii.* (Uchenye zapiski Tartuskogo gosudarstvennogo universiteta, 104), Tartu, 1961, pp. 3–57.

'Poeziia Karamzina'. Introduction to N. M. Karamzin. *Polnoe sobranie sochinenii.* (Biblioteka poeta. Bol'shaia seriia). Ed. Iu. M. Lotman 2nd edn Moscow, Sovetskii pisatel', 1966, pp. 5–52.

'Russo i russkaia kul'tura XVIII veka'. *Epokha prosveshcheniia. Iz istorii mezhdunarodnykh sviazei russkoi literatury.* Ed. M. P. Alekseev. Leningrad, Izdatel'stvo Nauka, 1967, pp. 208–81.

'The Stage and Painting as Code Mechanisms for Cultural Behavior in the Early Nineteenth Century'. Iu. M. Lotman and B. A. Uspenskii. *The Semiotics of Russian Culture.* Ed. Ann Shukman. (Michigan Slavic Contributions, 11). Ann Arbor, 1984, pp. 165–76.

*Sotvorenie Karamzina.* (Pisateli o pisateliakh). Moscow, Kniga, 1987.

Lotman, Iu. M. and Uspenskii, B. A. 'Spory o iazyke v nachale XIX v. kak fakt russkoi kul'tury. ("Proisshestvie v tsarstve tenei, ili sud'bina rossiiskogo iazyka" – neizvestnoe sochinenie Semena Bobrova)'. *Trudy po russkoi i slavianskoi filologii*, 24 (1975), 168–335.

Lupanova, I. P. *Russkaia narodnaia skazka v tvorchestve pisatelei pervoi poloviny XIX veka.* Petrozavodsk, Gosudarstvennoe izdatel'stvo Karel'skoi ASSR, 1959.

Makogonenko, G., ed. *Russkaia proza XVIII veka.* Moscow, Izdatel'stvo Nauka, 1971.

Marchenko, N. A. 'Istoriia teksta "Pisem russkogo puteshestvennika"'. N. M. Karamzin. *Pis'ma russkogo puteshestvennika.* (Literaturnye pamiatniki). Ed. Iu. Lotman; N. A. Marchenko; and B. A. Uspenskii. Leningrad, Nauka, 1984, pp. 607–12.

Marker, Gary. *Publishing, Printing, and the Origins of Intellectual Life in Russia, 1700–1800.* Princeton, Princeton University Press, 1985.

Matejka, Ladislav. 'Reported Speech in Contemporary Standard Russian'. Ph.D. Diss., Harvard University, 1960.

Meyer, Robert and Hopkins, Karen. 'A Speech-Act Theory Bibliography'. *Centrum*, 5, 2 (1977), 73–108.

Mordovchenko, N. I. *Russkaia kritika pervoi chetverti XIX veka.* Moscow, Izdatel'stvo Akademii Nauk SSSR, 1959.

Morson, Gary Saul and Emerson, Caryl, eds. *Rethinking Bakhtin: Extensions and Challenges.* Evanston, Northwestern University Press, 1989.

*Moskovskie Vedomosti.* Moscow, V Univ. tip., 1756–1800.

Murav'ev, M. N. *Sochineniia.* 2 vols. Izdanie Aleksandra Smirdina. Sanktpeterburg, v Tipografii Imperatorskoi Akademii Nauk, 1847.

Nazaretskaia, K. A. 'Ob istokakh russkogo sentimentalizma'. *Uchenye zapiski Kazanskogo universiteta*, 123, 8 (1963), 3–34.

'Poeziia i proza v moskovskikh zhurnalakh 60-kh godov XVIII v. (K voprosu o formirovanii sentimentalizma)'. *Uchenye zapiski Kazanskogo universiteta*, 124, 5 (1964), 3–25.

'Literaturno–khudozhestvennye vzgliady i tvorchestvo Masonov i ikh znachenii dlia formirovaniia sentimentalizma i predromantizma'. *Uchenye zapiski Kazanskogo universiteta*, 128, 4 (1969), 79–95.

Nebel, Henry M. *N. M. Karamzin: A Russian Sentimentalist.* The Hague, Mouton, 1967.

*Selected Aesthetic Works of Sumarokov and Karamzin.* Washington, D. C., University Press of America, 1981.

Neuhäuser, Rudolf. 'Periodization and Classification of Sentimental and Preromantic trends in Russian Literature between 1750 and 1815'. *Canadian Contributions to the Seventh International Congress of Slavists, Warsaw August 21–27, 1973.* The Hague, Mouton, 1973, pp. 11–39.

*Towards the Romantic Age. Essays on Sentimental and Preromantic Literature in Russia.* The Hague, Martinus Nijhoff, 1974.

'Karamzin's Spiritual Crisis of 1793 and 1794'. *Essays on Karamzin: Russian Man-of-Letters, Political Thinker, Historian, 1766–1826*. Ed. J. L. Black. (Slavistic Printings and Reprintings, 309). The Hague, Mouton, 1975, pp. 56–74.

Novikov, Ivan. 'Novgorodskikh devushek sviatochnyi vecher sygrannyi v Moskve svadebnoi'. *Pokhozhdenie Ivana gostinogo syna*. Vol. I. V Sanktpeterburge, 1785, pp. 112–52.

Ohmann, Richard. 'Speech Acts and the Definition of Literature'. *Philosophy and Rhetoric*, 4 (1971), 1–19.

'Literature as Act'. *Approaches to Poetics; Selected Papers from the English Institute*. Ed. Seymour Chatman. New York, Columbia University Press, 1973, pp. 81–107.

O'Neal, John C. *Seeing and Observing. Rousseau's Rhetoric of Perception*. (Stanford French and Italian Studies, 41). Saratoga, CA, Anma Libri, 1985.

Ong, Walter J. 'The Writer's Audience is Always a Fiction'. *PMLA*, 90, 1 (1975), 9–21.

Orlov, P. A. 'Ideinyi smysl povesti Karamzina "Bednaia Liza"'. *Uchenye zapiski Riazanskogo gosudarstvennogo pedagogicheskogo instituta*, 10 (1955). [Cited in Pavlovich, S. E. *Puti razvitia russkoi sentimental'noi prozy XVIII veka*. Saratov, Izdatel'stvo Saratovskogo universiteta, 1974, p. 155].

'Zhanr proizvedeniia N. M. Karamzina "Frol Silin, blagodetel'nyi chelovek"'. *Russkaia Literatura*, 4 (1976), 189–91.

*Russkii sentimentalizm*. Moscow, Izdatel'stvo Moskovskogo universiteta, 1977.

Page, Tanya. 'Karamzin's Immoralist Count NN or Three Hermeneutical Games of "Chinese Shadows"'. *Slavic and East European Journal*, 29, 2 (1985), 144–56.

Pavlovich, S. E. *Puti razvitiia russkoi sentimental'noi prozy XVIII veka*. Saratov, Izdatel'stvo Saratovskogo universiteta, 1974.

Piksanov, N. K. '"Bednaia Aniuta" Radishcheva i "Bednaia Liza" Karamzina (K bor'be realizma s sentimentalizmom)'. *XVIII vek*, 3 (1958), 309–25.

Poggioli, Renato. *The Oaten Flute*. Cambridge, MA, Harvard University Press, 1975.

Pogodin, M. *Nikolai Mikhailovich Karamzin, po ego sochineniiam, pis'mam i otzyvam sovremennikov*. Part I. Moscow, Tipografiia A. I. Mamontova, 1866.

Pospelov, G. N. 'U istokov russkogo sentimentalizma'. *Vestnik Moskovskogo universiteta. Seriia filologii*, 1 (1948). [Cited in Orlov, P. A. *Russkii Sentimentalizm*. Moscow, Izdatel'stvo Moskovskogo universiteta, 1977, p. 35].

*Problemy literaturnogo stilia*. Moscow, Izdatel'stvo Moskovskogo universiteta, 1970.

'Povest' o Frole Skobeeve'. *Russkaia povest' XVII veka*. Comp. M. O.

Skripil'. Ed. I. P. Eremin. Leningrad, Gosudarstvennoe izdatel'stvo khudozhestvennoi literatury, 1954, pp. 155–66.

Pratt, Mary L. *Towards a Speech Act Theory of Literary Discourse*. Bloomington, IN, Indiana University Press, 1977.

Predtechenskii, A. V. 'Obshchestvenno–politicheskie vzgliady N. M. Karamzina v 1790-kh godakh'. *Problemy russkogo Prosveshcheniia v literature XVIII veka*. Ed. P. Berkov. Leningrad, Izdatel'stvo AN SSSR, 1961, pp. 63–78.

*Priiatnoe i poleznoe preprovozhdenie vremeni*. 20 vols. Moscow, Univ. tip. u Ridigera i Klaudiia, 1794–80

Priima, F. Ia., ed. *Na putiakh k romantizmu. Sbornik nauchnykh trudov*. Leningrad, Nauka, 1985.

Prince, Gerald. 'Notes toward a Categorization of Fictional "Narratees"'. *Genre*, 4, 1 (1971), 100–6.

'On Readers and Listeners in Narrative'. *Neophilologus*, 55, 2 (1971), 117–22.

'Introduction to the Study of the Narratee'. *Poétique*, 14 (1973), 177–96.

Pukhov, V. 'Pervaia russkaia povest' o bednoi Lize'. *Russkaia literatura*, 1 (1965), 120–2.

Pumpianskii, L. V. 'Trediakovskii'. *Istoriia russkoi literatury*. Vol. I: *Literatura XVIII veka*. Ed. G. A. Gukovskii and V. A. Desnitskii. Moscow, Izdatel'stvo AN SSSR, 1941, pp. 215–63.

'Sentimentalizm'. *Istoriia russkoi literatury*. Vol. IV: *Literatura XVIII veka*. Ed. G. A. Gukovskii and V. A. Desnitskii. Moscow, Izdatel'-stvo AN SSSR, 1947, pp. 430–45.

Romberg, Bertil. *Studies in the Narrative Technique of the First-Person Novel*. Stockholm, Almqvist & Wiksell, 1962.

Rothe, Hans. *N. M. Karamzins europäische Reise: Der Beginn des russischen Romans. Philosophische Untersuchungen*. (Bausteine zur Geschichte der Literatur bei den Slaven, I). Bad Homburg v.d. H., Verlag Gehlen, 1968.

Rousseau, J. J. *Les Confessions de J. J. Rousseau, suivis des rêveries du promeneur Solitaire*. Vol. I. A Genève, 1782.

Rozova, Z. G. '"Novaia Eloiza" Russo i "Bednaia Liza" Karamzina'. *XVIII vek*, 8 (1969), 259–68.

S:Peterburgskii Merkurii. 2 vols. Sanktpeterburg, tip. I. Krylova s tova-rishchami, 1793.

Searle John R. *Speech Acts. An Essay in the Philosophy of Language*. London, Cambridge University Press, 1969.

'The Logical Status of Fictional Discourse'. *New Literary History*, 6, 2 (1975), 319–32.

'A Taxonomy of Illocutionary Acts'. *Minnesota Studies in the Philosophy of Science*, 7 (1975), 344–69.

Serman, I. Z. 'Iz istorii literaturnoi bor'by 60-kh godov XVIII veka (Neizdannaia komediia Fedora Emina "Uchenaia shaika")'. *XVIII vek*, 3 (1958), 207–25.

Bibliography 321

Bibliography 321

'Stanovlenie i razvitie romana v russkoi literature serediny XVIII veka'. *Iz istorii russkikh literaturnykh otnoshenii XVIII–XX vekov*. Moscow, Izdatel'stvo AN SSSR, 1959, pp. 82–95.

'Zarozhdenie romana v russkoi literature XVIII veka'. *Istoriia russkogo romana v dvukh tomakh*. Vol. I. Ed. A. S. Bushmin et al. Moscow, Izdatel'stvo AN SSSR, 1962, pp. 40–64.

Shamrai, D. D. 'Ob izdateliakh pervogo chastnogo russkogo zhurnala (Po materialam arkhiva Kadetskogo Korpusa)'. *XVIII vek*, 1 (1935), 377–85.

Siniavskii, Andrei [Abram Terts]. *Progulki s Pushkinym*. London, Overseas Publications Interchange, 1975.

Sipovskii, V. V. *N. M. Karamzin, avtor 'Pisem russkogo puteshestvennika'*. S.-Peterburg, Tipografiia u Demakova, 1899.

*Iz istorii russkogo romana i povesti (materialy po bibliografii, istorii i teorii russkogo romana)*. Vol. I: *XVIII vek*. Sanktpeterburg, Izdatel'stvo Imperatorskoi Akademii Nauk, 1903.

*Ocherki iz istorii russkogo romana*. Vol. I, Parts 1–2. S.-Peterburg, Trud, 1909–10.

Sipovskii, V. V., ed. *Russkie povesti XVII–XVIII vv*. S.-Peterburg, A. S. Suvorin, 1905.

Skipina, K. 'O chuvstvitel'noi povesti'. *Russkaia proza*. Ed. B. Eikhenbaum and Iu. Tynianov. (Voprosy poetiki, 8). Leningrad, Academia, 1926, pp. 13–41.

Smith, G. S. 'Sentimentalism and Pre-Romanticism as Terms and Concepts'. *Russian Literature in the Age of Catherine the Great: A Collection of Essays*. Ed. A. G. Cross. Oxford, Meeuws, 1976, pp. 173–84.

Städtke, Klaus. *Die Entwicklung der russischen Erzählung (1800–1825). Ein gattungsgeschichtliche Untersuchung*. (Deutsche Akademie der Wissenschaften. Veröffentlichungen des Instituts für Slawistik, 57). Berlin, Akademie-Verlag, 1971.

Starchevskii, A. *Nikolai Mikhailovich Karamzin*. S.-Peterburg, Pechatano v tipografii Karla Kraiia, 1849.

[Steele, Richard]. 'Idilliia. O svoistve idillii'. *Priiatnoe i poleznoe preprovozhdenie vremeni*, 7 (1795), 89–102.

Stepanov, V. P. 'Povest' Karamzina "Frol Silin"'. *XVIII vek*, 8 (1969), 229–44.

Sterne, Laurence. *A Sentimental Journey through France and Italy by Mr. Yorick*. 2 vols. London, Printed for T. Becket and P. A. De Hondt, 1768.

*The Life and Opinions of Tristram Shandy, Gentleman*. 9 vols. London, Printed for R. and J. Dodsley, 1760–7.

Streeck, Jürgen. 'Speech Acts in Interaction. A Critique of Searle'. *Discourse Processes*, 3, 2 (1980), 133–54.

Sumarokov, A. P. *Polnoe sobranie sochinenii v stikhakh i v proze*. 10 vols. Ed. and comp. Nikolai Novikov. Moscow, V universitetskoi Tipografii u N. Novikova, 1781.

S[umarok]ov, A. [P.] 'Zapiski otzhivshego cheloveka'. Part I: 'Istoriia moikh predkov'. *Vestnik Evropy*, 4 (1871), 694–6.

Thomson, James. *The Seasons*. London, 1730. Rpt. Menston, Yorkshire, The Scolar Press, 1970.

Titunik, I. R. 'The Problem of *Skaz* in Russian Literature'. Ph.D. Diss., University of California, Berkeley, 1963.

'Matvej Komarov's *Vanka Kain* and Eighteenth-Century Russian Prose Fiction'. *Slavic and East European Journal*, 18, 4 (1974), 351–66.

'Mikhail Chulkov's "Double-Talk" Narrative (Skazka o rozhdenii taftianoi mushki) (The Tale of the Origin of the Taffeta Patch)'. *Canadian–American Slavic Studies*, 9, 1 (1975), 30–42.

'The Problem of *Skaz* in Russian Literature of the Eighteenth Century'. *Forum at Iowa on Russian Literature*, 2 (1977), 87–103.

'The Problem of *Skaz* (Critique and Theory)'. *Papers in Slavic Philology*, 1 (1977), 276–301.

'Russian Sentimentalist Rhetoric of Fiction ("Image of Author")'. *Semiosis. Semiotics of Culture. In Honorem Georgii Lotman*. Ed. M. Halle; K. Pomorska; L. Matejka; and B. Uspenskii. (Michigan Slavic Contributions, 10). Ann Arbor, The University of Michigan, 1984, pp. 228–39.

Todd, William Mills III. *The Familiar Letter as a Literary Genre in the Age of Pushkin*. Princeton, Princeton University Press, 1976.

*Fiction and Society in the Age of Pushkin*. Cambridge, MA, Harvard University Press, 1986.

Todorov, Tzvetan. *The Fantastic: A Structural Approach to a Literary Genre*. Tr. Richard Howard. Ithaca, NY, Cornell University Press, 1975.

Tompkins, Jane P. *Reader-Response Criticism*. Baltimore, MD, Johns Hopkins University Press, 1980.

*Trudoliubivaia pchela*. Sanktpeterburg, tip. Akad. nauk, 1759.

Tynianov, Iurii N. *Arkhaisty i novatory*. Leningrad, 1929. Rpt. Munich, Wilhelm Fink Verlag, 1967.

Uspenskii [Uspensky], B. A. *A Poetics of Composition. The Structure of the Artistic Text and a Typology of a Compositional Form*. Tr. V. Zavarin and Susan Wittig. Berkeley, University of California Press, 1973.

*Iz istorii russkogo literaturnogo iazyka XVIII – nachala XIX veka. Iazykovaia programma Karamzina i ee istoricheskie korni*. Moscow, Izdatel'stvo Moskovskogo universiteta, 1985.

Vatsuro, V. E. 'Literaturno–filosoficheskaia problematika povesti Karamzina "Ostrov Borngol'm"'. *XVIII vek*, 8 (1969), 190–209.

Vinogradov, V. V. *O poezii Anny Akhmatovoi (stilisticheskie nabroski)*. (Trudy foneticheskogo instituta prakticheskogo ucheniia iazykov). Leningrad, 1925. Rpt. (Slavische Propyläen, 74). Munich, Wilhelm Fink Verlag, 1970.

*O khudozhestvennoi proze*. Moscow, Gosudarstvennoe izdatel'stvo, 1930.

*Ocherki po istorii russkogo literaturnogo iazyka XVII–XIX vv.* 2nd edn. Moscow, 1938. Rpt. Leiden, Brill, 1949.
'O iazyke Tolstogo (50 – 60-e gody)'. *Literaturnoe nasledstvo*, 35–36 (1939), 117–220.
*O iazyke khudozhestvennoi literatury*. Moscow, Gosudarstvennoe izdatel'stvo khudozhestvennoi literatury, 1959.
*Problema avtorstva i teoriia stilei*. Moscow, Gosudarstvennoe izdatel'-stvo khudozhestvennoi literatury, 1961.
'O stile Karamzina i ego razvitii (ispravleniia teksta povestei)'. *Protsessy formirovaniia leksiki russkogo literaturnogo iazyka (ot Kantemira do Karamzina)*. Moscow, Izdatel'stvo Nauka, 1966, pp. 237–58.
*O teorii khudozhestvennoi rechi*. Moscow, Izdatel'stvo Vysshaia shkola, 1971.
Voloshinov, V. N. 'Slovo v zhizni i slovo v poezii: k voprosam sotsiologi-cheskoi poetiki'. *Zvezda*, 6 (1926), 244–67.
*Marksizm i filosofiia iazyka. Osnovnye problemy sotsiologicheskogo metoda v nauke o iazyke*. 2nd edn. Leningrad, Priboi, 1930.
'Stilistika khudozhestvennoi rechi'. *Literaturnaia ucheba*, 2 (1930), 3–66; 3 (1930), 65–87; 5 (1930), 43–59.
'O granitsakh poetiki i lingvistiki'. *V bor'be za marksizm v literaturnoi nauke; sbornik statei*. Ed. V. Desnitskii; N. Iakovlev; and L. Tsyrlin. Leningrad, Priboi, 1930, pp. 203–40.
Young, Edward. 'Conjectures on Original Composition'. *The Complete Works, Poetry and Prose*. Ed. James Nichols. 2 vols. London, William Tegg, 1854. Facs. rpt. Hildesheim, George Olms, 1968. Vol. II, 547–86.
Zapadov, A. V. 'Tvorchestvo Kheraskova'. Introduction to M. M. Kher-askov. *Izbrannye proizvedeniia*. (Biblioteka poeta. Bol'shaia seriia). Leningrad, Sovetskii pisatel', 1961, pp. 5–56.

# Index

A. L., *Dobrada the Fairy or An Image of Virtuous Conduct Towards One's Neighbor (Dobrada volshebnitsa, ili obraz dobrodetel'stva blizhnemu)*, 100

Aesop, 2, 38, 263

Afanas'ev, E. L., 291n13, 305n53

album, 94, 113–14

Aleksei Mikhailovich, Tsar, 224

Al'tshuller, Mark, 292n40, 304n41

Anastasevich, B.,
'Letter to a Friend from the Capital' ('Pis'mo k drugu iz stolitsy'), 100

Anderson, Roger B., 182, 212, 246, 252, 279–80n18, 283–4n25, 288–9n43, 297n33, 298n37, 299n53, n54, 301n70, 302n19, 305n56, 306–7n69

Apuleius, Lucius, 2

*Arabian Nights*, 2

Austin, J. L., 15, 276–8n1

author utterance, definition, 22–5

autobiography, 95, 99, 281n30, 290n7, 306–7n69

Bakhtin, I.,
*I Too Am An Author (I ia avtor)*, 10

Bakhtin, M. M., 15–26, 155, 205, 276–8n1, 278n4
on bivocal speech (speech oriented towards another person's speech), 20–1, 128–30, 142–3, 205–6
on chronotope, 278n5
on dialogue, 15–17, 276–8n1

on direct author's speech (monologue; direct object oriented speech; univocal speech), 17–20, 278–9n12, 279–80n18
on direct speech of personages (represented speech; object speech), 17–18, 20
on epic, 17, 21, 32, 40–1, 50
on idyll, 46–50, 60, 87, 138
on image of author, 19, 278n8, 279n15
on heteroglossia, 17
on literature as utterance, 15–26
on novel, 17, 32
on speech genres, 16–17

Baklanova, N. A. , 303–4n37

Barclay, John,
*Argenis*, 2

Batiushkov, K. N.,
'Promenade to the Academy of Arts' ('Progulka v Akademiiu khudozhestv'), 285–6n32

Bayle, Pierre, 251

Belozerskaia, N. A., 222

Benitskii, A. P.,
'The Ox and the Sheep' ('Byk i ovtsa'), 121

Benveniste, Emile, 280–1n28

Berkov, P. N., 141–2, 305–6n64, 308n77

Beshenkovskii, E. B., 280n20

Bion, of Smyrna, 44

bivocal speech, 20–1, 128–30, 142–3, 205–6, 242–3, (*See also*: Bakhtin, M. M., on bivocal speech)

Blagoi, D. D., 122

324

Index                                325

Bobrov, Semen, 300n61, 309n82
Bogdanovich, I. F.,
  Dushen'ka', 232, 288n42,
    301–2n17
Bolotov, A. T., 192, 280n20,
    309n82
Bonnet, Charles, 251
Booth, Wayne, 279n13, 279–80n18
bouts-rimés, 94, 292n45
'Bova Korolevich', 1–2
Brang, Peter, 150, 210, 211, 225,
    252, 286n34, 288–9n43,
    294–5n11, 297n33, 298n37
Brissenden, R. F., 4–7, 13, 275n20
Bronson, B. H., 12
Brown, William Edward, 274n5,
    309n85
Brukhanskii, A. N., 48, 282–3n9
Bulich, N. V., 138, 294–5n11
Byronism, 26

Campe, J. H., 233, 234
caricature, 94, 98, 211, 218, 247,
    301–2n17
Cervantes Saavedra, Miguel de, 2
charade, 94
Chatman, Seymour, 279n13
Children's Reading for Heart and
    Mind (Detskoe chtenie dlia
    serdtsa i razuma), 10, 60, 133,
    135, 298n37
chronotope, 46–9, 93–101, 109,
    128, 161–4, 195, 205, 278n5,
    (See also: Bakhtin, M. M., on
    chronotope)
Chulkov, M. D., 3, 274–5n7
  The Comely Cook (Prigozhaia
    povarikha), 291n27
  The Mocker (Peresmeshnik), 99
Clarke, R. T., 107
Coiffier, Henri, 122
Cross, A. G., 50, 52–4, 61, 107,
    122–3, 133, 181, 182, 252,
    284n26, 288–9n43, 294n9,
    295n12, 305n57, 306n68,
    306–7n69, 307n74, 309n88
cult of friendship, 97, 108–9, 170,
    175, 266

Curtius, Ernst Robert, 284–5n31

Davidson, Dan D., 309n87
Demosthenes, 215, 219
Derzhavin, G. R., 192, 300n65
Dmitriev, I. I., 121–4, 167, 169,
    182
  My Trifles Too (I moi bezdelki),
    10, 99
Dmitriev, M. A., 121–4
Doležel, Lubomir, 15, 21, 27, 36,
    276–8n1
Dolgorukaia, N. D., 95
Dostoevskii, F. M., 241
  The Devils (Besy), 304n47
  The Village of Stepanchikovo
    (Selo Stepanchikova), 121–2
Drage, C. L., 274n5
Druids, 197

Eikhenbaum, B. M., 240, 298n37
Elagin, I. P., 1–3, 245–6, 265,
    305n53
Elizavetina, G. G., 95, 281n30
Emerson, Caryl, 276–8n1
Emin, F. A., 2–3, 61, 122, 214,
    215, 219–20, 231, 234, 264–5,
    272–3, 274–5n7, 280n20,
    302n19, 308–9n80
  The Adventures of Themistocles
    (Prikliucheniia Femistokla), 3
  Inconstant Fortune, or the
    Voyage of Miramond
    (Nepostoiannaia Fortuna, ili
    pokhozhdenie Miramonda),
    11, 26, 262–3, 291n26,
    302n19, 308n77
  Letters of Ernest and Doravra
    (Pis'ma Ernesta i Doravry),
    60, 98–9, 294n1
Emin, N.,
  The Game of Fate (Igra sud'by),
    294n1
  Roza, 294n1
epic, 17, 21, 32, 40–1, 49–50, 156

fairy tale, 114–20, 208–14,
    301–2n17

'The Grumbling Hive', 251
Marchesi, Luigi, 68, 74, 78,
    286n35
Maria Fedorovna, Dowager
    Empress, 191–2
Marker, Gary, 274n1, n2, 276n31
Marmontel, J.-F., 114, 122, 208,
    210, 274n5
Matejka, Ladislav, 282n49
Matveev, A. S., 224–5
Mendelssohn, Moses, 251,
    305n62
*Mercure de France*, 52
Meyer, Robert, 276–8n1
miniaturization, 47–8, 60, 79, 93,
    163–4
monologue 18–20, (*see also*
    Bakhtin, M. M., on direct
    author's speech)
Moritz, C. P., 233, 234
Morson, Gary Saul, 276–8n1
Moschus, 44
Moses, 73
Murav'ev, M. N., 4, 9, 282–3n9,
    284–5n31, 287–8n39
  'Emile's Letters' ('Emilievi
    pis'ma'), 87, 283n10
  'On Pastoral Poetry' ('O
    pastusheskoi poezii'), 283n10
  'The Suburban Dweller'
    ('Obitatel' predmest'ia'), 87,
    283n10
  'On Virgil' ('O Virgilii'), 283n10
  'My Cousin's Journey in [his]
    Pockets' ('Puteshestvie moego
    dvoiurodnogo brata v
    karmany'), 294n3

narrated event, definition, 22
narratee, definition, 21, 23–7,
    279n13
narrator, definition, 21, 23–7
narrator utterance, definition,
    23–6
Naryshkina, Natal'ia, 224–5
Nazaretskaia, K. A., 282n2
Nebel, Henry M., 305–6n64
Neoclassicism, 19, 75, 106

author-reader relationship,
    276n22, n31
genres, 9, 13, 44–6
prose, 1, 2–3, 26, 98, 206,
    265–73
style, 13, 28, 284–5n31
Neuhäuser, Rudolf, 182, 276n31,
    282n2, 296n19, 298n36, n37,
    299n53, 300n65, 301n6
norm text, definition, 21–2, 279n15
Novikov, Ivan, 234, 265, 308–9n80
  'The Novgorod Girls' Yuletide
    Evening' ('Novgorodskikh
    devushek sviatochnyi
    vecher'), 226–31, 303–4n37,
    n38
Novikov, N. I., 304n38

Oedipus, 260
O'Neal, John C., 286n36,
    286–7n37, 304n49, 304–5n52
Ong, Walter, 34
oration, 1, 123, 293n54
Orlov, P. A., 44–6, 122–3, 141,
    222, 282n2, 293n54, 295n16,
    297n35
Orpheus, 198–9, 215, 219
Ossian, 70, 73, 77, 114, 168
Ovid, 192, 272

Page, Tanya, 240, 305n55, n61
Pajon, H., 210
pamphlet, 98, 291n13
Pavlovich, S. E., 283–4n25,
    295n12, 298n37, 302n22
Pel'skii, P. A.,
    *My Something or Other (Moe
    koe-chto)*, 99
Pepelinière, J. de [?],
    *Daira, an Eastern Tale*, 262–3,
    302n19, 308n77
Perrault, Charles, 208, 210, 211,
    301n7
personage utterance, definition,
    20, 22–5
Petrine tales, 1, 206
Petronius, Gaius, 2, 248–9, 298n37
Petrov, A. A., 106, 168–9, 175